Paul de Cheun

A currency union is a geographical area throughout which a single currency circulates as the medium of exchange. Given the immediacy of the prospects for Economic and Monetary Union (EMU) among European Community countries, as well as the major political and economic developments in Central and Eastern Europe, the issue of currency unification – or diversification – has come to the forefront in economic research and in policy-making circles. This important and timely volume provides an assessment and critique of this research. In addition to a specially written survey article by the editors, it contains previously unpublished contributions by leading researchers in the field, discussing real and potential currency unions in the United States, the former Soviet Union, Europe, and Africa.

Policy issues in the operation of currency unions

Policy issues in the operation of currency unions

Edited by
PAUL R. MASSON
and
MARK P. TAYLOR

CAMBRIDGE
UNIVERSITY PRESS

Published by the Press Syndicate of the University of Cambridge
The Pitt Building, Trumpington Street, Cambridge CB2 1RP
40 West 20th Street, New York, NY 10011-4211, USA
10 Stamford Road, Oakleigh, Victoria 3166, Australia

First published 1993

Printed in Great Britain at the University Press, Cambridge

A catalogue record for this book is available from the British Library

Library of Congress cataloguing in publication data

Policy issues in the operation of currency unions / edited by Paul R.
Masson and Mark P. Taylor.
    p.   cm.
Includes bibliographical references.
ISBN 0 521 43455 6 (hardback)
1. Monetary unions. 2. Monetary unions – European Economic
Community countries. 3. Monetary policy – European Economic
Community countries. 4. Monetary unions – Soviet Union. 5. Dollar, American.
6. Dollar, Canadian. 7. French franc area. 8. Monetary unions – Africa.
I. Masson, Paul R. II. Taylor, Mark P., 1958–
HG3894.P65 1993
332.4'566–dc20   92-20210   CIP

ISBN 0 521 43455 6 hardback

VN

Contents

List of contributors   ix
Preface   xi

I Assessing the literature

1 Currency unions: a survey of the issues   3
   Paul R. Masson and Mark P. Taylor

II Existing currency unions

2 Costs and benefits of economic and monetary union: 55
   an application to the former Soviet Union
   Daniel Gros
3 Private capital markets and adjustment in a currency   75
   union: evidence from the United States
   Andrew Atkeson and Tamim Bayoumi
4 The economics of the CFA franc zone   96
   James M. Boughton

III Is Europe an optimum currency area?

5 Is Europe an optimum currency area?: evidence from   111
   regional data
   Paul de Grauwe and Wim Vanhaverbeke
6 Labor markets and European monetary unification   130
   Barry Eichengreen
7 European excess stock returns and capital market   163
   integration: an empirical perspective
   Patricia Fraser and Ronald MacDonald

IV   EMU: The road from Maastricht

8   The European System of Central Banks after   215
    Maastricht
    Charles A.E. Goodhart
9   A European money demand function   240
    Michael J. Artis, Robin C. Bladen-Hovell, and Wenda
    Zhang
10 Monetary union and fiscal union: a perspective from 264
    fiscal federalism
    Jürgen von Hagen

    Index   297

Contributors

Michael J. Artis	University of Manchester and Centre for Economic Policy Research
Andrew Atkeson	University of Chicago
Tamim Bayoumi	International Monetary Fund
Robin C. Bladen-Hovell	University of Manchester
James M. Boughton	International Monetary Fund
Paul de Grauwe	Catholic University of Leuven and Centre for Economic Policy Research
Barry Eichengreen	University of California, Berkeley and Centre for Economic Policy Research
Patricia Fraser	University of Dundee
Charles A.E. Goodhart	London School of Economics
Daniel Gros	Centre for European Policy Studies and Centre for Economic Policy Research
Ronald MacDonald	University of Dundee
Paul R. Masson	International Monetary Fund
Mark P. Taylor	International Monetary Fund and Centre for Economic Policy Research
Wim Vanhaverbeke	Catholic University of Leuven
Jürgen von Hagen	University of Mannheim, University of Indiana, and Centre for Economic Policy Research
Wenda Zhang	University of Manchester

Preface

Currency unions, or single currency areas, is a topic upon which both academics and policy-makers are now focusing a great deal of attention. This has perhaps been most marked in western Europe, given the immediacy of the prospects for Economic and Monetary Union (EMU) among European community countries. In parallel with the movement toward EMU, however, has come the unification of Germany, other major political and economic developments in central and eastern Europe, and increased economic integration in North America. These developments have naturally brought the issue of currency unification – or diversification – to the forefront.

It is in this context that a timely assessment and critique of the literature on common currency areas is needed, and this book provides a collection of recent research by leading scholars in this field.

The book is divided into four parts. The first part provides an assessment of the literature, while later parts look at existing currency unions, the issue of whether or not Europe is an optimum currency area, and the prospects for the establishment and operation of European Monetary Union in the wake of the Maastricht agreement of December 1991.

The opening chapter of the book, by Paul Masson and Mark Taylor, provides an overview and critical analysis of the currency union literature, focusing on a discussion of the conditions under which currency unions would be desirable and viable. Masson and Taylor discuss the empirical work – as well as presenting some new evidence – relating to the operation of existing currency unions in federal states and among regional country groupings. In particular, they examine the traditional criteria for the successful operation of optimal currency areas, the present evidence concerning the shock-absorbing properties of federal fiscal systems and the discipline imposed on the public sector by financial markets. Masson and Taylor also examine the implications of economic heterogeneity across a currency union, and whether or not convergence should be achieved before rather than after the union occurs. In addition, some issues relating to the possible transition toward monetary union in Europe are considered. The discussion is illustrated by reference to a number of actual or potential currency unions, including western Europe, the former Soviet Union, the United States, Canada, and the African CFA franc zone.

Part II, on existing currency unions, begins with a chapter by Daniel Gros, who examines whether there are any economic justifications for maintaining an economic and monetary union in the geographical area covered by the former Soviet Union. The main result of Gros' analysis is that the more developed republics located west of the Urals would benefit from leaving the rouble area. This conclusion follows from a close examination of the actual and potential economic structures of the various republics, as well as an analysis of the transition process toward a market economy. These republics, Gros argues, would likely want to proceed with structural reform at a different pace, and some republics would be able to operate tighter monetary policies than others, because of a lesser need to rely on the inflation tax. The Baltic republics would be expected to become highly open to the rest of the world, but not so some of the Asian republics. Gros notes that his conclusions thus run counter to the suggestions of the Commission of the European Communities, which has argued that the former Soviet Union should remain an economic and monetary union. The chapter also considers the long-run possibility of integration of some of the former Soviet republics into EMU.

Chapter 3, by Andrew Atkeson and Tamim Bayoumi, provides an empirical analysis of an existing currency union – the United States of America. A feature of most currency unions is that they contain an integrated capital market, which can be used by private individuals both to borrow and lend capital across regions within the union and to insure themselves against region-specific risk by holding a diverse portfolio of assets. Regional data for the United States are used to estimate the importance of these two factors. Atkeson and Bayoumi find that there have been large flows of capital between regions of the US over the last two decades, but that private capital markets provide only very limited insurance against regional fluctuations in income.

In the last chapter of this part, James Boughton examines the operation of a currency area in Central and West Africa, the CFA franc zone. These countries' currencies have been linked to the French franc since 1948. Though seemingly not an optimal currency area – having limited inter-regional trade, limited price flexibility, and marked differences in reactions to terms-of-trade shocks – CFA franc zone countries have nevertheless benefited from the discipline and stability of being associated with a major international currency.

Part III opens with an empirical piece by Paul de Grauwe and Wim Vanhaverbeke, in which they examine several issues relating to the optimality of Europe as a common currency area. In particular, two hypotheses are tested. The first relates to the presumption, implicit in the traditional optimum currency area literature that, in a monetary union, regional adjustment following asymmetric shocks will largely take the form of labor migration rather than real exchange-rate adjustment, while the opposite is true of countries with separate currencies. The second hypothesis examined concerns the frequency and size of asymmetric shocks: whether or not their occurrence differs as between regions of the same country and nations in Europe. De Grauwe and Vanhaverbeke find no evidence that asymmetric shocks are less important at the regional than at the national level, but also find that the presumption concerning labor mobility holds – with some qualifications – for Europe. The implications of these findings for European Monetary Union are sketched out in a concluding section.

In chapter 6, Barry Eichengreen provides a related analysis of European labor markets. Eichengreen begins by observing limited migration within the United Kingdom and Italy, especially relative to the United States. He argues that if labor mobility is low *within* European countries – where language and culture are relatively homogeneous – then it can hardly be expected to be high across the various countries making up a future European monetary union. Eichengreen notes, however, that comparisons of labor mobility should control for the strength of incentives to mobility. In fact, he finds that the dispersion of shocks to regional labor markets is quite similar across the UK, Italy, and the US. Moreover, he reports an elasticity of labor migration with respect to inter-regional wage differentials which is several times higher for the United States than it is in the UK and Italy. However, Eichengreen finds that these differences appear to have little impact on the persistence of deviations of unemployment rates from their long-term regional levels, when Europe is compared to the US.

In the final chapter of Part III, Patricia Fraser and Ronald MacDonald examine the degree of European capital market integration, by looking at the predictability of stock market returns in terms of common European factors. While Fraser and MacDonald report strong evidence of intra-European capital market integration, they find that the degree of integration of European capital markets with those in the United States is as strong as the degree of integration with Germany, suggesting a global, rather than a purely European, phenomenon.

Part IV, which is concerned with the prospectus for EMU in the light of the Maastricht Treaty of December 1991, opens with a chapter by Charles Goodhart, in which he analyzes the provisions of the Treaty as regards the

European System of Central Banks (ESCB). As well as discussing operational issues concerning the future ESCB, such as its operations in financial markets, clearing and settlement, and prudential regulations, Goodhart also discusses the modalities of transition from irrevocably fixed exchange rates to a single currency, as well as raising issues concerning the operational flexibility and democratic accountability of the ESCB.

In chapter 9, Michael Artis, Robin Bladen-Hovell and Wenda Zhang examine a key element of the feasibility of a single European monetary policy – the stability of EC-wide money demand. These authors apply recent econometric techniques to provide estimates of money demand over both the pre- and post-EMS period. The chapter also investigates the effect of disaggregating to the individual country level, revealing that conditions for aggregation may not be fully met within the system. The implications of this result for monetary policy after achievement of a monetary union are discussed in the final section of the chapter.

In the last chapter of Part IV, Jürgen von Hagen examines the so-called parallel-unification proposition: that successful currency union requires fiscal policy unification. This proposition has been justified on the grounds of the need to alleviate important allocative inefficiencies and enhance area-wide macroeconomic stabilization. Von Hagen argues that there are a number of fallacies lying behind the proposition. In particular, he argues that simple two-country models are inadequate to the purpose of analyzing this issue, and that static efficiency arguments neglect the synergetic gains from decentralization.

The editors are confident that the present volume will provide a significant contribution to the policy debate in this topical area. Although a number of the authors, including ourselves, are staff members of the International Monetary Fund, we wish to state that none of the papers contained in this volume is to be interpreted as representing the views or policies of the Fund or of its member country authorities.

I   Assessing the literature

1 Currency unions: a survey of the issues

PAUL R. MASSON
and MARK P. TAYLOR

I Introduction

A currency union may be defined as a geographical area throughout which a single currency circulates as the principal medium of exchange. Monetary, or exchange-rate unions, can be defined as areas within which exchange rates bear a permanently fixed relationship to each other. In the absence of capital controls, there can exist only one monetary policy in such areas.[1] In the limit, such areas of exchange stability might also involve the replacement of the currencies of member countries by a common currency, that is, the formation of a currency union. The implications for monetary policy independence are however the same for monetary and currency unions, so the two will be treated together in what follows.[2]

Interest in currency unions has grown steadily in recent years, following German unification and other developments in central and eastern Europe, as well as the emerging immediacy of the prospects for European Economic and Monetary Union (EMU). In our analysis, we discuss a number of issues relating to the operation of currency unions – in particular the conditions under which currency unions would be desirable and viable – and consider the operation of existing currency unions, in federal states and among regional country groupings.

Given the enormous recent growth in the relevant literature, it is inevitable that our chapter overlaps with several recent contributions, for instance, with the very comprehensive study by the EC Commission (1990), and with Eichengreen (1990a, 1990b). Our paper is somewhat more broad-ranging than those papers, however, as we attempt to analyze the various criteria for successful currency unions using the experience of other regions and then use them to consider EMU. In addition, we consider some issues relating to the transition toward monetary union in Europe. Provisions of the agreement to amend the Treaty of Rome (reached at Maastricht in December 1991) to achieve economic and monetary union by

3

January 1, 1999 at the latest, are mentioned at various points below. For a full discussion of the amendments, see the chapter by Goodhart in this volume.

The implications of currency unions for monetary policies and price stability are discussed in the next section. The desirable extent of currency unions has been the subject of an extensive literature on "optimum currency areas," which is surveyed in section III. Traditional criteria for the success of monetary unions in dealing with economic shocks include labor mobility, wage and price flexibility, diversification of the economies of member countries or regions and their interdependence (as measured by trade flows). Some empirical evidence relevant to these criteria is presented for Canada, the United States, and for other currency unions where requisite data are available; the same measures are also calculated for European countries which are members of the European Monetary System (EMS). Attempts to simulate macroeconomic models in order to analyze the nature of shocks facing economies are also surveyed.

Another means of improving the shock-absorbing ability of economies is through fiscal transfers among members. Until recently, the interaction between national fiscal policies and the credibility of the commitment of the union's monetary policy to price stability has received inadequate attention. This issue is especially relevant for the design of new monetary institutions in Europe, as well as for federations which may evolve toward a more decentralized division of fiscal powers between central and regional governments. Section IV therefore discusses some key issues relating to fiscal policies in monetary unions.

Section V addresses the implications of differences among members of a monetary union. Clearly, monetary union implies similar inflation rates for member countries or regions in the long run. However, it is less clear how much convergence has to be achieved *before* monetary union can occur. Economic development of poorer countries and regions is a desirable feature of any monetary system, and it is thus an important question whether currency union assists in the convergence of per capita income among the constituent parts. Such considerations are important, for example, for the EC, where some countries such as Greece and Portugal start from considerably lower income levels than those enjoyed by others, as well as for the former USSR, which has considerable diversity across republics. The evolution of regional disparities in the United States is reviewed in order to throw some light on this question.

Section VI considers issues that relate specifically to the transition in Europe toward Economic and Monetary Union. Topics discussed include the dangers of destabilizing speculation in a period in which there are no restrictions on capital movements and where parities are not viewed as irrevocably fixed, and the desired speed of the transition. A final section presents a summary and conclusions.

II Monetary policy issues

1 Facilitating transactions and ensuring price stability

Money facilitates transactions and thereby increases economic efficiency relative to a situation of barter. The social benefit derived from money is, moreover, enhanced by stability in its value, that is, by price stability. The widest possible use of a single money that exhibits such stability would minimize transactions costs and maximize its informational role. Indeed, this argument has motivated the call for a single world money, or global currency area (e.g., Cooper, 1990). In the next section, criteria that define "optimum currency areas" are discussed, and reasons are offered as to why the global economy is not likely to be such an area. Nevertheless, regional groups of countries may find it to their advantage to move to a common currency in order to reduce transactions costs and to reduce the unfavorable effects of exchange-rate uncertainty on trade and investment – provided that each such regional currency exhibits price stability.

Another important reason for a country to join a monetary union with a low-inflation country is to enhance the anti-inflationary *credibility* of its own monetary policy (Artis and Currie, 1983). The choice of exchange-rate regime necessarily conditions the choice of monetary policy. In a setting of high capital mobility – the situation facing most industrial countries – exchange-rate and monetary policies are closely linked. Therefore, fixing the exchange rate against a dominant currency means adopting monetary policies that are consistent with those of the country issuing the dominant currency. Tying the hands of the domestic monetary authority in this fashion may enhance its anti-inflationary credibility – provided of course that the monetary union is formed with a "hard" currency, so that price stability ensues. The credibility gain for the non-German members of the EMS is often cited as one of the important features of the Exchange Rate Mechanism (ERM) of the EMS, by which other central banks import the inflation stability of the Bundesbank.[3]

2 Monetary policy institutions in a currency union

Experience suggests that monetary policy in a currency union can be framed and implemented under several alternative institutional arrangements. If there is a dominant country, then that country's currency may or may not circulate in other countries. In either case, its central bank would to some degree set monetary policy for the union as a whole. As discussed above, advantages for other countries would clearly be enhanced if that currency were the most stable in value in terms of goods. The deutsche mark is an example of such a currency, and the countries of the EMS have gained credibility for their own monetary policies by being associated with those of Germany (albeit until now in a looser arrangement than that of currency union). The success of the Bundesbank in managing a stable currency is no doubt in large part a result of its formal independence from the Finance Ministry (aside from the general prescription that it should support government policy) and its legal responsibility to ensure the stability of the currency.[4]

The monetary policy of a currency union could alternatively be set by a supra-national institution. The CFA[5] Franc Arrangements, for instance, are composed of two groups of countries, the West African Monetary Union (WAMU) and the Central African Monetary Area (CAMA). Each of the areas has a central bank which sets, or coordinates, monetary policy for the area; given the exchange-rate arrangement followed, the room for maneuver of monetary policy is slight.[6] In the European Community, an Intergovernmental Conference on EMU reached agreement at Maastricht in December 1991 on amendments to the Treaty of Rome that lay down the principles of a common European monetary policy. A key requirement in establishing a European central bank would be to ensure an effective commitment to price stability. The ability to resist inflationary pressures will no doubt be enhanced by provisions establishing independence of the central bank from national governments (ruling out monetarization of government debt or indirect financing of national governments through interest subsidies, for instance) and enshrining the target of price stability in the central bank's statutes.[7] It is not clear, however, that such statutory guarantees of independence from fiscal policies are in fact sufficient, since indirect pressure can also be exerted. A further important question, which is discussed in section IV below, is therefore whether constraints such as those embodied in The Maastrict agreement are also needed on the fiscal policies of member countries.

3 Seigniorage

It is sometimes suggested that the goal of price stability may conflict with an attempt to use monetary expansion to finance government expenditure, as an alternative to raising revenue by conventional forms of taxation or issuing debt. This is the familiar case for an "inflation tax." Most forms of taxation produce distortions; moreover, the degree of distortion typically rises with the tax rate. Optimal tax policy is therefore said to imply "tax spreading," that is, equating the marginal costs of the various taxes – rather than relying solely on one or another form of taxation. Since countries face different collection costs for conventional taxes, their optimal inflation rates would, so the argument goes, differ; in some cases, the optimal inflation rate is argued to be non-zero. Others have, however, taken the view that the distortions associated with inflation are so high that it is apt to be optimal not to use it at all.[8]

The reliance on issuing money as a means of financing government expenditure varies considerably across European countries. Dornbusch (1988), Grilli (1989), and Giavazzi (1989) have all argued that the "southern tier" of EC countries – Portugal, Spain, Italy, and Greece – may face severe fiscal problems if they are forced to lower their rates of monetary expansion – and hence their rates of inflation – to the German level.[9] Dornbusch (1988, p. 26) estimates seigniorage to be of the order of 3 percent of GDP in these countries over the period 1976–84, as measured by the change in reserve money. However, with declines in inflation, seigniorage revenues have also declined. The EC Commission's estimate for the same four countries in 1988 is lower: ranging from 1.1 percent of GDP for Italy to 2.75 percent for Greece (EC Commission 1990, p. 122).[10]

The assumption that inflation rates, and hence seigniorage revenues, are optimally chosen is dubious. In many cases, inflation is an unintended consequence of undisciplined policies. The bias to overexpansionary monetary policies, whether for the purpose of increasing economic activity or for public finance reasons, is likely to be strong.[11] Furthermore, even if collection costs and distorting effects of conventional taxes might in principle justify some use of seigniorage, there is no presumption that these factors outweigh the costs of a significantly positive rate of inflation. On the contrary, the gains from price stability – assuming that the currency union establishes mechanisms to ensure it – are likely to dominate.

III Traditional criteria for successful currency unions

1 Factor mobility

The superiority of monetary exchange over barter is enhanced by widening the domain over which any single currency can be utilized. Nevertheless, as Mundell (1961) pointed out in a pathbreaking article, there are reasons related to macroeconomic shocks that constrain the size of an optimal currency area. In particular, Mundell argued that unless factors of production – labor and capital – can freely move between regions, shifts in demand facing one region relative to another may lead to unemployment in the absence of flexibility of the nominal exchange rate.[12] If wages and prices are sticky, real exchange-rate depreciation can only be accomplished through nominal exchange-rate changes. However, depreciation would be ruled out if the two regions were part of a currency union. Therefore, the criterion that Mundell proposed for an "optimum currency area" was a country or region in which factor mobility was high.

It is hard to obtain direct information on labor mobility. Barriers to migration may include formal immigration restrictions, social services or pensions that are not immediately available to migrants, and language or cultural differences. If employment were the only motive for migration, then mobility should narrow differences among unemployment rates.[13] Figure 1.1 presents data for the dispersion of unemployment rates across nine US census regions and ten Canadian provinces. Despite absence of formal barriers to mobility, the dispersion of unemployment rates is large in Canada – over 3 percentage points, or about 1/3 of the mean unemployment rate.[14] In contrast, dispersion has averaged a little over 1 percent in the United States, or 1/5 of mean unemployment. Furthermore, deviations from the average by individual states or provinces exhibit persistence. In the United States, the Pacific Northwest region is consistently above the national average, while the West North Central region is consistently below.[15] In Canada, the Maritime provinces (Newfoundland, Nova Scotia, New Brunswick, and Prince Edward Island) exhibit persistently higher unemployment, and Ontario, Manitoba, and Saskatchewan, generally lower unemployment. However, it is also the case that different regions have experienced a boom and a subsequent bust, leading their unemployment rates to dip below, and then rise substantially above, the national average.[16] Correspondingly, this would suggest that flows of population to and from these areas have on occasion been high.

In Europe, national unemployment rates exhibit greater dispersion than in either the United States or Canada, at least since 1979 (figure 1.1).[17] The greater dispersion in the EC may to some extent be attributed to the fact that migration among EC countries is clearly less substantial than within either the United States or Canada. A study cited by Eichengreen (1990b, p. 9) concluded that mobility in the United States was roughly 2 to 3 times as high as mobility *within* European states, as measured by the proportion of the population that changed region of residence;[18] migration *between* European states is no doubt much lower still. Relatively low mobility of labor is thus a potential handicap for the EC as it progresses toward monetary union.

When considering *capital* mobility, a distinction should be made between financial capital and physical capital. While expected rates of return on financial assets, such as bonds, tend to be equalized across countries, the same may not be true of expected returns on physical

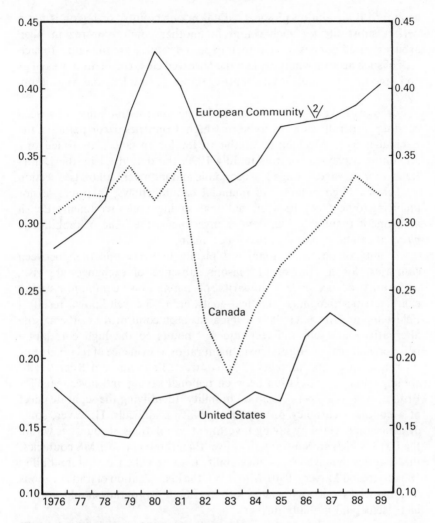

Figure 1.1 Dispersion of unemployment rates

Notes: [1]Coefficients of variation, i.e., deviations of unemployment rates, scaled by the mean (components are weighted by population).
[2]Twelve current members, excluding Luxembourg for which data were not available.

capital.[19] If a claim on physical capital in one country or region is not a perfect substitute for such claims in another country or region, then arbitrage need not ensure that their expected returns are the same. In fact, lack of such arbitrage may explain the observed close correlation of savings and investment in individual countries (Dooley, Frankel, and Mathieson, 1987).

For industrial countries without exchange controls, mobility of *financial* capital is generally thought to be very high. Countries participating in the Exchange Rate Mechanism of the EMS, for instance, abolished any remaining exchange controls in July 1990, the date fixed by the Delors Report for passage to stage 1 of economic and monetary union (see section VI below). High mobility of financial capital allows, in principle, for financing differences between national saving and investment. But if adjustment requires private sector investment, the issue of mobility of *physical* capital comes into play once again.

Mobility of physical capital is typically higher *within* than between countries, for a number of reasons: absence of exchange-rate risk, uniformity of tax codes, similarity of regulations, common national characteristics (language, political goals, etc.). The well-known result of Feldstein and Horioka (1980) – which has been confirmed by others using alternative data sets and techniques – points to the high correlation between national saving and investment ratios as evidence of relatively low international capital mobility.[20] In contrast, Bayoumi and Rose (forthcoming) find *no* correlation between regional saving and investment for Britain, suggesting perfect capital mobility. Identifying the separate effect of a common currency on capital mobility is difficult. However, some evidence is provided by saving/investment correlations of countries within the EMS, which are substantially lower than those of non-EMS countries; this suggests that exchange-rate stability tends to enhance capital mobility (Bhandari and Mayer, 1990). Moreover, the liberalization of trade in goods and financial services associated with the EC 1992 program should work to increase capital mobility further.

Capital accumulation may in principle substitute for labor mobility in accommodating some demand shifts and income shocks. However, given the lags involved in the installation of plant and equipment, capital mobility is likely to be helpful mainly for narrowing persistent regional disparities rather than for offsetting short-term shocks. A case in point is Germany, where one of the objectives of currency union was to encourage the capital flows needed to modernize the east German economy, and thereby stem massive migration to the west of the country.

Even within countries, movements of physical capital are often insufficient to ensure development of depressed areas, as witnessed by the persistence of low relative per capita income in the south of Italy, the north of England, the maritime provinces of Canada, and West Virginia in the United States (see the discussion of convergence in section V below). In a situation of regional specialization in goods which are no longer in high demand, there may not be incentives for productive investment. In these circumstances, labor and capital may both move out.[21] It is therefore doubtful that formation of a currency union can, in and of itself, lead to a sufficient mobility of physical capital either to cushion shocks completely or to lead to quick elimination of underdevelopment.

2 Openness and regional interdependence

Since one benefit of extending the use of a common currency is the reduction in transactions costs, the greater is the volume of inter-regional trade within a common currency area, the greater is the cost saving, other things equal, from the currency union. McKinnon (1963) also showed that the usefulness of exchange-rate flexibility to achieve external balance, without inducing large internal price level changes, is greater when an economy is relatively closed. In order to maintain external balance in the face of a fall in the real demand for the country's exports, resources in a fully employed economy must be shifted toward production of traded goods and away from non-traded goods sectors. The smaller the non-traded goods sector the larger the exchange-rate change needed to transfer a given amount of resources, and the larger the movement in internal prices that would result. Given the objective of price stability, therefore, very open economies (in the sense of having a relatively large tradables sector) are good candidates for fixed exchange rates against their trading partners. This includes possibly joining with them in a currency union, provided that the policies of their neighbors are consistent with price stability.

A comparison of the degree of openness between countries inside and outside existing currency unions is hampered by a relative paucity of data on trade flows within currency unions.[22] One can nevertheless examine the trade patterns of groups of countries, and calculate the proportion of their trade that is internal to the group. Some illustrative data are presented in table 1.1. It can be seen that the twelve EC countries, taken as a group, have a high proportion of internal, relative to external trade – as do the ten present participants of the Exchange Rate Mechanism of the EMS. Moreover, while all individual EC economies have a high degree of openness, the European Community as a whole is relatively closed to the rest of the world – with about the same ratio of external trade to GDP as the United States or Japan. On this criterion, the EC would seem to have the makings of natural common currency area.

Table 1.1. *Selected country groupings: intra-area trade as a share of total trade*

(Average, 1982–5)

	Percent of exports	Percent of imports	Percent of total trade
European Community			
EC 12[a]	54.3	51.4	52.8
ERM 10[b]	52.7	50.6	51.6
North America			
Canada and the United States	37.4	34.5	35.7
Canada, the United States and Mexico	39.0	35.5	37.0
CFA franc zone			
African countries only[c]	6.6	10.7	8.6
African countries including trade with France	27.9	38.6	37.8
CFA franc zone plus France	2.1	2.4	2.3

Notes: [a]Belgium, Denmark, France, Germany, Greece, Ireland, Italy, Luxembourg, Netherlands, Portugal, Spain, and the United Kingdom. Data for Belgium and Luxembourg are consolidated.
[b]EC 12 minus Greece and Portugal.
[c]Benin, Burkina Faso, Côte d'Ivoire, Mali, Niger, Senegal, Togo, Cameroon, Central African Republic, Chad, Congo, Gabon, and Equatorial Guinea.

Other European countries (for instance members of EFTA) also have close trading ties with EC countries, suggesting that even a wider currency area might be desirable. The importance of trade with EC countries no doubt is a primary reason for the explicit policy of "shadowing" of the deutsche mark by Austria, and of recent decisions by Norway, Sweden, and Finland to peg their currencies to the ECU. In the future, trade flows between Eastern European countries and the EC may also expand, raising the possibility of closer monetary integration.

Within the United States and Canada, states and provinces no doubt have a large amount of trade among themselves. One effect of currency union is to encourage integration. Looking at the two countries together, the United States and Canada also have a large proportion of bilateral trade, and this proportion may well increase as the Free Trade Agreement between the two countries comes into full force. However, the importance of the United States to Canada is much greater than the reverse. A North American free trade area that included these two countries plus Mexico would, on the basis of existing trade patterns, be more open than Europe.

Turning to the CFA franc zone, the extent of intra-union trade depends heavily on whether and how trade of the African countries with France is treated in the calculations (table 1.1). If only trade among African countries is considered, intra-union trade turns out to be relatively low. A larger proportion of trade is "internal" when trade with France is included in the numerator (but French overall exports and imports are not included in the denominator). The explanation lies in the fact that France is a much more important trading partner for each of the African countries than those countries are for France. As noted in table 1.1, once African countries and France are treated as a group, the share of internal trade is much reduced. Another currency union, that among Eastern Caribbean countries, also exhibits only a small amount of intra-regional trade; exports, which consist mainly of primary commodities, are directed primarily to the rest of the world.[23]

Clearly, in the cases of the CFA franc zone and the East Caribbean currency union, the size of intra-regional trade has not been the main motivation for currency union. More important has been the objective of enhanced monetary stability through a supra-national monetary institution.[24] This issue is discussed further below in section IV.

The former USSR provides yet another example of a currency union extending over a large geographical area. Data for trade among republics of the USSR confirm that production of particular goods is concentrated to a relatively high extent in single firms that supply the whole of the Soviet market, implying a high degree of inter-republic integration. Excluding the Russian Republic, the share of net material product of each republic delivered to the other republics ranges from 31 to 67 percent. For the Russian Republic, the share was 18 percent in 1988 (IMF, 1990). The high degree of integration suggests that separate currencies might, if exchange rates against the ruble varied sharply, greatly increase the uncertainty faced by producers. On the other hand, if the ruble continued to be associated with actual or repressed inflation resulting from monetary financing of central government deficits, pressures for republic currencies might intensify.

3 *Industrial and portfolio diversification*

The likelihood that an adverse shock would have a major impact on an economy will depend to some extent on how diversified is the economy's production structure.[25] If a country exports a wide variety of goods, and if shocks are primarily either to supply (i.e., technology) or to consumers'

14   Paul R. Masson and Mark P. Taylor

Table 1.2. *Selected industrial countries: shares of exports by commodity categories*

Country	Agricultural products[a]	Energy[b]	Other
Canada	19	9	72
United States	16	3	82
Japan	1	—[c]	99
France	17	2	81
Germany	6	1	93
Italy	7	2	91
United Kingdom	8	7	85
Australia	34	18	48
New Zealand	61	1	38

Notes: [a]Food, beverages, and tobacco; agricultural non-food (SITC 0, 1, 2, 4, less SITC 27, 28, 233, 244, 266, and 267).
[b]Mineral fuels, etc. (SITC 3).
[c]Less than 1 percent.
Sources: World Bank Trade System and Fund staff estimates. Based on data for 1988.

preferences (affecting relative demands for different goods), then the effect of any shock on output in the whole economy will be less (even in absolute terms) than the effect on individual industries. Other things equal, a diversified economy, therefore, has less need to retain exchange-rate flexibility in order to mitigate the effects of shocks.[26]

Countries whose production is not diversified, but instead is concentrated in a few goods, include a number of primary commodity exporters. Though industrial countries typically export a wider range of goods, there are some countries among them that are highly dependent on primary commodities: Australia for mineral resources and cereals, and Portugal, Greece, and New Zealand for agricultural products. Thus, Blundell-Wignall and Gregory (1990) argue, in the context of large and persistent commodity price fluctuations of the past two decades, that macroeconomic stabilization – in particular, the objective of price stability – calls for exchange-rate flexibility for Australia. Increases in world commodity prices raise domestic output prices, to a greater extent, the greater is the share of commodities in output; this pressure can be mitigated by exchange-rate appreciation. However, the appreciation will tend to crowd out other tradables production, in particular, manufactures, so that such sectoral

Table 1.3. *Selected industrial countries: shares of production by category in 1986ᵃ*

(In percent)

	Agriculture[b]	Construction	Energy and mining[c]	Manufacturing	Services[d]
Canada	4.0	7.6	9.0	23.4	56.0
United States	2.3	5.5	5.8	22.2	64.2
Japan	3.1	8.1	4.2	31.4	53.3
France	4.7	6.6	3.8	27.8	57.0
Germany	2.1	6.1	4.2	38.3	49.4
Italy	5.0	6.7	5.7	27.2	55.5
United Kingdom	2.1	6.7	7.8	27.6	55.9
Belgium	2.5	5.8	4.1	25.4	62.2
Denmark	6.6	8.3	3.0	24.6	57.5
Greece	17.3	7.4	5.1	21.1	49.1
Netherlands	5.2	6.3	9.1	23.4	56.0
Portugal	8.6	6.4	3.6	33.8	47.5
Spain	6.1	7.5	3.4	31.2	51.8

Notes: ᵃGDP at current prices. Shares are scaled to sum to 100.
[b]Including hunting, fishing, and forestry.
[c]Mining and quarrying (including petroleum and natural gas production), plus electricity generation and gas and water distribution.
[d]Excluding government services.
Source: OECD National Accounts.

considerations, to the extent they are judged important, may weigh *against* an appreciation. In addition, exchange-rate flexibility in the face of a *negative* commodity price shock may, through exchange-rate depreciation, increase the consumer price index by an amount proportional to the share of importables in consumption, and thereby exacerbate inflationary pressures. There thus are some qualifications to the argument for exchange-rate flexibility, even in this case; its relative advantages would depend on both the nature of shocks and the precise objectives of policy.

Canada and the United Kingdom are substantial exporters of energy, but in fact their net exports of energy goods are modest as a proportion of total exports (table 1.2). A broad impression of the diversification of domestic production can be obtained from industry output shares for a number of industrial countries (table 1.3). For the major industrial countries and for the other European countries for which data were available, the manufacturing sector constitutes between 1/5 and 1/3 of production.[27] Reliance on production of primary commodities (roughly agriculture, energy, and mining) is relatively small, except for Greece (where it is 22 percent of GDP), and, to a lesser extent, the Netherlands, Portugal, and Canada (between 12 and 14 percent of GDP). For the most part, the EC includes countries with a well-diversified structure of production. An interesting question is whether this diversification will continue with the abandonment of remaining trade barriers, making EC economies even more similar, or whether instead increased specialization will result, making the countries more dissimilar. Which of the two occurs will depend in large part on whether increased trade takes the form of inter- or intra-industry trade. In the latter case, specialization may occur, but with countries remaining diversified, so that shocks to the demand for a particular industry's product should not affect countries asymmetrically. The EC Commission (1990, p. 142) estimates that between 57 percent and 83 percent of intra-EC trade excluding Portugal and Greece was intra-industry. On the other hand, a comparison of *regional* output variability (within a given European country) with variability across European countries suggests that economic integration does not make the occurrence of asymmetric shocks less likely, and that divergence across countries may actually increase as a result of EMU (see chapter 5 below).

Another aspect to the issue is portfolio diversification. Adverse shocks to incomes in particular regions can be cushioned by holdings of assets which are claims to outside income streams. In principle, such diversification could provide insurance against purely regional shocks, and could make consumption independent of those shocks (Cochrane, 1988). Unfortunately, little is known about how widespread such portfolio diversification is in practice. There are likely to be great differences in the abilities of individuals and particular firms to hold diversified portfolios, due for instance to capital-market imperfections (preventing borrowing against future income) or transactions costs.

4   Wage/price flexibility

Implicit in the early literature on "optimum currency areas," which considered the value of exchange-rate adjustments for achieving internal and external balance, was the assumption that wages and domestic output prices were fixed, at least in the short run. It is now usual practice to regard wages and prices as "sticky" rather than fixed and to expect this stickiness to recede in the long run. Short-run stickiness may differ across countries.

In some countries the response of wages and prices to nominal exchange-rate changes could be large enough to limit the usefulness of nominal exchange-rate changes as an instrument of adjustment.

It is important to distinguish between two types of wage and price flexibility: real and nominal. Changes in a nominal price like the nominal exchange rate are a substitute for domestic price or wage changes, and may facilitate real adjustment. In the limiting case of real wage rigidity (for instance, due to complete indexation of wages), employment and net exports would, however, be unaffected by nominal exchange-rate changes, because rigidity of the real wage is tantamount to rigidity of the real exchange rate. In the other limiting case of perfect flexibility of real wages, the freedom to modify the nominal exchange rate can be helpful if nominal wages are sticky but redundant if nominal wages or prices are themselves flexible enough to do the job of altering real exchange rates.

On the spectrum stretching from perfect rigidity to perfect flexibility, evidence presented in Bruno and Sachs (1985) suggests that Europe is closer than the United States to the real wage rigidity end, while the reverse obtains for nominal wage rigidity.[28] This implies both that nominal exchange-rate changes would be a more effective tool in North America, and that the existence of higher real wage rigidity in Europe places a premium on other instruments to counter real shocks as well as on measures to improve labor-market flexibility.

5   An overview of the traditional criteria and the response to shocks

It is clear from the above discussion that there is no single over-riding criterion that could be used to assess the desirability or viability of a currency union. Some of the traditional flexibility criteria are favorable to existing and/or prospective currency unions, while others are adverse. Increasing analytical attention has therefore turned to analyzes of shocks affecting economies since shock-absorption combines the *net* influence of several of the traditional criteria.[29]

One central aspect of the question is whether shocks are symmetric or asymmetric (i.e., hit countries differently). Similar industrial structures may imply that real shocks facing industrial countries are symmetric. Another aspect is whether shocks are temporary or permanent. Temporary shocks may in principle be cushioned by financing, while permanent shocks require adjustment. A third issue is the origin of shocks: whether they are primarily nominal (i.e., to the price level) or real, domestic or foreign. Nominal exchange-rate flexibility is likely to do the best job in insulating the domestic economy from foreign, nominal disturbances. Fourth, there is the question of whether financial market shocks occur primarily in demands for money, or across domestic interest-bearing assets, or for foreign assets.[30] For example, if shocks occur in foreign exchange markets and are unrelated to economic fundamentals, then fixing the exchange rate may be the best solution.

Cohen and Wyplosz (1989) analyze shocks to real GDP, to the GDP deflator, to real wages, and to the current-account ratio, for both France and Germany. They decompose these shocks into permanent and temporary components, and also examine their degree of symmetry. They find that symmetric shocks to the two economies dominate the asymmetric ones; however, the same is not true when "Europe" (i.e., France and Germany taken together) is compared to the United States. Also, they find that symmetric shocks to France and Germany tend to be permanent, not temporary. Cohen and Wyplosz (1989) conclude from these results that monetary integration between France and Germany may be more viable than between Europe and the United States.

A recent study (Bayoumi, 1991) examines the nature of shocks hitting ERM countries since 1982 (arguably, the year when realignments became less frequent and the commitment to exchange-rate fixity was reinforced – Giavazzi and Spaventa, 1990), and compares responses to shocks of ERM countries to those of selected non-ERM countries. The main conclusions are as follows: (i) constraining the flexibility of exchange rates tends to produce a more drawn out response to shocks; (ii) price responses (in either direction) to shocks tend to be larger for ERM countries (aside from Germany) than for non-ERM countries; (iii) a comparison of the 1970s with the period since 1982 suggests that the formation of the ERM has made the *responses* of participating economies to shocks more similar; (iv) in contrast, the ERM does not seem to have increased the correlation across countries of the shocks themselves; and (v) already in the 1970s, shocks hitting ERM countries tended to be more symmetric than the shocks hitting non-ERM countries.

A complementary method for assessing the response to shocks within a currency union is to do stochastic simulations of an empirically based macroeconomic model. Repeated drawings are made from the estimated joint probability distribution of the shocks, the model is solved under different assumptions concerning the policy regime in place, and variances of variables of interest – for instance output and inflation – are calculated. This methodology was employed by Frenkel, Goldstein, and Masson (1989), using the International Monetary Fund's MULTIMOD model. They considered the use of both monetary and fiscal policy instruments to hit various intermediate targets. Shocks were applied to all the behavioral equations of the model, consistent with their historical distribution.[31] The results of that exercise suggested that fixing exchange rates among the United States, Japan, and Germany would lead to larger variances for key macroeconomic variables than maintaining flexible exchange rates accompanied by either monetary targeting or nominal GNP targeting. Again, these findings are consistent with the conclusion that the three largest economies may not constitute an optimal currency area.

A similar methodology was used by the EC Commission to analyze fixed exchange rates within the EMS.[32] Figure 1.2, which summarizes their results, is taken from that study. It suggests that a move from free floating of European currencies to the EMS system of infrequent and partial realignments increased average output variability in member countries, while reducing inflation variability.[33] The reduction in inflation variability is due to a reduction in asymmetric exchange-rate shocks and to an enhancement of price discipline in EMS countries other than Germany. Output variability increases outside of Germany because of the need to devote monetary policy in these countries to limiting currency movements against the deutsche mark (EC Commission, 1990, p. 154). A further move toward monetary union with irrevocably fixed exchange rates is argued to reduce *both* output and inflation variability. This would result from the disciplinary effects of narrower exchange-rate margins and from the implementation of a cooperative symmetric monetary policy. The EC Commission study highlights the following potential positive effects of currency union: (i) intra-EMS exchange-rate shocks (i.e., shocks to interest-rate parity) disappear; (ii) the elimination of expected devaluations dampens inflationary pressures;[34] and (iii) by enforcing coordination of monetary policies (making them identical, as a result of sharing the same currency), monetary union would reduce costs related to the attempt to use the exchange rate within the EC in a beggar-thy-neighbor fashion.[35] The negative effects of currency union are those associated with the loss of exchange-rate flexibility, as discussed above.

Despite the attractions of the simulation methodology, it is important also to recognize its limitations. First, the reduction in transactions costs resulting from the introduction of a common currency is not captured in such macroeconomic models.[36] Second, a comparison of different policy regimes, assuming that the structure of the rest of the economy is unaffected, may give misleading results. For instance, the degree of labor mobility or wage/price flexibility may respond endogenously to the elimination of exchange-rate fluctuations.[37] Third, there are other issues, concerning the credibility of the commitment to price stability and the need to discipline fiscal policy, that go beyond the scope of most empirical macro models.

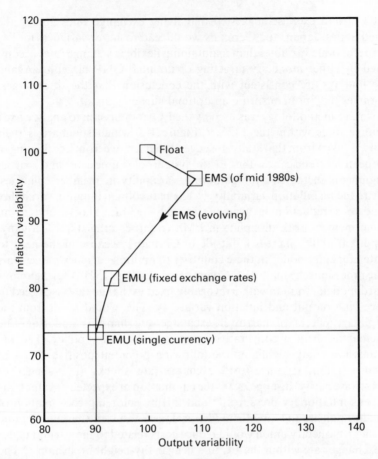

Figure 1.2 Macroeconomic stability of EMU
Notes: Indices EC average, free float = 100.
This figure plots the combinations of variability of output (GDP) and inflation for
the Community average in index form as resulting from the stochastic simulations.
The position of each of the four regimes ("free float," "EMS," "asymmetric EMU,"
and "EMU") corresponds to an intersection between a regime-dependent output–
inflation trade-off curve and a shifting preference curve.
Source: Stochastic simulations with the Multimod model of the IMF under the
responsibility of the Commission services. GDP is measured as a percentage
deviation from its baseline value, inflation is measured in percentage point
differences with respect to baseline inflation rates. The indices used in the figure are
obtained by averaging, first, the square of the deviations for forty-three simulations
over the period 1990–9 and by taking the square root. Dividing by the root
mean-squared deviations for the free float regime and multiplication by 100 then
gives the indices.
From EC Commission (1990), p. 154.

IV Fiscal policy within currency areas

Though a currency union makes monetary policy independence of member countries impossible, the same is not obviously true of fiscal policies.[38] If a well-developed financial market exists on which governments can borrow, they need not resort to monetary financing; hence it is sometimes argued that even independent and divergent fiscal policies will not disturb monetary conditions. However, the danger exists that governments would accumulate so much debt that they would not be able to service it or to borrow further at acceptable cost, and that as a result they would put pressure on the central bank to monetize that debt or to finance deficits through money creation. In these circumstances, the central bank could not credibly commit itself to price stability, and the private sector, recognizing this, would incorporate inflation into its expectations. Labor would demand higher wage settlements, and purchasers of government debt would demand higher interest rates to be compensated for expected inflation. The advantages of a stable currency would be lost.

It is useful in this context to consider more generally the role of fiscal policy in a currency union.[39]

1 Spillovers from national fiscal policies

The nature of the spillovers from national fiscal policies is likely to be different within a currency union than when countries are linked by flexible exchange rates. In the Mundell–Fleming model with perfect capital mobility and flexible exchange rates, a bond-financed increase in domestic government spending in the home country has *positive* transmission effects on output abroad because the domestic currency appreciates owing to a rise in domestic interest rates, leading to higher net exports in foreign countries. In contrast, under fixed exchange rates and in the absence of other structural changes, transmission effects are likely to be *negative*, since a fiscal expansion raises world interest rates, crowding out investment both at home and abroad, while foreign countries are likely to benefit much less from higher exports.[40]

Elaborations of the Mundell–Fleming model produce less clear-cut conclusions, as the channels of influence become more complicated.[41] However, the basic insights of the simpler model seem to be borne out by empirical estimates and simulations. For instance, simulations of fiscal stimulus using MULTIMOD suggest that increased government spending in Germany leads to increases in output in that country but to *falls* in output in EMS countries whose currencies are assumed to be tied to the deutsche mark.[42] In contrast, positive fiscal stimulus by the United States or Japan, whose currencies are modeled as being free to move flexibly against other currencies, generally cause output to expand in other countries initially – including the EMS countries. In a currency union, therefore, the absence of exchange-rate flexibility may "bottle up" to some extent the expansionary effects in the country undertaking fiscal stimulus – unless trade linkages are very strong or capacity utilization is very high. Also, the effects of higher interest rates will be spread to other member countries. In addition, if the temporary fiscal stimulus produces appreciation of the common currency, as implied by models with perfect capital mobility and rational expectations,[43] the other countries share in the appreciation, which tends to reduce their net exports. A mitigating effect results, however, from potentially tighter trade links between countries in a currency union, which would tend to increase trade elasticities and thereby spread the demand stimulus more widely.

Another spillover associated with monetary union concerns possible effects on the credibility of the joint monetary policy. In a country with a separate currency, the inflation problems associated with undisciplined fiscal policies that lead to unsustainable debt accumulation and eventual monetization are borne within the country itself. In a currency union, there is an externality from unsustainable fiscal deficits if they induce fears of monetization, since threats to price stability have consequences for *all* the countries in the union. How important this possibility is, of course, depends on the institutional structure, and in particular on the status of the union's central bank and its vulnerability to pressures from individual governments. There is an extensive literature on national central banks that suggests that the greater their independence from their fiscal authorities, the more successful they are in achieving low inflation.[44] The situation of a central bank in a monetary union is different, since it faces many national fiscal authorities: this may enhance its independence (Mélitz, 1991). Such reasoning would suggest that a European central bank might have a similar relationship with national fiscal authorities as the Federal Reserve *vis-à-vis* US state governments.

Unsustainable fiscal deficits in one country may, however, lead to pressures on other countries in the currency union to subsidize the errant government, either through monetary expansion, explicit fiscal transfers from other members, implicit interest subsidies, or loan guarantees. Monetary expansion may ensue, or at least be feared by the private sector, either because the profligate country may be able to exert pressure on the union's central bank, or because the objectives of the central bank may include employment and economic activity in member countries, which would tend to be adversely affected by the debt-servicing difficulties of the profligate member or by high interest rates. Given that solidarity among member countries is likely to be associated with the formation of a currency union, the pressures on the central bank to assist a country in difficulty may be quite strong.[45]

Ideally, the statutory position of the central bank would make it immune from such pressures. It has been argued that effective independence of a central bank from political authorities (including the personal independence of members of the governing bodies) is a necessary condition for monetary stability, and that in addition the central bank must be given the necessary instruments to achieve a monopoly over monetary creation.[46] However, it may be difficult to guarantee by statute alone that monetary policy is immune from pressures arising from lax budget discipline. A concern for other objectives in addition to price stability on the part of central bankers may lead them to respond to such pressures; this is the argument for making sure that central bankers are more "conservative" than other policy-makers. That is, by choosing officials who emphasize the goal of price stability (more than does society as a whole), governments may help to ensure that the temptation to engage in self-defeating monetary expansion is minimized.[47] Alternatively, a currency union may need to place some restrictions on the borrowing of member countries. This issue is considered in the next sub-section.

2 Prospects for budget discipline

There is the danger, raised by the Delors Committee Report, that, in the absence of supra-national controls, fiscal deficits might be excessive, endangering monetary discipline. As a result of this concern, the amendment to the Treaty of Rome, agreed at Maastricht in December 1991, stipulates that "member states shall avoid excessive government deficits" (Article 104 B.1). These are defined on the basis of two criteria in Article 104 B and in a protocol annexed to the treaty: (1) whether planned or actual deficits are in excess of 3 percent of GDP, if it is also the case that the deficit ratio "has not declined substantially and continuously" and that it is not a temporary and exceptional excess; and (2) whether the ratio of government debt to GDP exceeds 60 percent of GDP, if that ratio has not been declining at a satisfactory pace. The European Council will determine if governments have incurred excessive deficits, defined above, and, if so, will make recommendations to correct the situation. If those recommendations are not followed, then a number of sanctions on the offending government are possible, including modification of the European Investment Bank's lending policies to that country and the imposition of fines.

The tendency toward excessive deficits is modified by the formation of a currency union, in ways that are discussed below. However, it has also been argued that well-functioning capital markets should prevent such excessive borrowing. Well-informed investors in a free capital market impose discipline by raising the interest rates at which they are willing to lend, and by eventually cutting off lending to governments with unsustainable debt accumulation. This should occur before the problem becomes unmanageable, so the argument goes.[48] The experience of existing fiscal federations is relevant in assessing this argument.

Incentives for excessive deficits

Will the incentives to undertake unsustainable fiscal policies be modified in a currency union relative to a situation in which a country has its own currency? A number of factors come into play in addressing this question, some of which are hard to distinguish from those that result from greater integration generally, that is, from the creation of a common "economic space." First, a currency union, if it increases integration among member countries, may reduce the ability of countries to raise revenues. Factor mobility will make tax bases more mobile, and make it more difficult to levy non-benefit taxes, that is, taxes that are not linked to particular services.[49] As a result, shocks to the budget are more likely to lead to unsustainable deficits. On the other hand, increased factor mobility makes adjustment less difficult, reducing the need for·structural fiscal policies. Second, currency union will remove the freedom to use seigniorage as a flexible revenue source; as a result, it may force countries to rely more on issuing government debt, with dangers of unsustainable borrowing.[50] Third, if a country switches from borrowing in its own currency to borrowing in a common currency, debt-servicing costs may be affected. A larger capital market in the common currency may make interest costs less sensitive to the country's budgetary position; and nominal and real interest rates may also be lower if the common currency exhibits more price level stability. At the same time, the country concerned may no longer have the same captive market for its debt, for instance by issuing government securities to banks with high secondary reserve requirements or to individuals without access to other saving instruments.[51] Fourth, by increasing the effectiveness of fiscal expansion at home (see above), it may also increase the tendency to resort to fiscal stimulus. Fifth, by removing the very visible sanction of exchange-rate depreciation (though replacing it by the sanction of higher interest costs), currency union might decrease the political disincentives toward imprudent policies.

Government borrowing in fiscal federations

The experience of fiscal federations may provide some useful insights for other monetary unions. A preliminary empirical analysis of US data on state borrowing costs suggests that there is some evidence that higher debt burdens increase the cost of borrowing.[52] States typically run surpluses or small budget deficits, but it is not clear whether this is the result of market discipline or of constitutional provisions or statutes that aim at budget balance. Bishop, Damrau, and Miller (1989) argue that the Canadian example is more relevant for the operation of a currency union of independent countries, since Canada has a looser federal system than the United States, Australia, or Germany. In the latter countries, control over junior levels of governments by the federal government and restrictions on regional governments are both greater than in Canada. Moreover, the likelihood that the Government of Canada would feel obliged to honor provincial debts may be lower: "The lack of an explicit Federal Government guarantee to come to the assistance of a financially distressed province . . . has ensured that the market continues to send signals on the appropriateness of provincial budgetary policies" (Bishop, Damrau, and Miller, 1989, p. 13). However, in Canada fiscal transfers, or "equalization payments," to poorer regions are institutionalized to a greater extent than in the United States, and are larger in size than the EC Structural Funds (this is discussed more fully below), which may reduce the tendency for provinces to run excessive deficits. In addition, the mere fact that borrowing costs rise with increased deficits does not prove that those borrowing costs enforce discipline on the governments concerned; the latter would require that governments rein-in errant fiscal policies in response to increases in their borrowing costs.

The judgment that the market is always able to discipline governmental borrowers within a union seems too sanguine. More relevant perhaps than the experience within fiscal federations is the issuance of debt of independent states in foreign currency – for which there is no possibility for the country to reduce its real value through inflation. The experience of developing countries in the 1970s and 1980s suggests that market discipline is only applied after debt accumulation has reached clearly excessive levels; this is also suggested by examples of industrial countries, such as Ireland and Denmark, which incurred large foreign-currency debts in the late 1970s and early 1980s.

The CFA franc zone also provides some insights concerning the interaction of monetary and fiscal policies in a currency union. Unsustainable public sector imbalances in these countries have resulted in an overhang of external debt, in cost pressures, and in appreciation of real exchange rates relative to other Sub-Saharan countries. This has occurred despite the absence of monetization; statutory ceilings have allowed only limited access of governments to monetary financing, and these ceilings have been respected.

In sum, market forces do seem to play some role in disciplining governments' deficit spending. However, there does not appear to be a good case for arguing that problems of fiscal discipline disappear within currency unions in the absence of firm surveillance over policies or rules for limiting budget deficits. The next section considers the opposite question, namely whether the need for fiscal flexibility also increases within currency unions.

3   Fiscal flexibility and inter-regional transfers

In section III we discussed several characteristics that are helpful for the smooth functioning of currency unions, namely: labor mobility, industrial diversification, and wage and price flexibility. If these features are not present to a sufficient extent, then the fiscal instrument may be an especially important tool to cushion individual countries or regions from shocks, given the absence of the exchange-rate instrument for that purpose.[53] Such fiscal flexibility need not involve discretionary policy – often associated with the term "fine tuning" – but rather can be the result of the operation of automatic stabilizers. To the extent that fiscal policy is oriented toward medium-term objectives, however, the scope for fiscal flexibility is lessened.

An alternative (or possible complement) to larger national or regional deficits and surpluses for shock-absorbing purposes is a system of fiscal taxes and transfers between members of a currency union – a form of fiscal federalism. Such a mechanism is a feature of all political federations, to a lesser or greater extent. There is disagreement, however, on whether it is necessary for the successful operation of currency unions. Sala-i-Martin and Sachs (1992) show that, in the United States, the federal tax and transfer system serves as an important shock absorber by increasing federal tax payments from, and lowering transfer payments to, those regions that are prospering relative to the national average, and conversely for those that are relatively depressed. The federal tax system and outright transfers to states are estimated to cushion over *one-third* of the effects of region-specific shocks on disposable income.

Sala-i-Martin and Sachs (1992) conclude that the success of EMU requires a system of taxes and transfers on a similar scale in Europe. It is estimated that, at present, Community taxes compensate for no more than *1 percent* of an income loss from an unfavorable shock hitting any member country.[54] A contrasting view is that, even though transfers among EC countries are much lower than in the United States or Canada, the doubling of the size of structural funds by 1992 agreed in 1988 will provide sufficient fiscal resources to disadvantaged countries in the EC.[55]

It is also important to distinguish between income transfers induced by short-run effects of shocks from those that are related to persistent differences in prosperity – i.e., from richer to poorer regions. Von Hagen (1991) shows that, if the latter are omitted, and the effects of purely transitory shocks isolated, the stabilizing function of the US federal fiscal system is very small.

Canada also provides an interesting case study of federal taxes and transfers within a currency union. The cushioning effects of taxes on disposable income are larger for taxes than for transfers, as in Sala-i-Martin and Sachs (1992), but magnitudes of both seem to be lower in Canada than in the United States (Bayoumi and Masson, 1991). Thus, when only taxes from, and transfers to, households are considered the conclusions for Canada depart significantly from those for the United States. However, shock-absorbing properties of the federal tax and transfer system may also operate through corporate taxes and transfers to businesses and to provincial and local governments. Shocks to provincial income may be offset through these channels; effects may show up in household income, if only indirectly. For instance, transfer payments to provincial governments may allow them to continue to provide the same level of government services without raising provincial taxes. Indeed, the recently revised Canadian constitution enshrines the principle of equalization payments by the Government of Canada to ensure that comparable public services can be provided at "reasonably comparable levels of taxation."[56] While it is true that transfers to poorer provinces are a feature of Canadian fiscal federalism to a much greater extent than in the United States,[57] these transfers are intended to serve longer-run structural purposes rather than to offset cyclical fluctuations. These findings for the Canadian system suggest that, though the magnitude of the cushioning of shocks is somewhat smaller in Canada, the conclusion of Sala-i-Martin and Sachs, that a strong federal tax and transfer system is a key feature of viable currency unions, seems to be borne out.[58]

However, the smaller cushioning of shocks through the federal tax and transfer system, in Canada relative to the United States, has as its counterpart greater fiscal stabilization powers for provincial governments relative to state governments. Thus, provincial governments, unlike most US states, are not subject to balanced-budget limitations, and they have on occasion run substantial deficits. For example, in fiscal year 1987, the consolidated fiscal balance of all Canadian provinces amounted to 12 percent of provincial revenues.[59] Nevertheless, transfers from the federal government do provide a safety net. It can be argued that those transfers decrease the likelihood of financial crises and enable the fiscally weaker provincial governments to access global capital markets.[60] Without such transfers, the borrowing capacity of members of a currency area may be quite limited; individual states may not be able to commit themselves credibly to raising future taxes (to service borrowing) if factors of production are mobile.[61]

Such tax and transfer mechanisms are likely to be useful for reducing the costs of absorbing shocks. As noted in earlier sections, these costs are largest if shocks are asymmetric, if factor mobility is low, and if wages and prices are inflexible. To some extent, regional governments may be able to cushion shocks themselves, through running deficits and surpluses.

The issue of fiscal federalism is important not only for Europe, but also for federations that are transferring fiscal powers from the federal authority to regional governments. In Yugoslavia, fiscal federalism takes a highly decentralized form, with considerable spending undertaken by the republics and provinces. The tax resources of the central (federation) government are limited to a portion of indirect tax revenues. The federation has financed its expenditures in areas of defence, federal administration, veterans' and disability insurance, and financing of less-developed republics and the province of Kosovo, partly through "upward" transfers from the republics.[62] Transfers from the republics are determined in annual negotiations, and agreements must be ratified by the assemblies of all republics and autonomous provinces – an arduous process. From the Yugoslav experience, it appears that, in the context of a high degree of fiscal decentralization, the presence of upward transfers means that the effectiveness of federal fiscal policy is considerably reduced as an instrument of stabilization policy; moreover, fiscal decisions by individual republics can undermine federal monetary policy. Excessive fiscal decentralization may thus remove an instrument for cushioning regional shocks, as well as reducing the main advantage of a currency area – the wider circulation of a stable currency.

4   The case for fiscal policy coordination

The basic rationale for policy coordination is that national policy actions have non-trivial "spillover" effects on other countries; policy coordination is a mechanism for internalizing these externalities. Of course, policy spillovers exist among countries irrespective of whether they are members of a currency union.[63] However, the nature of these spillovers is affected by the exchange-rate regime in place; as pointed out above, for example, an expansionary fiscal policy may be negatively, not positively transmitted in a currency union. In addition, countries in a currency union may become more integrated economically, as well as more concerned about the welfare of their neighbors.[64]

The question arises as to the form that policy coordination should take to reduce unfavorable spillover effects. Two sorts of spillovers were discussed above: (i) macroeconomic spillovers associated with stabilization policy, and (ii) externalities related to budget discipline and credibility of monetary policy. The latter externalities imply a persistent bias in the direction of excessive deficits. In contrast, externalities related to stabilization policies in the face of shocks will depend on the sign of the shock: in one case a country's budget deficit will be excessive, while in another, the problem will be overcontractionary fiscal policies (for instance, in the case of higher oil prices discussed above). Therefore, rules or institutionalized procedures that put ceilings on deficits may be the solution for the first case, but not the second. It may be very difficult to define rules that are appropriate to all situations. A procedure that enables fiscal policies to be coordinated in a flexible fashion to minimize the unfavorable effects of both types of externalities has its advantages, but to the extent that it relies on discretion rather than rules, it may itself build in sub-optimal behavior. Discretionary policy coordination may not be put in place sufficiently quickly, may be subject to misinterpretation, and may be difficult to monitor.

Most federations have a combination of rule-based and discretionary coordination. For example, Canada has rules for making equalization payments to poorer regions, but they are renegotiated every five years. Coordination among federal and provincial governments also occurs through annual conferences of first ministers.[65] Such discretionary coordination has the drawback, compared to clear rules defining respective powers and responsibilities, that it is subject to the vagaries of successive renegotiation.

The discussion above suggests that currency unions cannot ignore the effects of fiscal policies on the exchange-rate mechanism. It seems clear that in order to discipline fiscal policies and reduce unfavorable regional effects, mechanisms for achieving both fiscal transfers and enhanced fiscal policy coordination are helpful. However, the decision to set up the institutions of fiscal federalism is essentially a political choice that balances loss of sovereignty against shared goals among members.

V Convergence issues

Issues of real and nominal economic convergence are central to any discussion of the formation of monetary unions.[66] It is perhaps intuitively obvious that monetary union implies convergence of inflation rates – at least in the long run. Indeed, convergence of both inflation rates and monetary policy has been a feature of the European Monetary System, particularly since 1982, despite some recent widening of the spread of inflation rates; see figure 1.3.[67] On the other hand, it is not clear whether

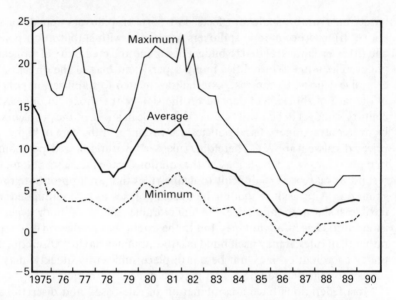

Figure 1.3 ERM: maximum and minimum rates of inflation (consumer price indices)
Source: International Monetary Fund, *International Financial Statistics*. Ungerer *et al.* (1990), p. 25.

real convergence is a prerequisite or a consequence of closer economic integration.

The Maastricht agreement specifies that a certain degree of convergence is needed before a country can proceed to economic and monetary union. Convergence is defined as follows: achievement of an annual rate of inflation that is no more than $1\frac{1}{2}$ percentage points above the average of the three best achievers; a sustainable fiscal position (defined as above, in section IV.2); observance of normal ERM fluctuation margins for the previous two years; and long-term interest rates that do not exceed the average for the three best-performing EC states by more than 2 percentage points.

The view that real convergence is a prerequisite for monetary and customs union would follow from the belief that the geographical location of economic activity is subject to centripetal forces arising from closer economic integration. Such forces might be due, for example, to the attractiveness of an already highly industrialized center – with an established infrastructure and other positive external economies – for the location of new activity (Myrdal, 1957; Perroux, 1959).

The opposing view – that closer economic and monetary integration is likely to lead to greater real economic convergence – follows from the neoclassical view that the free movement of goods and services in an environment not subject to exchange-rate risk will lead to an equalization of factor prices and per capita output.

Some clarification of the issues involved in this literature can be found in recent work by Krugman (1990) and Krugman and Venables (1990). They confirm two intuitive conclusions: (i) centralization is more likely the greater the size of available economies-of-scale and the greater the size of the mobile manufacturing sector; and (ii) it is less likely the greater the size and importance of transport costs.

Taking real output per capita (as a percentage of the national average) as the measure of real economic performance, figure 1.4 presents some evidence on the degree of real convergence during the last thirty years in a monetary union – the United States – and the European Community. It shows the cross-sectional standard deviation of regional real product per capita for US regions and of real GDP per capita for members of the European Community, including and excluding Greece, Portugal, and Spain, relative to the mean.[68] The figure suggests a significant degree of real economic convergence across the United States during this period, which concurs with the results of Barro and Sala-i-Martin (1990), who examine data for US states since 1840. The results of similar calculations using data for the countries of the European Community are interesting for a number of reasons. First they show that, on this measure, much of the dispersion in real economic performance across the EC is due to the southern countries – i.e., Greece, Portugal, and Spain. Excluding these countries, the standard deviation has remained reasonably constant at around 12 percent since the early 1960s, but including them causes the standard deviation to rise to between some 25 percent and 30 percent. There is some sign of real convergence across the EC in the 1970s; a comparison of the two lines suggests that this is due to faster growth in Greece, Portugal, and Spain.

Apart from these absolute differences in the patterns of real economic behavior across the two areas, the relative orders of magnitude are also worth noting. Thus, while the standard deviation of US regional real product per capita as a percentage of the national average varies between some 3 and 5 percent, the corresponding range for the European Community as a whole is between 22 and 35 percent or, excluding the southern countries, around 12 percent. There is certainly no presumption from the US data that currency union makes convergence of living standards difficult. However, how much of the convergence was facilitated by fixity of exchange rates – encouraging both capital and labor mobility – and how much was due to fiscal transfers from richer to poorer regions (discussed in section IV above), is unclear.

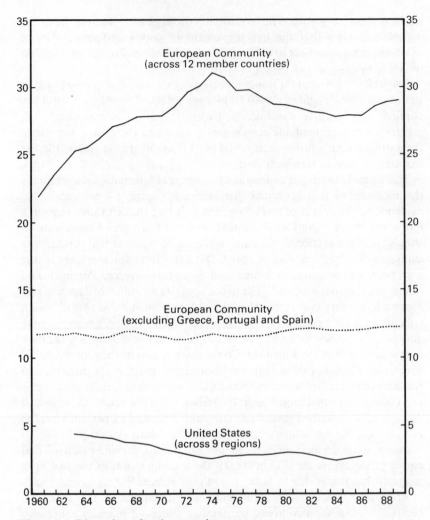

Figure 1.4 Dispersion of real per capita output
Note: Coefficients of variation, i.e., standard deviations of real per capita output, scaled by the mean (components are weighted by population).

Since monetary union implies intense pressure for convergence of inflation rates, a related question concerns the output costs of disinflation and whether or not nominal convergence should be achieved before or after monetary union. In a neoclassical framework, the output costs of disinflation are viewed as temporary, with output and employment returning in the medium term to the equilibrium, constant inflation rate level (Friedman, 1968). Recent work, however, suggests that European output and employment levels may display "hysteresis" effects (Blanchard and Summers, 1986; Gordon, 1988) – that is to say, the equilibrium level of unemployment or output is not independent of its time path. There are many competing theories of output and unemployment hysteresis, one of which is that the human capital – vocational skills and knowledge – of workers decays rapidly, making them difficult to re-employ and much less efficient workers after a certain period of unemployment. If this is the case, then it becomes dangerous to treat the output costs of disinflation as temporary. If output is reduced in order to disinflate, then in the absence of exogenous shocks and/or technological innovations it may stick at or near the new lower level until the authorities reflate. Evidence that reductions in inflation may generate permanent increases in unemployment is given by Sachs (1987) and Gordon (1988), both of whom employ European price and wage data.

Given, however, the perceived desirability of low inflation, the question is whether or not the output costs – temporary or permanent – of bringing down inflation are higher within monetary union than outside it. In large measure, the answer hinges on the credibility of the supra-national monetary authority to pursue the objective of price stability. If the commitment to price stability is perceived as strong and credible, then there may be a marked improvement in the output–inflation trade-off inside the monetary union as inflationary expectations are lowered – at least in countries with higher inflation rates.[69] This underlines the case for carefully examining the role and constitution of the European central bank.

VI Monetary union – transitional issues

1 European Monetary Union

Previous sections have considered a number of issues concerning currency unions, including: traditional criteria for their success, the conformity of existing unions to these criteria, the convergence of real economic performance before and after their establishment, and implications for fiscal policy. In this section, some of the issues concerning the transition to monetary union are discussed. The overwhelming case in point in this context is Europe, where agreement was reached at Maastricht in December 1991, to set up the "European Monetary Institute" on January 1, 1994, and to proceed to full monetary union by January 1, 1999.

A fundamental issue concerning the appropriate speed of transition toward full monetary union is whether or not it is necessary or desirable to achieve economic convergence *before* monetary union, or whether it can follow. This issue was discussed in section V. Another issue concerns whether or not, in stage 3, the supra-national authority responsible for monetary policy can be counted on to ensure price stability (section II above). A concern in progressing to a single money involves foregoing the monetary discipline presently imposed by the Bundesbank amongst the members of the ERM. While it may be argued that the existing members of the ERM have revealed a preference for price stability (Artis and Taylor, 1990), unless one can be sure that any new supra-national authority will do at least as well as the Bundesbank in this respect, there may be reasons for extending the transition period to full monetary union.

There are, clearly, two basic options available for the speed of transition – fast and slow. A third alternative (the so-called "two-track" approach) would be for an inner core group of countries to move rapidly to EMU with the remaining countries progressing toward monetary union less rapidly (see, e.g., Wolf, 1990). A major argument against such a scenario is that the outer core group may find themselves "outsiders" when they eventually come to full monetary union – i.e., a pattern of trading and other economic relationships may develop within the inner core, which members of the outer core may later find it hard to penetrate (see, e.g., Artis and Taylor, 1990). The slow option would allow time for the convergence of real and nominal economic variables and the development of other "prerequisites" of an optimal currency area. The argument against a slow transition, however, is based largely on the view that it is likely in some sense to be unstable.

The Maastricht agreement takes an intermediate position. As described in section V, certain criteria with respect to inflation, government deficits, exchange-rate margins, and long-term interest rates, are to be applied. These criteria are likely to be met quite easily for a core group of countries, but with much more difficulty by recent EC members (Portugal and Greece, especially) and some others. This suggests that a two-speed Europe is likely, though a degree of discretion is to be granted to the European Council to judge whether convergence has been achieved. In addition, a fixed timetable (mandating EMU by 1999) has been set; it is unlikely that *real* convergence, for instance of living standards, will have been achieved by then. Nevertheless, the length of "stage 2" (intermediate between the establishment of the European Monetary Institute and irrevocably fixed exchange notes) is long enough that the transition may be subjected to speculative pressures.

2   Sources of instability in the transition

There are at least two sources of instability which can threaten the transitional phase: instability arising from currency substitution and instability arising from speculative attack.

Currency substitution

In the absence of capital controls, it seems likely that a fully credible exchange-rate union will lead to a concentration of cash balances – especially those held by large corporations – in a small number of currencies in order to achieve benefits similar to some of those which accrue in monetary union (Giovannini, 1990; UK Treasury, 1990). This may generate large shifts in the demand for individual member currencies in the short run, with the instability becoming increasingly significant as the degree of European economic and financial integration rises.[70]

While these effects would not affect the overall stance of monetary policy across the exchange-rate union, they would make the interpretation of national monetary aggregates more difficult. Indeed, one recent study (Kremers and Lane, 1990) has produced econometric evidence that a single, stable aggregate demand function for narrow money expressed in a common currency already exists for the ERM membership as a whole, suggesting that problems arising from the imposition of a common set of parameters across the whole range of countries are more than compensated for by internalizing the effects of currency substitution and portfolio diversification.

Speculative attack

The possibility of instability arising from speculative attacks on the exchange rate relates to the markets' belief in the authorities' ultimate commitment – and ability – to maintain a certain parity. If successful, a speculative attack will be self-fulfilling in the sense that it will lead to a realignment of the currency.

One obvious scenario in which such an attack might occur is where the competitiveness of a high inflation member country has clearly been eroded by holding the nominal exchange-rate parity. This will therefore generate speculation that the currency will be devalued which, if it is intense, may lead to an eventual exhaustion of the authorities' foreign exchange reserves, so that they are then indeed forced to devalue. As noted by Giovannini (1990), such a situation may be exacerbated if price setters, producers, and unions "pencil in" a devaluation in their pricing and bargaining procedures, thereby adding further inflationary pressure. In this respect, it is worth noting that only a very small perceived probability of a sizable devaluation may be necessary to generate a significant skew in the distribution of expectations (a phenomenon related to the so-called "peso problem").[71]

A second scenario would be where a country has a very large stock of public debt, a substantial proportion of which is due to be refinanced (Giavazzi and Pagano, 1989). The markets may then perceive a reluctance on the part of the authorities to raise short-term interest rates in order to defend its currency because of the concomitant increase in debt service, and may believe that it would prefer, in the final analysis, to allow the debt to be eroded through a devaluation of the domestic currency. This perception may generate a capital flight from such a country which would initially lead to foreign intervention by the authorities and a consequent loss of reserves. The loss of reserves might then strengthen the perception that the parity cannot be held and so lead to an intensification of the attack.

As noted by Artis and Taylor (1988), it may be possible, at least in principle, to deter speculative attacks in the absence of capital controls by an appropriate design and mix of other measures such as realignment procedures, the degree of monetary policy convergence, and the intervention mechanism.[72]

With respect to realignment procedures, in the transition to monetary union, the option of frequent and "timely" realignments which avoid allowing rates to hit outer fluctuation limits and so offer speculators one-way bets is clearly not available.

With respect to foreign exchange market intervention arrangements, the literature on speculative attacks clearly identifies the trigger for an attack as the perception that reserves will be exhausted and the currency devalued.[73] While capital controls can limit the amount of speculative currency sales – preventing the trigger from being pulled by keeping the safety catch on – appropriate intervention arrangements can provide an assurance that reserve exhaustion will not occur – thereby alleviating pressure on the trigger. Thus, borrowing rights are a deterrent to attack and the limiting case – infinite borrowing rights – is indeed indistinguishable from an indissoluble exchange-rate union. The 1987 Basle–Nyborg Agreement, by increasing the availability of the "very short-term financing facility," was thus significant in reducing the vulnerability of the system to attack by increasing the funds immediately available to central banks in defence of their currency. To a large extent, however, the efficacy or otherwise of foreign exchange market intervention is an empirical question. (Unsterilized intervention, by definition, cannot be seen as independent of monetary policy.)

Sterilized foreign exchange market intervention can, in principle, be effective in stemming an attack in two ways. First, it alters the composition of the market portfolio and thereby its risk characteristics and so the equilibrium exchange rate (Branson and Henderson, 1985). Clearly, the effectiveness of such intervention will be weakened as interest-earning assets denominated in the various ERM currencies become closer substitutes for one another. Secondly, intervention may act as a signaling device (Mussa, 1981): if the authorities, acting on inside information, are prepared to bet against the market then intervention becomes a signal of future monetary policy (to the extent that the profitability of official intervention is publicly scrutinized).

The last official study of intervention, the Jurgensen Report (1983), concluded that sterilized intervention was a relatively weak instrument of exchange-rate policy. More recent empirical studies, in particular by Dominguez (1990) and Obstfeld (1990) (see Taylor, 1992 for a survey) essentially conclude that broad movements in exchange rates in the latter half of the 1980s have been largely attributable to monetary and fiscal policy developments rather than sterilized intervention; that the scale of sterilized intervention in recent years has generally been too small relative to the magnitude of outstanding asset stocks to have had significant portfolio effects (with the possible exception of 1987); that the signaling effect of sterilized intervention has only been effective when reinforced simultaneously by monetary policy or coincident news events (such as unexpectedly good trade figures); and that insofar as intervention does have any effect, it is likely to be considerably enhanced when undertaken by several countries in a concerted fashion.

This evidence therefore suggests that, notwithstanding the scope for concerted intervention to iron out short-term market fluctuations, the major route to avoiding the instability arising from speculative exchange-rate attacks in a transition to monetary union must be primarily via monetary policy coordination.

3 Arguments for and against a rapid transition
In the light of the above discussion, one can list at least four attractions of taking the fast route to monetary union: (i) maximum credibility to exchange-rate stability is generated since exchange rates are effectively eliminated; (ii) more of the efficiency gains associated with a single currency are obtained immediately; (iii) a central monetary authority may have more success in implementing area-wide monetary policy than individual country monetary authorities; and (iv) it could also avoid "beggar-thy-neighbor" interest rates and other policies.

The major argument against a rapid transitional phase is exactly that which is used in support of gradualism: it may be advisable to allow time for the "sufficient" convergence of economic performance and other conditions of successful monetary union, as discussed in section V. In the presence of persistent divergence of real economic indicators (such as per capita output) across Europe, some potential members may view the economic costs of joining EMU as outweighing the political costs of staying outside it.

A related argument is that, by imposing an administered, centralized approach to monetary management, there is the risk of achieving an *average* overall economic performance rather than the potential benefits of converging on "the best in the community" which a more autonomous, competitive approach may yield (UK Treasury, 1989). An alternative plan for a competitive, rather than administered, approach to the management of stage 3 (the Hard ECU Proposal) was put forward by the United Kingdom, but it did not achieve wide support and was not embodied in the Maastricht agreement.

VII   Summary and conclusions

The chapter has highlighted a number of the issues that arise in monetary unions, or common currency areas. The value of such unions clearly derives from the wider circulation of a stable currency; major benefits include reducing transactions costs, lowering price and exchange-rate variability, and enhancing the anti-inflationary credibility of monetary policy. For the latter to result from currency union, it is crucial that the proper incentives be provided for disciplined monetary policies. In this context, the institutional design of the central bank is of crucial importance. In particular, it seems likely that price stability is enhanced by *de facto* independence from fiscal authorities. Such independence may result from statutory provisions, but such provisions may not be sufficient if governments can exert indirect pressure on the central bank for easier monetary policy. The latter possibility is the reason for the argument, made in the Delors Committee Report, that constraints on fiscal deficits are also needed in the context of economic and monetary union in Europe; such constraints are embodied in the Maastricht agreement, though subject to a number of mitigating provisions.

The costs of currency union for a given country involve the loss of exchange-rate flexibility, which can be seen as providing an instrument to cushion "shocks" to the economy. The traditional literature on optimal currency areas considers the circumstances in which the loss of this instrument is the least costly: within currency unions exhibiting high factor mobility and wage/price flexibility, for economies that are relatively open, and for countries with a high degree of industrial diversification. Since these criteria are partial ones, an overall assessment requires a macroeconomic model and knowledge of the incidence of various shocks; some of this literature was surveyed above.

Another important macroeconomic tool is fiscal policy in its various aspects. It is possible that demands for the use of this tool might increase within a currency union, since the exchange-rate instrument is no longer available for cushioning shocks – at the risk, raised above, of interfering with monetary policy's objective of price stability. Even if the increased use of fiscal flexibility were desirable, the ability to service the debt resulting from large fiscal deficits incurred to cushion asymmetric national shocks might diminish in a currency union, especially if accompanied by increased economic integration and factor mobility, leading to mobility of tax bases. The fiscal issue is of considerable importance for Europe – hence the debate on whether monetary union needs to be accompanied by greatly expanded fiscal transfers or even a Community-wide system of taxation. In practice, there are relatively few examples of currency unions that are not also accompanied by some degree of political union. Evidence from existing federations (including new evidence provided in the chapter) suggests an important role for fiscal federalism in cushioning shocks, but the evidence is not conclusive as to the need for this feature, and more research is no doubt warranted. It seems likely, however, that for a currency union to be durable it must be accompanied by a degree of solidarity among member countries, and one manifestation of this solidarity is the willingness to make payments to members suffering from adverse circumstances.

Whether the exchange rate is an effective tool to cushion shocks has its counterpart in the debate on convergence: whether inherited nominal or real disparities – in rates of inflation, in levels of productivity and real per-capita incomes – need to be reduced before currency union occurs, or instead are reduced as a consequence of it. Evidence for the United States suggests that the forces for regional economic convergence are strong despite fixity of exchange rates between regions, but how much of this convergence is due to labor mobility or fiscal transfers is hard to assess. The experience of the former GDR in adopting the deutsche mark provides a cautionary example of the effects of lack of convergence – albeit an extreme one, given that the economic systems in the two parts of Germany were completely different.

A final issue treated in the chapter is how to assure a transition from a system of exchange-rate flexibility to a currency union; this issue is of direct relevance for Europe, where agreement has been reached on a timetable for transforming the EMS into a full currency union. That timetable balances the requirements of countries with very different economic positions. The transitional period permits achieving greater economic convergence and building new monetary institutions; however, the dangers from an extended transitional period include the possibility of speculative attacks and the need to avoid sharing ultimate responsibility for monetary policy.

Notes

We are grateful to a number of our colleagues for comments, and especially to Charles Adams, Tamim Bayoumi, Morris Goldstein, Jocelyn Horne, Peter Isard, George Kopits, Donald J. Mathieson, Patrice Muller, Kent Osband,

Horst Ungerer, and Jürgen von Hagen. Claire Adams provided expert research assistance. The views expressed in this paper are those of the authors and do not necessarily represent those of the International Monetary Fund.

1 Corden (1972, p. 3) calls areas with ostensibly fixed exchange rates but without integration of economic policies, or a common pool of foreign exchange reserves, or a single central bank, "pseudo-exchange-rate unions," because they cannot ensure the permanence of the relationship among currencies.

2 Allen (1976, p. 4), for instance, states: "in any monetary union either there must be a single currency, or, if there are several currencies, these currencies must be fully convertible, one into the other at immutably fixed exchange rates, creating effectively a single currency."

3 The issue then arises as to what makes it attractive for Germany to participate. Mélitz (1988) argues that Germany has gained competitiveness (and hence higher exports) because realignments have not completely offset inflation differentials. However, data for unit labor costs and value-added deflators suggest that, if anything, German competitiveness has deteriorated relative to its ERM partners since the formation of the EMS (Ungerer et al., 1990, p. 26). Giavazzi and Giovannini (1989) suggest that German participation increases the stability of Germany's overall effective exchange rate due to negative covariance between the EMS and non-EMS components. There is of course also the common political objective, which Goodhart (1990) argues is all too often ignored by economists.

4 This has both internal and external dimensions, but is primarily an injunction to maintain price stability. Government policy has also been strongly supportive of price stability.

5 CFA stands for "Communauté Financière Africaine."

6 Both areas use the same currency, the CFA franc, which is pegged to the French franc.

7 Eleven of the twelve member states agreed on these points at the Rome meeting of the European Council, October 27–8, 1990; the United Kingdom dispute the premise that a single currency is the ultimate goal, and argue for competition among currencies, focused on a "hard ECU." The treaty does not in fact incorporate provisions for currency competition, but does allow the UK to opt out of a single currency.

8 Canzoneri and Rogers (1990).

9 See also Xafa (1990) for an analysis of the Greek case.

10 Measured somewhat more precisely as the difference between the market interest rate and the rate paid on central bank liabilities, if any, multiplied by the monetary base.

11 Barro and Gordon (1983) and Gros (1989).

12 Clearly, wage and price flexibility makes exchange-rate flexibility unnecessary. See section III.4 below.

13 Eichengreen (1990a).

14 To some extent this has reflected unemployment insurance provisions that have been more generous in the less prosperous provinces.

15 The Pacific Northwest region consists of Alaska, Idaho, Montana, Oregon, Washington, and Wyoming. The West North Central region consists of Iowa,

Kansas, Minnesota, Missouri, Nebraska, North Dakota, and South Dakota.

16 Most notably (in the United States) the West South Central region which consists of Arkansas, Louisiana, Oklahoma, and Texas, and (in Canada) Alberta, related to oil price increases.

17 Estimates of dispersion of unemployment rates for German Länder however are similar to those for the twelve EC countries. See EC Commission (1990, p. 151).

18 See also EC Commission (1990, p. 151).

19 This is not to deny that equity prices (i.e., claims to physical capital) may vary in response to changes in the profitability of the capital stock; however, various lags and installation costs will make physical investment slow to adjust.

20 Other reasons may explain this correlation, for instance deliberate government policy to limit current-account imbalances, and shocks that have common effects on saving and investment.

21 Fiscal incentives may however be put in place to encourage investment and/or discourage outward migration.

22 See below, however, for a discussion of data for inter-republican trade within the USSR.

23 The East Caribbean Currency Area includes Antigua, Dominica, Grenada, Montserrat, St. Kitts, and St. Lucia.

24 Since 1983, the institutions of the East Caribbean currency union have included a common central bank.

25 Kenen (1969).

26 However, avoiding unemployment would depend on the existence of inter-sectoral factor mobility, so that sectors facing adverse demand shocks contract, and sectors with increased demand expand.

27 Of course, within the manufacturing sector, countries differ greatly in the range of goods produced, and also whether the goods produced are exported.

28 Studies of relative price flexibility that compare data for individual countries with those for Europe include Vaubel (1976), Poloz (1990), and Eichengreen (1990b). Though Vaubel concludes that the EC is in greater need of real exchange-rate adjustment than Germany, Italy, or the United States taken individually, the latter two studies are inconclusive as to whether the United States and Canada exhibit more relative price flexibility than Europe. The comparison is complicated by the fact that countries/regions differ in the extent to which price levels include traded goods (whose price may vary little relative to external prices) as opposed to non-traded goods (for which no arbitrage that would tend to equalize prices exists).

29 A critique of the single-criterion approach is given in Argy and de Grauwe (1990).

Attempts to provide a general theoretical framework are made by Ishiyama (1975), Tower and Willett (1976), and Argy (1990). Boyer (1978), Henderson (1979), Flood and Marion (1982), and Aizenman and Frenkel (1985) all examine the question of the optimal degree of exchange rate flexibility in response to shocks, using simple theoretical models. However, they do not attempt to quantify the relative variances, nor do they consider the benefits of a currency union in lowering transactions costs.

30 See Henderson (1979), Alexander and Henderson (1989).

31 Except for shocks to the interest-rate parity condition, which were set to zero in the fixed exchange-rate regime.

32 EC Commission (1990), chapter 6 and annex E. The simulations were also performed using the Fund's MULTIMOD model (see Masson, Symansky, and Meredith, 1990), by the staff of the EC Commission. The model does not include all the EMS members separately; results apply to Germany, France, Italy, the United Kingdom, and the Smaller Industrial Country Region. Implicitly, then, all EC member countries are assumed to participate in EMU.

33 Variability is an appropriate criterion if shocks do not affect long-run values of variables, so that the purpose of economic policy is to smooth the transition back to an unchanged long-run equilibrium. It is implicitly assumed that, in the long run, growth rates of monetary aggregates, and hence inflation rates, are unaffected.

34 This effect depends on some "forward-looking" behavior in wage setting.

35 See, for instance, Oudiz and Sachs (1984).

36 A more microeconomic approach was used to analyze the benefits of creating the single European market: see "The Economics of 1992," *European Economy*, No. 35 (March 1988).

37 A preliminary attempt to endogenize the degree of labor mobility in a theoretical model is made by Bertola (1989).

38 The term "fiscal policies" is used in its general sense to include both tax and spending policies; in Bovenberg, Kremers, and Masson (1991), which forms the basis of much of the material in this section, the term "budgetary policies" is used instead.

39 These issues are discussed in a European context by Bovenberg, Kremers, and Masson (1991). An early discussion of the role of fiscal policies in this context is given by Corden (1972); however, he does not consider possible effects on the credibility of the commitment to price stability.

40 A hybrid system in which some exchange rates are fixed, but others are flexible, might be expected to lead to a combination of positive and negative transmission effects.

41 Frenkel and Razin (1987) provide a detailed analysis of the various spillover effects in an expanded Mundell–Fleming model; transmission effects are shown to be uncertain as to sign.

42 This property of negative output transmission within the EMS is also evident in simulations reported in Roubini (1989). Similarly, analysis in Masson and Meredith (1990) of the increased demand emanating from east Germany (two-thirds of which is assumed directed to west Germany, the rest to other countries) suggests that it would reduce output in other EMS countries. This results from their real exchange-rate appreciation and higher real interest rates, which dominate the effects of increased demand from Germany.

43 See Dornbusch (1976). MULTIMOD has the property that fiscal expansion produces initial appreciation of the currency, but a long-run depreciation to bring about an improvement in competitiveness required to offset the deterioration in the country's interest service account. If the fiscal expansion also increases fears of monetization, it is quite possible that the currency could depreciate initially.

44 For recent contributions see Goodman (1989), Alesina (1989), and Grilli, Masciandaro, and Tabellini (1991), among others.

45 The availability of external financing to Greece despite unsustainable fiscal policies may be evidence that private capital markets expect an EC "bailout" in some form (see Xafa, 1990).

46 Pöhl (1990).

47 Rogoff (1985) has argued that appointing a "conservative" central banker may increase the welfare of society, because it may help to avoid the time-inconsistency problem facing monetary policy (see Barro and Gordon, 1983).

48 See Bishop, Damrau, and Miller (1989). However, these authors also discuss an example of failure of market discipline, the 1975 New York City debt crisis.

49 See Tanzi and Bovenberg (1990). However, incentives to migration in response to differences in local services or in taxation levels will be reduced if the latter are capitalized in house prices. See Bayoumi and Gordon (1991), who examine the relationship between UK local authority spending and house prices.

50 See Dornbusch (1988, 1989) and Giavazzi (1989). Alternatively, there may be pressures to cut government expenditures.

51 If monetary union is accompanied by free competition in financial services (as will be the case in Europe with the single market from the end of 1992), then countries with high reserve requirements may have to lower them to sustain the competitiveness of domestic banks.

  Capital controls in Italy until July 1990 limited the ability of domestic residents to acquire foreign currency assets. Giavazzi and Giovannini (1989) argue that this tended to keep down interest costs on government borrowing. Subsequent removal of capital controls has not, however, had an appreciable effect on borrowing costs.

52 Goldstein and Woglom (1991).

53 Corden (1972, p. 37) points out that aside from those policies that encourage labor mobility, fiscal flexibility will provide financing, not adjustment, and hence is only a temporary solution. The use of fiscal flexibility is illustrated in the European context by Masson and Mélitz (1991).

54 See Eichengreen (1990a, p. 142).

55 Bishop, Damrau, and Miller (1989, p. 24) estimate that the size of transfers to the four least-advanced EC members (Greece, Ireland, Portugal, and Spain) could be in the order of 2 percent of their combined GDP in 1992–3. This would constitute about 5 percent of those countries' government expenditures. In the United States, state receipts from the federal government were estimated by Eichengreen (1990a, p. 140) to be 21 percent of state expenditures in 1987.

56 Quoted in Graham (1982).

57 See Blank and Stanley (1990) and Boadway (1986).

58 Other federations, for instance Switzerland, Australia, and Germany, also have important inter-regional transfer mechanisms: it is interesting to see to what extent they offset regional shocks. See EC Commission (1990, pp. 166–8), and Bishop, Damrau, and Miller (1989).

59 Figure cited by Bishop, Damrau, and Miller (1989, p. 13). Balanced-budget changes in fiscal stance are of course still possible, but in practice do not seem to have been used for stabilization purposes by US states. An analysis of

government spending in Canada by province and by category is contained in Horry and Walker (1991).

60 Bishop, Damrau, and Miller (1989, p. 12).

61 See section IV.2 above, and Eichengreen (1990a).

62 The proportion of central government revenues accounted for by upward transfers was 14 percent in 1990.

63 Bredenkamp and Deppler (1990) argue that the externalities related to the use of fiscal policy for stabilization purposes are no more serious in a currency union.

64 Masson and Mélitz (1991) present a simulation of the response of two members of a currency union to an external oil price shock, which suggests that such a shock might lead to excessively tight policies in a currency union. Given a sufficient concern for negative effects on the trade balance or on inflation of higher oil prices, each country would tighten fiscal policy, exacerbating unfavorable effects on the other country (as captured by those targeted variables).

65 The federal prime minister and provincial premiers.

66 EC Commission (1990).

67 See also MacDonald and Taylor (1990).

68 These dispersion measures were calculated as the square root of the weighted variation around the weighted mean, with weights equal to the percentage of the total (i.e., EC or US) population in each country or region.

69 Giavazzi and Giovannini (1988) argue that ERM members may have improved the output–inflation trade-off by importing monetary policy credibility from the Bundesbank. Dornbusch (1989) and Weber (1991) however question whether costs of disinflation – especially in the early 1980s – were substantially reduced by EMS membership.

70 The discussion in this section is concerned with substitutability between national *monies*, as opposed to interest-bearing assets denominated in different currencies; on the latter see Artis and Taylor (1989).

71 Krasker (1980).

72 An additional means of raising policy credibility and thereby deferring speculative attack would be to manage the term structure of public debt such that the costs of reneging are very high (Calvo and Guidotti, 1990).

73 See, e.g., Buiter (1986), Driffill (1988), and Obstfeld (1988).

References

Aizenman, Joshua and Jacob A. Frenkel (1985), "Optimal Wage Indexation, Foreign Exchange Intervention, and Monetary Policy," *American Economic Review*, 75, June, pp. 402–23.

Alesina, Alberto (1989), "Politics and Business Cycles in Industrial Democracies," *Economic Policy*, No. 8, April.

Alexander, William E. and Dale W. Henderson (1989), "Liberalization of Financial Markets and the Volatility of Exchange Rates," in Robert M. Stern (ed.), *Trade and Investment Relations Among the United States, Canada, and Japan*, Chicago: University of Chicago Press, pp. 365–78.

Allen, Polly Reynolds (1976), "Organization and Administration of a Monetary Union," Princeton Studies in International Finance No. 38, Princeton University, June.

Argy, Victor (1990), "Choice of Exchange Rate Regime for a Smaller Economy: A Survey of Some Key Issues," in Argy and De Grauwe (eds.), pp. 6–81.

Argy, Victor and Paul De Grauwe (1990), "Introduction," in Argy and De Grauwe (eds.), pp. 1–5.

Argy, Victor and Paul De Grauwe (eds.) (1990), *Choosing and Exchange Rate Regime: The Challenge for Smaller Industrial Countries*, International Monetary Fund, Washington.

Artis, Michael J. and D.A. Currie (1983), "Monetary Targets and the Exchange Rate: A Case for Conditional Targets," in W.A. Eltis and P.J.N. Sinclair (eds.), *The Money Supply and the Exchange Rate*, Oxford: Oxford University Press.

Artis, Michael J. and Mark P. Taylor (1988), "Written Evidence," Report of the House of Lords Select Committee on the European Communities: The European Financial Area, House of Lords Paper 109, November.

(1989), "Some Issues Concerning the Long-Run Credibility of the European Monetary System," in Ronald MacDonald and Mark P. Taylor (eds.), *Exchange Rates and Open Economy Macroeconomics*, Oxford: Basil Blackwell.

(1990), "EMU: UK Should be Among the Leaders," *Financial Times*, December 14, p. 19.

Bank of England (1990), "The Exchange Rate Mechanism of the European Monetary System," *Bank of England Quarterly Bulletin*, 30, November, pp. 479–81.

Barro, Robert and David Gordon (1983), "Rules, Discretion and Reputation in a Model of Monetary Policy," *Journal of Monetary Economics*, 12, July, pp. 101–21.

Barro, Robert and Xavier Sala-i-Martin (1990), "Economic Growth and Convergence across the United States," mimeo, Harvard University, July.

Bayoumi, Tamim (1991), "The Effects of the ERM on Participating Economies," mimeo, International Monetary Fund, February.

Bayoumi, Tamim and James Gordon (1991), "The Determinants and Efficiency of Local Authority Spending in England," International Monetary Fund, Washington.

Bayoumi, Tamim and Paul R. Masson (1991), "Fiscal Flows in the United States and Canada: Lessons for Monetary Union in Europe," International Monetary Fund, November.

Bayoumi, Tamim and Andrew K. Rose (forthcoming), "Domestic and Intra-National Capital Flows," *European Economic Review*.

Bertola, Giuseppe (1989), "Factor Mobility, Uncertainty and Exchange Rate Regimes," in de Cecco and Giovannini (eds), pp. 95–118.

Bhandari, Jagdeep and Thomas Mayer (1990), "A Note on Saving-Investment Correlations in the EMS," International Monetary Fund, Washington, Working Paper No. WP/90/97, October.

Bishop, Graham, Dirk Damrau, and Michelle Miller (1989), "1992 and Beyond: Market Discipline CAN Work in the EC Monetary Union," Salomon Brothers, London, November.

Blanchard, Olivier J. and Lawrence H. Summers (1986), "Hysteresis and the European Unemployment Problem," in Stanley Fischer (ed.), *NBER Macroeconomics Annual*, Cambridge, Mass.: MIT Press, pp. 65–71.

Blank, Stephen and Guy Stanley (1990), "Is Canadian Federalism a Model for Europe and the Soviet Union?" *The International Economy*, October/November, pp. 73–5.

Blundell-Wignall, Adrian and Robert G. Gregory (1990), "Exchange Rate Policy in Advanced Commodity-Exporting Countries: Australia and New Zealand," in Argy and De Grauwe (eds.), pp. 224–71.

Boadway, Robin (1986), "Federal-Provincial Transfers in Canada: A Critical Review of the Existing Arrangements," in Mark Krasnick (ed.), *Fiscal Federalism*, Toronto: University of Toronto Press, pp. 1–47.

Bovenberg, A. Lans, Jeroen J.M. Kremers, and Paul R. Masson (1991), "Economic and Monetary Union in Europe and Constraints on National Budgetary Policies," IMF, *Staff Papers*, 38, June, pp. 374–98.

Boyer, Russell (1978), "Optimal Foreign Exchange Market Intervention," *Journal of Political Economy*, 86, December, pp. 1045–55.

Branson, William and Dale Henderson (1985), "The Specification and Influence of Asset Markets," in R. Jones and P. Kenen (eds.), *Handbook of International Economics*, Vol. II, Amsterdam: North-Holland.

Bredenkamp, Hugh and Michael Deppler (1990), "Fiscal Constraints of a Fixed Exchange Rate Regime," in Argy and De Grauwe (eds.), pp. 350–73.

Bruno, Michael and Jeffrey Sachs (1985), *Economics of Worldwide Stagflation*, Cambridge, Mass.: National Bureau of Economic Research.

Bryant, Ralph A., David A. Currie, Jacob A. Frenkel, Paul R. Masson, and Richard Portes (eds.) (1989), *Macroeconomic Policies in an Interdependent World*, International Monetary Fund, Washington.

Buiter, Willem H. (1986), "Fiscal Prerequisities for a Viable Managed Exchange Rate Regime: A Non-Technical Eclectic Introduction," Centre for Economic Policy Research, Discussion Paper Number 129, July.

Calvo, Guillermo and Pablo E. Guidotti (1990), "Credibility and Nominal Debt," International Monetary Fund, Washington, *Staff Papers*, 37, pp. 612–35.

Canzoneri, Matthew and Carol Ann Rogers (1990), "Is the European Community an Optimal Currency Area? Optimal Taxation Versus the Cost of Multiple Currencies," *American Economic Review*, 80, June, pp. 419–33.

Cochrane, John H. (1988), "Test of Consumption Insurance," NBER Working Paper No. 2642, July.

Cohen, Daniel and Charles Wyplosz (1989), "The European Monetary Union: An Agnostic Evaluation," in Bryant *et al.* (eds.), pp. 311–37.

Cooper, Richard N. (1990), "What Future for the International Monetary System?" mimeo, December, forthcoming in a *festschrift* for Jacques Polak.

Corden, W.M. (1972), "Monetary Integration," Essays in International Finance, No. 93, Princeton University, April.

de Cecco, Marcello and Alberto Giovannini (eds.) (1989), *A European Central Bank? Perspectives on Monetary Unification after Ten Years of the EMS*, Cambridge: Cambridge University Press.

Delors Committee Report (1989), *Report on Economic and Monetary Union in the European Community*, Committee for the Study of Economic and Monetary Union, June.

Dominguez, Kathryn (1990), "Market Responses to Coordinated Central Bank Intervention," *Carnegie-Rochester Conference Series on Public Policy*, No. 32, Spring, pp. 165–72.

Dooley, Michael, Jeffrey Frankel, and Donald J. Mathieson (1987), "International Capital Mobility: What Do Saving-Investment Correlations Tell Us?" IMF, *Staff Papers*, 34, September, pp. 503–30.

Dornbusch, Rudiger (1976), "Expectations and Exchange Rate Dynamics," *Journal of Political Economy*, 84, December, pp. 1161–76.

(1988), "The European Monetary System, the Dollar and the Yen," in Giavazzi, Micossi, and Miller (eds.), pp. 23–35.

(1989), "Credibility, Debt and Unemployment: Ireland's Failed Stabilization," *Economic Policy*, No. 8, April.

Driffill, John (1988), "The Stability and Sustainability of the European Monetary System with Perfect Capital Markets," in Giavazzi, Micossi, and Miller (eds.), pp. 211–28.

EC Commission (1990), "One Market, One Money: An Evaluation of the Potential Benefits and Costs of Forming an Economic and Monetary Union," *European Economy*, No. 44, Brussels, Commission of the European Communities, October.

Eichengreen, Barry (1990a), "One Money for Europe? Lessons from the U.S. Currency Union," *Economic Policy*, No. 10, April, pp. 117–87.

(1990b), "Is Europe an Optimum Currency Area?" University of California at Berkeley, Department of Economics, Working Paper No. 90-151, October.

Feldstein, Martin and Charles Horioka (1980), "Domestic Saving and International Capital Flows," *Economic Journal*, 90, June, pp. 314–29.

Flood, Robert P. and Nancy Marion (1982), "The Transmission of Disturbances under Alternative Exchange-Rate Regimes with Optimal Indexing," *Quarterly Journal of Economics*, 97, February, pp. 43–66.

Friedman, Milton (1968), "The Role of Monetary Policy," *American Economic Review*, 58, March, pp. 1–17.

Frenkel, Jacob A., Morris Goldstein, and Paul R. Masson (1989), "Simulating the Effects of Some Simple Coordinated Versus Uncoordinated Policy Rules," in Bryant *et al.* (eds.), pp. 203–39.

Frenkel, Jacob A. and Assaf Razin (1987), "The Mundell–Fleming Model A Quarter Century Later: A Unified Exposition," IMF, *Staff Papers*, 34, December, pp. 203–39.

Giavazzi, Francesco (1989), "The Exchange Rate Question in Europe," in Bryant *et al*, (eds.), pp. 283–304.

Giavazzi, Francesco and Alberto Giovannini (1988), "The Role of the Exchange Rate Regime in a Disinflation: Empirical Evidence on the European Monetary System," in Giavazzi, Micossi, and Miller (eds.).

(1989), *Limiting Exchange Rate Flexibility: The European Monetary System*, Cambridge, Mass.: MIT Press.

Giavazzi, Francesco and Marco Pagano (1989), "Confidence Crises and Public Debt Management," Centre for Economic Policy Research, Discussion Paper No. 318.

Giavazzi, Francesco, Stefano Micossi, and Marcus Miller (eds.) (1988), *The European Monetary System*, Cambridge: Cambridge University Press.

Giavazzi, Francesco and Luigi Spaventa (1990), "The New EMS," CEPR, Discussion Paper No. 369, January.

Giovannini, Alberto (1990), "The Transition to Monetary Union," CEPR, Occasional Paper No. 2, April.

Goldstein, Morris and Geoffrey Woglom (1991), "Market-Based Fiscal Discipline in Monetary Unions: Evidence from the U.S. Municipal Board Market," May.

Goodhart, Charles (1990), "Economists' Perspectives on the EMS: A Review Essay," *Journal of Monetary Economics*, 26, December, pp. 471–87.

Goodman, John B. (1989), "Monetary Politics in France, Italy and Germany: 1973–85," in Paolo Guerrieri and Pier Carlo Padoan (eds.), *The Political Economy of European Integration: States Markets and Institutions*, New York: Harvester Wheatsheaf.

Gordon, Robert J. (1988), "Back to the Future: European Unemployment Today Viewed from America in 1939," *Brookings Papers on Economic Activity*, 1, pp. 271–304.

Graham, John F. (1982), "Equalization and Canadian Federalism," *Public Finance*, 37(2), pp. 246–62.

Grilli, Vittorio (1989), "Seigniorage in Europe," in de Cecco and Giovannini (eds.), pp. 53–79.

Grilli, Vittorio, Donato Masciandaro, and Guido Tabellini (1991), "Political and Monetary Institutions and Public Finance Policies in the Industrial Democracies," *Economic Policy*, No. 13, October, pp. 341–92.

Gros, Daniel (1989), "Seigniorage in the EC: The Implications of the EMS and Financial Market Integration," International Monetary Fund, Washington, Working Paper No. WP/89/7, January.

Henderson, Dale (1979), "Financial Policies in Open Economies," *American Economic Review*, 69, May, pp. 232–9.

Horry, Isabella D. and Michael A. Walker (1991), *Government Spending Facts*, Vancouver: The Fraser Institute.

International Monetary Fund (1990), "The Economy of the USSR: A Study Undertaken in Response to a Request by the Houston Summit – Summary and Recommendations," International Monetary Fund, Washington, December.

(1991), The World Bank, Organization for Economic Co-operation and Development, and European Bank for Reconstruction and Development, *A Study of the Soviet Economy*, Paris.

Ishiyama, Yoshide (1975), "The Theory of Optimum Currency Areas: A Survey," IMF *Staff Papers*, 22, July, pp. 344–83.

Jurgensen, Philippe (1983), "Report of the Working Group on Exchange Rate Intervention," Washington: Board of Governors of the Federal Reserve System.

Kenen, Peter (1969), "The Theory of Optimum Currency Areas: An Eclectic View," in Robert Mundell and Alexander Swoboda (eds.), *Monetary Problems in the International Economy*, Chicago: University of Chicago Press.

Krasker, William S. (1980), "The 'Peso Problem' in Testing the Efficiency of Forward Exchange Markets," *Journal of Monetary Economics*, 6, pp. 269–76.

Kremers, Jeroen and Timothy Lane (1990), "Economic and Monetary Integration and the Aggregate Demand for Money in the EMS," IMF *Staff Papers*, 37, December, pp. 777–805.

Krugman, Paul (1990), "Increasing Returns and Economic Geography," NBER Working Paper No. 3275, March.

Krugman, Paul and Anthony Venables (1990), "Integration and the Competitiveness of Peripheral Industry," in Jorge Braga de Macedo and Christopher Bliss (eds.), *Unity with Diversity within the European Economy: The Community's Southern Frontier*, Cambridge: Cambridge University Press.

MacDonald, Ronald and Mark P. Taylor (1990), "Exchange Rates, Policy Convergence, and the EMS," *Review of Economics and Statistics*, 73, pp. 553–8.

Masson, Paul R. and Jacques Melitz (1991), "Fiscal Policy Independence in a European Monetary Union," *Open Economies Review*, No. 2, pp. 113–36.

Masson, Paul R. and Guy Meredith (1990), "Domestic and International Macroeconomic Consequences of German Unification," in Leslie Lipschitz and Donogh McDonald (eds.), *German Unification: Economic Issues*, International Monetary Fund, Occasional Paper No. 75, December, pp. 93–114.

Masson, Paul R., Steven Symansky, and Guy Meredith (1990), *MULTIMOD Mark II: A Revised and Extended Model*, IMF Occasional Paper 71, July.

McKinnon, Ronald I. (1963), "Optimum Currency Areas," *American Economic Review*, 53, September, pp. 717–25.

Mélitz, Jacques (1988), "Monetary Discipline and Cooperation in the European Monetary System: A Synthesis," in Giavazzi, Micossi, and Miller (eds.), pp. 51–78.

(forthcoming), "Brussels on a Single Money," *Open Economics Review*.

Mundell, Robert A. (1961), "A Theory of Optimum Currency Areas," *American Economic Review*, 51, September, pp. 657–65.

Mussa, Michael (1981), "The Role of Official Intervention," Occasional Paper No. 6, New York: Group of Thirty.

Myrdal, Gunnar (1957), *Economic Theory and Underdeveloped Regions*, London: Duckworth.

Obstfeld, Maurice (1988), "Competitiveness, Realignment, and Speculation: The Role of Financial Markets," in Giavazzi, Micossi, and Miller (eds.), pp. 232–46.

(1990), "The Effectiveness of Foreign-Exchange Intervention: Recent Experience," in William Branson, Jacob Frenkel, and Morris Goldstein (eds.), *Policy*

Coordination and Exchange Rate Fluctuations, Chicago: NBER and University of Chicago Press.

Oudiz, Gilles and Jeffrey Sachs (1984), "Macroeconomic Policy Coordination among the Industrial Economies," *Brookings Papers on Economic Activity*, 1, pp. 1–76.

Perroux, François (1959), "Les Formes de Concurrence dans le Marché Commun," *Revue d'Economie Politique*.

Pöhl, Karl Otto (1990), "Address by the President of the Deutsche Bundesbank in Paris on 16/1/90," BIS Review, No. 12, January 17.

Poloz, Stephen S. (1990), "Real Exchange Rate Adjustment Between Regions in a Common Currency Area," mimeo, Bank of Canada, Ottawa, February.

Rogoff, Kenneth (1985), "The Optimal Degree of Commitment to an Intermediate Monetary Target," *Quarterly Journal of Economics*, Vol. 100, pp. 1169–89.

Roubini, Nouriel (1989), "Leadership and Cooperation in the European Monetary System: A Simulation Approach," NBER Working Paper No. 3044, Cambridge, Massachusetts, July.

Sachs, Jeffrey D. (1987), "High Unemployment in Europe: Diagnosis and Policy Implications," in Claes-Henric Siven (ed.), *Unemployments in Europe: Analysis and Policy Issues*, Timbro.

Sala-i-Martin, Xavier, and Jeffrey Sachs (1992), "Fiscal Federalism and Optimum Currency Areas: Evidence for Europe from the United States," in Matthew B. Canzoneri, Vittorio Grilli, and Paul R. Masson (eds.), *Establishing a Central Bank: Issues in Europe for Lessons from the U.S.*, Cambridge: Cambridge University Press.

Tanzi, Vito and A. Lans Bovenberg (1990), "Is There a Need for Harmonizing Capital Income Taxes Within EC Countries?" International Monetary Fund, Washington, Working Paper No. WP/90/17, March.

Taylor, Mark P. (forthcoming), "Sterilized Intervention," in P. Newman, M. Milgate, and J. Eatwell (eds.), *The New Palgrave Dictionary of Money and Finance*, London: Macmillan.

Tower, Edward and Thomas D. Willett (1976), "The Theory of Optimum Currency Areas and Exchange-Rate Flexibility," Special Papers in International Economics No. 11, Princeton University, May.

UK Treasury (1989), *An Evolutionary Approach to EMU*, London: HMSO.
    (1990), *Treasury Bulletin*, London: HMSO.

Ungerer, Horst, Jouko J. Hauvonen, Augusto Lopez-Claros, and Thomas Mayer (1990), *The European Monetary System: Developments and Perspectives*, International Monetary Fund, Washington, Occasional Paper No. 73, November.

Vaubel, Roland (1976), "Real Exchange-Rate Changes in the European Community: The Empirical Evidence and Its Implications for European Currency Unification," *Weltwirtschaftliches Archiv*, Bd. 112, pp. 429–70.

Von Hagen, Jürgen (1991), "Fiscal Arrangements in a Monetary Union: Evidence from the U.S.," mimeo, Indiana University, March.

Weber, Axel A. (1991), "Reputation and Credibility in the European Monetary System," *Economic Policy*, No. 12, April.

Wolf, Martin (1990), "Champions Enter the Lists for EMU," *Financial Times*, December 12, p. 15.

Xafa, Miranda (1990), "EMU and Greece: Issues and Prospects for Membership," Woodrow Wilson School, Discussion Papers in Economics No. 155, Princeton University, Princeton, New Jersey, July.

II Existing currency unions

2 Costs and benefits of economic and monetary union: an application to the former Soviet Union

DANIEL GROS

1 Introduction

What keeps an "Economic Union of ex-Soviet Republics" together? Western experts (and the union government) have often argued against the dissolution of the Soviet Union on the ground that it would involve large economic costs. The purpose of this chapter is to discuss whether this is indeed true; i.e., the chapter tries to determine whether some republics would gain by leaving the Soviet (economic) Union. In analytical terms this is equivalent to asking whether economic considerations could provide a justification for keeping the Soviet Union at least an economic and monetary union.

The main result of the analysis is that the more developed republics west of the Urals would be better off outside the Soviet economic sphere. These republics would want to liberalize their economies faster, they would need to rely less on the inflation tax, and they could expect to trade more with the outside world than with the rest of the ex-Soviet Union once their economies have been liberalized.

The Commission of the European Communities (and other western economic institutions) have argued all along during the dissolution process that it would be preferable to keep the former Soviet Union an economic and monetary union (EMU). This chapter comes to a different result because it argues that competition in reform can be useful. Moreover, this chapter also considers explicitly an alternative which was neglected (perhaps for obvious political reasons) in the report of the EC Commission, namely that some republics might prefer to integrate their economies more with the emerging European economic and monetary community than with the rest of the ex-Soviet Union.

This chapter takes the existing republics of the former Soviet Union as natural lower level economic units, because only at the republican level can there exist the administrative and political structures necessary to create the institutional and legal framework for the functioning of a market economy.[1] Moreover, most republics (except Russia) are economic regions that are as homogenous as most European countries.

The remainder of the chapter is organized as follows. Section II starts with the issue that dominates the present political agenda, namely whether a centralized approach to reform is preferable to leaving this decision to individual republics in order to introduce competition in reform. Section III then discusses very briefly the lessons that can be drawn from the literature on fiscal federalism. Section IV analyzes the importance of maintaining the "Soviet" common market, i.e., the costs and benefits for any individual republic of participating in a Soviet customs union. Section V discusses the incentives for individual republics to keep the ruble as their currency. Finally, section VI concludes with a reflection about reasons why the European Community is moving in the opposite direction, i.e., why western Europe is a process of integration whereas the Soviet Union has disintegrated.

II Centralization or competition in reform?

The union–republic controversy has undoubtedly delayed the implementation of fundamental economic reforms. However, this does not necessarily imply that a centralized reform plan is the best option. Fundamentally the issue is the following: at present (i.e., in early 1992) there is a large area with completely distorted prices and without the necessary legal and institutional framework for a market economy. Can any sub-unit of this area gain by implementing reforms on its own and thus allowing its inhabitants to trade freely at "true" market prices? In general the answer should be yes.

For example, it is often alleged that price reform has to be implemented at the union level because differences in prices would lead consumers to buy where the goods are cheapest. As long as the ruble remains the common currency of the ex-Soviet Union and there are no restrictions on inter-republican trade, price reform in one republic alone would indeed lead to large-scale attempts to arbitrage price differences. However, this arbitrage is the essence of a market economy and should not be regarded a cost.

If any republic were to implement a radical reform its price structure would be different from that of the rest of the union. Residents of other republics would then certainly come to "plunder" its shops for those goods that are cheaper in that particular republic. However, this "plunder" is in reality an advantage since all these goods will be sold at their marginal cost of production and an increase in demand for local products can only lead to an increase in the surplus of domestic producers.[2]

Vice versa, consumers of the republic that initiated a reform in isolation would gain by buying goods in the rest of the union at the old subsidized prices. In reality, however, shops in the ex-Soviet Union are now mostly empty. This implies that the impact of a radical reform on the supply of new goods and the distribution system should be more important than changing the price structure of the limited number of old goods that are actually available at their official price. Entrepreneurs in a republic that was the first to implement fundamental reforms would therefore gain by being able to satisfy a pent-up demand for diversified products coming from the entire union area.

The rest of the union loses from an uncoordinated reform process to the extent that residents of the republic that initiated reforms on its own then buy (or rather attempt to buy) goods that are priced below cost in other republics. However, this is a consequence of the distorted old union price structure and should not be regarded as a cost of an uncoordinated price reform. On the contrary, this effect has the advantage that it constitutes an incentive to implement reforms in the remainder of the union as well.

The spillover effects through goods arbitrage that arise from an uncoordinated reform process do thus not constitute a valid argument for a centralized reform process. Moreover, experience has shown that a credible reform strategy has to be adapted to the specific local circumstances. Some competition to find out the best way toward a market economy should therefore be beneficial.

If there were a credible commitment by the union authorities to implement a radical reform plan the issue of a decentralized transition to a market economy would not even arise. However, there are some considerations which suggest why the union authorities might always be more cautious in their approach to reform than the authorities of the smaller republics. The creation of a market economy should benefit all citizens in the longer run. However, some groups are bound to lose in the short run and during the initial transition period it is even possible that the majority of the population is worse off for a limited period of time because it always takes more time to create new and efficient enterprises than to liquidate the existing inefficient ones. This makes a fast transition more difficult since the authorities that now have to obtain democratic approval for their actions will try to shelter most groups from the adverse effects of the transition.[3] It is apparent that the problem increases with the degree of heterogeneity of the economy. This explains why the smaller republics, which are the more homogeneous regions, are generally willing to go faster and take more radical measures.[4]

Moreover, as has been often emphasized the creation of a market economy is impossible without the support from an administration that executes and interprets the new laws in the new spirit.[5] It is much easier to set up and control such an administration in a small country than in the entire ex-Soviet Union whose total administrative body is said to run into the millions. The authorities of the smaller and therefore more homogeneous republics have the additional advantage that action can be concentrated on a smaller number of important sectors (e.g., some republics do not have to deal with the issue of how to convert defense industries or they do not have an energy sector that needs their attention). This is a further argument for allowing the republics to implement their own reforms.

Finally the large military–industrial complex that dominated the economy of the Soviet Union represents a powerful obstacle to the radical reforms which can only diminish the power of the bureaucrats and military that run it. The large expenditures on the military are only in the interest of the leaders of the union which are concerned about their global role. However, individual republics do not see the need to maintain a large military–industrial complex and are therefore more likely to overcome the resistance against radical reform from this sector.

All these arguments suggest that the implementation of the reforms should therefore be left to the republics unless the union authorities take radical measures.

III   Fiscal federalism

A central aspect of the power struggle between the union and the republics concerns the distribution of expenditure and taxes. Although this issue has been very much politicized it is useful to bring out the underlying economic considerations by applying the fiscal federalism arguments to the case of the ex-Soviet Union.

The main insight coming from the literature on fiscal federalism is that the authority to tax should be delegated to lower levels of government to the extent that the public goods produced by these levels of government can be appropriated mainly by the tax payers of their own jurisdiction. This general principle suggests that a large degree of fiscal decentralization would be appropriate for the ex-Soviet Union, since, given its size and heterogeneity, there are large differences in the needs of the different republics. For example, a more developed republic might want to levy higher taxes to finance the expenditure on social infrastructure (higher education, telecommunications, etc.) that is needed to sustain a modern industrial sector.

From a pure efficiency point of view the direct taxing authority of the union government (or the power to coordinate the actions of the republican governments) would thus be justified only in the case of indivisibilities and external effects. This implies that the direct role of the union government should be limited to defense, environment, long-distance transport infrastructure, etc. Beyond these areas it might also be necessary to allow the union government to coordinate republican fiscal policy to limit the effect of tax competition (for example, establishing a common system of a value added tax or in the taxation of financial capital).

This argument for a fundamental shift in fiscal authority to the republics might seem to be inconsistent with the dominant share of the federal government in large western states. However, most of the powers at the federal level over taxes and expenditures in western societies have nothing to do with efficiency arguments, since they are used to redistribute income. Income redistribution on such a large scale is motivated by the perception that all citizens of the country belong to one community which cares about its weaker members. This is certainly not the case between the inhabitants of most of the republics of the ex-Soviet Union. This is why it would be appropriate to limit the role of the union government to those areas where a central authority is necessary on efficiency grounds alone.

IV   A "Soviet" custom union?

Despite the customs ports instituted by some smaller republics, goods and services could by early 1992 still move freely across republican boundaries. The ex-Soviet Union is thus still an *economic union* (which is usually defined as "a unified market inside which goods, services, capital, and people can move without any obstacles"). To obtain an idea of the order of magnitude of the efficiency gains an integrated market can yield it is useful to recall that the elimination of the remaining, small, barriers to intra-EC trade by the 1992 programme is estimated to bring large economic benefits (up to 4–6 percent of the Community's GDP according to Emerson (1988)). If the ex-Soviet Union had already a market economy the kind of trade barriers contemplated by some republics should thus imply very large economic costs indeed. There is therefore, a priori, a strong case against the imposition of customs borders between republics (as opposed to a general protection against competition from western producers) which would break up the Soviet economic union.

An exception to this general presumption is warranted, however, in two cases which are now discussed in turn:

Temporary regional protectionism during the transition

Most theoretical arguments in favor of protectionism are based on the absence of a well-developed capital market that allows producers to finance an initial period of "learning by doing" and to finance the investment in capital and technology that is necessary to be able to withstand international competition. Experience shows that it takes some time before an efficient capital market can be created, even within those republics that want to reform their economies as fast as possible. There is therefore a strictly economic rationale for regional protectionism during the transition. This applies, however, only to those goods for which the price is set administratively at a lower level in the rest of the union. In these cases some temporary controls on the inter-republican movements of goods might be justified because domestic producers would otherwise go bankrupt. However, since in reality very few goods are actually available on a large scale at their official price it is not likely that there are many cases in which domestic producers need to be protected against "unfair" competition from the rest of the union. On the contrary, experience has shown that other republics will impose a ban on the export of subsidized products. It is therefore likely that a republic that initiates reforms on its own does not even need to erect customs barriers to protect its "infant" industries. If the reform is successful the rest of the union will do it.

Moreover, the creation of a customs border represents also a temptation to extend trade barriers to all trade, not just the goods where some restrictions are unavoidable for the reasons mentioned. A fast transition toward a market economy would have the additional advantage that the disruption of internal trade through internal customs borders would be only temporary and would be limited to a small number of goods. This would also minimize the temptation for individual republics to use overall protectionism to raise or preserve employment (which will be difficult to resist since there will be considerable unemployment during the transition). The economic difficulties faced by central Europe because of the disruption of established trade patterns (through national protectionism) after the First World War are a good example of the damage that could result if regional protectionism were to spread too far.[6]

Is the ex-Soviet Union an optimal customs union?

A second reason why a number of republics may want to conduct their own commercial policy is that any republic that participates in the Soviet economic sphere would have to adopt the same barriers (tariffs or quotas) for trade with the rest of the world as the rest of the ex-Soviet Union.[7] Once the transition period is over (and regional protectionism loses its justification) the fundamental question for each republic is therefore whether it gains more from participating in world trade than from participating in intra-union trade.

The standard analysis of customs unions shows that the benefits from joining a customs union depend on a number of factors: (1) the degree of protectionism practised by the union, (2) the size of the union, (3) the size and economic structure of the participating economies.

Provided some sort of union continues to exist it will with all likelihood be some time before this new union adopts a liberal trade regime. This implies that the smaller republics would prefer to conduct their own commercial policy since inside a Soviet customs union they would import more high-cost products from the other republics and would thus lose from trade diversion.

The size of the union is also an important factor because the larger the customs union the more likely it is that it contains the lowest-cost producers of most goods and therefore the less likely it is that trade diversion takes place. However, this aspect does not favor the ex-Soviet Union because, given the available estimates, Soviet output is less than one fifth of that of the European Community. Moreover, the ex-Soviet Union will also for some time not be the lowest-cost producer for the capital equipment that most republics need to modernize their manufacturing industries. Remaining in the Soviet customs union would thus imply potentially important costs in the form of the large trade diversion effect.

For these two reasons alone the ex-Soviet Union (in its former extension) is not an attractive area for a customs union. But there are other considerations which suggest even more strongly that some republics would definitely gain from leaving a Soviet customs union.

By now a widely accepted synthesis of the traditional comparative advantage view and the modern view based on economies of scale and product differentiation suggests that there will be intensive intra-industry trade between highly developed countries and that there will also be inter-industry trade between countries with different capital/labor ratios.[8] However, there should be little trade between countries with a similar capital/labor ratio that are not developed enough to specialize in the industrial goods exchanged within the group of rich countries.[9] In this view the trade between developed countries consists of the exchange of differentiated industrial goods produced with economies of scale but similar capital intensities, whereas the trade between rich (high capital/labor ratio) countries and less-developed countries (low capital/labor ratio) consists of the exchange of products with different capital/labor ratios.

This view of international trade can also explain why regional integration in Latin America has consistently failed. Numerous attempts to create customs unions in Latin America have all failed, suggesting that regional integration among less-developed economies is not very useful. The richer Latin American countries are a particularly useful base for comparison

Table 2.1. *Trade and economic centers*

Panel A

	Brazil (%)	Latin America (%)	US (%)	EC (%)
Argentina	11.0	26.7	15.5	28.7
Chile	7.6	20.5	20.7	27.5

Panel B

	Germany (%)	USSR (%)	US (%)	EC (%)
Finland	13.5	16.4	5.5	41.8
Greece	21.6	2.3	5.3	60.2
Yugoslavia	12.9	19.9	5.7	33.3

Note: Percentage of trade (average of imports and exports) of country listed on the left with the countries or regions in the top row.
Source: International Monetary Fund, Direction of Trade Statistics 1989 Yearbook. All data refer to 1985–88 averages.

because they have a GDP per capita that is close to the more realistic estimates for the ex-Soviet Union, i.e., about 2,000 US dollars. A simple comparison of trade flows suggests the reasons for this result.[10]

As shown in panel A of table 2.1, Chile, for example (which has one of the highest GDP per capita in the region) conducts only 20 percent of its trade with all of Latin America, but over 27 percent with the European Community (and another 20 percent with the United States).[11] The bilateral trade flows between Argentina and Brazil are also interesting because these two countries are in a similar relationship as the Ukraine and Russia, at least in terms of population:[12] only about 11 percent of the trade of Argentina is with Brazil, but more than 28 percent is with the European Community. A customs union between these two countries is therefore not likely to yield large economic benefits (unless the common external rate of protection is much lower than the present average of the two national tariffs and quota systems). On the contrary such a customs union (as opposed to a free trade zone) might actually be welfare reducing because it might lead to more trade diversion than trade creation.

Inside a group of richer countries (e.g., the OECD countries) intra-industry trade dominates and the geographical distribution of trade flows is determined primarily by the so-called "gravitational factors," i.e., distance, cultural affinity, and size of the different markets. Simple gravity equations that embody these factors can account for about 80 percent of the cross-sectional variations in the size of bilateral trade flows among European OECD countries.[13] These equations suggest that the overwhelming factor in determining the geographical distribution of trade flows is market size. For all European countries, and the European Soviet republics, this implies that the Community is likely to become the dominant trade partner in the future.

The data on three European countries (Finland, Greece, and Yugoslavia) in panel B of table 2.1 confirm that trade with the Community is very important even for countries that are at its periphery. Indeed, Germany alone is almost as important as the ex-Soviet Union even for a country like Finland that is not a member of the Community. More recent data show that Finnish trade with the ex-Soviet Union has been reduced to about 10 percent of overall Finnish trade since part of the Finnish–Soviet trade in the past had been politically motivated.

The Finnish example is particularly interesting because the Baltic republics are in a similar position and of a similar size (Lithuania has about the same population as Finland). This example suggests that the Baltic republics would trade primarily with western Europe if they were to become independent and that they would lose considerably if they participated in a Soviet customs union.

The central Asian republics seem to represent another clear case. They can always be expected to trade intensively with the ex-Soviet Union because of their different level of development and their geographical position.

The Ukraine and the trans-Caucasian republics are in an intermediate position. For the latter geography suggests intensive trade with the rest of the ex-Soviet Union, but also with the Middle East. The Ukraine (as well as Belorussia) has an industrial structure that suggests intensive trade with western Europe, but geography and cultural factors favor also strong integration with Russia. The Argentina–Brazil example reported above, suggests, however, that the first effect might be stronger.

An interesting application of the so-called "peripherality index" in the EC Commission's evaluation of the economy of the ex-Soviet Union confirms this impression.[14] These calculations, which take into account only the ex-Soviet Union and the former COMECON partners, suggest that the three Baltic republics are as "peripheral" to the center of the trade bloc that was centered around the ex-Soviet Union as some of the central-Asian republics whereas the Ukraine is the republic with the lowest index of peripherality.

This section has argued so far that the trade patterns of established

Table 2.2. *Regional distribution of Yugoslav trade*

Percentage of trade with	Exports		Imports	
	1982	1988	1982	1988
EC	21.0	38.7	34.6	40.5
COMECON	44.8	26.3	29.8	21.0

Source: International Monetary Fund, Directions of Trade Statistics 1989 Yearbook.

market economies suggest that a number of republics on the western edge of the ex-Soviet Union might in the future trade much more with western Europe (essentially the Community) than with each other. This argument is, of course, valid only if the trade links that have been created in the past can be changed rather quickly. Indeed Krugman (1991) suggests that historical accidents may even have a permanent impact on trade. It is therefore interesting to consider the case of Yugoslavia where the reform process started earlier. The Yugoslav experience can thus be taken as an indicator of the speed with which the regional distribution of trade can change.

Since changes over time do not show up in the four-year averages used in table 2.1 it is useful to consider the regional distribution of Yugoslav trade at two points in time as done in table 2.2.

Between 1982 and 1988 the share of trade with the COMECON declined from 44.8 to 26.3 percent on the export side and from about 30 to 21 percent on the import side. At the same time the share of the Community increased from 21 to almost 40 percent on the export side and from about 35 percent to over 40 percent on the import side. This rather substantial change in relative trade patterns (the Community and the COMECON essentially switched places) as a result of only partial reforms suggests that radical reforms might have a very substantial impact on trade patterns of some republics in the five years which the union government considers to be necessary for a smooth transition to independence.

The experience of Poland shows, however, that the redirection of trade patterns can at times be much more dramatic as shown in table 2.3. In only one year, 1987 (i.e., before the "big bang" of 1990), the share of industrial countries in Polish trade (the average of exports and imports) increased by over 10 percentage points (their share went from 31 to 44 percent), while the share of the ex-Soviet Union and other ex-COMECON countries fell by

Table 2.3. *Regional distribution of Polish trade*

	1987	1988	1989	1990
Industrial countries	31.2	44.1	45.1	55.5
COMECON*	46.7	39.4	38.6	25.0

Note: Percent distribution of trade, average of exports and imports.
*IMF definition: "USSR plus other non-members," i.e., excludes Hungary and after July 1990 the ex-GDR.
Source: International Monetary Fund, Directions of Trade Statistics 1989 Yearbook.

7 percentage points (from 46.7 to 39.4 percent). The reform of 1990 only continued this movement and the share of industrial countries in Polish trade is now above 55 percent, whereas the share of the ex-COMECON countries fell to 2.5 percent.[15]

Redirecting trade flows at this scale involves, of course, substantial adjustment costs which might be lower if the adjustment is slower than in the case of Poland, but the data presented here suggest that trade with the west can very rapidly displace the established, planned, trade flows whose disruptions should thus not be as catastrophic as often argued; provided, of course, that it is not imposed overnight but the outcome of a market-led process.

V A "Soviet" common currency?

The introduction of a national currency signifies for some republics an important symbol of their independence. Not to retain the rouble and thus leave the "Soviet" monetary union is therefore an important political decision. However, the analysis of this section shows that for some republics the introduction of a national currency can also be justified on purely economic grounds.

The literature on optimal currency areas argues that the main advantage of having a national money is that the exchange rate can be a useful adjustment instrument in the case of nationally differentiated shocks.[16] However, this advantage has to be weighted against the gains from the ultimate degree in economic integration that is provided by a common currency. This standard economic analysis of the costs and benefits of a monetary union can also be applied to the case of the ex-Soviet Union.[17]

Introducing separate republican currencies would create a barrier for inter-republican trade because it would increase transactions costs. The importance of this disadvantage of splitting up the ruble area depends on the intensity of (inter-republican) trade and the efficiency of the payment and transactions system provided by the ruble. In evaluating these two effects it is convenient to distinguish between the short run (i.e., the situation as of early 1992), the medium run (i.e., the transition period to a market economy, perhaps two to three years) and the long run.

Short-run considerations

It is apparent that the present monetary regime of the ruble area (which still encompasses the whole territory of the ex-Soviet Union) is not tenable. Republican central banks compete against each other for credit (and the supply of banknotes) from the central bank of the union. Each republican central bank has the incentive to obtain as much credit as possible since the consequences in terms of higher inflation are spread over the entire union.

This externality is rapidly leading to hyperinflation, which implies that the ruble is losing its function as "money." This is especially true for inter-republican trade which is increasingly not conducted by enterprises working with rubles, but through a complicated web of contracts that involve republican and regional ministries (or other official bodies) as well as individual enterprises which are owned by the state (the union, republic, or region) on the basis of barter or hard currency. In trade among republics the ruble thus does not fulfil the main function of money (i.e., it is not the medium of exchange) and cannot therefore provide the benefits that otherwise arise from a common currency.

Unless the monetary constitution of the union is changed there is therefore little prospect that the ruble can be stabilized. Under the current circumstances, however, it seems that it is impossible to introduce the kind of central control over money creation that is necessary for a functioning monetary union. Republican currencies would not suffer from this externality and should thus be more stable.

The republics are thus faced with a dilemma since intra-ex-Soviet Union trade amounts to more than 30 percent of output of most smaller republics (including the three Baltic republics for which it amounts to about 50 percent of output, see table 2.4). A collapse of inter-republican trade would thus be catastrophic to these smaller republics. The sharp contraction in trade between the ex-Soviet Union and the former COMECON countries shows that this could happen if some republics introduce their own currencies which would probably be initially inconvertible. However, this does not imply that the only alternative is to retain the ruble, however

Table 2.4. *Soviet republics: trade with the union and the rest of the world*

| | Trade as a percentage of GNP(*) | | | |
	Total	Domestic	Foreign	Population
USSR total	30	21	8	284,500,000
RSFSR	22	13	9	146,500,000
Ukraine	34	27	7	51,400,000
Belorussia	52	45	7	10,100,000
Uzbekistan	40	34	5	19,600,000
Kazakhstan	34	29	4	16,500,000
Georgia	44	38	5	5,300,000
Azerbaijan	41	35	5	6,900,000
Lithuania	55	47	7	3,700,000
Maldavia	52	46	6	4,200,000
Latvia	54	47	7	2,700,000
Kirghizia	46	40	5	4,200,000
Tadzhikistan	44	38	6	5,000,000
Armenia	54	48	5	3,500,000
Turkmenistan	42	38	4	3,500,000
Estonia	59	50	8	1,600,000

Note: *Assuming the same GNP/NMP ratio as for the USSR as a whole.
Source: Statistical abstract.

inflationary it has become. As argued more in detail in Gros (1991) and Bofinger and Gros (1991) inter-republican trade could be maintained by a Soviet payments union so that the introduction of republican currencies does not have to lead to a collapse of inter-republican trade.

Medium-run consideration: the transition

Are these circumstances likely to change in the near future? New reform plans are introduced with a certain regularity (initially at the union level, but now also at the republican level) but given that most of them remain on paper and given the delays that have already arisen in the implementation of ones that are actually supposed to be implemented it must be assumed that it will be some time before a functioning market economy is established in the union or at least in most republics.

Assuming that through a change in the monetary constitution of the rest of the union the rouble could be stabilized, the question arises whether it would be useful to retain it as a common currency during the transition period. This is probably not the case because a common currency also has a cost.

The main cost of a common currency is that exchange-rate changes can facilitate the adjustment to nationally differentiated shocks. In the case of the transition period this argument is particularly relevant since the reform process in itself will provide a source for large regionally differentiated shocks.

The domestic aspects of the reform process are already a source of regionally differentiated shocks because price reform will lead to large changes in relative prices and therefore an important redistribution of income given the high degree of specialization of many republics and regions. Moreover, important aspects of the overall reform process might be determined and implemented at the level of the republic (or even region). Smaller republics with a more developed administrative structure would therefore be able to reform their economies much faster than the larger ones. But this implies that their exchange rate *vis-à-vis* the rest of the ex-Soviet Union might have to adjust considerably in the short run. This could be achieved also through movements in domestic prices, but given the size of the adjustment that might be required substantial inflation or deflation might be the result. If wages adjust less easily downwards, this argument suggests that those republics that either lose from the freeing of prices or are slower to implement reforms would benefit most from having a currency they could devalue *vis-à-vis* the rest of the union. This would probably be the case for the central Asian republics. For the Baltic republics the income loss from price reform (principally because of higher energy prices) might be offset by a faster reform process.

Even after the initial shock of creating a market economy has been at least partially absorbed, the process of opening the Soviet Union to international trade will create another reason why the exchange rate between different regions and/or republics might have to change considerably in the medium run. Republics that are close to the major world markets for industrial goods (e.g., the EC) and have a diversified industrial structure underpinned by a well-educated workforce can expect to adapt much easier to international competition. This would require a real appreciation *vis-à-vis* the less-developed republics. Retaining the rouble would therefore imply potentially large domestic wage and price inflation, which could be avoided with different currencies in some republics. The opposite would, of course, hold for those republics that would face a deterioration of their terms of trade once they have to adapt to international competition.[18] This might be the case for some of the commodity exporting republics of central Asia.

The long run

Only in the long run (i.e., when all parts of the Soviet Union have become a market economy and are integrated in the world economy) can one expect that the rouble could potentially provide the traditional benefits of a common currency. At first sight this seems to suggest that the smaller republics, which are already now very open to trade, should at least have a long-run interest in remaining in the rouble area. It has even been suggested that in the long run most of the republics might have an interest in forming a monetary union again.

However, even a small republic, that is not a viable currency area on its own, has an alternative to remaining in the rouble area: it can join another currency area. Whether this is an attractive alternative depends on the geographical distribution of its trade. At present all republics trade more with each other than with the outside world, but as argued above this is likely to change radically in the long run. For example, only about 15–20 percent of the total trade of the Baltic republics is now with the outside world. For a country like Finland (which is in a similar geographical position and has about the same population as Lithuania) the opposite is true as illustrated already above. At present only about 11 percent of Finnish trade is with the ex-Soviet Union, trade with the European Community is four times as important since it accounts for about 45 percent of Finnish trade.

Once the Baltic republics are integrated into the world economy their trade patterns are likely to resemble that of Finland today for the reasons outlined in the previous section. In that case they would gain more from joining the emerging European economic and monetary union (EMU) than from remaining in the rouble area. However, this would not be the case for the central Asian and Transcaucasian republics, for which it is more likely that they will trade more with (the rest of) the ex-Soviet Union than with the European Community (or other industrialized countries).

For the larger republics (i.e., mainly the Ukraine) intra-ex-Soviet Union trade is less important relative to output (a bit under 30 percent, comparable to the ratio for France, which has approximately the same population) so that the economic argument against a separate currency is weaker. The larger republics are therefore probably viable currency areas of their own. The previous section has argued, however, that even a republic like the Ukraine might trade more with western Europe than Russia once the transition to a market system is completed. Even for the Ukraine (and Belorussia) it is therefore not self-evident, that it would gain from rejoining (or even staying in) a Soviet monetary union.

In summary, the arguments discussed in this section suggest that for any time horizon one wishes to consider, a number of republics would gain from leaving the rouble area.[19] This result is reinforced if one takes into account labor mobility, which is another important criterion according to the optimum currency area literature (because a lack of wage flexibility could be made up by migration). However, labor mobility will probably remain limited due to the housing shortage for some time even though there are few legal obstacles to labor mobility within the ex-Soviet Union.[20] Moreover, in some republics large-scale inter-republican migration would not be acceptable on political grounds.

In the European context it is also often argued that a monetary union should be supported by a fiscal framework that provides some implicit insurance mechanism so that a region that is hit by an adverse shock receives a transfer of income that compensates at least partially for the inability to devalue the regional exchange rate. Such a mechanism would probably not exist in a reformed Soviet Union because Russia, which would be the main contributor to such a scheme, does not want to finance other republics.

The most important consideration for most republics can perhaps be illustrated with a comparison: what central American country would like to link its currency to the Mexican peso? Russia, which will undoubtedly dominate whatever remains of the union, is essentially an energy-based economy (similar in size to Mexico) and one would expect the real value of the Russian rouble to fluctuate with world energy prices. The real exchange rates of the other republics, most of which are intensive net energy importers, would thus have to move frequently in the opposite direction to that of the Russian rouble. Given this likelihood of large asymmetric shocks any monetary union between Russia and other republics would involve large adjustment problems for the other participants.

VI Concluding remarks: are the ex-Soviet Union and western Europe moving in opposite directions?

An analysis of this chapter suggests that economic arguments cannot be expected to provide an underpinning for an "Economic and Monetary Union of Sovereign Republics" covering the entire area of the old Soviet Union. This seems to be in contrast to developments in western Europe where the construction of the Community has always been underpinned by strong economic arguments. What accounts for this difference?

Comparing the costs and benefits of a Soviet and a European economic and monetary union (EMU) reveals two main differences:

First, the union government has always hesitated with regard to the introduction to a market economy. The individual republics differ radically in their willingness and capacity to take this step quickly. Separate currencies (and to some extent temporary customs borders) would allow them to implement economic reforms at their own pace. This consideration is not relevant for the European Community since all member countries have a market economy.

Second, once the transition to a market economy is complete, some republics will probably trade more with the outside world (especially the European Community), than with the ex-Soviet Union. This is also not the case for the European Community where even the peripheral countries (in geographical terms) trade much more with the Community than the rest of the world.

In general terms, however, the crucial difference between Europe and the ex-Soviet Union is that in Europe the center, in geographical and numerical terms, is also the strongest part of the Community, not only in terms of income, but also in terms of macroeconomic stability. The center of the Community, which corresponds roughly to the initial narrow band EMS members, therefore not only attracts most trade flows but it also provides an anchor in terms of sound macroeconomic stability for the weaker, peripheral regions. In the ex-Soviet Union there is no such centre.[21] Russia is less developed than some of the peripheral republics and is also not necessarily more stable. This implies that for the western republics integration with the Community is more attractive, from an economic point of view, than integration with Russia. The central Asian republics do not have an alternative large economic area into which they could integrate, they are therefore more interested in remaining in the Soviet economic monetary union.

A final warning seems appropriate: as in the case of the Community the assessment of the costs and benefits of forming an economic and monetary union depends crucially on the alternatives considered. If the only alternative to keeping the ex-Soviet Union as it exists at present is the creation of states that conduct economic warfare against each other it is apparent that the present misery represents a lesser evil.

Notes

I wish to thank Paul de Grauwe, Jean Pisani-Ferry, Peter Kenen, Jørgen Mortensen, and Alfred Steinherr for helpful comments and discussions. Throughout this chapter, for stylistic reasons, we occasionally refer to "the union" in place of "the ex-Soviet Union" or "the economic union of countries which formerly comprised the Soviet Union."

1 The declarations of sovereignty of some of the autonomous republics (most of which are located inside the Russian republic) can apparently not be taken seriously, see Uibopuu (1990).

2 This argument holds under the assumption that price reform had been implemented together with other structural reforms, see Gros and Steinherr (1991b) for details.

3 Western societies have always had to face a similar problem that is analyzed in the literature on the political economy of protection: measures that hurt a small group, but benefit the rest of the economy are often not taken even if the net gain to society is large because the resistance from the small group is well organized whereas the support from the rest of the society is weak since the gain for each individual agent is small.

4 Differences in local attitudes toward the market economy are often used as excuses by politicians, but this is doubtful in the light of the results of Shiller *et al.* (1990) which suggest a surprising degree of similarity in popular attitudes toward market mechanisms in the United States and the ex-Soviet Union.

5 See for example Gros and Steinherr (1991a and b) and Sachs (1990).

6 See Kaser (1986) for a detailed account of the inter-war difficulties faced by central European countries.

7 Another, more remote, possibility, which is not discussed here is that of a mere free trade area without any common external trade policy. A free trade zone would represent the optimal solution from a theoretical point of view, but this is a policy any republic could pursue even in isolation by a policy of unilateral free trade with all trading partners.

8 See Helpman and Krugman (1985) for an exposition.

9 Balassa and Bauwens (1988) provide extensive test of this view. Möbius and Schumacher (1990) provide a sectoral analysis of the trade of eastern European countries that also confirms this general view.

10 The following discussion is meant to provide an informal approximation of the result one would obtain by using a formal gravity model of trade flows.

11 The Andean Pact provides an even more striking example since only 4 percent of the foreign trade of its five members is within the area.

12 The population of the Ukraine is 55 million (versus 30 million for Argentina) and that of Russia is 140 million, the same as Brazil.

13 See, for example, Aitken (1973), Balassa and Bauwens (1988) provide a confirmation of the importance of gravitational factors on an industry by industry basis.

14 See Commission of the European Communities (1990b) Annex VII.

15 See Lipton and Sachs (1990) and Sachs (1990) for an account of the Polish experience.

16 This is the fundamental insight from Mundell (1961). The European Commission has recently published an evaluation of the economic costs and benefits of forming an economic and monetary union in the European Community, see Commission of the European Communities (1990a).

17 In the European context two definitions of monetary union are often used: irrevocably fixed exchange rates (plus full capital mobility) and the introduction of a single common currency. Given that the ex-Soviet Union starts with a single currency the first definition of a monetary union is not interesting since a republic that introduces its own currency would surely not do so with the aim of

keeping the exchange rate with the rouble irrevocably fixed. In the case of the ex-Soviet Union the term monetary union must therefore mean a common (and single) currency.

18 Except if they can expect large fiscal transfers.

19 Commission of the European Communities (1990b) recognizes that only a stable rouble can be a useful money. But it does not really take into account that at least some republics have the alternative of joining another regional block.

20 Residency permits for Moscow, which are accorded only in special cases, constitute one example of legal restrictions of labor mobility within the ex-Soviet Union.

21 The fact that the ex-Soviet Union cannot provide a "pole of attraction" in economic terms also explains why all central and eastern European countries are orienting themselves toward the Community.

References

Aitken, D. (1973), "The Effect of the EEC and EFTA on European Trade: A Temporal Cross-Section Analysis," *American Economic Review*, 63, pp. 881–92.

Balassa, B. and L. Bauwens (1988), *Changing Trade Patterns in Manufactured Goods: An Econometric Investigation*, Amsterdam: North-Holland.

Bofinger, P. (1991), "Options for a New Monetary Framework for the Area of the Soviet Union," Centre for Economic Policy Research, Discussion Paper No. 604, London, October.

Bofinger, P. and D. Gros (1991), "A Multilateral Payments Union of the Republics of the Soviet Union," manuscript, Centre for European Policy Studies, Brussels, November.

Collins, S. and D. Rodrik (1991), "Eastern Europe and the Soviet Union in the World Economy," Institute of International Economics, Policy Analysis in International Economics No. 32, Washington, DC, May.

Commission of the European Communities (1990a), "One Market, One Money," *European Economy*, No. 44, October.

(1990b), "Stabilisation, Liberalisation and Devolution: Assessment of the Economic Situation and the Reform Process in the Soviet Union," *European Economy*, No. 45, December.

De Grauwe, P. (1990), "The Economic Integration of West and East Germany. Two tales based on trade theory," Catholic University of Leuven, CES International Economics Research Papers, No. 72.

Emerson, M. (1988), "The Economics of 1992," *European Economy*, No. 35, October.

Gros, D. (1991), "A Soviet Payments Union?" manuscript, Centre for European Policy Studies, Brussels, October.

Gros, D. and E. Jones (1991), "Price Reform and Energy Markets in the Soviet Union and Central Europe," Centre for European Policy Studies, Working Document No. 57, August.

74   **Daniel Gros**

Gros, D. and A. Steinherr (1991a), "From Centrally-planned to Market Econo-
· mies: Issues for the Transition in Central Europe and the Soviet Union," CEPS
Paper 51, Centre for European Policy Studies and Brassey's.
(1991b), "Economic Reform in the Soviet Union: Pas-de-Deux between Disin-
tegration and Macroeconomic Destabilization," Princeton Studies in Interna-
tional Finance No. 71, Princeton University, November.
Havrylyshyn, O. and J. Williamson (1991), "From Soviet disUnion to Eastern
Economic Community," Institute for International Economics, Policy Analy-
sis in International Economics No. 35, Washington, DC, October.
Helpman, E. and P. Krugman (1985), *Market Structure and Foreign Trade*, Boston,
Mass.: MIT Press.
Kaser, M.C. (ed.) (1986), *The Economic History of Eastern Europe 1919–1975*,
Oxford: Clarendon Press.
Krugman, P. (1990), "Increasing Returns and Economic Geography," NBER
Working Paper 3275, Cambridge, Mass.: National Bureau of Economic
Research, March.
Lipton, D. and J. Sachs (1990), "Creating a Market Economy in Eastern Europe:
The Case of Poland," *Brookings Papers on Economic Activity*, Vol. I,
pp. 75–135.
Möbius, U. and D. Schumacher (1990), "Eastern Europe and the EC: Trade
Relations and Trade Policy with regard to Industrial Products," Paper for the
Joint Canada Germany Symposium, Toronto, November.
Mundell, R. (1961), "A Theory of Optimum Currency Areas," *American Economic
Review*, 51, September, pp. 657–65.
Sachs, J. (1990), "Political and Economic Reconstruction in Eastern Europe and
the Soviet Union: The Role of the European Communities," Paper prepared
for the Seventh Annual Conference of CEPS, November.
Shiller, R., M. Boycko, and V. Korobov (1990), "Popular Attitudes towards Free
Markets: The Soviet Union and the United States Compared," NBER
Working Paper No. 3453, September.
Uibopuu, H.-J. (1990), "In Zukunft ein Commonwealth sowjetischer Nationen?"
Frankfurter Allgemeine Zeitung, October 18.

3 Private capital markets and adjustment in a currency union: evidence from the United States

ANDREW ATKESON
and TAMIM BAYOUMI

I Introduction

One of the features of most currency unions is that they contain an integrated national capital market, which can be used by private individuals to borrow and lend capital across regions within the union. In addition to allowing capital to be transferred across regions, the existence of an integrated capital market also allows individuals to insure themselves against region-specific risk by holding a diverse portfolio of assets. The extent to which individuals actually use capital markets in these ways is the focus of this chapter.

Regional data for the United States of America are used to estimate the importance of these two factors. The United States is an obvious candidate for such an investigation, since it is a large, well-integrated currency area with freely functioning capital markets.[1] Examining behavior within the United States sheds light on the importance of private capital markets in economic adjustment within market economies in general. It also gives pointers as to the probable impact of more open international capital markets on behavior across countries, particularly in Europe where the progress toward Economic and Monetary Union (EMU) is rapidly creating an integrated capital market.

We begin by examining regional data from the United States on product and income for evidence of intertemporal trade among the regions of the United States. The regional data are collected on a basis similar to that under which components of the national data on gross national product (GNP) and gross domestic product (GDP) are calculated, so that these data allow rough calculations of the magnitude of inter-regional net factor payments. These calculations indicate that inter-regional net factor payments, and thus, presumably, net asset positions, are large. Back of the

75

envelope calculations indicate that on average a region in the US is a net debtor or creditor to the tune of one-sixth of its capital stock. Changes in these measures of inter-regional net factor flows over time give some indication of the magnitude of capital flows between regions. Rough calculations indicate that several regions of the United States have experienced large and persistent inflows or outflows of capital over the last two decades.

We next turn our attention to studying the extent of inter-regional portfolio diversification within the United States. While we do not have direct estimates on inter-regional gross capital holdings within the United States, we are able to use the rich regional data on income and product to obtain indirect evidence of the extent of these holdings. The method that we use for our measurements is as follows. Regional income can be divided into categories derived from payments to labor, payments to capital, and taxes and transfers. Regional product can be similarly divided into payments to labor and payments to capital. To examine whether these differences between capital income and capital product reflect some behavioral pattern of gross capital holdings (and not simply measurement error) we apportion the fluctuations in regional capital income into parts consistent with the portfolio choices of three prototypical consumers: (1) those who derive the bulk of their income from capital and invest in the national portfolio, (2) consumers who derive the bulk of their income from labor and who invest their capital nationally in order to offset changes in their labor income, and (3) consumers who, for informational or other reasons, simply invest locally. The presumption is that consumers who derive most of their income from capital should choose similar portfolios regardless of their region of residence, while consumers who derive most of their income from labor should attempt to construct capital portfolios generating income flows with a negative correlation with their own labor income while consumers who invest locally should have capital income that fluctuates with the capital product in their region of residence.

We find that a substantial fraction of the fluctuations in regional income from capital are uncorrelated with fluctuations in region capital product and are highly correlated with fluctuations in national income paid to capital. In general, only a tiny fraction of the fluctuations in regional capital income are accounted for by attempts of consumers to smooth regional labor income or by fluctuations in regional capital product. However, there is evidence that in states with a large agricultural sector there is considerably more insurance of labor incomes.

Finally, we address the question of whether the greater integration of the capital market linking the regions of the United States actually allows consumers, in the aggregate, to insulate their consumption from regional fluctuations. Unfortunately, we have no data on regional consumption at business cycle frequencies. But we are able to use some regional retail sales data (as a proxy for regional consumption data) and income and product data to see whether at longer horizons consumers use the opportunities for inter-regional intertemporal trade and risk-sharing that are available to insulate their consumption from regional fluctuations in income and product. If consumers do use such opportunities to a large extent, then aggregate consumption growth should be correlated across all of the states of the United States and should be independent of regional fluctuations in income or product growth.[2] The US regional data do not coincide with these predictions of such a model of inter-regional risk-sharing. Over the long run, regional aggregate consumption growth is not highly correlated across regions and is highly correlated with fluctuations in regional income and product growth. Hence, even within the unified market of the United States, there would appear to be severe limitations on the smoothing of regional consumption over regional fluctuations.

This paper is organized as follows. The next section outlines the regional income and product data and discusses our calculations of the inter-regional net factor flows within the United States. The third section investigates the extent of inter-regional gross capital holdings, while the fourth section examines the relationship between regional consumption and regional income and product. The final section concludes.

II Net capital flows within the United States

There are two ways that the movement of capital within regions of a currency union could be calculated. The first, deriving from the expenditure data, would be to calculate regional saving and investment data. The difference between these two series would then be a measure of regional "current accounts" and hence capital flows.[3] Unfortunately, the requisite data simply do not exist for regions in the US. The alternative is to look at net factor payments, which can be derived from the difference between income and output. Net capital positions can then be inferred from these factor payments. This is the approach taken in this section.

Ideally, in order to calculate the size of net factor flows across US regions, it would be useful to have estimates of both state product (regional GDP) and state income (regional GNP), and calculate flows of factor payments directly. Unfortunately, while data on state product exist and are published by the Commerce Department we are unaware of any such data on total regional incomes. What do exist on a regional basis, however, are data on total personal incomes, which we will use as a proxy for total income.[4]

The principal differences between personal income and a comprehensive

Table 3.1. *Ratio of personal income to regional product, 1963–86*

(Percent, relative to US average)

Region	Ratio	Ratio excl. labor transfers	Ratio excl. labor and Govt. Trans.
N. England	9.7	8.0	8.6
Mid East	4.4	5.4	5.9
Grt. Lakes	−0.8	−1.0	−1.8
Plains	−0.2	0.4	−0.2
South East	−1.9	−2.5	−1.5
South West	−9.8	−9.8	−10.6
Rocky Mnts	−4.3	−4.3	−5.5
Far West	2.1	2.1	2.1
Mean abs. value	4.2	4.2	4.5

measure of income on a state or regional basis that would be comparable with GNP are contributions to social insurance less transfer payments, corporate retained earnings (including allowances for depreciation and net interest receipts), and indirect taxes. Data exist on regional contributions for social insurance less transfers, and are analyzed below. We do not have data on corporate retained earnings or indirect taxes. By making no adjustment for these factors we implicitly assume that they represent the same fraction of total regional income that they do in national income.[5]

Table 3.1 gives some data on the size of the differences between regional production and regional income for the eight standard regions of the United States used by the Bureau of Economic Analysis, averaged over the period 1963–86. The first column shows the percentage deviation between this ratio for a particular region and for the US as a whole. For example, the value of 9.7 for New England indicates that the ratio of personal income to state product for New England is 9.7 percent above the corresponding ratio for the US as a whole, and hence indicates that relative to its output New England has a relatively high level of personal income. By contrast a negative figure (as in the case of, say, the South East region) indicates that relative to its production per head the South East region has relatively low income.

The data show large differences between regional income and regional production over the period 1963–86. New England has an average income some 10 percent above their relative product; by contrast, the South West has a similar sized deficit. While other regions have smaller deviations, only two have ratios with absolute values below 1 percent. To get a sense of the average size of these differences, the last row of the table shows the mean absolute value of the figures. This indicates that the average ratio between income and product for a region diverges by over 4 percent from value for the US as a whole. These data indicate large and persistent net factor flows across regions of the United States.[6]

The North Eastern states (New England and the Mid East), and to a lesser extent those in the Far West, receive income from the other regions of the country. These net flows could reflect three different effects, namely labor income, capital income, or net transfers (which are dominated by government payments). The second and third columns in table 3.1 investigate the relative importance of these factors. In column 2 the income–production ratios are recalculated using labor income by work place, rather than by residence, in order to see if these differences in relative incomes reflect workers who live in one region and work in another. The data do show some differences, in particular the relative income of New England falls somewhat, possibly reflecting the fact that parts of the region are wealthy suburbs of New York. However, the mean absolute value of the ratios remains unchanged, indicating that overall this is not an important factor in explaining the results.

In column 3 the data are further adjusted for transfers (net of personal payments for social insurance). Excluding the effect of such transfers tends to make the difference between income and product larger, indicating that net transfers play a role in lowering regional disparities between income and product. However, the role is reasonably small; when they are excluded the mean absolute value of the differences rises from 4.2 percent to 4.5 percent. Hence it appears that most of the large regional disparities between income and product emanate from net flows of income from capital.

The regional data imply that there are large differences in net capital ownership across different regions of the United States. To get an idea of the orders of magnitude involved it may be useful to make some back of the envelope calculations. If the rate of return on capital is assumed to be 10 percent, a 1 percentage net capital flow implies that a region is a net capital creditor to the tune of 10 percent of its regional product. Further assuming a capital–output ratio of 3, this implies it is a net capital creditor of 3.3 percent of its domestic capital stock. Since the mean absolute value across regions (adjusting for labor incomes and transfers) is 4.5 percent, these assumptions imply that the average region in the United States either owns (in the case of the North East and Far West) or owes (for the other regions) some one sixth of its capital stock.

Looking at averages over the entire data period shows a snapshot of net

Table 3.2. *Income product ratio over time (ratio of personal income to state product relative to US averages)*

Region	1966–70	1971–5	1976–80	1981–6	Diff. 1966/70– 1981/6
N. England	9.6	9.9	10.6	8.7	−0.9
Mid East	3.3	3.7	5.5	5.1	1.8
Grt. Lakes	−4.0	−1.5	0.9	3.3	7.3
Plains	0.2	−0.3	−1.2	−0.7	−0.9
South East	−2.5	−2.1	−1.0	−1.4	0.9
South West	−6.2	−8.3	−12.7	−13.3	−7.1
Rocky Mountains	−1.4	−2.7	−6.4	−7.5	−6.1
Far West	3.4	1.5	0.7	2.2	−1.2

capital positions across region. It is also of interest to look at movements in these net capital positions over time. Table 3.2 shows the ratio of personal income to state product but this time reported for successive five-year periods, starting in 1966–70 and ending with 1981–6. Changes in the ratio of personal income to state product should reflect changes in the ownership of assets, with the ratio deteriorating in the case of regions which are importing capital from the rest of the United States, and rising in regions which are lending capital. Hence the movement of these ratios should tell us something about the movement of capital within the regions of the United States over the last two decades. The table shows a marked deterioration in the relative income of the South West and Rocky Mountain regions over time, balanced by a gain for the Great Lakes (and, to a lesser extent, the Mid East). These data appear to chart a steady flow of capital from the established regions of the economy to new and relatively unexploited regions.[7]

As before, it is useful to gain an impression of the orders of magnitude involved in these flows. Unfortunately, there are many factors which might change the ratio of income and product for regions of the United States that are not related directly to current accounts, so that it would be difficult to determine the size of regional current accounts from the figures presented in table 3.2. On the other hand, it is clear that the evidence of continuing capital flows presented in the table is qualitatively different than analogous evidence in international data.[8] Hence it appears that, in addition to the existence of large capital positions across states, there is also evidence of continuing large inter-regional capital flows over the period since 1965, implying large and persistent regional "current accounts."

III Measuring inter-regional gross capital positions

In the previous section, we have seen that there are large net capital flows representing substantial intertemporal trade among the regions of the United States. This section uses the income and product data to look at the extent of inter-regional portfolio diversification. In particular, we examine the degree to which the unified US capital markets are used by individuals to insure themselves against region-specific disturbances to production. By doing this, unified private capital markets provide one avenue by which individuals can ease adjustment to regional disturbances within a currency union.

Consider a model with three types of individuals, called capitalists, workers, and local investors. Capitalists derive all their income from the ownership of capital; since they have no income from labor they will invest in the average national portfolio,[9] and hence their capital income will vary with national capital income. Workers, on the other hand, attempt to insure themselves against movements in their own local labor income. They will choose a portfolio whose returns are negatively correlated with regional labor income and hence their capital income will be negatively correlated with regional labor income. Finally, there are some investors who invest in the regional economy, due to factors such as superior information about local investment options. Their capital income is assumed to be correlated with that of the region.[10] Formally, giving these three types of individuals superscipts 1, 2, and 3:

$$\Delta I^1_{Ki} = \Delta I_{Kn}$$
$$\Delta I^2_{Ki} = -\beta \Delta I_{Li} \qquad (3.1)$$
$$\Delta I^3_{Ki} = \Delta P_{Ki}$$

where I_{Ki} represents per capita income from capital in state i, I_{Kn} is national per capita income from capital, I_{Li} is per capita income from labor in state i, P_{Ki} is capital product per capita from state i, and Δ is the first difference operator. Thus I represents personal incomes, while P represents income from the production side of the accounts.

If it is assumed that these three types of individuals each receive a fixed proportion of total capital income,[11] then writing these proportions as λ^{1i}, λ^{2i}, and $(1 - \lambda^{1i} - \lambda^{2i})$ for capitalists, workers, and local investors respectively in region i, then the process for total capital income in regions i becomes,

$$\Delta I_{Kit} = \lambda^{1i} \Delta I_{Knt} - \beta \lambda^{2i} \Delta I_{Lit} + (1 - \lambda^{1i} - \lambda^{2i}) \Delta P_{Kit} \qquad (3.2)$$

Including a constant term in each equation (α^i), to represent unmeasured factors, produces estimating equations for regions $a, b, \ldots, i$,

$$\Delta I_{Kat} = \alpha^a + \lambda^{1a}\Delta I_{Knt} - \beta\lambda^{2a}\Delta I_{Lat} + (1 - \lambda^{1a} - \lambda^{2a})\Delta P_{Kat}$$
$$\Delta I_{Kbt} = \alpha^b + \lambda^{1b}\Delta I_{Knt} - \beta\lambda^{2b}\Delta I_{Lbt} + (1 - \lambda^{1b} - \lambda^{2b})\Delta P_{Kbt} \qquad (3.3)$$
$$\vdots$$
$$\Delta I_{Kit} = \alpha^i + \lambda^{1i}\Delta I_{Knt} - \beta\lambda^{2i}\Delta I_{Lit} + (1 - \lambda^{1i} - \lambda^{2i})\Delta P_{Kit}$$

These are the basic estimating equations used in this section of the chapter.

For the regions of the United States we can use the data on personal incomes and state product referred to earlier to provide the four series required to estimate equation (3.3), namely state personal income derived from capital (the dependent variable), national personal income derived from capital, state personal income derived from labor, and state product accruing to capital. The first three series were calculated from the personal income data by state. Total personal income is divided into four major categories: total earnings (further sub-divided into wages, other labor income, and proprietors' income); dividends, interest, and rent; transfers; and personal charges for social insurance. *Personal income derived from capital* was calculated as the sum of dividends, interest, and rent, while national capital income was calculated in the same way but using the aggregate US data. It should be stressed that such data are collected individually for each state, and hence we do have independent observations on these flows.[12] *Personal income derived from labor* was defined as total earnings (excluding payments for social insurance). Data on state product accruing to capital were obtained from the data on state product also discussed above. The state product data differentiate between compensation to labor, proprietors' income, and income from various other sources. *State product accruing to capital* was calculated as the state product less compensation to labor and proprietors' income. All the series were calculated on a per capita basis and converted into real terms using the product deflator for the US as a whole.

Equations (3.3) were estimated as a block using three-stage least squares, in order to exploit the existence of data across different states. To increase the power in the estimation of the parameters of interest (λ^{1i}, $-\beta\lambda^{2i}$, and $(1 - \lambda^{1i} - \lambda^{2i})$), a cross equation restriction was imposed that these coefficients were the same across states. Instrumental variable techniques were used because, in the absence of full contingent claims markets, equations (3.2) and (3.3) only hold in expected value terms; the instruments used were a constant, a time trend, and the first and second lags of the change in US personal income derived from labor and capital.

Table 3.3 shows the results of running equations (3.3) using annual regional data over the period 1966–86 for the twenty largest states by

Table 3.3. *Regression results from US regional private sector capital income*

$$\Delta I_{Kit} = \alpha_i + \lambda^1 \Delta I_{KNt} - \beta \lambda^2 \Delta I_{Lit} + (1 - \lambda^1 - \lambda^2) \Delta P_{Kit}$$

	Largest 20 states	8 BEA regions
Nat. cap. inc. λ^1	0.9838 (0.0016)**	0.9909 (0.0108)**
Labor inc. $-\beta\lambda^2$	−0.0040 (0.0002)**	−0.0011 (0.0024)
Cap. prod. $(1-\lambda^1-\lambda^2)$	0.0216 (0.0003)**	0.0132 (0.0044)*
R^2	0.66–0.94	0.76–0.97
DW	1.04–2.49	1.08–2.22

Notes: The equations were estimated using three-stage least squares. I_{Kit} is real per capita income from dividends, interest, and rent for state i in period t, and subscript N refers to the national value, I_{Lit} is income from labor for state i in period t, while P_{Kit} is state product accruing to capital for state i in period t. Standard errors for coefficients are reported in parentheses. * and ** indicate significance at the 5% and the 1% level, respectively. Constant terms for the individual equations not reported.

population and for the eight standard regions of the US, as defined by the Bureau of Economic Analysis (BEA). The regression using the twenty most populous states has the advantage of using more data, while the regional regressions are more comprehensive (the twenty largest states cover about 80 percent of the population).[13] The table reports the estimated coefficients and associated standard errors for the three independent coefficients (λ^1, $-\beta\lambda^2$, and $(1-\lambda^1-\lambda^2)$). In addition, the range of the R^2 and Durbin–Watson statistics for the individual equations in the system are reported, to give a sense of the fit of the equations and degree of autocorrelation in the residuals.

Looking at the results for the largest twenty states, it is clear that the most important influence on changes in personal income from capital across states is the change in national personal income from capital. The estimated coefficient λ^1 is 0.9838, with a standard error of 0.0016. Given the interpretation of λ^1 as the proportion of capital flows associated with "capitalists" (people who are not using their capital income to insure against regional shocks to their labor income), this implies that the vast majority of fluctuations in personal income from capital are not associated with region specific economic shocks.

Personal income from capital does, however, have a small but detectable role in insuring against shocks to regional labor income. The coefficient on the change in personal income from labor $(-\beta\lambda^2)$, at -0.0040, has the expected negative sign and is significant at conventional levels.[14] The coefficient implies that a dollar fall in labor income produces a 0.4 cent increase in personal income from capital. While capital flows do provide some insurance against regional shocks to labor income, this insurance is clearly extremely partial. Finally, the coefficient on the change in state product accruing to capital was also found to be small (0.0216) but significant in the regression. Agents do appear to have a slight tendency to invest more heavily in local enterprises.

The descriptive statistics indicate that the individual equations fit reasonably well and are not clearly misspecified. The R^2 statistics indicate that between 79 and 94 percent of the variance in the original series are explained by the regressions, while the Durbin–Watson statistics, which vary between 1.00 and 2.59, show no clear or systematic problems with autocorrelation.

The results for the regression using data on BEA regions confirm those from the twenty largest states. All the coefficients from the regional regression are within one standard error of those estimated using the state-by-state data, while the descriptive statistics are again satisfactory. Hence it appears that the results for the twenty largest states are a relatively good indicator of behavior in the US as a whole, as might be expected given their size.

One interesting feature of the regional results, which is not apparent in table 3.3, is the relatively poor performance of the regression for the Plains states. This equation has both the lowest R^2 and the lowest Durbin–Watson statistics of any of the eight individual equations. It is possible that this deterioration in fit reflects differences in behavior across regions, and in particular differences between agricultural areas and other regions.

In order to investigate this possibility more fully, equations (3.3) were re-estimated using data from the states comprising each of the BEA regions. The results from this exercise are reported in table 3.4. These more detailed regressions generally confirm the earlier findings: the coefficients on aggregate US personal income are consistently large and significant, indicating "capitalists" are the dominant factor in regional behavior; and the coefficient on local product is consistently small and positive, indicating a weak preference for local investment. In the coefficients on state labor income, however, there are some interesting indications of differences in regional behavior. Both the Plains states and, to a lesser extent, the South-Eastern states (which are relatively agricultural) attract large negative coefficients which are significantly larger than the coefficients for the US as a whole, reported in table 3.3. The other regions, on the other hand, generally show results not dissimilar from aggregate US behavior, although the Far West region attracts a significantly positive coefficient.

Table 3.4. *Regression results for individual regions' private sector capital flows*

$$\Delta I_{Kit} = \alpha_i + \lambda^1 \Delta I_{KNt} - \beta\lambda^2 \Delta I_{Lit} + (1 - \lambda^1 - \lambda^2)\Delta P_{Kit}$$

Region	Nat. cap. inc. λ^1	Labor income $-\beta\lambda^2$	Cap. prod. $(1-\lambda^1-\lambda^2)$
New England	0.912 (0.132)**	0.015 (0.023)	0.011 (0.051)
Mid East	1.281 (0.090)**	−0.008 (0.021)	0.058 (0.033)
Great Lakes	0.839 (0.041)**	−0.015 (0.016)**	0.031 (0.011)*
Plains	1.029 (0.066)**	−0.061 (0.013)**	0.043 (0.018)*
South East	0.758 (0.040)**	−0.035 (0.008)**	0.014 (0.007)
South West	0.984 (0.132)**	0.019 (0.028)	0.019 (0.026)
Rocky Mnts.	0.639 (0.090)**	−0.016 (0.020)	0.019 (0.012)
Far West	0.834 (0.111)**	0.054 (0.019)**	0.009 (0.030)
Farm states	0.871 (0.052)**	−0.045 (0.007)**	0.009 (0.030)

Notes: See table 3.3.

It appears that primarily agricultural areas have different behavior from the US as a whole. This is confirmed by the last row in table 3.4, which shows reports a regression using data from eleven "farm states," defined as those states where farm proprietors' income make up more than 2 percent of total income.[15] The coefficient on income from labor is again negative and significant. At −0.0452, compared with −0.0040 for the largest twenty states, the point estimate indicates that farm states exhibit a level of insurance against changes in labor income which is ten times larger than that for the US as a whole, with each 1 dollar fall in income from labor being associated with a 4.5 cent rise in income from capital.

This difference between behavior in the US as a whole and the eleven farm states prompts two questions. Why is the insurance to changes in labor income generally so small, and why is it so much larger for the farm states. Clearly, there are many possible explanations, however two factors may be worth highlighting.

First, to the extent that capital flows are related to retirement income they are likely to reflect highly diversified portfolios, and hence these payments are unlikely to vary with changes in labor income. Second, and more importantly, regional economic disturbances tend to produce unemployment rather than changes in real wages.[16] While it is possible to think of regional portfolios that could insure against a general fall in regional wages, it is much more difficult to think of the private sector portfolio which can insure against unemployment. This hypothesis can also explain the different behavior found in the farm states. To the extent that ·farm wages are relatively flexible, as would appear likely given the highly variable prices for agricultural products, individuals are more able to insure themselves against regional fluctuations in labor income. Furthermore, given the derivative markets for agricultural products, the portfolio is relatively easy to construct. It appears probable, therefore, that the different behavior of farm states reflects the different nature of the labor market in these regions.

If it is correct that, because most regional adjustment is reflected in unemployment rather than real wages, individuals find it difficult to protect themselves from regional economic disturbances, then such protection may be provided by government. National and regional fiscal systems cushion to some extent against regional economic difficulties in the form of income-related taxes and transfers. The importance of net government transfer payments as a cushion for regional incomes was investigated by re-running equation (3.3), but with net transfers (transfers less taxes and payments for social insurance) substituted for private capital income. Specifically, the following set of regressions were estimated,

$$\Delta I_{Gat} = \alpha^a + \lambda^{1a}\Delta I_{Gnt} - \beta\lambda^{2a}\Delta I_{Lat} + (1 - \lambda^{1a} - \lambda^{2a})\Delta P_{Kat}$$

$$\Delta I_{Gbt} = \alpha^b + \lambda^{1b}\Delta I_{Gnt} - \beta\lambda^{2b}\Delta I_{Lbt} + (1 - \lambda^{1b} - \lambda^{2b})\Delta P_{Kbt}$$

$$\vdots$$

$$\Delta I_{Git} = \alpha^i + \lambda^{1i}\Delta I_{Gnt} - \beta\lambda^{2i}\Delta I_{Lit} + (1 - \lambda^{1i} - \lambda^{2i})\Delta P_{Kit}$$

(3.4)

where I_G represents real per capital government net transfers, and the other variables are as in equation (3.3).

The regression relates the change in real per capita net government transfers for each state to a constant, the change in national net transfers, the change in real labor income for the state, and the change in real state capital product; three stage least squares was used with the same instruments as in the earlier regressions. The interpretation of the regression coefficients in this case is somewhat different from that in the earlier regressions. In particular the coefficient λ^1, which measures the connection between local and national transfer payments, no longer represents "capitalist" behavior, it is simply a term used to take the effect of the national business cycle, and other changes in national fiscal policy, out of the regressions. The parameters of most interest in these regressions are those on labor and capital product, since they measure the degree to which government transfers insure local labor income and local returns to capital, respectively.

The regressions were estimated for the same sets of regions and states as

Table 3.5. *Regression results from US regional transfer less direct tax payments*

$$\Delta TR_{it} = \alpha_i + \lambda^1 \Delta TR_{Nt} + \lambda^2 \Delta IL_{lit} + \lambda^3 \Delta P_{Kit}$$

	Largest 20 states	Farm states
Nat. trans. less taxes λ^1	0.763 (0.005)**	0.704 (0.059)**
Inc. from labor λ^3	−0.136 (0.002)**	−0.037 (0.019)*
Capital prod. λ^3	−0.056 (0.002)**	−0.101 (0.030)**
R^2	0.53–0.89	0.24–0.93
DW	1.18–2.63	1.11–2.29

Notes: The equations were estimated using three-stage least squares. TR_{it} represents real per capita net transfer payments in state i in time period t, other variables are defined above for table 3.3. Standard errors for coefficients are reported in parentheses. * and ** indicate significance at the 5% and the 1% level, respectively. Constant terms for the individual equations not reported.

the earlier ones related to private capital markets. As in the earlier estimation, a significant difference was found between the behavior of farm states and other regions. For the sake of brevity, only the results for the largest twenty states (which are taken as a proxy for the country as a whole) and the farm states are reported.

The results in table 3.5 indicate that the government plays a significant role in insuring against localized income shocks. For the twenty largest states, the coefficient associated with changes in personal labor income is −0.136, implying that each 1 dollar fall in labor income produces a 13.6 cent rise in transfers net of taxes, while that associated with changes in income accruing to capital is −0.056, implying that each 1 dollar fall in product accruing to capital results in a 5.6 cent increase in transfers less taxes. The government appears to be the principal provider of insurance against regional economic fluctuations, although, at $13\frac{1}{2}$ cents in the dollar for fluctuations in labor income, this insurance is also relatively partial.

The results for the farm states show a somewhat different picture. In these states the insurance provided for changes in labor income is relatively small (−0.037), while that for income accruing to capital is much larger (−0.101). This implies that while a 1 dollar fall in labor income produces only a 3.7 cent rise in transfers, a dollar fall in income accruing to capital produces a 10.1 cent rise in transfers. The sizeable transfers associated with capital product for the farm states presumably reflects the fact that much of the variation in farm income is reflected in the data on income accruing to capital. Transfers associated with farm support are therefore related to changes in income accruing to capital, not with income earned by labor. Given the size of farm support payments, the large coefficient on capital product probably reflects these transfer payments.

The results for the twenty largest states can be compared with other papers looking at relationship between fluctuations and fiscal policy across regions of the US. Sachs and Sala-i-Martin (1992) and Bayoumi and Masson (1992) estimate that a 1 dollar fall in local income results in a 30–5 cent rise in federal transfers less taxes, while von Hagen (1992) reports a figure of 10 cents. All of these studies focus on federal fiscal payments and include federal grants to states in their calculations. In addition, they do not differentiate between personal income from labor and capital product, but rather look at total personal income; hence the results are not directly comparable with those reported in this chapter. However, our results would appear to be closer in magnitude to those reported by von Hagen than to those reported by Sachs and Sala-i-Martin and Bayoumi and Masson. Clearly, this is an area for future investigation.

IV   Fluctuations in regional consumption

The data on regional product and income presented so far indicate that there are substantial opportunities for individual consumers within the United States to geographically diversify their holdings of capital and to engage in inter-regional borrowing and lending, but that in practice consumers have relatively little insurance against fluctuations in regional income. In this section, we examine data on regional aggregate consumption to see if, on balance, consumers are able to insulate their consumption from fluctuations in regional income and product.

In a world of complete contingent markets, two individuals who trade two goods in a single market should choose their consumption to equate their marginal rates of substitution between those two goods to the common price ratio they face for those two goods. If the two goods are apples and oranges, for instance, consumers' observed consumption of these goods should be explained by some demand system and should be independent of the ratio of apples to oranges in their endowments. If the two goods are consumption in the present and consumption in the future, in a deterministic setting consumers' observed consumption should be explained by some theory of their marginal rate of substitution between consumption at these different dates and the interest rate. There should be no particular relationship between the timing of consumption and the timing of income. If consumption today and consumption tomorrow are traded in a setting with uncertainty but complete markets, then observed consumption should still be explained by some theory of the marginal rate of substitution between consumption today and consumption tomorrow in the different states of nature and the full range of asset prices. Again, the theory would predict that there should be no particular relationship between the realization of a consumer's uncertain income growth and his/her consumption growth.

This implies that, in a world with complete markets, no variable should help to explain the growth rate of an agent's consumption except to the extent that it is correlated with variables that affect that agent's marginal rate of substitution between consumption today and consumption tomorrow.[17] Thus, the growth rate of a region's income, for instance, should have no impact on the growth rate of its consumption. We test the degree to which consumers use markets to smooth their consumption path by looking at whether, in practice, relative growth in income is a useful predictor of the relative growth of consumption across regions or not.[18]

Unfortunately, there are no direct measures of total consumption available on a regional basis for the United States. However, retail sales data have been collected on a state by state, county and city basis in Censuses conducted by the Commerce Department in various years between 1929 and 1987, using an extensive survey of retail establishments. Originally, the data were collected at irregular intervals; subsequently they have been taken at five-year intervals in years ending with digits 2 and 7. We use revised Census data published in Winston and Hertzberg (1956) for sales data for 1929, 1933, 1935, 1939, 1948, and 1954, and direct Census data for the years 1958, 1963, 1972, 1977, 1982, and 1987.

Regional price data are problematic. CPI data for selected cities extending back beyond 1929 from the Bureau of Labor Statistics indicate that long-term differences in regional price levels is not an important issue in examining these consumption and income data. In the reported results we use regional price indices to deflate the income and consumption data; results using national price indices produced very similar results. Population totals on a state-by-state basis are available from the Commerce Department's Bureau of Economic Analysis. They are supplied on the diskettes describing personal income by state from 1929.

We examine the connection between regional consumption growth and regional income and product growth with some simple regressions. The regressions are of the following form: let C_t^j denote the ratio of per capita retail sales in state j at time t to national per capita retail sales at time t, and DY_t^j to denote the ratio of per capita disposable personal income in state j

Table 3.6. *Regression results from state level data with regional deflators*

Years	Coeff.	s.e.	Years	Coeff.	s.e.
1929–87	0.83**	0.14	1929–35	1.10**	0.21
1929–58	0.60**	0.14	1933–9	0.27*	0.10
1958–87	0.95**	0.18	1954–8	0.59**	0.10
1929–39	0.88**	0.19	1958–63	0.82**	0.13
1939–48	0.45**	0.17	1963–7	0.97**	0.13
1948–58	−0.05	0.27	1967–72	0.22	0.19
1958–67	0.87**	0.1	1972–7	0.70**	0.15
1967–77	0.31	0.25	1977–82	0.95**	0.10
1977–87	1.14**	0.08	1982–7	1.26**	0.07

Notes: The regressions show the coefficients from running a regression of the change in consumption across states on the change in personal disposable income, for the time periods specified. * and ** indicate significance at the 5% and the 1% level, respectively. Constant terms for the individual equations not reported.

at time t to the national figure for per capita disposable personal income. For several pairs of dates t and s, the vector C_s^j/C_t^j was regressed on the vector DY_s^j/DY_t^j using ordinary least squares.

Table 3.6 presents regressions using state level data for the United States. These regressions use data from forty-nine states (excluding Hawaii and Alaska, but including the District of Columbia). The results indicate a strong relationship between consumption and income growth at horizons of five years or more across regions of the United States; all but two of regression coefficients are significantly different from zero at the conventional levels of significance, while most are not significantly different from unity. Given that the complete markets model predicts no relationship between the two variables, the evidence clearly rejects the hypothesis.[19] It appears that consumers do not use capital markets to smooth their consumption patterns in the way predicted by the complete markets model.

V Conclusion

Our examination of the role of capital markets in the US currency union leads to three conclusions about the role of these markets in regional adjustment. First, these markets do play an important role in allowing net transfers of capital within the US currency union. This contrasts with the situation across individual countries, where net capital positions in the post-war period have generally been small.[20]

Second, despite the opportunities for diversifying regional risk in private capital markets, the bulk of individuals do not appear to use such markets in this way. Regional flows of private sector income from capital are highly correlated with national flows, and do little to insure against local fluctuations in labor income. This may well reflect the importance of unemployment rather than real wages in regional adjustment (a hypothesis supported by the larger insurance of labor income evident in farm states). Most of the limited amount of insurance for regional labor income appears to be carried by the government. Finally, consumers do not appear to use capital markets to smooth consumption in the way predicted by the complete markets model with an infinitely lived consumer.

All of these conclusions have implications for the integration of capital markets both within existing currency unions and across international boundaries. Integrated capital markets are likely to produce large flows of capital across regions or national boundaries. However, they are unlikely to provide a substantial degree of insurance against regional economic fluctuations, except to the extent that capital income flows become more correlated across regions. This task will continue to be primarily the business of government. Nor do they imply an end of the tight link between changes in regional personal income and regional consumption.

Notes

1 Unlike many other currency unions, however, it does have a relatively splintered banking system.
2 A number of authors have examined the implications of models of consumption risk-sharing using data both at the individual and the international level. Mace (1991), Cochrane (1991), and Townsend (1991) explicitly examine the correlation of consumption growth and income growth across consumers in individual level panel data. Caroll and Summers (1991) and others have used international data on aggregate consumption and income at the country level to reject the hypotheses of representative consumer complete markets models of aggregate consumption growth. Backus, Kehoe, and Kydland (1989) and Stockman and Tesar (1990) have examined the correlation of consumption growth across countries empirically in the context of international business cycle models. Most authors have concluded that the complete markets model is not an adequate description of the international data.
3 Bayoumi and Rose (forthcoming) use this approach for UK data.
4 The May 1988 *Survey of Current Business* describes the Gross State Product data. For a description of the personal income data see US Department of Commerce (1984).

5 It is, of course, possible to think of connections between relative personal income and the omitted data. One way of gauging the possible size of such biases is to look at the relationship between compensation and state product. If compensation is a relatively constant proportion of total product across regions it would indicate that omitted variables were unlikely to be important since the product accounts would indicate little variation in the proportion of non-labor product across regions; if compensation varies considerably as a proportion of state product, on the other hand, then these omitted variables could be important. From the state product data it is possible to calculate the ratio of all compensation to labor (the sum of compensation of employees and proprietors' labor income) to overall state product for the standard regions of the United States used by the Bureau of Economic Analysis; averaged over the full period 1963–86 this ratio varies from 66 percent in the South West to 73 percent in New England. This range of 7 percent of state product is relatively small compared to the 20 percent variation in ratios between personal income and state product reported below. Hence we believe the reported results are not dominated by biases in the data.

6 These differences are an order of magnitude larger than the equivalent differences across countries, see Atkeson and Bayoumi (1991).

7 The nineteenth century also saw large international capital flows from the developed to the new world, Imlah (1958).

8 Examination of the ratio of net factor payments abroad to GNP for many of the major industrialized countries indicates that there are only a few instances in which this ratio has changed by more than 1 percentage point over the last fifteen or twenty years.

9 This exposition assumes identical preferences.

10 The division of individuals into these three rigid types is made purely for analytic convenience, in practice one would expect most people to have a mixture of motives for holding assets.

11 Since these investors hold different portfolios, these proportions could change over time. The assumption that they are fixed is made for analytic convenience.

12 See US Department of Commerce (1984).

13 The twenty largest states are MA, PA, NJ, NY, MA, IL, IN, MI, OH, WI, MO, CA, WA, FL, GA, LA, NC, TE, VA, and TX. The eight regions are New England, the Mid East, Great Lakes, Plains, South East, South West, Rocky Mountains, and Far West.

14 This is not simply a reflection of the behaviour of regional capital product. When capital product was substituted for capital income in the regressions the coefficient on labor income was positive, indicating that regional rewards to capital and income are positively correlated.

15 The 11 farm states are KS, MN, NE, ND, SD, ID, MT, AR, OK, IA, and WI. Only one farm state, Wisconsin, is also a member of the twenty largest states.

16 See Blanchard and Katz (1992).

17 If other factors, such as leisure, are not separable from consumption in the utility function, then labor income growth may well be correlated with consumption growth. However, since we look at correlations across different regions of the

United States, such non-separabilities would only matter if there were substantially different trends in leisure across regions, an unlikely hypothesis.

18 Migration or demographic change could cause average income per capita and average consumption per capita to be correlated on a regional basis without violating the principle that each individual was fully insured against income fluctuations. But, since our regression results indicate a high correlation between consumption and income growth at intervals as short as five years, we do not regard migration or demographic change as a likely explanation for our findings.

19 Similar results are obtained when food sales are used as the proxy for consumption, so these results do not appear to be an artifact of the choice of total retail sales, which includes durable goods purchases, as a proxy for consumption. We also obtained similar results when state product, as opposed to state income, was used in the regressions.

20 This is not true of the nineteenth century, however, when there were large international transfers of capital, see Imlah (1958).

References

Artis, M. and T. Bayoumi (1990), "Saving, Investment, Financial Integration and the Balance of Payments," in *Staff Studies for the World Economic Outlook*, International Monetary Fund, September.

Atkeson, A. and T. Bayoumi (1991), "Do Private Capital Markets Insure Against Regional Risk? Evidence from the United States and Europe," unpublished manuscript, University of Chicago.

Backus, David, Patrick Kehoe, and Finn Kydland (1989), "International Real Business Cycles," Federal Reserve Bank of Minneapolis, Working Paper No. 426.

Barro, Robert and Xavier Sala-i-Martin (1991), "Economic Growth and Convergence Across the United States," *Journal of Political Economy*, 100(2), pp. 233–51.

Baxter, Marianne and Mario J. Crucini (1990), "Explaining Saving-Investment Correlations," mimeo, University of Rochester and Rochester Center for Economic Research.

Bayoumi, T. and P. Masson (1991), "Fiscal Flows in the United States and Canada. Lessons for Monetary Union in Europe," unpublished manuscript, International Monetary Fund.

Bayoumi, T. and A. Rose (forthcoming), "Domestic Saving and Intra-National Capital Flows," *European Economic Review*.

Blanchard, O. and L. Katz (1992), "Regional Evolutions," *Brookings Papers on Economic Activity I*, pp. 1–61.

Caroll, C. and L. Summers (1991), "Consumption Growth Parallels Income Growth: Some New Evidence," in D. Bernheim and J. Shoven (eds.), *National Saving and Economic Performance*, University of Chicago Press.

Cochrane, John (1991), "A Simple Test of Consumption Insurance," *Journal of Political Economy*, 99(5), pp. 957–76.

Cole, Harold and Maurice Obstfeld (1991), "Commodity Trade and International Risk Sharing: How Much do Financial Markets Matter?" *Journal of Monetary Economics*, 28(1), pp. 3–24.

Easterlin, Richard (1957), "Regional Growth of Income: Long Run Tendencies," in S. Kuznets and D. Thomas (eds.), *Population, Redistribution, and Economic Growth in the United States*, The American Philosophical Society, Philadelphia.

Eichengreen, B. (1990a), "One Money for Europe? Lessons from the US Currency Union," *Economic Policy*, 10, pp. 119–86.

   (1990b), "Is Europe an Optimal Currency Area?" Centre for Economic Policy Research, Discussion Paper 478.

Feldstein, M. and C. Horioka (1980), "Domestic Saving in International Capital Flows," *Economic Journal*, 90, pp. 314–29.

Garnick, Daniel (1990), "Accounting for Regional Differences in Per Capita Income Growth: An Update and Extension," *Survey of Current Business*, January, pp. 29–40.

von Hagen, J. (1992), "Fiscal Arrangements in a Monetary Union: Evidence from the US," in Don Fair and Christian de Boissieux (eds.) *Fiscal Policy, Taxes and Financial Systems in an Increasingly Integrated Europe*, (Deventer; Kluwer 1992).

Imlah, A. (1958), *Economic Elements in the Pax Britannica: Studies in British Foreign Trade in the Nineteenth Century*, Harvard University Press.

Institute of International Finance (1991), *External Assets and Liabilities of Industrial Countries*.

Lucas, R. (1978), "Asset Prices in an Exchange Economy," *Econometrica*, pp. 1429–45.

Lucas, Robert E. Jr. (1987), *Models of Business Cycles*, New York: Basil Blackwell.

Mace, Barbara (1991), "Full Insurance in the Presence of Aggregate Uncertainty," *Journal of Political Economy*, 99(5), pp. 928–56.

Masson, P. and J. Melitz (1991), "Fiscal Policy Independence in a European Monetary Union," *Open Economy Review*, pp. 113–36.

Mitchell, B. (1988), *British Historical Statistics*, Cambridge: Cambridge University Press.

Portes, R. (1989), "Macroeconomic Policy Coordination and the European Monetary System," Centre for Economic Policy Research Discussion Paper No. 342, September.

Sachs, J. and X. Sala-i-Martin (1992), "Fiscal Policies and Optimum Currency Areas: Evidence from Europe and the United States," in M. Canzeroni,V. Grilli and P. Masson (eds.) *Establishing a Central Bank: Issues in Europe and Lessons from the US* (Cambridge: Cambridge University Press, 1992) pp. 1950–219.

Stockman, Alan and Linda Tesar (1990), "Tastes and Technology in a Two Country Model of the Business Cycle: Explaining International Co-movements," NBER, Working Paper No. 3566, December.

Summers, L. (1988), "Tax Policy and International Competitiveness," in Jacob Frenkel (ed.), *International Aspects of Fiscal Policies*, University of Chicago Press.

Tesar, Linda (1992), "Saving, Investment, and International Capital Flows," *Journal of International Economics*, Forthcoming.

Townsend, Robert (1991), "Risk and Insurance in Village India," Manuscript.

Winston, Clement and Marie Hertzberg (1956), "Regional Trends in Retail Sales," *Survey of Current Business*, September, pp. 11–20.

US Department of Commerce (1984), *State Personal Income: Estimates for 1929–1982*, February.

4 The economics of the CFA franc zone

JAMES M. BOUGHTON

I Introduction

The economic rationale for the existence of the CFA (Communauté Financière Africaine) franc zone in Africa is not so much that it constitutes an optimal currency area among its member countries, but rather that it provides an effective monetary standard for them. This currency union comprises seven countries that are members of the West African Monetary Union and that use a common central bank (the Central Bank for West African States) and six countries that use the Bank for Central African States as their central bank. The two banks issue distinct but equivalent currencies, each of which is known colloquially as the CFA franc. Both currencies are pegged firmly to the French franc; although the rules of the system allow each bank to change the rate independently of the other, there has not been a single parity change since 1948. Furthermore, after an early period when some countries had opted out of the system and established independent currencies, membership in the zone increased by two countries during the 1980s. Despite the diversity of economic structure across the zone, despite the massive terms-of-trade losses experienced by some member countries in the 1980s, despite the lack of intra-regional trade, thirteen sovereign countries have elected to forego the exchange rate as an instrument of external adjustment, choosing instead to moor expectations and ensure a measure of policy discipline by tying their hands – not just together, but to a well-anchored post.[1]

The phenomenal persistence of the CFA franc zone is all the more remarkable in view of the magnitude of the problems that the region has faced in recent years. Without any doubt, the past decade or so has been extraordinarily difficult for the franc zone, as it has for many developing countries. The predominant adverse economic shock has been a prolonged, severe decline in the terms of trade, which resulted essentially from the global weakness in primary commodity prices. That decline produced a gap between the value of output and the initial level of real incomes, a consequent deterioration in the balance of payments, and – to the extent that domestic costs did not fall commensurately with the drop in export values – a loss of international competitiveness. It of course does not follow that exchange-rate depreciation would have been a useful means of restoring competitiveness and external balance, but it does raise the question of whether the policy of refusing to consider that possibility in order to preserve the stabilizing role of the exchange rate has imposed extra adjustment costs on these economies. The goal of this chapter is to review the economic performance of the countries in the zone and to examine the relationship between performance and the zone's institutional arrangements.

II Economic performance

Much of the criticism of the franc zone as an economic structure has been based on the observation that the two largest countries – Cameroon and Côte d'Ivoire – have experienced a severe loss of competitiveness in recent years and have been hamstrung in trying to offset the loss while keeping the exchange rate fixed against the French franc (which itself became a "hard" currency around the same time as the terms-of-trade shock). Using the real effective exchange rates reported in the IMF's *International Financial Statistics* as the measure of international competitiveness, one finds that from 1982 to 1987 Cameroon experienced a real effective appreciation of 37 percent; from 1985 to 1988, Côte d'Ivoire underwent a real appreciation of a similar magnitude. Certainly these losses were substantial and had serious deleterious effects on these countries. The aggregate current-account balance for the zone, which from 1971 through 1977 had averaged just $3\frac{1}{2}$ percent of GDP, averaged more than 7 percent of GDP for the period 1978–89. The deterioration thus preceded any loss of competitiveness, but the lack of exchange-rate adjustment could be cited as a factor in prolonging the problem into the second half of the 1980s and beyond.

Three cautionary points must be noted before one concludes that the exchange regime has inhibited external adjustment. First, once a country with a floating exchange rate loses control over domestic prices, regaining competitiveness will require not just a devaluation but massive and continuing depreciation of the currency. In neighboring Zaïre, for example, the exchange rate was allowed to depreciate by an average of 115 percent *per annum* from 1985 through 1990, while the real effective exchange rate depreciated by a *total* of 27 percent. To sacrifice price stability to correct an external imbalance is unlikely to be of more than palliative assistance. Second, many of the smaller countries in the franc zone, including Gabon and Togo, managed to avoid real appreciation throughout the 1980s and even realize substantial gains in competitiveness. Third, even Cameroon and Côte d'Ivoire experienced a measure of real exchange-rate stability over the longer run. From 1978 to 1990, the net real appreciation in both cases was around 10 percent.

Given the difficulty of assessing the behavior of real exchange rates and the limited amount of data available for statistical analysis, the value of the exchange rate as an anchor can best be seen by comparing economic performance between the members of the franc zone and their neighbors. In so doing, it is important to choose the comparator countries carefully. A number of studies have taken the rest of sub-Saharan Africa as the basis for comparison. The choice, however, is problematic because it includes countries that are much more heavily industrialized or otherwise more diversified than those in the zone and that therefore have been less subject to terms-of-trade shocks; and because some of the comparator countries have had exchange arrangements similar to those in the zone. Another avenue has been to compare against selected high-inflation countries, in Africa or elsewhere in the developing world; again, it is difficult to isolate the effects of the currency system from those of other aspects of policy regimes or external conditions.

A natural choice does turn out to be available, because all of the *contiguous* neighbors of the zone have had independent currencies and have pursued relatively flexible exchange-rate policies. In addition, that group of countries has had a quite similar experience to the CFA countries regarding economic development and diversity and the effects of terms-of-trade shocks. As a first approximation, therefore, the predominant factor that distinguishes the countries in the franc zone from their contiguous neighbors is that the former have consistently pursued a policy regime that eschews the exchange rate as a policy instrument. As for the neighbors, five have independently floating currencies, and all of those experienced relatively high inflation in the 1980s: the Gambia, Ghana, Nigeria, Sierra Leone, and Zaïre. The other five for which enough data are available have managed their currencies to varying degrees. Two countries – Guinea-Bissau and Mauritania – have pursued managed floats. The Guinea-Bissau peso is adjusted to the SDR on the basis of estimates of the domestic inflation rate, while the Mauritanian ouguiya is adjusted on the basis of movements in a basket of currencies. One currency (the Libyan dinar) is pegged to the SDR. The remaining two – the Algerian dinar and the Moroccan dirham – are pegged to other currency baskets.[2]

An ideal set of comparators would have been subject to similar shocks during the period being examined, but that raises the question of what the right period is. The World Bank data base for Africa spans the period from 1965 through 1987. For that full period, both groups of countries suffered a decline in the terms of trade, but the loss was relatively large for the franc-zone countries (30 percent, compared with 12 percent for the comparators). The zone also experienced a larger variance around the downward trend in the terms of trade; the standard deviation for the twenty-three years was 25 percentage points, compared with 14 points for the neighboring countries as a group. Also of interest is the Hamada–Iwata ratio, which gives the impact of the change in the terms of trade on a country's GDP; by that measure, the loss amounted to 0.4 percent per annum for the CFA zone and 0.3 percent for the neighbors. Shortening the period to the last decade (1977–87) brings the two groups closer together: a total drop of 27 percent in the terms of trade, equivalent to 0.8 percent of GDP per annum, for both groups. The neighboring countries experienced slightly larger volatility, with a standard deviation around the negative trend of 9 percentage points, compared with 7 percentage points for the franc zone. Nonetheless, by any reasonable standard, it seems that adverse shocks have been at least as severe for the CFA countries as for the other countries in the region. The comparison is especially close for the more recent period, which is also the period when the most severe shocks occurred.[3]

So how have these two groups compared in performance? The clearest advantage enjoyed by the franc-zone countries is in price stability. From 1980 through 1989, inflation – measured by GDP deflators – ranged from − 1 percent annually in Gabon to a maximum of 7.5 percent in Benin. The zone average, at 4.2 percent per annum for the decade, was well below that of France (6.5 percent). In contrast, four of the ten neighbors experienced inflation in excess of 40 percent per annum, and two others were in double digits. Only the four Northern neighbors, those listed above as linking their currencies closely to a basket of currencies, came close to achieving price stability, and even two of those had inflation rates higher than the highest rate within the franc zone. The overall mean inflation rate for the ten comparators was 26 percent.

Comparison of real growth rates is more mixed, but on average the franc-zone countries did as well as the others in the 1980s. Except for Niger, all of the countries in the zone experienced positive real growth for the decade as a whole, and in six cases output growth exceeded the rate of population growth. The average annual growth rate for the zone was 2.5 percent, compared with 2 percent for the eight contiguous countries for which output data are available. Domestic investment has also been relatively high, averaging 23 percent over the period 1976–87, compared with 19 percent in neighboring countries. The bottom line is that the countries in the zone achieved relatively greater success in stabilizing prices, while suffering no loss in output growth compared with their neighbors.

The degree of external imbalance has been somewhat greater for the CFA franc zone than for the neighboring countries. For example, over the period 1978–88, the overall current-account deficit averaged nearly $7\frac{1}{2}$ percent of GDP for the zone, compared with $4\frac{1}{2}$ percent for the neighbors. This difference is attributable in large measure to the weaker constraints facing the franc-zone countries, owing to the greater availability of concessionary external finance (see the discussion of official assistance, below). The consequences should not be minimized on that score; although growth has held up reasonably well, most of the member countries, like their neighbors, have had difficulties servicing external debts in recent years and have had recourse to debt rescheduling through the Paris Club. Unlike several of their neighbors, however, debt servicing difficulties have not generally extended to the IMF or the World Bank. Only the Congo has been classified by the World Bank as being in non-accrual status, and none has had arrears of six months or more to the IMF; four neighboring countries have had such arrears: Liberia, Sierra Leone, Sudan, and Zaïre.

This generally upbeat picture of the low real cost of price stabilization in the zone conflicts with some other studies, including notably the recent paper by Devarajan and Rodrik (1991).[4] That paper develops a framework in which countries attempt to minimize welfare losses that result from departures of real growth from its potential or departures of inflation from a target rate. Fixing the exchange rate promotes price stability at the expense of destabilizing real growth, owing to the loss of an output-stabilizing policy instrument. Since the data presented just above suggest that there may be no *long-run* trade-off between price stability and growth, it is important to note that the real costs in this framework are inherently temporary.[5]

Devarajan and Rodrik's model and assumptions imply that the authorities in the franc zone could improve welfare by switching to a more flexible exchange regime if they are prepared to tolerate at least 1.5 percent higher annual inflation in order to reduce departures of output growth from the potential rate by an average of 1 percentage point. The authors conclude that the current regime implies an "excessive anti-inflation bias" (p. 24). That conclusion, however, relies on an implicit assumption that the output costs of inflation control are persistent as well as a number of explicit assumptions about the inflation and output targets and the relationships between outcomes and the choice of regime.

III   The role of the currency arrangements

Given that the countries in the CFA franc zone have performed reasonably well under difficult circumstances in the 1980s, it remains to establish a link between the exchange regime and economic performance. There are three major positives. First, adherence to an external monetary standard, especially to a currency that itself is a member of a successful hard-currency club, conveys a measure of discipline to financial policies that would otherwise be difficult for the authorities of an embattled economy to maintain. The evidence for that discipline is simply that prices have been stable throughout the region for at least the past decade, as described above.

The discipline argument should not be oversold. As Corden (1990) has noted, financial pressures that arose in Côte d'Ivoire in the late 1970s led to increases in tariffs and non-tariff barriers, with negative effects on growth. Similar pressures in the mid 1980s led to a banking crisis in Cameroon. More generally, a country's exchange arrangements may promote but do not guarantee discipline; imbalances may result in repression or a liquidity squeeze rather than open inflation. Even so, the overall growth record of the countries in the zone was sufficiently strong in the 1980s to suggest that price stability was more than an illusion.

The second positive aspect, closely related to the first, is that policies are more credible when they are constrained by a multinational institutional structure. Giavazzi and Pagano (1988) developed a theoretical framework related to the European Monetary System (EMS) that illustrated how such a framework would enhance credibility both through the existence of the institutionalized constraints and by making the public more aware of the constraints. Agenor (1991) developed a model of developing countries in which joining a currency union was one form of reputation-enhancing policy that could help to overcome behavior that would otherwise undermine the credibility of a fixed exchange-rate regime. Within the recent history of the franc zone, it is noteworthy that press reports of possible devaluations of the CFA franc have tended to generate capital flight from domestic banks in the more vulnerable countries, in contrast to normal periods when the convertibility and stability of the franc have contributed to confidence in the currency as a store of value. Again, the difficulty of finding a measurable effect of the hard-currency policy on longer-term growth is the clearest indication of its credibility.

Finally, the positive factor that may be the most important in the context of the CFA franc zone is that membership in the zone has given these countries access to France and to Europe. This access has taken several forms. First and foremost, it has generated a great deal of trade. Roughly two-thirds of the total international trade of the CFA franc countries is with France, within the franc zone, or with European countries whose exchange rates are closely linked with the franc. And growth in trade has been strong, typically outstripping the growth in output, whereas in the neighboring countries trade growth has been erratic and on balance has been much slower than output growth. For example, from 1976 through 1987, real trade growth (measured in 1980 US dollars) averaged about $3\frac{1}{4}$ percent for the franc-zone countries and just $\frac{3}{4}$ of 1 percent in the contiguous neighbors.

Second, access to Europe has enabled the countries in the zone to maintain currency convertibility and open capital movements, which has further promoted the growth of trade and output. Full convertibility within the franc zone (i.e., among the countries in the CFA zone and between those countries and France, Monaco, and other "operations account countries" such as the Comoros) has been a fundamental principle of the zone since its inception. France undertakes to guarantee convertibility at the fixed parity by permitting overdrafts in the operations accounts that each regional central bank maintains at the French Treasury. All of the member countries maintain some restrictions on payments for capital-account transactions, and several also maintain some limited restrictions on payments for current-account transactions. (For details, see the International Monetary Fund's Annual Report on Exchange Arrangements and Exchange Restrictions.) But these exceptions are minor, and the system is essentially open.

Third, the CFA franc countries have benefited from important financial support from France through the overdraft facilities mentioned just above. An external deficit for a member country will result in a loss of reserves and thereby a drop in the balance held by the regional central bank on behalf of the country in the Operations Account at the French Treasury. When that balance falls below specified levels, the central bank must tighten monetary policy, normally through a rise in rediscount rates for the country in question and restrictions on the availability of rediscounting facilities. But the central banks have automatic access to (interest-bearing) overdrafts and thus to whatever financing is required for the external deficits of member countries.

In addition to the Operations Accounts, France provides substantial official develpment assistance (ODA) to these and other Francophone African countries. Overall, France is by far the largest single bilateral donor to sub-Saharan Africa, accounting for nearly a third of ODA to that region in 1990, and more than $3\frac{1}{2}$ times as much as the next highest donor (the United States). The majority of that aid, perhaps as much as three quarters, went to the CFA franc countries. Partly because of that strong support from France, perhaps partly because the relatively greater financial stability in the zone was conducive to aid flows from other donors as well, total availability of ODA has been much higher for this region than for the neighboring countries. For the period 1986–9, ODA to the CFA franc countries averaged nearly 8 percent of GDP, compared with just over 2 percent for the neighboring countries.[6]

The two major potential weaknesses of the system as a monetary standard – the loss of the exchange rate as a policy instrument and the risk of overvaluation – have, as discussed above, turned out to be of limited empirical consequence. There is some evidence that the system may have contributed to some cyclicality in key economic variables. As would be suggested by the Devarajan–Rodrik model, output growth has been more variable than in neighboring countries: the 1971–87 standard deviation of annual growth rates of real GDP averaged nearly 7 percentage points for the CFA franc countries and just $4\frac{1}{2}$ percent for the contiguous neighbors. On the other hand, the standard deviation for investment/GDP ratios was lower (19 percentage points, compared with 28).

The weaknesses of the CFA franc zone derive more from its not being an optimum currency area. There is, of course, no single standard for making such a judgment, but three features of the franc zone may be singled out in this context. First – and this is the biggest contrast with Europe – there is a lack of intra-regional trade and therefore relatively little to gain from the use of a single currency in settling payments within the region. Whereas intra-regional trade accounts for more than half of the international trade of the EMS countries, the figure for the CFA franc zone is well under 10 percent.

Second, price flexibility has been limited, and that in turn has strengthened the case for relying on the exchange rate to correct the level of real incomes. For example, from 1984 to 1987 the world market price of robusta coffees, measured in CFA francs, fell by about half its initial value. During that same period, prices paid to coffee growers rose in every major coffee-exporting country in the CFA zone, by amounts ranging from two percent in Cameroon and the Congo to 40 percent in Benin. By the end of the period, coffee growers throughout the region were receiving three to five times the world market price for their product. As for urban wages, while wage cuts were fairly common in the 1970s and early 1980s (see Levy and Newman (1989) for a detailed study of Côte d'Ivoire), resistance seems to have stiffened in the wake of the severe external shocks of the more recent period. In 1990, for example, the authorities in Côte d'Ivoire announced plans to cut wages by up to 40 percent but then postponed implementation indefinitely in response to strikes and other disturbances.

Third, the production and trade structure and hence the incidence of terms-of-trade losses has varied widely across the region. All of the countries in the zone are heavily dependent on exports of primary commodities, but there is a diversity of exported products ranging from coffee (nearly 60 percent of Côte d'Ivoire's exports) to fish (30 percent for Sénégal) to cotton (two thirds or more for Chad and Mali) to petroleum (the predominant export for Cameroon, the Congo, and Gabon) and even uranium (80 percent of Niger's exports).

World market prices of most of these commodities were weak throughout much of the 1980s, but the extent of that weakness was far from uniform. From 1980 to 1990, the price of uranium was the weakest, falling by more than 60 percent. Coffee prices fell by more than 40 percent, and petroleum and fishmeal prices fell by around 20 percent. Cotton prices, in contrast, fell by just 13 percent, and in the second half of the decade both cotton and fishmeal prices rose while most others continued to fall. Correspondingly, the terms of trade experience of the countries in the zone varied widely. Every member country experienced declines in the 1980s, but through 1987 the declines ranged from 10 percent for Sénégal to 44 percent for Cameroon.

The obvious implication of this diversity is that, if the exchange rate were to be changed in an attempt to adjust real incomes to movements in the terms of trade, the required magnitude of the devaluation would, in all likelihood, not be uniform across countries. It of course does not follow that the optimum policy would be for each country to adopt an independent policy with respect to currency arrangements and the exchange rate, only that each country must develop an independent response with respect to deflation of real incomes in the face of terms-of-trade losses, whether through exchange-rate policy or domestic policies.

There are factors that tend to favor the smooth functioning of the franc zone as a currency union. Factor mobility is an important element in adjustment to external shocks for countries in a currency union. Over a reasonable time period, labor and/or physical capital should be able to move between regions within the union to compensate for rigidities in relative prices. The CFA franc zone is a huge territory, almost twice the total land mass of Western Europe, and the transportation systems are not well developed. Nonetheless, substantial movements of labor do occur. In Côte d'Ivoire, for example, at least one of six workers will have come from Burkina Faso, Mali, or elsewhere in the CFA franc zone. Typically, these workers stay for relatively brief periods and move in response to shifts in economic conditions (see Zacharia and Condé, 1985). Thus in spite of obvious difficulties the functioning of the currency union does not seem to be hampered particularly by a lack of factor mobility.

Of greater importance is the uniformity of the direction of trade. It is certainly true that the importance of France as a trading partner has tended to diminish over time. Whereas in the mid 1960s France accounted for nearly half of all international trade of the CFA countries, by the mid 1980s the portion had fallen to 30 percent. But much of that decline was attributable to growth in trade with other countries whose currencies in the meantime had become closely linked to the French franc, either through the EMS or through unilateral exchange-rate policies (such as with Austria). This broader stable-currency area accounts for well over half of total trade for all of the countries in the zone. In no case is Japan a major trading partner, and in very few cases does the United States play a large role.

Because of this fairly uniform trading pattern, all of the CFA franc countries are able to conduct the majority of their trade at fixed or nearly fixed exchange rates. Furthermore, monetary shocks such as shifts in exchange rates between Europe and other regions, while they could affect the competitiveness of the region as a whole, will not have major implications for relative positions within the zone.

IV Conclusions

What can one conclude? The CFA franc zone is far from qualifying as an *optimum* currency area, owing particularly to the very small degree of intra-regional trade, some inflexibility of prices and wages, and a wide diversity of incidence of shifts in the terms of trade. The unavailability of the exchange rate as a policy tool has doubtless placed an extra burden on fiscal policies, factor mobility, and support from abroad. These burdens have been especially serious for those countries that have suffered especially large deteriorations in the terms of trade – notably Cameroon, the Congo, and Gabon – or that have had difficulty containing financial pressures, including Côte d'Ivoire as well as Cameroon. It does not follow, however, that a different system would serve them better, because it is not clear whether the abandonment of the multilateral currency arrangements would weaken the discipline or the credibility of stabilization policies, or whether it would weaken the ties to Europe that the zone enjoys through trade and financial support.

What is clear, both from the theoretical literature on exchange regimes and from observation of the functioning of the CFA franc zone, is that the key issue is the ability of the authorities to *stabilize* economic activity within the confines of the current system; economic growth over the longer run has not been undermined. Simple comparisons with neighboring countries, such as those discussed above, as well as simulation models such as that of Devarajan and Rodrik, do suggest an impairment of the stability of output as the cost of price stabilization. Improving that trade-off so as to reduce reliance on outside support in response to adverse shocks is the major challenge facing those who would seek to preserve and strengthen the franc zone.

Notes

1 For a more detailed description and for references on the history of the zone, see Boughton (1992).
2 Three other countries adjoin the zone but have insufficient data for a comparison of economic performance; these comprise Guinea, Liberia, and the Sudan. For some series, data are missing for Libya and the Gambia as well. In most cases, data also are unavailable for the smallest CFA franc country, Equatorial Guinea (which joined only in 1985).
3 It has not been feasible to use the same data periods for all of the comparisons made here, owing to differences in coverage among the principal data sources.
4 The conclusion that growth has not been lower than in similar countries elsewhere is, however, robust with respect to the choice of comparators. Specifically, the finding is consistent with studies that have compared growth against other sub-Saharan African countries (i.e., not just those contiguous to the zone, and excluding the Northern tier) over varying time periods. Notable examples include Devarajan and de Melo (1987, 1990) and Guillaumont et al. (1988).
5 A common feature of models of exchange-regime choice is that the trade-off is between stability of prices and stability of output, holding fixed the long-run rate of output growth. For examples, see Flood and Marion (1982) and Aizenman and Frenkel (1986).
6 Sources: OECD (1991a), tables 38 and 43; OECD (1991b). The averages mask a wide range of experience, especially for the neighboring countries, where ODA ranged from near zero for Libya to more than half of GDP for the Gambia and Guinea-Bissau. The range within the zone was from around 3 percent for Cameroon and Gabon to 22 percent for Mali. The medians were 13 percent for the CFA franc zone and 8 percent for the neighbors. The differences between the two groups are not attributable to income levels, which were around $600 per capita for both groups.

References

Agenor, Pierre-Richard (1991), "Credibility and Exchange Rate Management in Developing Countries," International Monetary Fund, Working Paper WP/91/87, September.
Aizenman, Joshua and Jacob A. Frenkel (1986), "Supply Shocks, Wage Indexation and Monetary Accommodation," Journal of Money, Credit and Banking, 18, August, pp. 304–22.
Boughton, James M. (1992), The CFA Franc Zone: Currency Union and Monetary Standard, IMF Working Paper WP/91/133, December. Forthcoming in Monetary Integration, edited by Anthony Courakis and George Tavlas, to be published in 1992 by Cambridge University Press.

Corden, W. Max (1990), "Exchange Rate Policy in Developing Countries," World Bank, *Policy, Research, and External Affairs Working Papers*, WPS 412, April.

Devarajan, Shantayanan and Jaime de Melo (1987), "Evaluating Participation in African Monetary Unions: A Statistical Analysis of the CFA Zones," *World Development*, 15, April, pp. 483–96.

(1990), "Membership in the CFA Zone: Odyssean Journey or Trojan Horse?" World Bank, *Policy, Research, and External Affairs Working Paper*, WPS 482, August.

Devarajan, Shantayanan and Dani Rodrik (1991), "Do the Benefits of Fixed Exchange Rates Outweigh Their Costs? The Franc Zone in Africa," National Bureau of Economic Research, Working Paper No. 3727, June.

Flood, Robert P. and Nancy Peregrim Marion (1982), "The Transmission of Disturbances under Alternative Exchange Rate Regimes with Optimal Indexing," *Quarterly Journal of Economics*, 97, February, pp. 43–68.

Giavazzi, Francesco and Marco Pagano (1988), "The Advantage of Tying One's Hands: EMS Discipline and Central Bank Credibility," *European Economic Review*, 32, June, pp. 1055–82.

Guillaumont, Patrick, Sylviane Guillaumont, and Patrick Plane (1988), "Participating in African Monetary Unions: An Alternative Evaluation," *World Development*, 16, May, pp. 569–76.

Levy, Victor and John L. Newman (1989), "Wage Rigidity: Micro and Macro Evidence on Labor Market Adjustment in the Modern Sector," *The World Bank Economic Review*, 3, January, pp. 97–117.

Organization for Economic Cooperation and Development (1991a), *Development Co-operation: Efforts and Policies of the Members of the Development Assistance Committee,* Paris: OECD.

(1991b), *Geographical Distribution of Financial Flows to Developing Countries,* Paris: OECD.

Zacharia, K.C. and Julien Condé (1985), *Migration in West Africa: Demographic Aspects,* New York: Oxford University Press.

III Is Europe an optimum currency area?

5 Is Europe an optimum currency area?: evidence from regional data

PAUL DE GRAUWE
and WIM VANHAVERBEKE

I Introduction

The traditional theory of optimum currency areas, as developed by Mundell (1961), has identified the conditions under which a monetary union between regions or countries will work smoothly.[1] In a nutshell this theory says that when regions or countries are subjected to different disturbances (asymmetric shocks) the adjustment process will require either real exchange rates to adjust, or factors of production to move, or a combination of these two. In the absence of real exchange-rate flexibility and factor mobility, regional or national concentrations of unemployment will be inevitable.

The theory of optimum currency areas has also established a presumption that in a monetary union the adjustment mechanism will rely more on factor mobility than on real exchange-rate flexibility. Of course, in a monetary union the real exchange rates of regions can change, because of divergent regional movements of prices.[2] However, it is likely that the regional adjustment process following asymmetric shocks will rely less on these relative price changes than on mobility of labor. Exactly the opposite holds for countries with separate currencies. The presumption here is that more of the adjustment to asymmetric shocks will take the form of real exchange-rate changes than of labor mobility. The reason is that countries can change their nominal exchange rates. (For a fundamental contribution see Vaubel, 1976. See also Meltzer, 1986.)

The purpose of this chapter is twofold. First it aims at contrasting the nature of the adjustment mechanism between regions of the same country, and between countries in Europe. Is this presumption as described by their theory of optimum currency areas correct?

Second, we want to find out whether the occurrence of asymmetric shocks is different as between regions of the same country and nations in

111

Europe. Recently the European Commission (1990) has forcefully argued that further economic integration of Europe will reduce the likelihood of asymmetric shocks in European countries. If this is so, it may not matter much whether there is sufficient real exchange-rate flexibility and labor mobility. European countries may form a monetary union without fear that they will face large adjustment costs, because they will typically face the same shocks with similar effects in all countries. In this chapter we provide some evidence that can shed light on this issue. More particularly, we systematically compare the divergent movements of regional and national output and employment trends. We will ask the question of whether output and employment changes tend to be more asymmetric between countries than between regions of the same country. This issue of the asymmetry of shocks has recently been analyzed by several researchers (see Cohen and Wyplosz, 1989; Weber, 1990; EC-Commission, 1990; Eichengreen, 1990). The value added of the present chapter is that it contrasts the experience of regions with those of countries in Europe. (For a similar recent study see von Hagen and Neumann, 1991.)

In sections II and III we focus the attention on the nature of the regional and national adjustment processes by presenting data on real exchange-rate variability (section II) and labor mobility (section III). In section IV we study the occurrence of asymmetric shocks by analyzing the degree of regional and national dispersion of output and employment trends. Finally in section V the implications for economic and monetary union in Europe are drawn.

II Real exchange-rate variability – regional and national

In this section we compare systematically the degree of real exchange-rate variability of regions (within countries) and of countries.

Definitions and data

We concentrate our attention on the real exchange rates using *unit labor costs* as the price variable. We chose this definition because of data availability: using unit labor costs allowed us to cover a wider group of countries and regions than if we had used other price variables. In addition the unit labor cost is the most comprehensive measure of competitiveness.

For each country we define the real (effective) exchange rate as follows:

$$R_{it} = \sum_j \alpha_{ij}(S_{ijt}.P_{jt}/P_{it}) \tag{1}$$

where R_{it} is the real effective exchange rate of country i in period t; S_{ijt} is the nominal exchange rate of currency i with respect to currency j in period t expressed as an index; P_{jt} and P_{it} are the unit labor costs of country j and i respectively; α_{ij} is the weight of currency j in the effective exchange rate of country i, as measured by the share of trade of country j in country i's total trade.

In a similar way we define a real effective exchange rate of a region k in a particular country as follows:

$$R_{kt} = \sum_{m} \alpha_{km}(P_{mt}/P_{kt}) \tag{2}$$

Note that, since the currency is the same in that country, the nominal exchange rate is irrevocably fixed and drops out of the formula. Note also that α_{km} is defined here as the weight of region m in the effective exchange rate of region k. In this case of regional exchange rates we used the shares of region m in the total GDP of the country.[3]

The regional data come from Eurostat, *Banque de données régionales*. We used regional data of Germany, France, Spain, the UK, and the Netherlands. For the regions of the other countries we lacked the necessary data on unit labor costs. This yielded data of fifty regions during the sample period 1977–85. (As a result of the limitations of regional data, this is the longest sample period that could be constructed.) The complete list of these regions is given in the appendix.

The data source of the national data is OECD, Economic Outlook. We used data of the following countries: Belgium, Denmark, France, Germany, Greece, Italy, Japan, the Netherlands, Portugal, Spain, the United Kingdom, and the United States.

Measures of real exchange-rate variability

We computed different measures of real exchange-rate variability. At first one aims at capturing the long-run variations of the real exchange rates. This measure should give us an idea of whether these real effective exchange rates of countries and regions have a tendency to move in a trend-like fashion or whether they return to some constant value.[4] We define this variability concept (LVR) as follows:

$$LVR = \sum_{i=1} \frac{1}{n}\frac{1}{m}\frac{|R_{i,tn}-R_{i,t0}|}{R_{i,t0}}$$

where n is the length of the period expressed in years, $R_{i,t0}$ and $R_{i,tn}$ are the real exchange rates in the beginning and at the end of the period (respectively), and m is the number of countries (regions).

Two other measures of variability concentrate on the short-term

Table 5.1. *Real exchange-rate variability*

(in yearly percentage change)

Countries	Whole sample (1977–85)	EMS (1977–85)
Long-run variability:		
LVR	2.01	1.99
Short-run variability:		
MAYC	4.4	3.3
SDYC	4.5	3.6

Regions in	W. Germany (1977–88)	Spain (1980–5)	Netherlands (1977–88)	UK (1980–5)
Long-run variability:				
LVR	0.4	1.0	0.7	0.7
Short-run variability:				
MAYC	0.8	1.8	2.2	1.6
SDYC	0.9	1.9	1.5	1.6

Notes: MAYC is the mean absolute yearly change.
SDYC is the standard deviation of yearly changes.
Sources: The national data are from OECD, Economic Outlook.
The regional data are from Eurostat, Banque de données régionales.

movements of the real exchange rates. The first one is the mean of the absolute yearly changes of the real exchange rate (MAYC). The second one is defined as the standard deviation of the yearly changes of the real exchange rate (SDYC).

Empirical results

In table 5.1 we present the results of computing the average variability of the real exchange rates during 1977–85.

We observe that the variability of the real exchange rates of nations is about twice as large as the one observed at the regional level.[5] In order to test for the significance of these differences we computed t-ratios testing for differences in the mean. The results are presented in table 5.2.

The results of table 5.2 confirm that the differences in the mean between regions and countries are significant. All the t-ratios indicate that these differences are significant at the 1 percent level. Thus, during the sample

Table 5.2. *Real exchange-rate variability (1980–5): Tests of significance of differences in the mean*

Variability measures	Mean value		*t*-ratio
	Regions	Countries	
Long-run variability:			
LVR	0.75	2.01	−3.0
Short-run variability			
MAYC	1.76	4.70	−4.4
SDYC	1.70	4.84	

Notes: See table 5.1.
Sources: See table 5.1.

Table 5.3. *Real exchange-rate variability: tests of significance of differences in the mean*

Variability measures	Mean value		*t*-ratio
	EMS-Regions	EMS-Countries	
Long-run variability			
LVR	0.55	1.99	−3.4
Short-run variability			
MAYC	1.58	2.82	−1.9
SDYC	1.24	3.09	

Notes: See table 5.1.
Sources: See table 5.1.

period 1977–85 the long-run variability of the real exchange rates between regions of the same monetary union tended to be less than half as large as the one observed between sovereign nations. The same holds for the short-run variability measures.

Since the group of countries in the sample involve both EMS and non-EMS countries we also wanted to find out whether this significant difference between regional and national exchange-rate variability may not be affected by the fact that the real exchange-rate variability in the non-EMS countries was very high. We therefore computed the same average variability measures restricting ourselves to the EMS countries and the regions in EMS countries. The results are given in table 5.3.

Table 5.4. *Average flows of immigrants plus emigrants of regions to and from the rest of the country*

(as a percent of population of the region)

	1975	1980	1987	1975–87 (yearly average)
Belgium	0.92	0.89	0.84	0.87
Denmark	1.29	1.12	1.17	1.17
W. Germany	1.32	1.33	1.07	1.21
	(1.06)*	(1.06)*	(0.85)*	(0.98)*
Spain	N.A.	0.40	0.46	0.36
France	1.24	1.15	N.A.	1.20
Italy	0.78	0.68	0.53	0.66
Netherlands	2.02	1.63	1.66	1.68
UK	N.A.	1.51	1.81	1.54

Notes: N.A. = not available.
* = these numbers exclude the German "city-states" Bremen, Hamburg, and West Berlin.
Source: Eurostat, Banque de données régionales.

As expected, we observe from table 5.3 that the variability of the real exchange rates is lower in the EMS than in the non-EMS countries. However, the difference between regional and national variability measures remains and is of a similar order of magnitude as in the previous table.

III   Regional and national labor mobility

The degree of labor mobility is an important factor in determining the nature of the adjustment when asymmetric shocks occur in regions or in countries. In this section we contrast the evidence about labor mobility between regions of the same country and between countries.

Our measure of labor mobility between regions will be the flow of migrants in one region from and to the other regions expressed as a percent of the population of the former region. Thus this measure is the sum of the immigrant and emigrant *flows* of a particular region (as a percent of the population of that region). Table 5.4 presents these measures of regional mobility for a number of European countries.

Table 5.4 allows to note some striking differences in inter-regional mobility of European countries. The two southern countries, Spain and

Table 5.5. *Stock of a country's immigrants plus emigrants from and to the rest of the EC, in 1984*

(as a percent of population of the country)

Belgium	1.59
W. Germany	0.57
France	0.41
Italy	0.72
Netherlands	0.70
EC-6 average	0.64

Source: Calculations based on Straubhaar (1988).

Italy, have a much lower degree of inter-regional mobility than northern countries such as Germany, the UK, and France.

These differences are not due to aggregation bias, i.e., the size of the regions in these countries is approximately the same. This cannot be said of the smaller countries in the sample, whose regions are typically much smaller than regions in the larger countries. The smaller size of regions in small countries helps to explain the greater degree of inter-regional labor mobility observed in these countries. For West Germany we have also computed the same measures of inter-regional mobility after excluding the three "city-states" of the Federal Republic (Bremen, Hamburg, and West Berlin). These cities experience a much higher degree of mobility. The results are presented between brackets.

The differences in the intensity of inter-regional mobility of labor between the south and the north of Europe is surprising. It is surprising because the regional differences in per capita income tend to be higher in the south than in the north.[6] These differences would tend to produce larger migratory flows in the south than in the north of Europe. The perception of a high inter-regional mobility in the south and a low one in the north does not correspond to the facts.

We next compare the inter-regional mobility measures of table 5.4 to similar *inter-country* mobility measures in Europe. We could not find yearly *flow* data of inter-country mobility, however. Instead we had to rely on *stock* figures in a given year. These stock figures express the total number of migrants of a given country to and from the rest of the Community (as a percent of the population of the former country). Thus, these numbers have to be interpreted as the *cumulative flows* of all the preceding years. The results are given in table 5.5. Due to data limitations we could only construct data for the original EC countries.

Comparing table 5.5 with table 5.4 leads to the following conclusion. The migratory flows between regions of the same country are low and of a different order of magnitude than those between countries of the Community. This can be seen from the fact that the stock data of table 5.5 are smaller (on average) than the yearly flow data of table 5.4. If the average length of stay of migrants in EC countries is, say, ten years, this would imply that the yearly flows of migrants between the EC countries is less than one tenth of the yearly flow of migrants between regions.

The results presented so far can be summarized as follows. Adjustment mechanisms that can be relied upon to absorb shocks in regions and countries in Europe differ significantly. European countries experience a significantly higher degree of real exchange-rate variability than European regions. Conversely, regions experience a degree of labor mobility that is much higher than the one observed between countries in Europe. It is fair to say that the latter is almost absent as an adjustment mechanism.[7] These results confirm the presumption of the traditional optimum currency theory.

We have also observed that the degree of inter-regional mobility of labor is higher in the north than in the south of Europe (Spain and Italy). We will take up this point when we consider the implications for European monetary unification.

IV   Asymmetric shocks in regions and in countries

The theory of optimum currency areas stresses that when asymmetric shocks occur, regions of an "optimal" monetary union are likely to adjust mainly by migration of the labor force, whereas countries that are not part of an "optimal" monetary union will rely more on real exchange-rate changes to adjust to those shocks. The empirical evidence discussed in the previous sections seems to confirm this traditional view.

Much of the recent discussion of the issue whether the EMS countries should form a monetary union has focused on the question whether large asymmetric shocks are likely to occur in a future European monetary union. If these are unlikely to happen, the lack of labor mobility between EMS countries may not matter much.

The recent European Commission's report "One Market, One Money" has taken a strong stand on this issue. It argues that the continuing economic integration in the Community will make the EC countries more alike, so that asymmetric shocks will become less important. The existing instruments of policy will be able to deal with these disturbances (see EC Commission, 1990, p. 136).

A major difficulty in identifying asymmetric shocks is that we only observe their effects on some endogenous variable (e.g., output and

Table 5.6. *Short-term and long-term divergencies in regional and national growth rates of output*

(in yearly percentage change)

Countries (76–90)	Long-run divergence	Short-run divergence
Whole sample	0.48	1.66
EMS	0.48	

Regions in	Long-run divergence	Short-run divergence
France (76–86)	0.78	2.04
W. Germany (76–86)	0.51	1.09
Netherlands (76–86)	0.71	3.85
Spain (81–6)	1.45	3.59
UK (76–88)	0.72	1.40

Note: The long-run divergence of regions is defined as the standard deviation of the average regional growth rates over the relevant periods. For nations we have the same definition. The short-run divergence is defined as the average of the yearly standard deviations of the regional (resp. the national) growth rates.
Sources: The national data are from OECD, Economic Outlook. The regional data are from Eurostat, Banque de données régionales.

employment). These variables, however, are also influenced by economic policies. As a result, divergent movements in these variables can be evidence both of exogenous asymmetric shocks and of different national economic policies.

In this section we present some data on regional output and employment growth and compare these with the corresponding national data.

Regional and national output growth

Table 5.6 presents some evidence about divergencies in the growth rates of output between regions and between countries. We compute measures of short-term and of long-term variability. As our measure of short-term regional divergencies of output growth, we take the average of the yearly standard deviations of the regional growth rates of output. We do the same for the short-term divergencies of national output growth.

As our measure of the long-term divergencies we compute the standard deviation of the average growth rate of regional output. We use a similar measure of long-term divergencies in growth rates of countries. Thus, this measure gives us insight into the question of whether long-term growth rates tend to diverge more between countries than between regions.

The results of table 5.6 lead to some surprising conclusions. It appears that the long-run divergencies in *national* growth rates are substantially lower than the long-run divergencies in *regional* growth rates. Thus, regions belonging to the same countries in Europe tend to have a more unequal development of their output than nations.

As far as the short-term divergencies in growth rates are concerned, we find that there are fewer differences between regions and countries. The short-term deviations of the regional and the national growth rates are of comparable orders of magnitude.

We also note the special position of West Germany, where the regional dispersion of growth rates (both long-run and short-run) is small in comparison of what one observes in other countries.

Regional and national employment growth

In this section we present data on the regional and national dispersion of the growth rates of employment. We use the same measures of dispersion as in the previous section. The results are presented in table 5.7. Note that the sample of countries is not the same as in table 5.6. This has to do with the different availability of regional employment data.

The conclusions that can be drawn from table 5.7 are almost identical to the ones derived from table 5.6. The long-run dispersion of employment growth between regions of the same country is substantially larger than the dispersion of these growth rates between countries. For the short-term measures of dispersion we do not find the same pronounced difference between regions and countries.

Note again the special position of West Germany, which experiences a much more balanced regional development of employment than most other countries. Noteworthy is also the fact that the regional dispersion of employment growth is particularly pronounced in the southern European countries (Spain and Italy). Earlier we noted that the regional labor mobility is relatively low in these southern countries. These two features (unbalanced regional growth in employment and low mobility of labor) helps to explain the relatively large regional concentration of unemployment in these southern European countries. We show some evidence in table 5.8. The differences between the north and the south of Europe are

Table 5.7. *Short-term and long-term divergencies in regional and national growth rates of employment*

(in yearly percentage change)

Countries (1976–90)	Long-run divergence	Short-run divergence
Whole sample	0.30	1.13
EMS	0.26	

Regions in	Long-run divergence	Short-run divergence
W. Germany (76–87)	0.38	0.63
France (76–87)	0.38	0.70
Italy (84–7)	0.89	2.18
Spain (81–8)	2.00	2.88
UK (82–6)	0.96	1.11

Note: The long-run divergence of regions is defined as the standard deviation of the average regional growth rates over the relevant periods. For nations we have the same definition. The short-run divergence is defined as the average of the yearly standard deviations of the regional (resp. the national) growth rates.

Table 5.8. *Regional unemployment rates in 1989*

(in percent)

	Standard deviation	Maximum	Minimum	Difference
France	2.4	14.7	6.7	8.0
W. Germany	2.3	10.9	3.2	7.7
Great Britain*	2.3	10.5	4.0	6.5
Italy	6.4	21.8	4.1	17.7
Spain	4.5	26.5	13.7	12.8

Note: *Contrary to the data on the United Kingdom in the previous tables, the data in this table exclude Northern Ireland.
Source: Eurostat, Banque de données régionales.

striking. The regional dispersion of unemployment appears to be much more substantial in Spain and especially in Italy as compared to Germany and Great Britain.

V   Real exchange-rate flexibility and asymmetric shocks

In a previous section we observed that the degree of real exchange-rate flexibility between regions of the same country is (on average) smaller than between countries. This, however, does not imply that real exchange-rate movements have no role to play in the regional adjustment process. In this section we provide some additional empirical evidence highlighting the role of real exchange-rate changes. We computed the correlations between variability measures of real output and of real exchange rates, for both regions and countries. We did the same exercise with employment. The results are shown in tables 5.9 and 5.10.

We observe that the regional variability of output is relatively well correlated with the regional variability of the real exchange rates. The surprising thing is that this correlation is stronger and more significant at the regional than at the national level.[8] This suggests that, although the regional variability of real exchange rates is relatively small, it nevertheless plays a significant role in regional adjustment.

The correlations between the variability of real exchange rates and employment is much weaker. In addition, no strong differences are observed between the regional and the national correlations.

On the whole the evidence of tables 5.9 and 5.10 suggests that real exchange rates do play some role in the adjustment process at the regional level. Regions experiencing large disturbances in real output tend to have relatively large movements in their real exchange rates. This is consistent with the hypothesis that asymmetric regional disturbances are absorbed by regional changes in the real exchange rates. And, since nominal exchange rates are fixed between regions, this can also be seen as evidence that relative prices play a role in the adjustment process. It is clear, however, that this evidence can only be called suggestive. Correlation coefficients do not tell us anything about the direction of the causality. These correlations can also be interpreted to mean that relative price shocks cause variability in output and employment.

The evidence of this section adds some nuance to the presumption of the traditional optimum currency theory. It suggests that real exchange-rate changes continue to play a role in the adjustment process of regions. This has also been found by researchers in the context of other regions (see Poloz, 1990, for the Canadian provinces).

In this connection it is important to stress that there is evidence (which is

Table 5.9. *Correlations between measures of dispersion in real exchange rates and growth rates of output*

	Short term	Long run
All countries and regions	0.27**	0.23*
All countries	−0.03	−0.16
All regions	0.73***	0.28*
Regions in		
Germany	0.60**	0.07
Spain	0.79***	0.47**
Netherlands	0.95***	−0.2
UK	−0.41	0.18

Notes:
*** = significant at 1% level.
** = significant at 5% level.
* = significant at 10% level.
Source: Eurostat, Banque de données régionales.

Table 5.10. *Correlations between measures of dispersion in real exchange rates and growth rates of employment*

	Short term	Long run
All countries and regions	0.22*	0.06
All countries	0.53*	0.10
All regions	0.50***	0.17
Regions in		
Germany	0.03	0.04
Spain	0.53**	−0.07
Netherlands	0.20	0.44
UK	−0.38	0.27

Notes:
*** = significant at 1% level.
** = significant at 5% level.
* = significant at 10% level.
Source: Eurostat, Banque de données régionales.

not revealed by our correlation analysis) that real exchange-rate changes have also been quite important in the adjustment process of individual EMS countries, that have chosen to limit the changes in their nominal exchange rates. Countries like Belgium and the Netherlands, for example, allowed significant real depreciations of their currencies of 20–30 percent to occur during the early part of the eighties. These real depreciations were instrumental in the adjustment process of these countries following asymmetric shocks to which these countries were subjected at the start of the eighties.[9]

It is fair to conclude from this empirical evidence that real exchange-rate changes (relative price changes) will continue to play a role in regional adjustment in the future.

VI   Conclusion: implications for EMU

In this chapter we have presented descriptive statistics about regions and countries in Europe. This statistical analysis helps us to shed some light on the question of whether Europe is an optimal currency area. Our main findings are the following.

First, we have found that the presumption of the optimum currency theory holds for Europe provided some nuances are made. At the level of regions of the same country (monetary union) labor mobility plays a role in the adjustment process. Although the degree of real exchange-rate flexibility between regions is limited, it does appear to play some role in the adjustment process of regions. At the national level, there is almost no labor mobility but significantly more exchange-rate variability. As the EMS moves toward monetary union the question arises whether and to what extent the smaller reliance on real exchange-rate flexibility can be compensated for by more labor mobility.

Second, there is no evidence that asymmetric shocks occur less at the regional than at the national level. The opposite seems to be the case. We found larger and more sustained divergencies of the growth rates of output and employment at the regional level than at the national level. Thus, national growth rates of output and employment tend to diverge less than the same growth rates at the level of regions of the same countries.

This evidence can lead to two interpretations about the prospects of a future EMU in Europe. One is optimistic, the other is pessimistic. The optimistic view, which can also be found in the recent "One Market, One Money" report of the EC Commission, is that the low occurrence of asymmetric shocks at the national level (which we find in our paper) makes it possible to move ahead with monetary union without one having to fear that major adjustment problems will arise in the future. In this view, as economic integration moves forward, the occurrence of asymmetric shocks will even decline in the future, reducing the adjustment costs.

There is, however, also a pessimistic interpretation of our results. Regions of the same country today are certainly more economically integrated with each other than countries in the Community. The large occurrence of asymmetric shocks at the regional level observed today suggests that economic integration does not make the occurrence of asymmetric shocks less likely. The opposite seems to be the case. Thus, a future EMU in Europe may be confronted with the same kind of divergencies in national output and employment trends as the one observed today at the regional level. This may lead to major changes in the adjustment process between countries, and may force labor mobility to play a greater role than it does today.

This more pessimistic view of the integration process stresses that the latter typically leads to regional concentration and agglomeration effects.[10] As a result, shocks that affect one particular industry also tend to have concentrated effects on particular regions. The experience of the US tends to confirm this view. The economic integration in the US is certainly more advanced than the integration achieved in the Community. At the same time one observes that the regional concentration of industrial production is much more pronounced in the US than in Europe (see Krugman, 1990, for evidence). As a result, sectoral shocks (say in the automobile industry, or in the textile industry) have pronounced regional effects, and require major regional adjustment efforts.

The interesting aspect of this phenomenon is that one finds evidence of relatively strong divergence of economic developments of highly integrated regions both at a relatively disaggregated level (i.e., regions within existing European countries) and at a more aggregated level (regions in the US of the size of existing European countries). This suggests that, if European countries integrate further, they are likely to move toward a model in which asymmetric shocks become more rather than less important.

Third, there are clearly two models of regional development in Europe. One is northern as typified by West Germany, the other is southern. The northern model of regional development is balanced. It involves a relatively large regional mobility of labor and low divergencies in output and employment. As a result, regional unemployment rates are relatively uniform. The southern model is one where labor is relatively immobile, divergencies in output and employment are relatively pronounced, and large regional concentrations of unemployment exist.

The major issue is to what model the monetary union in Europe will tend to converge. Neither of the two models will be without costs for individual countries. The northern model appears most attractive. One should bear in mind, however, that this model involves a sizeable amount of regional labor mobility. Thus, if this is the model to which Europe converges, relatively large movements of labor between countries will be necessary. The southern model does not require so much mobility of labor. It does lead to large regional divergencies in unemployment rates.

Which of the two models of monetary union will prevail in Europe is difficult to predict. If the mobility of labor between countries cannot be increased sufficiently, the southern model of monetary union may prevail. In that case not all regions and countries in Europe will profit from monetary union.

Appendix: List of regions

BR Deutschland

R11	Schleswig-Holstein
R12	Hamburg
R13	Niedersachsen
R14	Bremen
R15	Nordrhein-Westfalen
R16	Hessen
R17	Rheinland-Pfalz
R18	Baden-Württemberg
R19	Bayern
R1A	Saarland
R1B	Berlin (West)

France

R21	Ile de France
R22	Bassin Parisien
R23	Nord-Pas-de-Calais
R24	Est
R25	Ouest
R26	Sud-Ouest
R27	Centre-Est
R28	Méditerranée
R29	Départements d'Outre-Mer

Italia

R31	Nord Ovest
R32	Lombardia
R33	Nord Est

R34	Emilia-Romagna
R35	Centro
R36	Lazio
R37	Campania
R38	Abruzzi-Molise
R39	Sud
R3A	Sicilia
R3B	Sardegna

Nederland

R41	Noord-Nederland
R42	Oost-Nederland
R47	West-Nederland
R45	Zuid-Nederland

United Kingdom

R71	North
R72	Yorkshire and Humberside
R73	East Midlands
R74	East Anglia
R75	South East
R76	South West
R77	West Midlands
R78	North West
R79	Wales
R7A	Scotland
R7B	Northern Ireland

Espana

RB11	Galicia
RB12	Asturias
RB13	Cantabria
RB21	Pais Vasco
RB22	Navarra
RB23	Rioja
RB24	Aragon
RB41	Castilla-Leon
RB42	Castilla-La Mancha
RB43	Extremadura
RB51	Cataluña

128   **Paul de Grauwe and Wim Vanhaverbeke**

RB52   Comunidad Valenciana
RB53   Baleares
RB61   Andalucia
RB62   Murcia
RB63   Ceuta Y Melilla

Notes

This paper is produced as part of a CEPR research programme on "Financial and Monetary Integration in Europe" supported by a grant from the Commission of the European Communities under its SPES Programme (no. E8900105/RES). We are grateful to Veerle Vermeulen for research assistance, and to Jürgen von Hagen and Ivo Maes for useful comments and suggestions.
 1 See also McKinnon (1963), Kenen (1969).
 2 A recent paper by Poloz (1990) provides evidence that changes in these regional exchange rates in Canada are substantial.
 3 This implies that in equation (2) $a_{km} = a_m$ for all k.
 4 It would have been more appropriate to use unit root tests. However, the limited number of (yearly) observations precluded such an approach.
 5 We also observe that the degree of variability of the regional exchange rates in West Germany is substantially lower than the one observed in other countries. We return to the differences between German regions and the other regions in Europe in a later section.
 6 See, e.g., EC Commission (1990) for evidence of regional disparities of income per capita.
 7 These results confirm the recent empirical studies of Eichengreen. See Eichengreen (1990b). In a recent study von Hagen and Neumann (1991) came to similar conclusions. However, from their study it appears that the degree of real exchange-rate variability among a core group of countries (Germany, Benelux, Austria) has declined significantly during the eighties.
 8 The EC Commission (1990) also found no evidence of a significant relationship between real exchange-rate changes and national growth rates of output. See EC Commission, 1990, p. 147.
 9 See De Grauwe and Vanhaverbeke (1990) for case studies of Belgium and the Netherlands.
10 For a recent formalization of this view see Krugman (1990). There are of course older writers who have stressed these effects of integration. See Giersch (1949), Myrdal (1957), and Scitovsky (1958).

References

Balassa, B. (1961), *The Theory of Economic Integration*, New York: Irwin.
Cohen, D. and C. Wyplosz (1989), "The European Monetary System: An agnostic evaluation," in R. Bryant, D. Currie, J. Frenkel, P. Masson, and R. Portes

(eds.), *Macroeconomic Policies in an Interdependent World*, International Monetary Fund, Washington, pp. 311–37.

De Grauwe, P. and W. Vanhaverbeke (1990), "Exchange Rate Experiences in Small EMS Countries: Belgium, Denmark and the Netherlands," in V. Argy and P. De Grauwe (eds.), *Choosing an Exchange Rate Regime. The Challenge of Smaller Industrial Countries*, International Monetary Fund, Washington.

Eichengreen, B. (1990a), "One Money for Europe? Lessons from the US Currency Union," *Economic Policy*, No. 10, April, pp. 117–87.

(1990b), "Is Europe an Optimum Currency Area," CEPR Discussion Paper, No. 478, November.

European Commission (1990), "One Market. One Money," *European Economy*, No. 44, October.

Giersch, H. (1949), "Economic Union between Nations and the Location of Industries," *Review of Economic Studies*, 17, pp. 87–97.

Kenen, P. (1969), "The Theory of Optimum Currency Areas: An Eclectic View," in R. Mundell and A. Swoboda (eds.), *Monetary Problems of the International Economy*, Chicago: University of Chicago Press.

Krugman, P. (1990), "Geography and Trade," Gaston Eyskens Lectures, University of Leuven, (to be published by MIT Press).

McKinnon, R. (1963), "Optimum Currency Areas," *American Economic Review*, 53, pp. 717–25.

Meltzer, A. (1986), "Size, Persistence, and Interrelation of Nominal and Real Shocks," *Journal of Monetary Economics*, 17, pp. 161–94.

Mundell, R. (1961), "A Theory of Optimum Currency Areas," *American Economic Review*, 51 September.

Myrdal, G. (1957), *Economic Theory and Underdeveloped Regions*, London: Duckworth.

Poloz, S. (1990), "Real Exchange Rate Adjustment between Regions in a Common Currency Area," in V. Argy and P. De Grauwe (eds.), *Choosing an Exchange Rate Regime. The Challenge of Smaller Industrial Countries*, International Monetary Fund, Washington.

Scitovsky, T. (1958), *Economic Theory and Western European Integration*, Stanford.

Straubhaar, T. (1988), "International Labour Migration within a Common Market: Some Aspects of the EC Experience," *Journal of Common Market Studies*, 27.

Vaubel, R. (1976), "Real Exchange Rate Changes in the European Community. The Empirical Evidence and Its Implications for European Currency Unification," *Weltwirtschaftliches Archiv*, 112, pp. 429–70.

von Hagen, J. and M. Neumann (1991), "Real Exchange Rates Within and Between Currency Areas: How Far Away is EMU? Indiana Center for Global Business," Discussion paper no. 62, April.

Weber, A. (1990), "Emu and Asymmetries and Adjustment Problems in the EMS: Some Empirical Evidence," CEPR Discussion Paper No. 448, August.

6 Labor markets and European monetary unification

BARRY EICHENGREEN

I Introduction

Monetary unification promises to revolutionize the conduct of macro-economic policy in Europe. Countries previously free to pursue independent monetary policies will be forced to toe a common line. New constraints will be placed on the conduct of fiscal policy, whether the monetary union treaty incorporates explicit ceilings on budget deficits or governments are simply precluded from printing money to finance public spending.[1] Economic and Monetary Union, or EMU, insofar as it entails a loss of policy autonomy, may involve real economic costs as well as the convenience and efficiency gains of transacting in one rather than several national currencies.

In his seminal article on optimum currency areas, Mundell (1961) identified two criteria useful for evaluating such costs. The first is the incidence of shocks. If disturbances are distributed symmetrically across countries, a common policy response will suffice. In response to a negative aggregate demand shock, for example, that is common to all EMU countries, a common policy response in the form of a simultaneous monetary and/or fiscal expansion may be all that is required. Only if disturbances are distributed asymmetrically across countries will there be occasion for an asymmetric policy response and may the constraints of monetary union bind.

The second criterion identified by Mundell is the extent of labor mobility. The more mobile is labor the less is the need for different policy responses to prevent the emergence of regional problems. Labor can simply move from the depressed to the booming region, eliminating the need for an asymmetric policy response. When labor mobility is limited, in contrast, regional unemployment problems may persist unless the depressed region is allowed to pursue independent policies and, if necessary, to depreciate its currency.

130

Recent researchers have devoted considerable attention to the incidence of shocks.[2] Bayoumi and Eichengreen (1991a, 1991b), for example, found that shocks to eleven EC member countries have been more asymmetrically distributed than shocks to the eight census regions of the United States. Whereas common factors account for 49 percent of the variance of supply shocks to US regions from the 1960s through the 1980s, they explain only 33 percent of the variance of supply shocks to EC countries.[3] In the case of demand shocks, common factors account for 51 and 33 percent of the variance for the US and Europe, respectively. According to Mundell's first criterion, then, the EC is less of an optimum currency area than the United States.

In comparison, little systematic attention has been directed toward the analysis of labor mobility. Previous studies cited in Eichengreen (1991) indicate that observed migration rates are lower in Europe than in the US. Not only are migration rates between European nations relatively low, but so are migration rates within those nations. Americans move between US states about three times as frequently as Frenchmen move between *départements* and Germans move between *lander*. If Europeans move little among regions of European nations within which culture and language are relatively minor barriers to mobility, they can hardly be expected to move between European nations once statutory barriers to migration are removed. On the basis of this evidence, Mundell's second criterion also suggests that the EC is less of an optimum currency area than the United States.

One problem with simple comparisons of migration rates is that the geographic units of analysis may not be strictly comparable. Another is that the economic determinants of labor mobility are not held constant. Labor may move less within European countries not because it is less mobile intrinsically but because it has less incentive to move. While previous work on the incidence of disturbances has shown shocks to European countries to be distributed asymmetrically, it still could be that shocks to regions within individual European countries are relatively symmetric.[4] Hence labor may not move between regions within European countries because it has no reason to do so, not because it is unwilling or unable.

If labor really is mobile within European countries, then it may become almost as mobile among them once remaining statutory barriers to migration come down.[5] Relinquishing the exchange rate as a policy instrument may then be of no more consequence than it is for the regions of the United States. Asymmetric policy responses will not be required in response to asymmetric shocks, since labor can simply move from depressed to booming regions. The benefits of EMU are then likely to dominate the costs.

This paper presents a preliminary exploration of the implications of European labor-market performance for EMU. The analysis comes in three parts. The first part investigates shocks to regional labor markets in Great Britain, Italy, and the United States. Britain and Italy are two countries where the regional problem is prominent, while the US is the obvious basis for comparison. The second part of the analysis considers the migratory response in the three countries. Migration is not the only way in which regional labor-market disequilibria can be eliminated, of course; others include adjustments in regional wages and prices, inter-regional capital movements and inter-regional fiscal transfers. The third part of the analysis therefore asks directly how quickly regional labor-market equilibrium is restored. This three-part analysis is preceded by an overview of regional labor-market conditions and followed by a brief conclusion.

The results are striking. First, the dispersion of shocks to regional labor markets is quite similar across the three countries. The variability of the response of regional unemployment to changes in national unemployment is smaller in the US than in Britain, and smaller in Britain than in Italy, but the differences are minor. Moreover, the variability of the response of regional unemployment to changes in the nation's real exchange rate is the same for Italy and the US and somewhat lower for Britain. On the basis of these results, there is little reason to think that labor-market disturbances are more asymmetrically distributed within Britain and Italy than within the United States.

Second, the responsiveness of migration to regional labor-market disequilibria is greater in the US than in either Britain or Italy. The elasticity of migration with respect to inter-regional wage differentials is at least five times as large for the US as for Britain. The estimated wage elasticity for Italy is smaller still. International variations in the elasticity of migration with respect to inter-regional unemployment differentials are less pronounced, but they too point to the greater responsiveness of labor flows in the United States. The implication is that labor mobility works less powerfully in Europe than in the US to eliminate regional labor-market disequilibria.

The third finding is surprising in light of the previous two. Despite that shocks to regional labor markets in the US and Europe are of comparable magnitude and that migration in the US responds more powerfully to those shocks, it is not obvious that deviations from the long-term relationship among regional unemployment rates are more persistent in Europe than in the US. Though the evidence on this question is not clearcut, it appears that, when disturbances cause regional unemployment rates within European countries to diverge, other mechanisms, perhaps including relative wage adjustments, labor–leisure choice, inter-regional capital mobility,

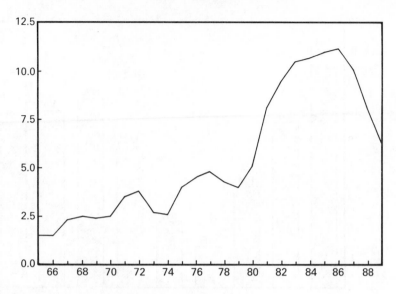

Figure 6.1 UK unemployment rate, 1966–88

and government policy, substitute adequately for Europe's limited labor mobility in order to bring them back into line.

II   An overview of regional labor markets

The last decade and a half in the industrial economies has been characterized by volatile unemployment fluctuations at both the national and regional levels. This section sketches the outlines of those fluctuations and provides some discussion for Britain, Italy, and the United States.

Unemployment in Britain, displayed in figure 6.1, is dominated by the steady rise after 1974, reflecting first the oil shock and then the Thatcher disinflation.[6] Figure 6.2 shows the very different rates of unemployment that prevailed in different regions at the end of the period.[7] Prominent in that figure is the north–south divide, with unemployment well below the national average in the South and East Anglia, slightly below average in the East Midlands, and above average in the West Midlands, the North, Wales, and Scotland.

In part, the varying fortunes of different regions reflect the composition of economic activity. Wales for example relies for much of its income and employment on metal manufacturing and on the energy sector (coal mining and oil refining), which fell on hard times in the 1980s. The North and Yorkshire–Humberside are similarly oriented toward energy and heavy

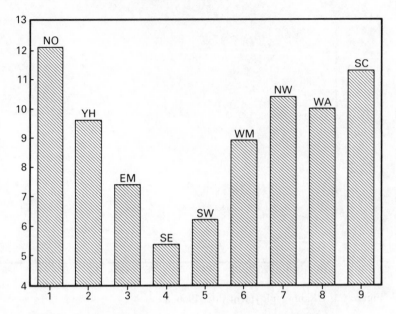

Figure 6.2 UK regional unemployment rates, 1988

manufacturing, particularly minerals, metals, and chemicals. Unemployment in the West Midlands is associated with a higher share of employment in the manufacturing sector than any other Britain region, and with the fact that it depends on a relatively narrow range of industries centering on engineering and motor vehicles which were depressed for most of the 1980s.

Sectors dependent on light manufacturing and services were less severely affected by the post-1979 slump. Employment in the South East, dominated by London, is concentrated in banking, insurance, finance, business services, and leasing. The South West relies on public administration, agriculture, and defense. In the East Midlands, a higher-than-average share of regional GDP is generated by manufacturing industry (31 percent in 1986 compared to a UK average of 25 percent); those industries are predominantly engaged in light manufacturing, of products such as textiles, clothing, and footwear. East Anglia was similarly insulated by its specialization in light manufacturing (primarily food and beverages) and agriculture.

Figure 6.3 for Italy shows a dramatic increase in unemployment in the mid seventies, followed by a further increase through the first half of the 1980s. Figure 6.4 shows the different levels of unemployment prevailing in different Italian regions in 1988.[8] Their standard deviation is 6.40, or nearly twice the comparable figure for Britain (3.46), despite that the average

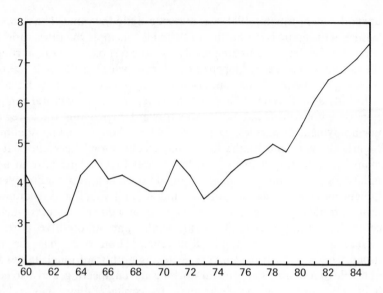

Figure 6.3 Italian unemployment rate, 1960–84

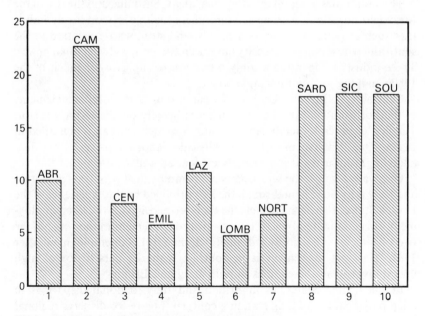

Figure 6.4 Italian regional unemployment rates, 1988

unemployment rate for 1988 was almost exactly the same. The dominant feature of the figure is the north–south divide: unemployment was above 15 percent in Sardinia, Campania, Sicily, and the rest of the south; at roughly the national average of 11 percent in Lazio (which includes Rome) and Abruzzi; but below 10 percent elsewhere in the center and in the north.

In Italy as in Britain, differences across regions in the sectoral composition of employment go some way toward explaining these regional unemployment disparities. The north, defined here to include Piedmont, Liguria, Veneto, and Emilia-Romagna, accounts for 70 percent of Italy's manufacturing employment.[9] Piedmont and Liguria specialize in heavy industries such as motor vehicles, iron and steel, and shipbuilding, Veneto in light industries, such as footwear and apparel. Small and medium-size firms producing labor-intensive, high-value added products such as ceramics, furniture, scientific instruments, and automotive parts are increasingly evident in Emilia-Romagna.[10] Lombardy has the most broadly based industrial structure, featuring both traditional staples such as textiles, food processing, metal working and engineering, and also newer light industries, such as electronics. Its capital, Milan, has a highly developed service sector: it is the seat of the Italian stock exchange, the site of the country's leading trade fair, and the host of the head offices of most important Italian corporations.

The situation is different in Campania, Sicily, Sardinia, and the rest of the Mezzogiorno. Along with agriculture, these regions rely on heavy industries such as petroleum, petrochemicals, and steel, whose location in the south and whose capital intensity have been encouraged by regional policy. These industries operated at only a fraction of capacity for much of the 1980s, making for high unemployment.

Central Italy (Marche, Umbria, Tuscany, and Lazio) combines elements of the north and south. The region relies heavily on the tertiary sector. Textiles, chemicals, metallurgy, and motor vehicles are all represented in Lazio. The "Emilian model" of small-scale, labor-intensive, high-value-added light industry is increasingly evident as well.

One way to gauge the seriousness of unemployment problems in Britain and Italy is to view them through the lens provided by the experience of the United States. Figure 6.5 depicts the time-series behavior of US unemployment. It is dominated by a dramatic upward movement in the wake of the two oil shocks, but also by a dramatic decline in US unemployment after 1981. This last movement is in contrast with the persistence of high unemployment in the eighties in both Italy and Britain.

In the United States, as in Britain and Italy, regional disparities in unemployment are of long-standing concern. Figure 6.6 displays regional unemployment rates in 1988.[11] These vary from a low of 3.1 percent in New

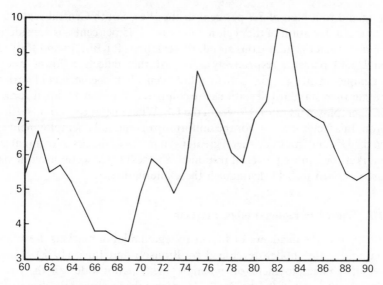

Figure 6.5 US unemployment rate, 1960–90

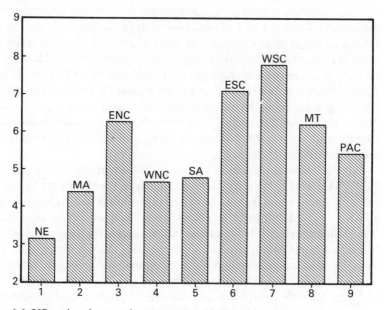

Figure 6.6 US regional unemployment rates, 1988

England to a high of 7.8 per cent in the West South Central region. The standard deviation of the regional figures – 1.45 per cent – is considerably smaller than the analogous standard deviations for Britain and Italy (3.46 and 6.40 percent, respectively). In part this reflects a lower national unemployment rate (5.5 percent), but even when coefficients of variation rather than standard deviations are compared, the inter-regional variation in unemployment rates is lower in the US. What inferences should be drawn from this fact is unclear, for the uniformity of regional unemployment rates in the US could reflect either a greater symmetry of shocks to regional labor markets or a more powerful response. The next three sections of the paper are designed to help distinguish these alternatives.

III   Shocks to regional labor markets

To analyze the incidence of shocks to regional labor markets, I estimate a variant of the model developed by Branson and Love (1988). I regress regional unemployment on unemployment nationwide, on the real exchange rate, and on the real price of energy. I then examine the dispersion of regional responses to shocks to the common explanatory variables. Following Branson and Love, a time trend is included where necessary to pick up secular trends not captured by the other variables. Regressions are estimated using ordinary least squares.[12]

The dependent variable is the number of workers unemployed (in thousands). Regional and national unemployment are expressed in logs. Insofar as the cyclical sensitivity of regional unemployment exceeds (falls short of) the cyclical sensitivity of national unemployment, the coefficient on the log of national unemployment should exceed (fall short of) unity. The coefficient on the real exchange rate should be positive (negative) for regions specializing in the production of non-traded (traded) goods, since a decline in the real rate signals an appreciation. The coefficient on the real energy price should be positive for energy-using regions, negative for energy-producing regions.

Table 6.1 reports regression results for Britain for the period starting in 1974.[13] The elasticity of regional unemployment with respect to national unemployment varies from a low of 0.85 in the North to a high of 1.21 in the South East. Scotland has a relatively low cyclical sensitivity, the East and West Midlands relatively high ones. Industrial composition goes some way toward explaining these regional characteristics. The tendency for employment to hold up relatively well in Scotland, for example, reflects the economy's diversification out of traditional staples (textiles, shipbuilding, and metals) into electronics and services.[14] The cyclical sensitivity of unemployment in the Midlands reflects the importance of manufacturing

Table 6.1. *Covariates of regional unemployment in Britain, 1974–87*

(unemployment in logs)

Region	Constant	National unemploy-ment	Real exchange rate	Real energy price	R^2
East Anglia	− 5.299	1.147	0.003	0.001	0.99
	(16.68)	(44.39)	(2.87)	(0.13)	
East Midlands	− 3.800	1.146	− 0.001	− 0.001	0.99
	(13.54)	(50.25)	(1.06)	(0.96)	
West Midlands	− 3.652	1.186	− 0.002	0.001	0.99
	(7.51)	(29.98)	(1.40)	(0.24)	
North	− 0.719	0.849	− 0.002	0.001	0.99
	(1.98)	(28.73)	(1.43)	(0.31)	
North West	− 1.293	0.946	0.001	0.001	0.99
	(12.22)	(109.87)	(0.07)	(1.98)	
York & Humberside	− 2.899	1.112	− 0.002	− 0.002	0.99
	(9.15)	(43.44)	(1.712)	(1.61)	
South East	− 4.036	1.206	0.005	0.001	0.99
	(13.60)	(49.96)	(5.17)	(1.13)	
South West	− 2.912	0.971	0.005	0.001	0.99
	(5.62)	(23.02)	(2.86)	(0.45)	
Wales	− 1.740	0.914	− 0.001	0.001	0.99
	(7.07)	(45.68)	(1.27)	(0.62)	
Scotland	− 0.830	0.910	− 0.001	− 0.001	0.99
	(1.63)	(21.95)	(0.45)	(0.60)	

Note: t – statistics in parentheses.
Source: See text.

industries (motor vehicles and engineering in the West Midlands, textiles in the East Midlands).[15] The standard deviation of the table 6.1 coefficients on national unemployment for British regions is 0.13.[16]

These results differ from those reported in previous studies of cyclical sensitivity. For example, Armstrong and Taylor (1985) found, by regressing regional unemployment on national unemployment, that cyclical sensitivity was lowest in the North West, South East, and East Anglia, highest in the North, Wales, and the West Midlands. Differences between their results and mine are attributable to the fact that previous studies fail to control for determinants of regional unemployment other than unemployment nation-wide, whereas the results in table 6.1 are partial correlations controlling for the real exchange rate and the real price of energy.

Only one of the ten coefficients on the real price of energy, that for the North West, differs significantly from zero at the 90 percent level. Although this plausibly reflects the energy-using character of the region's industries, it is not clear why the same relationship is not evident for other industrial areas like Yorkshire and the Midlands.

Three of the ten coefficients on the real exchange rate in table 6.1 differ significantly from zero at the 90 percent confidence level, and a fourth, that for Yorkshire and Humberside, comes close to significance at that level. Six of the ten coefficients are negative, four positive, indicating considerable regional heterogeneity in the unemployment response to real exchange-rate shocks. Thus, even after controlling for the business cycle and the relative price of energy, the real exchange rate significantly affects regional unemployment differentials in Britain.

The signs of the coefficients on the real exchange rate can be interpreted in terms of sectoral composition: employment in regions with positive coefficients is concentrated disproportionately in sheltered sectors (services in the South East, public administration and defense in the South West, agriculture and light manufacturing in East Anglia). The positive coefficient for the North West is an anomaly, but unlike the other three positive coefficients it differs insignificantly from zero.

Table 6.2 adds a time trend to the basic regression. Six of the ten coefficients on the real exchange rate now differ from zero at standard confidence levels. Their magnitude remains basically unchanged from table 6.1. The positive coefficient for the North West turns negative, reassuringly, although that for Scotland turns positive, albeit insignificantly so.

For Italy, there exist separate definitions of unemployment for the pre- and post-1975 periods. Surveys for the post-1975 period added a third category of unemployed workers to the two categories reported previous-ly.[17] Insofar as the national unemployment rate included as an explanatory variable in the regressions is an aggregation of the dependent variable for the individual regions, the coefficient on unemployment nationwide may capture any implications of the shift. This is not true, of course, to the extent that the change in definition affected measured unemployment differently in different regions. I therefore estimated two variants of the basic equation, one which included among the unemployed only the two categories of workers considered before 1975, the other which included also the third category of unemployed workers for the post-1975 years.

The variation across regions in the cyclical sensitivity of local unemploy-ment to national unemployment is almost exactly the same for Italy as for

Table 6.2. *Covariates of regional unemployment in Britain, 1974–87, including trend*

(unemployment in logs)

Region	Constant	National unemploy- ment	Real exchange rate	Real energy price	Time	R^2
East Anglia	−6.187	1.335	0.003	−0.002	0.021	0.99
	(33.55)	(45.71)	(6.09)	(3.23)	(6.94)	
East Midlands	−3.427	1.067	−0.001	−0.001	0.009	0.99
	(9.26)	(18.21)	(0.96)	(0.15)	(1.44)	
West Midlands	−4.564	1.379	−0.003	−0.002	0.021	0.99
	(8.13)	(15.51)	(1.92)	(0.92)	(2.34)	
North	0.171	0.660	−0.001	0.003	0.021	0.99
	(0.54)	(13.20)	(1.84)	(2.47)	(4.02)	
North West	−1.192	0.924	0.001	0.001	0.002	0.99
	(8.11)	(39.68)	(0.17)	(2.21)	(1.00)	
York & Humber.	2.195	0.970	−0.002	−0.001	0.016	0.99
	(6.91)	(19.28)	(2.02)	(0.32)	(3.19)	
South East	4.688	1.344	0.005	−0.001	−0.015	0.99
	(15.57)	(28.20)	(6.71)	(0.24)	(3.12)	
South West	−4.25	1.255	0.005	−0.002	−0.031	0.99
	(10.51)	(19.58)	(4.57)	(1.71)	(4.76)	
Wales	−1.800	0.927	−0.001	0.001	−0.001	0.99
	(5.01)	(16.29)	(1.23)	(0.39)	(0.24)	
Scotland	0.086	0.716	−0.001	0.001	0.021	0.99
	(0.14)	(7.50)	(0.30)	(0.50)	(2.19)	

Note: t – statistics in parentheses.
Source: See text.

Britain. In table 6.3, which uses only pre-1975 categories of unemployment, the elasticity of regional unemployment with respect to national unemployment ranges from a high of 1.28 for Lombardy to a low of 0.80 for Abruzzi and Molise, with a standard deviation for the nine regions of 0.16. In table 6.4, which uses the alternative definition of unemployment, this elasticity ranges from 1.23 (again for Lombardy) to 0.83 (this time for Puglia, Basilicata, and Calabria), with a standard deviation of 0.14.[18] Recall that for Britain the comparable high and low values of this elasticity were 1.21 and 0.85, with a standard deviation of 0.13. Thus, the variability in regional

Table 6.3. *Covariates of regional unemployment in Italy, 1960–84, pre-1978 definitions of unemployment*

(unemployment in logs)

Region	Constant	National unemployment	Real exchange rate	Real energy price	R^2
Piedmont, Valle d'Aosta, Liguria	−4.067 (6.67)	1.182 (14.33)	0.005 (1.76)	−0.001 (0.74)	0.97
Lombardy	−3.215 (2.41)	1.275 (7.09)	−0.009 (1.45)	0.001 (0.003)	0.86
Tre Venezie	−1.476 (1.03)	1.095 (5.67)	−0.011 (2.36)	−0.001 (0.02)	0.77
Emilia-Romagna, Marche	−0.049 (0.61)	0.889 (8.19)	−0.012 (2.98)	−0.001 (0.34)	0.87
Tuscany, Umbria, Alto Lazio, Lazio Meridionale, Campania	−1.732 (3.07)	0.990 (12.98)	0.007 (2.60)	−0.001 (0.65)	0.97
Abruzzi, Molise	−2.389 (3.96)	0.800 (9.28)	0.004 (1.45)	−0.001 (1.52)	0.92
Puglia, Basilicata, Calabria	−1.259 (1.28)	0.817 (6.14)	0.006 (1.25)	−0.001 (0.008)	0.88
Sicily	−1.596 (2.72)	0.828 (10.47)	0.001 (0.27)	0.003 (3.33)	0.97
Sardinia	−5.459 (5.07)	1.231 (8.46)	0.005 (0.87)	0.002 (1.11)	0.94

Note: t – statistics in parentheses.
Source: See text.

responses to the business cycle is almost exactly the same across the two countries.

Only for Sicily and for Abruzzi-Molise is there evidence of a differential response to real energy prices. In contrast, four of the nine coefficients on the real exchange rate in table 6.3 differ significantly from zero at the 90 percent level; in table 6.4, six of the nine are statistically significant. (The pattern of signs is identical across the two tables.) Of the six significant

Table 6.4. *Covariates of regional unemployment in Italy, 1960–84,
post-1977 definitions of unemployment*

(unemployment in logs)

Region	Constant	National unemploy- ment	Real exchange rate	Real energy price	R^2
Piedmont,	−3.880	1.148	0.006	−0.001	0.98
Valle d'Aosta,	(8.69)	(18.71)	(1.90)	(1.06)	
Liguria					
Lombardy	−2.692	1.228	−0.012	−0.001	0.94
	(3.02)	(10.01)	(1.94)	(0.06)	
Tre Venezie	−1.214	1.041	−0.016	0.001	0.89
	(1.25)	(7.77)	(2.34)	(0.22)	
Emilia-Romagna,	−1.176	0.940	−0.007	0.001	0.95
Marche	(2.19)	(12.75)	(1.94)	(1.03)	
Tuscany, Umbria,	−1.533	0.978	0.006	−0.001	0.98
Alto Lazio,	(4.04)	(18.73)	(2.19)	(0.66)	
Lazio Meridionale,					
Campania					
Abruzzi, Molise	−3.452	0.937	0.007	−0.002	0.97
	(7.45)	(14.71)	(2.07)	(1.93)	
Puglia,	−1.353	0.827	0.006	0.001	0.94
Basilicata,	(2.04)	(9.08)	(1.32)	(0.47)	
Calabria					
Sicily	−2.301	0.907	0.003	0.003	0.99
	(5.77)	(16.53)	(1.17)	(3.27)	
Sardinia	−5.114	1.198	0.003	0.001	0.97
	(6.88)	(11.71)	(0.65)	(0.91)	

Note: t – statistics in parentheses.
Source: See text.

coefficients in table 6.4, three are positive, three negative, again suggesting considerable regional heterogeneity in unemployment responses to changes in the real exchange rate.

The signs of the coefficients are generally plausible, although there are anomalies. The negative real exchange-rate coefficients are for Lombardy, Veneto, and Emilia-Romagna, which produce a variety of manufactures and thus should be adversely affected by a real appreciation.[19]

How does the regional variation in the response of unemployment to real exchange-rate shocks differ between Italy and Britain? Regional disparities created by real exchange-rate shocks are more important for Italy. The standard deviation of the real exchange-rate coefficients is 0.028 for Britain but 0.0074 for Italy when table 6.3 data are used and 0.0087 for Italy when table 6.4 data are used. Thus, while roughly comparable regional unemployment disparities emerge in the two countries in response to business cycle fluctuations (holding the real exchange rate constant), larger regional unemployment differentials emerge in Italy than Britain in response to real exchange-rate fluctuations (holding aggregate unemployment constant).

Table 6.5 summarizes the results for the United States. The dispersion of regional unemployment responses to national unemployment is remarkably similar to those for Britain and Italy. The elasticity of regional unemployment with respect to national unemployment ranges from 1.12 for the East North Central (home of the cyclically sensitive motor vehicle complex), to 0.81 for the Mountain states. These findings are consistent with the conclusions of Gellner (1974), who emphasized the cyclical sensitivity of unemployment in the North Central and Northeast for the first half of the period. The standard deviation for the nine regions is 0.12. Recall that the analogous estimates for Britain and Italy were 0.13 and 0.14–0.16, respectively, only slightly larger.

There is evidence of a tendency for higher energy prices to raise regional unemployment only for the East North Central (again reflecting the importance of the motor vehicle production) and the East South Central (which traditionally relies on the energy-using steel sector and other industries that act as suppliers to the automotive complex). The negative coefficient for the West South Central borders on significance, reflecting the tendency for higher energy prices to reduce unemployment in oil-patch states like Texas and Oklahoma.

Six of the nine coefficients on the real exchange rate differ significantly from zero at the 95 percent level or better. Three of the six significant coefficients are positive, three negative, again indicating considerable diversity of regional response to real exchange-rate shocks. Of all nine coefficients, five are positive.

The standard deviation of the nine estimated coefficients for the real exchange rate is 0.0089, matching almost exactly the table 6.4 estimate for Italy. Thus, holding the economy-wide level of unemployment constant, a real exchange-rate shock has the same tendency to create regional unemployment disparities in Italy as in the US. In contrast, Britain is less vulnerable to regional problems caused by real exchange-rate disturbances than the United States.

Table 6.5. *Covariates of regional unemployment in the United States,*
1960–89

(unemployment in logs)

Region	Constant	National unemploy- ment	Real exchange rate	Real energy price	Time	R^2
New England	−4.073	1.104	0.014	−0.572	−0.032	0.78
	(3.50)	(6.70)	(3.26)	(1.46)	(5.46)	
East North Central	−2.931	1.119	−0.002	0.330	0.001	0.98
	(5.91)	(16.22)	(0.97)	(1.98)	(0.22)	
East South Central	−1.379	0.849	−0.011	0.882	0.012	0.95
	(1.59)	(6.90)	(3.42)	(3.03)	(2.69)	
Middle Atlantic	−2.389	1.034	0.008	0.189	−0.027	0.96
	(4.97)	(15.20)	(4.25)	(1.17)	(11.06)	
South Atlantic	−2.691	1.021	0.005	0.184	−0.001	0.99
	(7.33)	(19.64)	(3.42)	(1.49)	(0.17)	
West North Central	−0.726	0.816	−0.008	0.212	0.007	0.98
	(1.99)	(15.80)	(6.22)	(1.73)	(3.85)	
West South Central	−0.783	0.942	−0.013	−0.566	0.028	0.93
	(0.74)	(6.31)	(3.19)	(1.61)	(5.19)	
Mountain	−1.700	0.807	−0.002	−0.057	0.025	0.98
	(3.08)	(10.33)	(0.75)	(0.31)	(8.94)	
Pacific	−0.800	0.874	0.002	−0.345	0.009	0.94
	(1.02)	(7.86)	(0.64)	(1.30)	(2.13)	

Note: t – statistics in parentheses.
Source: See text.

Overall, then, the dispersion of shocks to regional labor markets is
remarkably similar across countries. The variability of the response of
regional unemployment to changes in national unemployment is smaller in
the US than in Britain, and smaller in Britain than in Italy, but the
differences are minor. The variability of the response of regional unemployment to changes in the real exchange rate is the same for Italy and the US,
and somewhat lower for Britain than for the other two countries.

On the basis of these results, then, there is no reason to think that
labor-market disturbances are more asymmetrically distributed within
Britain and Italy than within the United States. On the contrary, the
regional variability of shocks looks remarkably similar across countries.

This creates a presumption that observed high rates of inter-regional migration in the US reflect higher labor mobility, not a similar response to dissimilar shocks. The next section asks whether this presumption can be documented systematically.

IV   The migratory response

To analyze the migratory response to regional labor-market disturbances, I estimate a variant of the model of inter-regional migration utilized by previous authors in studies of Britain and Italy. Given the persistence of regional problems in Europe, there exists an extensive literature on the subject. For Britain, a first generation of studies used aggregate Census data to measure the capacity of regional and local labor-market variables to explain migration patterns.[20] More recent studies utilize micro-data. Hughes and McCormick (1981), for example, considered the impact of council housing policies on the propensity for individuals to migrate between regions. They found that council tenants are less likely to relocate than other renters, presumably reflecting their fear of losing the benefits of sub-market rents.

A particularly simple and intuitive model is that applied to British data by Pissarides and McMaster (1990). Pooling data for nine British regions for the years 1961–82, they relate net immigration (as a share of population) in each region at each date to the natural logarithm of the relative wage of that region (its wage divided by the average wage in Great Britain), and to the unemployment ratio of that region (its unemployment rate divided by the British unemployment rate). Both variables are entered with one-year lags to permit the relationship to be estimated by ordinary least squares, while the log of relative wages is entered in first-difference form.[21] In-migration is hypothesized to rise with the relative wage and fall with the relative unemployment rate.

For Italy, a number of migration models have been estimated using data disaggregated to the regional level. Salvatore (1981) estimated a time-series model relating the number of emigrants from the south to the north to unemployment rates, the growth of the non-agricultural labor force, and the real industrial wage in each region. Low unemployment, rapid labor force growth and high wages locally all were found to discourage emigration. A'Hearn (1991) estimated similar equations using pooled data for a larger set of Italian regions, relating migration to the level and change in relative wages, relative unemployment rates, and relative consumption levels. Both unemployment and wages (the level of the local–national differential but not the change) had statistically significant effects on migration.

Attanasio and Padoa Schioppa (1991) estimate a model for Italy broadly similar to the Pissarides–McMaster model for Britain. Using annual data for six geographic regions for the years 1960–86, they relate net immigration to the log of local wages, the log of national wages, local unemployment, and national unemployment.[22] Comparisons with the Pissarides–McMaster model are complicated by the fact that Attanasio and Padoa Schioppa enter log wages in level rather than first-difference form, do not hypothesize that local and national conditions affect migration symmetrically, and estimate contemporary rather than lagged effects.

Moreover, there does not appear to exist a comparable model for the United States. There is an extensive literature on inter-regional migration in the US (see the survey by Greenwood, 1975), but to date most of it has utilized micro-data or Census data disaggregated to the metropolitan level. Two exceptions are Miller (1973) and Barro and Sala-i-Martin (1991). Miller used state-level data from the 1960 Census, where median family income was his proxy for regional wages. Despite little correlation between migration rates and family income, upon controlling for other determinants of migration propensities (extent of previous migration and college attendance, among other variables), he identified a consistently significant relationship. Using annual data for 1950 through 1987, Barro and Sala-i-Martin similarly find a strong relationship between inter-state migration and personal income. International comparisons are again difficult, however, by virtue of the fact that local economic conditions are measured differently than in the studies of Britain and Italy described above (personal income rather than wages is used to measure compensation, while unemployment rates are not considered).

I have therefore estimated migration equations for the three countries, attempting to make the data and specification as closely comparable as possible. My point of departure is the Pissarides–McMaster model, since theirs is a particularly parsimonious specification. The first column of table 6.6 reports the results of my effort to replicate their basic regression. As in their paper, immigration responds positively to changes in local wages relative to national wages, negatively to local unemployment relative to national unemployment. There is considerable persistence in migratory patterns, as reflected in the coefficient on the lagged dependent variable of 0.61.[23]

The second column presents comparable estimates for the nine Census regions of the United States. Most of the coefficients have the same signs and the same significance levels as in the Pissarides–McMaster study of Britain. The economic implications are different, however. The elasticity of immigration with respect to the change in relative wages is an order of magnitude larger.[24] The elasticity with respect to relative unemployment

Table 6.6. *Basic migration models for Britain, the US, and Italy*
(*dependent variable is immigration scaled by population*)

	(1) Britain (1961–82)	(2) US (1962–88)	(3) Italy (1962–85)
Constant	0.12	1.50	0.01
	(2.32)	(5.76)	(0.06)
Change in log	0.42	15.13	0.23
wages lagged	(1.76)	(2.52)	(0.30)
Unemployment	−0.17	−0.37	−0.04
lagged	(2.87)	(1.92)	(0.48)
Migration lagged	0.58	−0.05	0.73
	(9.56)	(0.77)	(21.82)
Number of obs.	180	243	144

Notes: *t*-statistics in parentheses. Change in wages and unemployment variables both denote ratio of local value to national average. Dummy variables for regions are included in each regression but not reported.
Source: See text.

rates is twice as large, although the magnitude of the standard errors suggests caution when comparing elasticities. In contrast to the result for Britain, there appears to be little persistence in US migratory patterns after controlling for wage and unemployment differentials. (The coefficient on the lagged dependent variable is essentially zero.) This is systematic evidence, then, that migration is more sensitive to current economic conditions in the US than in Britain.

The Pissarides–McMaster specification performs poorly on data for six Italian regions.[25] Neither the change in the relative wages of industrial and agricultural workers nor relative unemployment rates appears to have much impact on Italian migration, which displays even more persistence than in Great Britain. It could be that Italian labor simply does not respond to these variables. But Attanasio–Padoa Schioppa and A'Hearn have shown that the explanatory power of Italian migration equations can be enhanced by substituting the level of the wage differential for its first difference. The first column of table 6.7 displays the results of estimating this variant of the model. When the log of the local–national wage differential is entered in levels rather than changes, it has a statistically significant positive impact on immigration. Still, the wage elasticity of

Table 6.7. *Alternative migration models for Italy (dependent variable is immigration scaled by population)*

	First wage series (1)	Second wage series (2)	Second wage series (3)
Constant	0.18	0.01	0.37
	(1.49)	(5.76)	(2.70)
Level of log wages lagged	1.35		1.07
	(3.71)		(4.43)
Change in log wages lagged		0.22	
		(0.45)	
Unemployment lagged	−0.11	−0.04	−0.20
	(1.27)	(0.50)	(2.31)
Migration lagged	0.63	0.73	0.62
	(15.37)	(21.98)	(16.01)
Number of obs.	144	144	144

Notes: t-statistics in parentheses. Sample period is as in table 6.6. Change in wages and unemployment variables both denote ratio of local value to national average. Dummy variables for regions are included in each regression but not reported. Column 1 utilizes the same definition of wages as in the previous table, while columns 2 and 3 use the alternative definition.
Source: Author's estimates, as described in the text.

migration is only half that for Britain and less than a tenth that for the United States. The unemployment differential enters with the anticipated sign, but its coefficient is small relative to that in the US and British equations and remains statistically indistinguishable from zero.

The second and third columns of table 6.7 substitute an alternative definition of Italian wages. Previous regressions used the effective daily wage paid to industrial and agricultural employees, a series that excludes the service sector and includes only firms covered by the provisions of the public insurance system. The alternative series used in the second and third columns of table 6.7 is the compensation of all employees, inclusive of social security contributions. When this series is entered in difference form, the results are essentially identical to those in table 6.6. When it is entered in level form, its point estimate is slightly smaller; in addition, however, the unemployment differential is statistically different from zero at standard confidence levels. The point estimate on the unemployment differential is comparable to that for Britain, which means that it is little more than half the size of that for the United States.

To summarize, the models estimated here confirm the tendency for inter-regional labor flows to respond to economic conditions. In all three countries, immigration is encouraged by relatively high wages and relatively low unemployment. But the elasticity of migration with respect to wage differentials is very much larger in the United States. Similarly, US labor exhibits a greater tendency to move in response to regional unemployment differentials. This, then, is systematic evidence in support of the presumption of greater labor mobility in the US.

V   Restoring regional labor-market equilibria

Migration is not the only mechanism whereby divergences among regional unemployment rates can be eliminated. Even if labor fails to flow from high to low unemployment regions, capital may flow in the other direction to make use of idle labor. The increase in capital/labor ratios in depressed regions should enhance the productivity of labor there, reducing unemployment. Alternatively, wages may fall in high unemployment regions, pricing unemployed labor back into the market.[26] A third possibility is that labor–leisure choice responds elastically to regional unemployment, with labor supply rising in low unemployment regions, thereby increasing the pool of individuals seeking work, and conversely in high unemployment regions. Finally, fiscal transfers to depressed regions, operating through either the federal fiscal system or explicit regional policies, may boost purchasing power and labor demand. Thus, it need not follow from the fact that European labor is less mobile between regions that regional problems are more persistent than in the United States.

To analyze the speed with which regional labor-market disequilibria are eliminated, I extend the approach taken in Eichengreen (1990). Given large literatures for all three countries suggesting that local unemployment differentials persist, it is inappropriate to assume that unemployment rates converge to the same level. Instead, I adopt the more general assumption that there is a stable long-run relationship between unemployment in a region and the average unemployment rate in the nation of which that region is a part. In other words, regional and national unemployment rates are cointegrated. I therefore estimate for each region a cointegrating regression of the form:

$$U^R = a + bU^N \tag{1}$$

where U^R is the regional unemployment rate, U^N is the national unemployment rate, and a and b are parameters to be estimated. If regional and national unemployment rates are cointegrated, then the associated error correction form can be used to identify the speed of adjustment of regional unemployment rates:

$$dU^R = a + bdU^N + ce_{t-1} \qquad (2)$$

where d is the difference operator, e is the residual from equation 1 above, and a, b, and c are again parameters to be estimated. c captures the speed with which regional labor markets respond to divergencies between local and national unemployment rates.

For Britain and Italy, the analysis is straightforward. Despite the notoriously low power of tests for the cointegration of short time series, for all nine British regions it is impossible to reject the null that regional unemployment rates are cointegrated with the national rate.[27] Cointegration obtains for five of the six Italian regions, and for the sixth (the Italian North) the Durbin–Watson statistic falls just short of the critical value provided by Dickey and Fuller. Results are summarized in table 6.8. For the nine British regions, the unweighted average of the error correction term c is 0.47. The analogous average for Italy is 0.34. This means that about a half of any divergence between regional and national unemployment rates in Britain, and about a third in Italy, is eliminated in the next year.

Analyzing the US data is more complex, for evidence of cointegration ranges from weak to non-existent. Of nine US regions, unemployment rates in only three (East North Central, South Atlantic, and Mountain) are clearly cointegrated with the national rate. This fact was previously noted in Eichengreen (1990) and, using another approach, by Hall (1972). Following Eichengreen (1990), I therefore add additional regressors to the right-hand side of equation 1 in order to produce a cointegrated vector. Specifically, I add the real energy price and real exchange-rate variables used section III.

With the addition of these variables, the hypothesis of cointegration can no longer be rejected for any of the nine US regions.[28] Equation 2 can then be estimated, including on its right-hand side all of the differenced variables. As shown in the first column of table 6.9, the error correction terms again vary across regions. They are largest, plausibly, for three regions whose unemployment rates were cointegrated with the national average even before the additional regressors were added to equation 1.

The unweighted average of the error correction terms for the nine US regions is 0.26, smaller than the comparable averages for Britain and Italy. This striking result suggests that some other mechanism besides labor mobility works to restore regional labor-market equilibrium in the European countries.

Table 6.8. *Cointegration and error correction parameters for Britain and Italy*

UK	Cointegrating regression		Durbin–Watson statistic	Error correction term
	Constant	Slope		
North	0.94	1.32	0.67	−0.30
	(5.43)	(48.73)		(1.94)
Yorkshire–Humberside	−0.50	1.15	1.19	−0.97
	(2.36)	(34.92)		(5.96)
East Midlands	−0.47	0.95	1.15	−0.87
	(9.18)	(120.28)		(3.85)
South-East–East Anglia	−0.73	0.92	0.52	−0.34
	(2.86)	(22.91)		(2.08)
South-West	0.77	0.76	0.45	−0.21
	(4.34)	(27.34)		(1.50)
West Midlands	−1.37	1.31	0.51	−0.46
	(10.24)	(62.84)		(2.66)
North-West	−0.37	1.30	0.59	−0.15
	(3.23)	(72.73)		(0.92)
Wales	0.76	1.15	0.83	−0.57
	(5.92)	(57.19)		(2.75)
Scotland	1.31	1.09	0.46	−0.32
	(6.28)	(33.49)		(1.89)
Italy				
North-East	−0.01	0.71	0.92	−0.54
	(0.70)	(14.43)		(3.15)
North	0.01	0.61	0.30	−0.17
	(1.37)	(5.09)		(1.73)
East-Central	0.01	0.53	0.67	−0.29
	(3.99)	(8.13)		(2.04)
Lazio	0.04	0.54	0.46	−0.23
	(4.95)	(3.66)		(1.72)
South-East	−0.01	1.18	1.07	−0.58
	(0.47)	(17.95)		(2.92)
South	−0.01	1.69	0.70	−0.26
	(3.56)	(20.57)		(1.88)

Note: *t*-statistics in parentheses. Samples are as in table 6.6.

Table 6.9. *Error correction parameters from augmented specification*

United States		Great Britain		Italy	
NE	−0.26	NO	−0.44	NE	−0.65
	(3.08)		(2.57)		(3.23)
MA	−0.24	YH	−1.14	NO	−0.21
	(2.16)		(5.72)		(1.60)
ENC	−0.31	EM	−0.99	CE	−0.39
	(2.37)		(4.02)		(2.13)
WNC	−0.19	SE	−0.56	LA	−0.25
	(1.44)		(2.73)		(1.55)
SA	−0.43	SW	−0.72	SE	−0.69
	(3.13)		(4.49)		(3.21)
ESC	−0.31	WM	−1.06	SO	−0.43
	(2.99)		(4.51)		(2.37)
WSC	−0.19	NW	−0.22		
	(2.03)		(0.97)		
MT	−0.40	WA	−0.71		
	(2.38)		(3.33)		
PA	−0.18	SC	−0.69		
	(1.42)		(3.93)		

Note: t-statistics in parentheses. Sample periods are as in table 6.6.
Source: See text.

To check the robustness of these results, I re-estimated the cointegrating regressions and error correction forms for Britain and Italy including also the real energy price and real exchange rate. With the addition of these variables, the hypothesis of cointegration could not be rejected for any Italian region. In the case of Britain, in contrast, the addition of the real energy price (alone or in conjunction with the real exchange rate) caused the hypothesis of cointegration to be rejected for York, where it had been accepted before.

Estimates of the error correction term from the augmented model are summarized in the last two columns of table 6.9. Compared to the first column for the US, they continue to show relatively rapid adjustment. The unweighted average for Britain is 0.73, for Italy 0.44.[29] This confirms the results reported above.

This section, along with its substantive results, also suggests an agenda for research. That regional unemployment rates are cointegrated with the national rate in Britain and Italy but not in the United States warrants further analysis. The idea that one US region's unemployment rate can diverge indefinitely from the national average is not plausible. Eventually that differential must become so conspicuous that some adjustment mechanism will begin to bring it back into line. That the US data appear inconsistent with the hypothesis of cointegration may simply reflect that existing time series are short and that regional unemployment differentials in the US show relatively little variation. More data acquired with the passage of time may allow the hypothesis of cointegration to be resurrected.[30]

Even so, the absence of cointegration for the United States is indicative of more than data problems. Within European nations, regions characterized by unusually high unemployment in one year (or one decade) also tend to be characterized by unusually high unemployment in the next. The hypothesis of cointegration is readily accepted for Italy and Britain because unemployment rates in high unemployment regions tend to maintain a relatively stable relationship to unemployment rates nationwide, and similarly for low unemployment regions. In the US in contrast, one decade's high unemployment regions can become the next decade's low unemployment regions.[31] The transformation of New England, for example, from a textile- and boot-and-shoe-based economy in the 1960s and early 1970s to a center of high-technology industries in the 1980s converted it from a relatively high to a low unemployment region. With unemployment rates in New England moving from well above the national average to well below it over the sample period, it is not surprising that the hypothesis of cointegration is rejected. Why the identity of relatively high and relatively low unemployment regions should persist in Europe but shift repeatedly in the United States remains inadequately understood.

The other item for research is to identify and analyze the mechanisms that substitute for labor mobility in bringing Britain and Italy's regional labor markets back into line. What we know about wage flexibility and private investment suggests that neither one furnishes the critical mechanism. Most observers believe that wages are less, not more, flexible in Europe than in the US. Similarly, policy-makers complain of the death of private capital flows to depressed regions to make use of idle labor. It could be that individuals enter the labor force in disproportionate numbers in regions where unemployment is low, augmenting the stock of idle workers, and that they exit the labor force in regions where unemployment is high, reducing numbers measured as out of work. Alternatively, fiscal transfers to depressed regions within Britain and Italy are sufficiently flexible and generous that region-specific shocks are eliminated as quickly as in the US. But again, further analysis is required.

VI   Conclusion

The literature on optimum currency areas points to the symmetry of shocks and the mobility of factors of production as two criteria for evaluating the costs of EMU. This chapter has analyzed both criteria from a labor-market perspective. Since the United States forms a currency area, the evidence for Britain and Italy is compared systematically with evidence for the US. The dispersion of shocks to regional labor markets was found to be similar across countries. But the responsiveness of migration to regional labor-market disequilibria was found to be much greater in the US. International variations in the elasticity of migration with respect to inter-regional unemployment differentials, while less pronounced, point similarly to the greater responsiveness of labor flows in the United States.

Yet despite that shocks to regional labor markets in the US and Europe are of comparable dispersion, and that US migration responds more powerfully to those shocks, it is not obvious that deviations from the long-term relationship among regional unemployment rates are more persistent in Europe than in the US. When disturbances cause regional unemployment rates within European countries to diverge, it appears that other mechanisms, perhaps including relative wage adjustments, inter-regional capital mobility, and government policy, substitute adequately for Europe's limited labor mobility in order to bring them back into line. Further analysis of those alternative mechanisms forms the obvious agenda for research.

Data Appendix

1   Post-war Britain

Data on British unemployment were drawn from Department of Employment and Productivity (1971), supplemented by various issues of the Department of Employment *Gazette*. The regions distinguished by the Department of Employment are the South East, East Anglia, South West, West Midlands, East Midlands, Yorkshire (including Humberside), North West, North, Wales, Scotland, and Northern Ireland. (Given changes in regional definition in 1974, for that portion of the analysis (tables 6.6–6.9) where longer time series are important, East Anglia and the South East were combined.) I excluded Northern Ireland on the grounds that its labor market is very imperfectly integrated with that of Great Britain, although in principle Irish data could be used.

Data on number of migrants as a share of regional population were constructed as described in Pissarides and McMaster (1990).

To construct a time series for the real exchange rate, nominal exchange rates and consumer price indices were first gathered for Britain's ten leading trading partners. Trade was measured as the sum of imports and exports in 1980. A consumer price index for Saudi Arabia is not available for the early part of the sample period; I therefore dropped Saudi Arabia from the initial list of ten trading partners. (Since British imports from Saudi Arabia are almost entirely oil, the impact of conditions there on the British economy should be captured by real energy prices.) I then computed the real exchange rate as the trade-weighted arithmetic average of foreign consumer prices, converted into sterling using the spot rate, relative to the British consumer price index. For energy prices I drew the prices of fuel purchased by manufacturing industry from the *Annual Statistical Abstract of the United Kingdom*, deflated by consumer prices, from Feinstein through 1965, from Mitchell (1988) for 1966–70, and from *IFS* thereafter.

2   Italy

The surveys used to gather labor market statistics for Italy were revised in 1977 to reflect new definitions of unemployment. For prior years, two categories of unemployed persons were distinguished: persons separated from a previous position, and new entrants to the labor force in search of their first position. Much of the rise in Italian unemployment in the 1970s is concentrated in the second category, reflecting legally mandated severance pay provisions which discouraged layoffs and made it more difficult for recent school leavers to find a first position. The revised surveys after 1976 distinguish persons recently separated from a previous position, new entrants in search of a first position, and other persons in search of work. These data are drawn from *Annuario Statistico del Lavoro*. Problems of comparability between pre- and post-1975 data are discussed and an attempt to reconcile the two is made by Massarotto and Trivellato (1983).

The Italian real exchange rate was calculated identically to that for Britain, except that Saudi Arabia and Libya were excluded from the initial list of ten leading trade partners due to the absence of a continuous consumer price index.

No energy price index appears to be available for Italy for the entire period. I spliced the following series: the price of fuel oil in Turin for 1958–62, the arithmetic average of separate indices for crude petroleum and for petroleum products for 1963–74, and the published index for crude oil and petroleum products for 1975–84. All series were taken from the *Annuario Statistico Italiano* (various issues). The resulting index was deflated by Italian consumer prices as published in *IFS*.

Data on domestic migration were drawn from *Popolazione e Movimento*

Anagrafico dei Comuni (various issues). The net migration rate was calculated as the percentage of the total resident population per administrative region tabulated in the *Ricostruzione della Popolazione Residente per Sesso, Eta' e Regione* (1960–72), *Popolazione e Bilanci Demografici per Sesso, Eta' e Regione* (1973–81), *Popolazione Residente per Sesso, Eta' e Regione* (1982–5), and *Statistiche Demografiche* (1986–7).

Two series are used for nominal wages by region. The first is the effective daily wage paid to the injured-at-work employees of industry and agriculture, which appears in the *Notiziario Statistico* (various issues). This series excludes the service sector and includes data only for firms complying with the rules of the public insurance system. The second series is the compensation of employees, inclusive of social security contributions, drawn from the *Annuario di Contabilita' Nazionale* (1974, 1986). There are two regional series, one for 1961–70 and one for 1970–84, but they are not homogeneous. See Attanasio and Padoa-Schioppa (1991) for details about the construction of consistent series.

3 United States

Data for the US on unemployment by state, based on the Current Population Survey, have been published by the US Department of Labor since the early to mid 1970s (depending on the state and the size of the CPS sample). These data appear in the Labor Department's *Geographic Profile of Employment and Unemployment* (various issues). For prior years I rely on the estimates of state agencies, as tabulated in the *Manpower Report of the President* (various issues).

The real exchange rate for the US was constructed to be comparable to those for Britain and Italy, starting with consumer price indices and exchange rates for the country's ten leading trade partners in 1980, excluding Saudi Arabia for lack of a continuous consumer price index, and using trade weights to aggregate. The real price of energy is computed as the consumer price index for energy relative to the consumer price index for all items, both from Council of Economic Advisors (1991).

Series P-20 of Current Population Reports, which provides direct data on domestic migration patterns, distinguishes four regions only. For finer geographic breakdowns like those utilized here, one has to rely on residual computations. Total population change was first calculated taking mid-year population estimates for each region. Natural population change was then computed as the average of births minus deaths for end-year observations, since births and deaths are over the entire year whereas population is computed at mid year. The difference between total and natural migration was attributed to net migration.

Data on population are based on the *Current Population Survey*, while data on births and deaths were drawn from the *Vital Statistics of the U.S.* Average hourly earnings of production workers in manufacturing industries were drawn from the *Employment and Earnings*. Since these data were provided by state, we constructed a weighted average for each division; the weight used for each state was the number of employees in non-agricultural establishments, whose source was again *Employment and Earnings*.

Notes

I thank Orazio Attanasio and Christopher Pissarides for help with data and Luisa Lambertini for expert research assistance. Financial support was provided by the Center for German and European Studies of the University of California at Berkeley.

1 The extent to which fiscal convergence is a necessary concomitant of monetary union remains a debated point. See Eichengreen (1991), Bayoumi and Russo (1991), and Goldstein and Woglom (1991).

2 Early contributions include Cohen and Wyplosz (1989) and Weber (1990). For a more detailed review of the literature than is presented here see Bayoumi and Eichengreen (1991a).

3 Common factors are measured by the share of the cross-country variance explained by the first principal component.

4 De Grauwe and Vanhaverbeke in chapter 5 of this volume examine growth rates of output and employment for a number of European countries, and find that they vary more at the regional than at the national level. From this they conclude that shocks are more asymmetric at the regional than at the national level. They do not, however, provide systematic comparisons between Europe and the United States.

5 Those impressed by the importance of cultural and linguistic differences would probably anticipate that migration between European countries will remain lower than migration within them even after statutory barriers are removed.

6 The data upon which these and subsequent figures are based are described in the data appendix.

7 The labels denote, reading left to right, North, Yorkshire–Humberside, East Midlands, South East, South West, West Midlands, North West, Wales, and Scotland.

8 The labels denote, reading left to right, Abruzzi, Campania, Center, Emilia, Lazio, Lombardy, North, Sardinia, Sicily, and South.

9 Following King (1985), I also include as part of the North Val d'Aosta, Trentino-Alto, Adige, and Friuli-Venezia Giulia.

10 See Bianchi and Gualtieri (1990).

11 The labels denote, reading left to right, New England, Middle Atlantic, East North Central, West North Central, South Atlantic, East South Central, West South Central, Mountain, and Pacific.

12 Endogeneity of the explanatory variables, notably the real exchange rate, is

unlikely to be a problem insofar as explanatory variables are measured for the entire economy while the dependent variables are for relatively small regions. Any one region's unemployment is unlikely to have a discernible impact on real wages economy-wide and hence on the nation's real exchange rate, for example. An exception to this statement is when workers in the industries that dominate economic activity in a particular region set the tone for wage negotiations economy-wide.

13 Standard definitions of regions used by the Ministry of Labour were revised in 1974, rendering problematic the use of pre- and post-1974 data together. There were also a variety of procedural changes in the measurement of British unemployment in the 1980s, which inevitably complicates the interpretation of its time series behavior.

14 North Sea oil provided an additional boost to Scottish employment in the early 1980s. Townsend (1983, p. 98).

15 Townsend (1983, pp. 118–19).

16 All subsequent comparisons across countries also refer to table 6.1 estimates for Britain.

17 See the data appendix for further discussion.

18 The relatively low coefficients for Abruzzi, Calabria, and the rest of the South are consistent with the results of Caroleo (1990), who regressed unemployment in the Mezzogiorno on national unemployment and a time trend, obtaining coefficients on national unemployment in the neighborhood of 0.8.

19 Insofar as workers in these manufacturing industries set the tone for wage negotiations nationwide, a rise in their unemployment may put downward pressure on real wages, leading to real exchange-rate depreciation. This positive correlation between unemployment and the real exchange rate is the opposite of the sign of the estimated coefficient on the real exchange rate, suggesting that the estimated effect represents a lower bound on the real exchange-rate effect. On the other hand, reverse causation may help to explain the positive coefficient for Piedmont-Liguria, the home of much of Italy's heavy industry.

20 See for example Creedy (1974), Hart (1970), and Langley (1974).

21 A lagged dependent variable and regional dummy variables are also included.

22 First and second lags of the dependent variable are also included. I refer in the text to the equations reported in their table 6.2.

23 The only respect in which my estimates differ from Pissarides and McMaster is in the coefficient on relative wages. My point estimate is only about a fifth the size of theirs and it is statistically different from zero at the 90 rather than the 95 percent level.

24 According to my point estimates, the elasticity for the US is about 25 times as large as for Britain. If that of Pissarides and McMaster is used instead, the US wage elasticity is still larger by a factor of five.

25 For the remainder of this chapter I follow Attanasio and Padoa Schioppa's scheme for consolidating Italian regions. The six regions are Northeast (Tre Venezie: Veneto, Trentino-Alto, Adige, Friuli-Venezia Giulia), Northwest (Piedmonte, Valle d'Aosta, Lombardia, Liguria), Center (Emilia-Romagna, Toscana, Umbira, Marche), Lazio, Southeast (Abruzzo, Molise, Puglia), and Southwest (Calabria, Basilicata, Campania, Sicilia, and Sardegna).

26 Alternatively, wages may rise in the booming region, pricing its labor out of the market and thereby eliminating the differential.

27 After the first draft of this chapter was written, I came across Chapman (1991), who undertakes a similar cointegration analysis of regional and national unemployment rates for the UK. Despite slight differences in implementation, his results are consistent with mine: unemployment rates in the UK are cointegrated, although "regional and national unemployment are not as closely related as might have been supposed . . ." Chapman (1991, p. 1059).

28 I used the test statistics developed by Engle and Yoo (1987).

29 As further sensitivity analysis, I re-estimated these models adding the real exchange rate *or* the real energy price, but not both, to the basic cointegrating regression and the associated error correction form. For Italy, the results were essentially unchanged. (The average value of the error correction term was 0.39 when the real energy price was added, 0.41 when the real exchange rate was added instead.) For Britain, the error correction terms tended to shrink noticeably (to 0.56 and 0.55, respectively) but remained larger than the corresponding values for the United States.

30 See Frankel (1990) for a discussion of the sensitivity of such tests to the limited availability of data.

31 For further discussion, again see Eichengreen (1990).

References

A'Hearn, Brian (1991), "Migration and Economic Convergence in Post-War Italy," unpublished manuscript, University of California at Berkeley.

Armstrong, Harvey and Jim Taylor (1985), *Regional Economics and Policy*, London: Philip Allan.

Attanasio, Oarzio P. and Fiorella Padoa Schioppa (1991), "Regional Inequalities, Migration and Mismatch in Italy, 1960–86," in Fiorella Padoa Schioppa (ed.), *Mismatch and Labor Mobility*, Cambridge: Cambridge University Press, pp. 237–321.

Barro, Robert and Xavier Sala-i-Martin (1991), "Convergence Across States and Regions," *Brookings Papers on Economic Activity*, 1, pp. 107–58.

Bayoumi, Tamim and Barry Eichengreen (1991a), "Shocking Aspects of European Monetary Unification," unpublished manuscript, International Monetary Fund and University of California at Berkeley.

(1991b), "Is There a Conflict Between EC Enlargement and European Monetary Unification?" unpublished manuscript, International Monetary Fund and University of California at Berkeley.

Bayoumi, Tamim and Massimo Russo (1991), "Fiscal Policy and EMU," paper presented at a conference on European Economic and Monetary Union, Barcelona, July 1–5.

Bianchi, Patrizio and Guiseppina Gualtieri (1990), "Emilia-Romagna and its Industrial Districts: The Evolution of Model," in Robert Leonardi and

Raffaella Y. Nanetti (eds.), *The Regions and European Integration: The Case of Emilia-Romagna*, London: Pinter, pp. 83–108.

Branson, William and James Love (1988), "U.S. Manufacturing and the Real Exchange Rate," in Richard Marston (ed.), *Exchange Rate Misalignment*, Chicago: University of Chicago Press, pp. 241–70.

Caroleo, Floro E. (1990), "Le Cause Economiche Nei Differenziali Regionali Del Tasso Di Disoccupazione," *Economia & Lavoro*, 23, pp. 41–53.

Chapman, Paul G. (1991), "The Dynamics of Regional Unemployment in the UK, 1974–89," *Applied Economics*, 23, pp. 1059–64.

Cohen, Daniel and Charles Wyplosz (1989), "The European Monetary Union: An Agnostic Evaluation," CEPR Discussion Paper No. 306.

Council of Economic Advisors (1991), *Economic Report of the President*, Washington, DC: GPO.

Creedy, J. (1974), "Inter-Regional Mobility: A Cross-Section Analysis," *Scottish Journal of Political Economy*, 21, pp. 41–53.

Department of Employment and Productivity (1971), *British Labour Statistics: Historical Abstract 1886–1968*, London: HMSO.

Eichengreen, Barry (1990), "One Money for Europe? Lessons from the U.S. Currency and Customs Union," *Economic Policy*, 10, pp. 117–87.

(1991), "Is Europe an Optimum Currency Area?" in Herbert Grubel (ed.), *European Economic Integration: The View From Outside*, London: Macmillan (forthcoming).

Engle, R.F. and B.S. Yoo (1987), "Forecasting and Testing Co-integrated Systems," *Journal of Econometrics*, 85, pp. 143–59.

Frankel, Jeffrey A. (1990), "Quantifying International Capital Mobility in the 1990s," in Dilip Das (ed.), *Current Issues in International Trade and International Finance*, Oxford: Oxford University Press.

Goldstein, Morris and G. Woglom (1991), "Market-Based Fiscal Discipline in Monetary Unions: Evidence from the U.S. Municipal Bond Market," unpublished manuscript, International Monetary Fund.

Greenwood, M.J. (1975), "Research on Internal Migration in the United States: A Survey," *Journal of Economic Literature*, 8, pp. 397–433.

Hall, Robert (1972), "Turnover in the Labor Force," *Brookings Papers on Economic Activity*, 1, pp. 709–56.

Hart, R.A. (1970), "A Model of Inter-Regional Migration in England and Wales," *Regional Studies*, 4, pp. 279–96.

Hughes, Gordon and Barry McCormick (1981), "Do Council Housing Policies Reduce Migration Between Regions?" *Economic Journal*, 91, pp. 919–37.

International Monetary Fund (various years), *International Financial Statistics*, Washington, DC: IMF.

Istituto Centrale di Statistica (various years), *Annuario Statistico del Lavoro*, Rome: ISTAT.

(various years), *Annuario Statistico Italiano*, Rome: ISTAT.

(various years), *Popolazione e Movimento Anagrafico dei Comuni*, Rome: ISTAT.

(various years), *Popolazione e Bilanci Demografici per Sesso, Eta' e Regione*, Rome: ISTAT.

(various years), *Statistiche Demografiche*, Rome: ISTAT.

(various years), *Annuario di Contabilita Nazionale*, Rome: ISTAT.

(various years), *Ricostruzione della Popolazione Residente per Sesso, Eta' e Regione*, Rome: ISTAT.

Istituto Nazionale per l'Assicurazione Contro gli Infortuni sul Lavoro (various years), *Notiziario Statistico*, Rome: INAIL.

King, Russell (1985), *The Industrial Geography of Italy*, London: Croom Helm.

Langley, P.C. (1974), "The Spatial Allocation of Migrants in England and Wales," *Scottish Journal of Political Economy*, 21, pp. 259–77.

Massarotto, Guido and Ugo Trivellato (1983), "Un Metodo Per il Raccordo delle Serie Regionali Sulle Forze di Lavoro Senze Informazioni Estranee," *Economia & Lavoro*, 4, pp. 67–77.

Miller, Edward (1973), "Is Out-Migration Affected by Economic Conditions?" *Southern Economic Journal*, 39, pp. 396–405.

Mitchell, B.R. (1988), *British Historical Statistics*, Cambridge: Cambridge University Press.

Mundell, Robert (1961), "A Theory of Optimum Currency Areas," *American Economic Review*, 51, 657–65.

Pissarides, Christopher and Ian McMaster (1990), "Regional Migration, Wages and Unemployment: Empirical Evidence and Implications for Policy," *Oxford Economic Papers*, 42, pp. 812–31.

Salvatore, Dominick (1981), *Internal Migration and Economic Development: A Theoretical and Empirical Study*, Washington, DC: University Press of America.

Townsend, Alan R. (1983), *The Impact of Recession*, London: Croom Helm.

United Kingdom (various years), *Annual Abstract of Statistics of the United Kingdom*, London: HMSO.

United States Department of Health, Education and Welfare (various years), *Vital Statistics of the United States*, Washington, DC: GPO.

United States Department of Labor (various years), *Geographical Profile of Employment and Unemployment*, Washington, DC: GPO.

United States Department of Labor (various years), *Employment and Earnings*, Washington, DC: GPO.

United States, President (various years), *Manpower Report of the President*, Washington, DC: GPO.

Weber, A. (1990), "EMU and Asymmetries and Adjustment Problems in the EMS: Some Empirical Evidence," Centre of Economic Policy Research, Discussion Paper No. 448.

7 European excess stock returns and capital market integration: an empirical perspective

PATRICIA FRASER
and RONALD MACDONALD

I Introduction

Perfectly integrated capital markets may be described as markets in which financial assets, with identical risk characteristics but traded in different national capital markets, have identical expected returns: domestic financial markets will be linked such that expected returns on similar assets will not move independently. While the degree of capital market integration (and the efficiency of financial markets) has implications for the pricing of financial assets, and ultimately the allocation of resources, it is particularly important when viewed from a European perspective. By late 1992 barriers to the free movement of goods and services within the European Community (EC) should have been abolished and this should be reflected in increasing integration of EC members' goods markets. However, for goods market integration to develop smoothly there should exist a European-wide pool of capital to finance European-wide investment projects. In fact the existence of the European Monetary System (EMS) since 1979 and the gradual relaxation of capital controls which this has entailed should indeed have resulted in greater European capital-market integration.[1]

In this chapter we consider the extent of capital-market integration for certain key European countries during the recent period of floating exchange rates. This is achieved by, first, examining the extent to which excess stock returns are predictable for a number of key European countries (France, Germany, Italy, and the UK) and the US[2] and, secondly, examining the extent to which any such predictability is explicable in terms of international factors. To the extent that they are affected by these latter factors, we interpret this as evidence of capital-market integration (see

163

following paragraph for a further discussion); that is, a common co-movement of equilibrium excess returns indicates capital-market integration. Furthermore, if there is evidence of such integration for European countries, we try to determine if it is international excess returns as measured by US excess returns or, alternatively, German excess returns which are most important. One key feature of our analysis concerns the effect that the Exchange Rate Mechanism of the European Monetary System has had on the integration process in Europe.

As we have suggested, we take the common movement of expected excess returns as our main indicator of capital-market integration. Such common movement simply suggests that there is some underlying factor which moves excess returns in two or more countries in the same way. There are a variety of interpretations as to what this factor might be: movements in the international business cycle, which may impart a common risk factor into world stock returns (from a European perspective, is the German business cycle more important in this regard than the US equivalent?);[3] changes in the volatility of stock returns; some sort of contagion effect on the part of noise traders. In this chapter we take no particular position on the interpretation of the causal factor.

The remainder of this chapter is organized as follows. In section II we present a review of the recent evidence on capital-market integration.[4] The econometric methodology which we employ is outlined in section III. The data used in our study are described in section IV and some descriptive statistics are also presented. In sections V and VI our econometric results are discussed. Section VII offers some preliminary conclusions.

II Capital-market integration: a review of recent evidence

Empirical evidence on capital-market integration may be drawn from both the economic and the finance literatures. The purpose of this section is to bring together these two strands of literature in order to highlight the way in which capital-market integration has been measured. Essentially, the economic literature on capital-market integration can be distinguished by studies that focus on the extent of international capital mobility, or, the degree of international financial market linkages. The literature on the former has generally taken the form of Saving–Investment (S–I) correlation analysis, the argument being that if there exists an international pool of capital alongside international investment opportunities, domestic saving and investment are unlikely to be correlated. The size of such correlation coefficients, therefore, indicates the degree of international capital mobility. The literature on financial market linkages has taken the form of the analysis of international parity conditions, where linkages are measured by the extent to which rates of return on financial assets are equalized, and by the correlations and predictability of international share prices. We summarize recent evidence on both these approaches below.

Savings–investment correlations

In a cross-sectional study which examined world-wide S–I correlations for the period 1960–74, Feldstein and Horioka (1980) challenged the view of a highly elastic supply of foreign capital so popular in textbook expositions of the Mundell–Fleming model. In their regressions, of national investment against national savings, they report coefficient estimates of 0.887 (gross savings and investment) and 0.938 (net savings and investment), both of which are significant at conventional levels. Feldstein (1983) reported further evidence for the period 1960–79 which reinforced these findings, the coefficients on gross and net savings being 0.796 and 0.993, respectively. Other cross-sectional studies report similar findings to Feldstein (see, for example, Summers, 1989), but Dean *et al.* (1989) report that the coefficient estimate on savings appear to have a declining trend when estimated over the sub-periods 1963–7, 1968–72, 1973–7, and 1983–7 (see Cooper, 1991 for a survey).

However, the S–I regressions conducted by Feldstein and Horioka and others have been heavily criticized, especially in terms of the econometric methodology. Usefully, Frankel, Dooley, and Mathieson (1989) summarize such criticisms, indicating that most of the problems with this approach arise because of the endogeneity of national savings to the economic system. The authors point out that simultaneous equation bias, and the resulting inconsistent coefficient estimates, is likely to be present as S–I will only be independent if: investment is a function of a representative real rate of return which is uncorrelated with national savings; international real rates of returns are equalized; the foreign real rates of return on such assets are determined exogeneously and hence the domestic country is "small" economically and cannot affect the world interest rate. Bayoumi (1989), when estimating S–I correlations for the period 1965–86, attempted to overcome the endogeneity problem by using instrumental variables. He found that OLS regression results were not changed in any significant manner; that is, investment and savings were highly correlated. Bayoumi suggested that Ricardian equivalence may also be a problem and tested for this by private saving–public saving regression analysis. Overall, the results tended to support the Ricardian equivalence argument. Using an adjusted savings variable in the cross-sectional S–I analysis Bayoumi reported reduced correlations for the data period (1965–86).

Time series regressions, while avoiding the endogeneity, suffer from the stylized fact that savings and investment, however expressed, are strongly pro-cyclical in nature and therefore a researcher may be in danger of accepting the null hypothesis of strong correlation between series when it is in fact false. Frankel (1989), using cyclically adjusted instrumental variables for the US, reports that S–I correlations were decreasing overtime: for 1956–73 the coefficient estimate on the savings variable was 0.872 while for the period 1975–87 the estimate was 0.311. Obstfeld (1986), using data for Germany, UK, and the US, also found S–I correlations to be falling over time. This view of increasing capital mobility was, however, challenged by Bayoumi (1989). Using private sector savings and changes in private fixed investment for ten OECD countries over the period 1966–86, he reports F tests for the sub-periods 1960–73 and 1984 and 1986 that suggest parameter stability. The evidence using S–I analysis remains, therefore, inconclusive. Our approach to capital-market integration is in some ways analogous to the S–I approach, but it does not suffer from the deficiencies of the latter.

Parity conditions

Capital-market integration can also be assessed by examining the extent to which international rates of return are equalized. A number of inter-related parity conditions suggest the use of different types of returns.

Covered interest parity

The computation of Covered Interest Parity (CIP) facilitates a test of financial integration in terms of short-run efficient arbitrage and hence can be thought of as testing the short-run integration of capital markets. The CIP condition equates the forward exchange-rate premium with nominal interest-rate differentials. Essentially, the evidence suggests that the general relaxation of capital controls have led to more efficient arbitrage between financial markets. Tests have been conducted in two ways. (1) Using financial assets that are identical in every respect except currency of denomination (Aliber, 1973; Frenkel and Levich, 1975, 1977; Taylor, 1987, 1989a; Fraser and Taylor, 1991). Aliber, for instance, explains any apparent deviations from CIP as reflecting *political risk*, such as expected changes in tariff structures or capital controls. Hence deviations from parity represent risk premia imposed by agents who engage in arbitrage. Frenkel and Levich (1975, 1977), in their study of CIP, allow for costs associated with foreign exchange transactions by creating a neutral band around the interest parity line concluding that allowance for such costs and the degree of market turbulence account for most of the deviations from CIP. Taylor (1987, 1989a) and Fraser and Taylor (1991), using high frequency data sampled during periods of turbulence, also report support for the CIP condition. (2) Tests have also been carried out where the assets are identical in currency of denomination but issued in different countries (Frankel, 1989). Such an activity is often described as onshore–offshore arbitrage (Cooper, 1991). Empirical evidence for deviations from onshore–offshore arbitrage indicate differentials are diminishing over time. Tests of CIP would seem, therefore, to indicate a movement toward short-run integration of capital markets.

Uncovered interest parity
Uncovered Interest Parity (UIP) denotes "speculative efficiency": capital flows equalizing expected rates of return on international financial assets under the joint hypothesis that agents are rational and risk neutral. There now exists a substantial body of literature which seeks to test UIP. Under rationality and risk neutrality UIP simply reduces to testing the forward exchange rate as an optimal predictor of the future spot rate. Generally, tests for 1920s data (MacDonald and Taylor, 1988) and for the more recent float (MacDonald and Torrance, 1989), have tended to reject UIP. More recent literature on the issue has tended to look at whether the rejection is due to the failure of rationality, risk aversion or both (MacDonald and Taylor, 1989, and MacDonald and Torrance, 1989) and whether the risk premium can be modeled (Wolfe, 1987 and Fraser and Taylor, 1990a). MacDonald and Torrance, for example, reject both rational expectations and risk neutrality for the mark, yen, Swiss franc, and sterling against the US dollar for the period 1984–7 while Taylor (1989b), testing US dollar–sterling effective exchange rates for the period 1979–85, was unable to reject the rationality of expectations. Fraser and Taylor (1990a), using GARCH and latent variable models, have limited success in modeling risk premia for the 1920s period of floating exchange rates. Tests of the UIP condition remain ambiguous and do not therefore help gauge the extent of capital-market integration.

Real interest-rate parity
Real Interest Parity (RIP) (under the maintained hypothesis of Uncovered Interest Parity (UIP) and Purchasing Power Parity (PPP)) exists if capital is perfectly mobile. RIP is linked to the S–I analysis discussed above by the consideration that if capital markets are integrated an important element of the saving/consumption decision will have been set in international markets, hence the scope for effective macroeconomic stabilization policy is severely limited. Artis and Taylor (1989) argue that it is of interest to see if members of the EMS conform more closely to RIP than non-members as differentials within such a currency union would suggest that financial

disturbances in one country are being reflected in the other union members' labor markets rather than being reflected in cross rates. Such a conclusion is motivated by the fact that members of the EMS strive to make their currencies perfect substitutes for one another thus protecting cross-rates from movements in and out of the dollar (Canzoneri, 1982). The extant empirical evidence on RIP has not, by and large, been favorable to the hypothesis and this, perhaps, is not surprising given the stringent underlying assumptions. For example, Mishkin (1981 and 1984) convincingly rejects the hypothesis when testing the US against six OECD countries. Mishkin regresses the *ex-post* differentials on four "Time" variables which proxy past real rates of return. The author reports significant correlation between current and past real interest differentials. Real interest differentials, therefore, would not appear to be random occurrences.

Cumby and Obstfeld (1984), using both domestic and Euro-currency rates of return, strongly reject RIP for several major economies. Isard (1983) focuses directly on long-run interest rates for the US/Germany country pair. Using survey data to construct a series of inflationary expectations, the author rejects the hypothesis that real interest differentials can be expected to disappear within a two-year horizon. Fraser and Taylor (1990b), using the bivariate vector autoregressive (BVAR) methodology, concentrate on Euro-interest rates of six and twelve month maturity for the period July 1979 to December 1986, for all country pair combinations of six European countries and the US. In every case they convincingly reject RIP. However, as RIP rests on UIP and PPP, the validity of such assumptions is important. Frankel and MacArthur (1988), address this particular issue, concluding that the source of the real interest differential is the failure of PPP (thus the imperfect integration of goods markets rather than financial markets).

Finance based tests

As indicated in the introduction to this review, there is considerable empirical evidence on capital-market integration reported in the finance literature. While the economic literature on capital-market integration has been motivated by macroeconomic issues, the finance strand of the literature has been directed toward microeconomic issues and, in particular, it has focused on national stock-market segmentation and the resulting potential gains from international portfolio diversification. More recently, however, "finance" research has been directed toward an investigation of whether integration is the result of economic "news" being very quickly assimilated into the international system, or if any co-movement in share prices is driven by contagion effects (Jeon and Furstenberg, 1990). Much of the former analysis has been tested by presenting evidence on the correlation of stock returns. Artis and Taylor (1990), for example, assess the impact of the abolition of UK exchange controls on portfolio investment under the hypothesis that such policies should have led to closer integration of UK and overseas stock markets after 1979. They tested this proposition in two ways. First, the extent of short-run stock-market integration was assessed by testing for significant shifts in the correlation of monthly stock returns after 1979. Second, by employing the two-stage cointegration methodology proposed by Engle and Granger (1987), Artis and Taylor test for long-run stock-market integration. The tests were implemented for five major stock markets, including the European countries of Germany, Netherlands, and the UK, for sub-periods October 1976–June 1986 and April 1973–September 1979. The authors report little evidence to suggest national stock markets are converging. Jeon and Furstenberg (1990), focus on the world's four largest stock exchanges (New York, London, Paris, and Tokyo) assessing the extent of their integration by constructing a four variable VAR system. Using daily data and accounting for the sequence of trading hours across markets, they regress the logarithm of stock index returns against lagged values of all variables in the system for the period January 1986 through November 1987. An increase in international co-movements is reported since the October 1987 crash. Further, volatility studies, which assess the extent to which the volatilities of share prices in national markets lead to an increase in volatility in other national markets, also indicate increasing covariance of major stock markets (Goodhart, 1988; King and Wadhwani, 1989).[5]

Howe and Mandura (1989), analyze the impact of international listings on common-stock risk by examining whether the risk characteristics of firms change as a result of foreign listings. The authors point out that, in the presence of segmented capital markets, foreign listings can serve to increase international integration and therefore cause a change in the equilibrium prices for dual listed firms: if markets are perfectly integrated then there should be no effect on the dual listed firms' share price. Using quarterly data over the period 1969–84 and constructing various measures of risk, their evidence suggests that dual listings do not seem to cause significant shifts in risk. They conclude that markets may be reasonably well integrated.

Campbell and Hamao (1989) study US and Japanese stock markets over the period 1971–89. They estimate a model in which excess stock-market returns (risk adjusted returns) in Japan and the US are driven by an unobservable variable so that they move together over time. By exploiting the time series properties of the data and estimating a highly restricted single latent variable model they then test the restrictions. The major findings of Campbell and Hameo are: (1) It is generally possible to forecast excess returns in both countries using similar sets of domestic variables and, furthermore, small stocks appear to have a greater predictable element than large stocks; (2) Japanese variables do not help to forecast US excess returns, but US variables appear to help forecast Japanese excess returns; (3) Excess returns are positively correlated although they are not perfectly correlated. The authors conclude that US and Japanese stock markets appear to be substantially integrated.

Generally, the above review of capital-market integration literature suggests that the evidence in favor of integration is mixed and appears mainly to concentrate on world-wide integration. Our empirical analysis is directed largely toward European stock-market integration. We employ a variety of econometric techniques all of which are designed to extract optimal information from the data in order to compute indirect tests of European capital-market integration.

III Econometric methodology

Our initial task was to compute some descriptive statistics and some simple correlations of the series in order to characterize and assess the co-movement of individual data series. As is now commonplace we also tested for the orders of integration of the series. To this end, we follow the strategy outlined in Perron (1988) of constructing a number of statistics based upon the following two regression equations:

$$s_t = \mu^* + \alpha^* s_{t-1} + u_t \tag{1}$$

$$s_t = \tilde{\mu} + \tilde{\beta}(t - T/2) + \tilde{\alpha} s_{t-1} + \tilde{u}_t \tag{2}$$

where s denotes the variable of interest. The statistics are: $Z(t\alpha^*)$ and $Z(t\tilde{\alpha})$, which are standard t-tests for testing $\alpha = 1$ in (1) and (2); $Z(\Phi_1)$, which tests the null that $(\mu,\alpha) = (0,1)$ in (1); $Z(\Phi_2)$ which tests the null that $(\mu,\beta,\alpha) = (0,0,1)$ in (2); $Z(\Phi_3) = (\mu,0,1)$ in (2). The strategy first involves estimating model (2) and using the statistics $Z(t\tilde{\alpha})$ and $Z(\Phi_3)$ to discern whether there is evidence which would allow rejection of the null hypothesis of a unit root. If it is not possible to reject the unit root hypothesis, then greater power may be obtained by moving to equation (1) and using the associated statistics. Before using (1), however, we must check that $\tilde{\mu} = 0$, since the statistics based on this equation are not invariant to a non-zero drift. An insignificant value for $Z(\Phi_2)$ means we may proceed to estimate $Z(t\alpha^*)$ and $Z(\Phi_1)$.

We extend our simple correlation analysis by conducting multivariate cointegration tests (for example see MacDonald and Taylor, 1991). This involves testing for the number of stochastic trends in a data set, using the methods proposed by Johansen (1988) and Johansen and Juselsius (1990) so we may ascertain joint co-movement of the series during our chosen sample period. Briefly, if there exists a linear combination of two or more $I(1)$ series which is itself stationary, then the series are cointegrated, that is, they have a stable long-run relationship. For $NI(1)$ series it is possible for there to be up to $N-1$ stationary linear combinations or cointegrating vectors (Engle and Granger, 1987). Consider an $N \times 1$ vector of $I(1)$ variable X which has an autoregressive representation with Gaussian errors ε_t:

$$X_t = \Pi_1 X_{t-1} + \Pi_2 X_{t-2} + \ldots + \Pi_k X_{t-k} + \varepsilon_t \qquad t = 1, 2, \ldots, T \quad (3)$$

Within this framework the cointegrating matrix is:

$$I - \Pi_1 - \Pi_2 - \ldots - \Pi_k = \Pi \qquad (4)$$

will be an $N \times N$ matrix whose rank determines the number of distinct cointegration vectors which exist between the variable X. Define two $N \times r$ matrices α and β, such that:

$$\Pi = \alpha \beta' \qquad (5)$$

The rows of β' form the distinct cointegration vectors such that, if β' is the ith row of β':

$$\beta_i' X_t \sim I(0) \qquad (6)$$

Johansen (1988) and Johansen and Juselsius (1990) demonstrate that the stochastic matrix trace test for the hypothesis that there are at most r distinct cointegrating vectors can be carried out by constructing a likelihood ratio test statistic:

$$(T) = T \sum_{i=r+1}^{N} \ln(1 - \hat{\lambda}_i) \qquad (7)$$

where $\hat{\lambda}_{r+1}, \ldots, \hat{\lambda}_N$ are the $N-r$ smallest squared canonical correlations between the X_{t-k} and ΔX_t series, corrected for the effect of the lagged differences of the X process. Johansen (1988) shows that the trace statistic as defined by (7) will have a non-normal distribution under the null hypothesis. He does however provide approximate critical values for the statistic, generated by the Monte Carlo method.

We next compute regressions of excess stock-market returns on domestic and international variables to assess their power in forecasting excess returns. Following Campbell and Hamao (1989), if we consider a K-factor intertemporal asset pricing model:

$$R_{i,t+1} = E_t(R_{i,t+1}) + \sum_{k=1}^{K} \beta_{ik} F_{k,t+1} + \varepsilon_{t+1} \qquad (8)$$

where R_i is the excess return on asset i, between t and $t+1$, E_t is the expectations operator at time t, F_{t+1} is the factor realization at $t+1$, and ε_t is a white-noise error term, then the excess return on asset i will be determined by the expected excess return plus the sum of the products of constant betas and the k-factor realizations. Any deviation from this will be because of "news" occurring between t and $t+1$, ε_{t+1}. If we restrict the expected excess return so that:

$$E_t(R_{i,t+1}) = \sum_{k=1}^{k} \beta_{ik}\lambda_{ki} \tag{9}$$

where λ_{kt} is a market risk premium for the kth factor at time t and further assume that the information set available to agents consists of a vector of N forecasting variables and that agents are rational, then:

$$\lambda_k = \sum_{n=1}^{N} \theta_{kn}X_{nt} \tag{10}$$

and (9) becomes:

$$E_t(R_{i,t+1}) = \sum_{k=1}^{K} \beta_{ik} \sum_{n=1}^{N} \theta_{kn}X_{nt} \tag{11}$$

Thus by regressing I excess returns on N forecasting variables we can compute estimates of the product of the beta and risk coefficient in (9):

$$E_t(R_{i,t+1}) = \sum_{n=1}^{N} \alpha_{in}X_{nt} + \mu_{t+1} \tag{12}$$

We then extend the model by estimating an "Observable Factor" model. The extension simply involves adding in the "foreign" excess stock return, (R_f), as an independent variable in addition to the domestic and foreign forecasting variables:

$$E_t(R_{i,t+1}) = \beta_{if}R_{f,t+1} + \sum_{n=1}^{N} \alpha_{in}^*X_{nt} + \mu_{i,t+1}^* \tag{13}$$

The idea is that, if the predictability of the forecasting variables is simply reflecting the changing risk of an international factor, the addition of such a factor should destroy the statistical significance of the forecast variables. In our analysis the international factor is proxied by a foreign excess stock return.

The observable factor model, however, assumes that foreign excess returns can successfully proxy the international factor in the asset pricing model outlined above. We concur with Campbell and Hamao (1989) that this is a strong assumption to make and we therefore also estimate an unobservable factor model. In this model we focus on the common movement of expected excess returns in response to changes in the price of risk of a single world factor which is "latent." If we consider pairs of excess stock returns and N forecasting variables, then from (12), β_i and θ_n can only be identified up to a normalization. Therefore if we place overidentifying restrictions on the model by normalizing $\beta_1 = 1$, we can write the system:

$$
\begin{bmatrix} R_{1,t+1} \\ R_{2,t+2} \end{bmatrix} = \begin{bmatrix} \theta_2 & \theta_2 & \dots & \theta_N \\ \beta_2\theta_1 & \beta_2\theta_2 & \dots & \beta_2\theta_N \end{bmatrix} \begin{bmatrix} X_{1t} \\ \vdots \\ X_{Nt} \end{bmatrix} + \begin{bmatrix} \omega_{1,t+1} \\ \omega_{2,t+1} \end{bmatrix} \tag{14}
$$

The first row of the coefficient matrix identifying the coefficients θ_n and the first column, the coefficients β_2. The remaining $N-1$ coefficients in (14) being restricted and forcing the two excess returns to be perfectly correlated. We estimated this model and tested the overidentifying restrictions using Generalized Method of Moments (Hansen, 1982). The estimated coefficients from such a model may also be of interest as they are estimates of any common international component present in our excess returns. We use two different specifications for the unobservable factor model; foreign and domestic short-run interest rates and foreign and domestic spreads are used as instruments for both US and German excess stock returns. We now turn to a description of the data used in this study and our empirical results.

IV The data and some descriptive statistics

The data for this chapter were all extracted from the International Monetary Fund's International Financial Statistics and consist of monthly observations of four variables for six countries. The variables are a short interest rate (a Treasury Bill rate, where available), a long interest rate (a twenty-year bond), and an aggregate stock price index. From these variables we constructed two additional variables, namely the spread between long and short interest rates and the excess return of stock returns over a risk-free rate of interest (where the latter is taken to be the Treasury Bill rate or equivalent). Stock returns are calculated simply as the (logarithmic) change in the stock price index.[6]

The countries considered are France, Germany, Italy, the US, and the UK. The first three countries are of special interest since they have formed the core of the EMS since its inception and we refer to them in what follows as the "European countries"; the UK and US are added as "control" countries, their inclusion allows us to examine issues of whether integration is greatest with Germany as anchor or with the US as anchor and the effects of non-ERM membership (our sample period coincides with the period in which the UK was not a member of the ERM). Our full sample is from January 1972 through 1990. The start date coincides with the general movement to a more flexible exchange-rate regime via the "Smithsonian realignment," when exchange rates could fluctuate 2.25 percent around central rates and the European "snake in the tunnel" where some European countries (including Germany and France but excluding Italy and the UK) agreed to be more closely aligned but could fluctuate with non-aligned countries according to the 2.25 percent band proposal. We also consider two sub-samples which coincide with the non-EMS period within our full sample (January 1972 to February 1979) and an "EMS period" (March 1979 through 1990). Our prior is that the EMS period should be one in which European integration is greatest; however, as discussed above, we recognize that for the first sub-sample some of our chosen "European" countries operated the "Snake in the Tunnel" system of exchange-rate fixity. Given that the EMS is a more formal mechanism of exchange-rate flexibility we would expect the extent of any integration to be greatest under this system.

As discussed above, as a preliminary exercize to our tests for the degree of capital-market integration we conducted a number of descriptive statistics on our data set. Reported in tables 7.1a–7.1c are the means and standard deviations of our statistics for both full and sub-samples and in all cases these statistics are close to zero. For stock returns there is the interesting result that monthly mean returns become positive for our European countries during the EMS sub-sample; however, this is also true for the UK and US, so such changes are not perhaps attributable to an "EMS effect." The ARCH statistics are also reported in tables 7.1a–7.1c and indicate that heteroscedasticity is prevalent for all our series for the full sample period and a similar pattern is evident for both the sub-samples, although, interestingly, it is a little less prevalent for the sample period corresponding to the existence of the EMS.

Our results from estimating the statistics based on (1) and (2) for lag lengths 0, 1, 2, 4, 8, and 12 are reported in tables 7.2a–7.2c for the interest-rate and share price series. The overwhelming impression gained from these tables is that our interest-rate and share price series are almost all $I(1)$ process; that is, integrated of order one (hence the excess return series will also be stationary). The exception is the UK short-term interest rate which would appear to be stationary around some non-zero mean (although this would appear to be dependent on the chosen lag depth).[7]

In tables 7.3a–7.3c some simple correlation statistics are reported for the changes of the interest-rate series and for our two transformed variables. In terms of the excess returns correlations, we note that for the full sample the European countries generally have higher correlations with the non-European set than on an intra-European comparison. This pattern is

Table 7.1a. *Descriptive statistics for excess returns and interest rates*[a]

	Mean	S.D.	ARCH(4)		Mean	S.D.	ARCH(4)
France				**US**			
Shares	−0.001	0.005	51.149	Shares	−0.002	0.003	13.135
			(0.000)				(0.010)
i^{LR}	0.009	0.000	9.618	i^{LR}	0.008	0.000	23.501
			(0.047)				(0.000)
Δi^{LR}	0.000	0.000	16.767	Δi^{LR}	0.000	0.000	54.132
			(0.002)				(0.000)
i^{SR}	0.008	0.000	64.063	i^{SR}	0.007	0.000	11.274
			(0.000)				(0.024)
Δi^{SR}	0.000	0.000	12.215	Δi^{SR}	0.000	0.000	59.389
			(0.016)				(0.000)
Long-short spread	0.000	0.000	24.496	Long-short spread	0.000	0.000	23.145
			(0.000)				(0.000)
Germany				**UK**			
Shares	0.000	0.003	25.616	Shares	−0.001	0.004	32.278
			(0.000)				(0.000)
i^{LR}	0.006	0.000	9.641	i^{LR}	0.009	0.000	15.048
			(0.047)				(0.005)
Δi^{LR}	0.000	0.000	16.380	Δi^{LR}	0.000	0.000	6.779
			(0.002)				(0.148)
i^{SR}	0.005	0.000	19.937	i^{SR}	0.010	0.000	21.699
			(0.001)				(0.000)
Δi^{SR}	0.000	0.000	29.783	Δi^{SR}	0.000	0.000	39.644
			(0.000)				(0.000)
Long-short spread	0.001	0.000	10.591	Long-short spread	0.001	0.000	35.433
			(0.032)				(0.000)
Italy							
Shares	−0.003	0.004	19.880				
			(0.001)				
i^{LR}	0.011	0.000	15.827				
			(0.003)				
Δi^{LR}	0.000	0.000	25.627				
			(0.000)				
i^{SR}	0.011	0.000	14.036				
			(0.007)				
Δi^{SR}	0.000	0.000	48.503				
			(0.000)				
Long-short spread	0.001	0.000	8.815				
			(0.066)				

Note: [a]The mean of the series is the equally weighted average of the observations. S.D. denotes standard deviation. ARCH(.) is a test of Autoregressive Conditional Heteroscedasticity of up to 4 lags. Figures in parenthesis below the ARCH statistics are marginal significance levels. Sample periods are as follows: France – January 1972 to August 1990, Germany – January 1972 to July 1990, Italy – January 1972 to May 1990, US – January 1972 to November 1990, UK – January 1972 to October 1990.

Table 7.1b. *Descriptive statistics for excess returns and interest rates (1972–9)[a]*

	Mean	S.D.	ARCH (4)		Mean	S.D.	ARCH (4)
France				**US**			
Shares	−0.005	0.009	19.799 (0.001)	Shares	−0.006	0.004	13.521 (0.009)
i^{LR}	0.008	0.000	23.769 (0.000)	i^{LR}	0.006	0.000	4.046 (0.399)
Δi^{LR}	0.000	0.000	8.004 (0.091)	Δi^{LR}	0.000	0.000	2.485 (0.647)
i^{SR}	0.007	0.000	0.713 (0.950)	i^{SR}	0.006	0.000	8.774 (0.067)
Δi^{SR}	0.000	0.000	12.845 (0.012)	Δi^{SR}	0.000	0.000	3.570 (0.467)
Long-short spread	0.000	0.000	2.434 (0.657)	Long-short spread	0.000	0.000	11.441 (0.022)
Germany				**UK**			
Shares	−0.004	0.004	9.129 (0.058)	Shares	−0.005	0.008	17.639 (0.001)
i^{LR}	0.007	0.000	10.097 (0.039)	i^{LR}	0.011	0.000	12.247 (0.016)
Δi^{LR}	0.000	0.000	12.918 (0.012)	Δi^{LR}	0.000	0.000	8.974 (0.062)
i^{SR}	0.005	0.000	29.875 (0.000)	i^{SR}	0.008	0.000	8.865 (0.069)
Δi^{SR}	0.000	0.000	3.398 (0.494)	Δi^{SR}	0.000	0.000	11.946 (0.018)
Long-short spread	0.001	0.000	16.964 (0.002)	Long-short spread	0.003	0.000	6.837 (0.145)
Italy							
Shares	−0.014	0.008	8.805 (0.066)				
i^{LR}	0.009	0.000	20.972 (0.000)				
Δi^{LR}	0.000	0.000	10.172 (0.038)				
i^{SR}	0.009	0.000	4.344 (0.361)				
Δi^{SR}	0.000	0.000	18.674 (0.001)				
Long-short spread	0.000	0.000	2.999 (0.558)				

Note: [a]See note to table 7.1a. The sample period in all cases is from January 1972 to February 1979.

Table 7.1c. *Descriptive statistics for excess returns and interest rates* (1979–90)[a]

	Mean	S.D.	ARCH(4)		Mean	S.D.	ARCH(4)
France				**US**			
Shares	0.002	0.006	29.172	Shares	0.000	0.003	7.642
			(0.000)				(0.106)
i^{LR}	0.010	0.000	2.993	i^{LR}	0.009	0.000	8.083
			(0.559)				(0.089)
Δi^{LR}	0.000	0.000	9.397	Δi^{LR}	0.000	0.000	28.628
			(0.052)				(0.000)
i^{SR}	0.009	0.000	64.098	i^{SR}	0.008	0.000	6.128
			(0.000)				(0.189)
Δi^{SR}	0.000	0.000	8.399	Δi^{SR}	0.000	0.000	35.915
			(0.078)				(0.000)
Long-short spread	0.001	0.000	24.168	Long-short spread	0.000	0.000	12.659
			(0.000)				(0.013)
Germany				**UK**			
Shares	0.002	0.004	15.875	Shares	0.001	0.004	9.875
			(0.003)				(0.043)
i^{LR}	0.006	0.000	5.933	i^{LR}	0.009	0.000	4.136
			(0.204)				(0.388)
Δi^{LR}	0.000	0.000	8.789	Δ^{LR}	0.000	0.000	2.619
			(0.067)				(0.623)
i^{SR}	0.006	0.000	3.588	i^{SR}	0.010	0.000	13.862
			(0.465)				(0.008)
Δi^{SR}	0.000	0.000	19.089	Δi^{SR}	0.000	0.000	28.068
			(0.001)				(0.000)
Long-short spread	0.001	0.000	3.169	Long-short spread	0.000	0.000	27.113
			(0.530)				(0.000)
Italy							
Shares	0.003	0.006	11.812				
			(0.019)				
i^{LR}	0.012	0.000	7.112				
			(0.130)				
Δi^{LR}	0.000	0.000	12.714				
			(0.013)				
i^{SR}	0.012	0.000	6.428				
			(0.169)				
Δi^{SR}	0.000	0.000	9.699				
			(0.046)				
Long-short spread	−0.001	0.000	1.431				
			(0.839)				

Note: [a]See note to table 7.1a. Sample periods are as follows: France – March 1979 to August 1990, Germany – March 1979 to July 1990, Italy – March 1979 to May 1990, US – March 1979 to November 1990, UK – March 1979 to October 1990.

Table 7.2a. Unit root tests (bills)

$$s_t = \mu^* + \alpha^* s_{t-1} + \mu_t$$

$$s_t = \tilde{\mu} + \tilde{\beta}(t - T/2) + \tilde{\alpha} s_{t-1} + \tilde{\mu}_t$$

Country	l=0 s	l=0 Δs	l=1 s	l=1 Δs	l=2 s	l=2 Δs	l=4 s	l=4 Δs	l=8 s	l=8 Δs	l=12 s	l=12 Δ
France												
$(t\alpha')$	2.041	-10.798	-2.208	-10.795	-2.278	-10.728	-2.471	-10.985	-2.537	-10.972	-2.546	-10.94
(ϕ_1)	2.228	58.301	2.552	58.266	2.744	57.536	3.139	60.377	3.299	60.233	3.322	59.94
Germany												
$(t\alpha')$	-1.324	-9.147	-1.595	-9.116	-1.755	-9.078	-1.966	-9.190	-2.209	-9.519	-2.305	-9.6
(ϕ_1)	0.957	41.838	1.330	41.547	1.590	41.195	1.975	42.238	2.475	45.354	2.691	46.5
Italy												
$(t\alpha')$	-2.047	-9.123	-2.206	-9.167	-2.301	-9.089	-2.407	-9.117	-2.446	-8.990	-2.406	-8.0
(ϕ_1)	2.269	41.622	2.558	42.025	2.755	41.302	2.990	41.564	3.080	40.394	2.988	39.0
US												
$(t\alpha')$	-2.302	-9.956	-2.600	-10.121	-2.684	-9.980	-2.628	-9.605	-2.436	-9.220	-2.460	-9.2
(ϕ_1)	2.696	49.566	3.420	51.252	3.641	49.814	3.492	46.050	3.011	42.212	3.068	42.0
UK												
$(t\alpha')$	-2.698	-11.837	-2.865	-11.834	-2.954	-11.861	-2.972	-11.784	-3.042	-11.765	-3.013	-11.68
(ϕ_1)	3.977	70.068	4.385	70.023	4.621	70.366	4.727	69.409	4.867	69.181	4.785	69.19

The null hypothesis is discussed in section III and defined in Perron (1988). The critical values at 5% level of significance are as follows (Fuller, 1976, Dickey and Fuller, 1981):

Critical values	5%
$Z(t\alpha')$ $(\alpha^* = 1)$	-2.88
$Z(\phi_1)$ $(\mu^*, \alpha^*) = (0,1)$	4.63

Note: See table 7.1a for sample periods.

Table 7.2b. Unit root tests (bonds)

$$s_t = \mu^* + \alpha^* s_{t-1} + \mu_t$$
$$s_t = \tilde{\mu} + \tilde{\beta}(t - T/2) + \tilde{\alpha} s_{t-1} + \mu_t$$

Country	$l=0$ s	Δs	$l=1$ s	Δs	$l=2$ s	Δs	$l=4$ s	Δs	$l=8$ s	Δs	$l=12$ s	Δs
France												
$Z(t\alpha^*)$	−1.313	−21.958	−1.389	−22.852	−1.426	−11.553	−1.538	−11.855	−1.662	−12.210	−1.746	−12.56
$Z(\phi_1)$	0.987	241.093	1.067	260.745	1.111	66.711	1.258	70.407	1.443	74.808	1.580	78.49
Germany												
$Z(t\alpha^*)$	−1.233	−9.193	−1.509	−9.287	−1.636	−9.224	−1.745	−9.108	−1.843	−9.046	−1.941	−9.1
$Z(\phi_1)$	0.797	42.258	1.167	43.144	1.364	42.549	1.547	41.462	1.720	40.886	1.904	41.8
Italy												
$Z(t\alpha^*)$	−0.941	−8.508	−1.046	−8.513	−1.112	−8.496	−1.191	−8.473	−1.286	−8.640	−1.346	−8.8
$Z(\phi_2)$	2.134	24.131	1.594	24.160	1.422	24.064	1.299	23.932	1.222	24.897	1.200	25.8
$Z(\phi_3)$	2.959	36.196	2.230	36.240	2.001	36.097	1.840	35.899	1.746	37.346	1.722	38.8
US												
$Z(t\alpha^*)$	−1.708	−11.466	−1.833	−11.549	−1.838	−11.375	−1.822	−11.207	−1.860	−11.207	−1.922	−11.27
$Z(\phi_1)$	1.521	65.747	1.733	66.728	1.741	64.666	1.713	62.688	1.781	62.688	1.893	63.43
UK												
$Z(t\alpha^*)$	−3.011	−18.426	−3.121	−10.732	−3.148	−10.608	−3.115	−10.293	−3.089	−10.151	−3.085	−10.13
$Z(\phi_2)$	3.556	113.175	3.653	38.407	3.690	37.510	3.645	35.264	3.615	34.260	3.610	34.11
$Z(\phi_3)$	5.223	169.762	5.397	57.601	5.456	56.266	5.383	52.896	5.332	51.390	5.325	51.16

The null hypothesis is discussed in section III and defined in Perron (1988). The critical values at 5% level of significance are as follows (Fuller, 1976; Dickey and Fuller, 1981):

Critical values

		5%
$Z(t\alpha^*)$	$(\alpha^* = 1)$	−2.88
$Z(\phi_1)$	$(\mu^*, \alpha^*) = (0,1)$	4.63
$Z(t\tilde{\alpha})$	$(\tilde{\alpha} = 1)$	−3.43
$Z(\phi_2)$	$(\tilde{\mu}, \tilde{\beta}, \tilde{\alpha}) = (0,0,1)$	4.75
$Z(\phi_3)$	$(\tilde{\mu}, \tilde{\beta}, \tilde{\alpha}) = (\mu,0,1)$	6.34

Table 7.2c. Unit root tests (share price)

$$s_t = \mu^* + \alpha^* s_{t-1} + \mu_t$$
$$s_t = \tilde{\mu} + \tilde{\beta}(t - T/2) + \alpha s_{t-1} + \tilde{\mu}_t$$

Country	$l=0$ s	Δs	$l=1$ s	Δs	$l=2$ s	Δs	$l=4$ s	Δs	$l=8$ s	Δs	$l=12$ s	Δs
France												
$Z(t\tilde{\alpha})$	−2.001	−15.184	0	0	0	0	0	0	0	0	0	0
$Z(\phi_2)$	0.000	0.000	0	0	0	0	0	0	0	0	0	0
$Z(\phi_2)$	2.313	115.305	0	0	0	0	0	0	0	0	0	0
Germany												
$Z(t\tilde{\alpha})$	−1.381	−11.113	−1.372	−11.106	−1.464	−11.093	−1.542	−11.089	−1.520	−10.941	−1.586	−11.00
$Z(\phi_2)$	2.827	41.186	2.464	41.133	2.356	41.035	2.292	41.074	2.308	39.892	2.265	40.33
$Z(\phi_2)$	2.128	61.776	2.055	61.697	2.068	61.551	2.098	61.608	2.088	59.835	2.123	60.50
Italy												
$Z(t\alpha)$	−1.441	−11.509	−1.521	−11.552	−1.535	−11.422	−1.582	−11.459	−1.665	−11.629	−1.713	11.73
$Z(\phi_2)$	2.449	44.157	2.186	44.495	2.152	43.473	2.065	43.763	1.966	45.104	1.933	45.94
$Z(\phi_3)$	2.114	66.234	2.023	66.741	2.016	65.208	2.006	65.643	2.025	67.655	2.054	68.91
US												
$Z(t\tilde{\alpha})$	−2.088	−11.286	−2.216	−11.327	−2.255	−11.247	−2.273	−11.132	−2.266	−11.035	−2.240	−10.96
$Z(\phi_2)$	3.580	42.467	3.307	42.783	3.262	42.173	3.246	41.287	3.252	40.549	3.278	39.89
$Z(\phi_3)$	3.211	63.701	3.268	64.174	3.306	63.259	3.325	61.930	3.318	60.823	3.290	59.97
UK												
$Z(t\tilde{\alpha})$	−2.670	−10.395	−2.814	−10.506	−2.854	−10.305	−2.908	−10.267	−2.869	−10.054	−2.843	−9.99
$Z(\phi_2)$	4.047	36.025	3.884	36.810	3.881	35.389	3.895	35.123	3.883	33.642	3.881	33.26
$Z(\phi_3)$	4.018	54.037	4.302	55.215	4.396	53.083	4.528	52.685	4.431	50.462	4.368	49.89

Note: See note to tables 7.2a and 7.2b for critical values.

Table 7.3a. *International correlation of series*[a]

	France	Germany	Italy	US	UK
Excess stock-market returns					
France	1.000				
Germany	0.325	1.000			
Italy	0.143	0.296	1.000		
US	0.347	0.412	0.306	1.000	
UK	0.218	0.405	0.339	0.568	1.000
Change in long-term interest rates					
France	1.000				
Germany	0.407	1.000			
Italy	0.182	0.090	1.000		
US	0.304	0.427	0.093	1.000	
UK	0.142	0.180	0.753	0.185	1.000
Change in short-term interest rates					
France	1.000				
Germany	0.137	1.000			
Italy	0.092	0.045	1.000		
US	0.169	0.089	0.100	1.000	
UK	0.064	0.065	0.081	0.085	1.000
Long–short interest-rate spread					
France	1.000				
Germany	0.486	1.000			
Italy	0.367	−0.017	1.000		
US	0.542	0.680	0.039	1.000	
UK	0.157	0.367	0.280	0.193	1.000

Note: [a]The sample periods are as follows: excess stock returns – January 1972 to May 1990. Interest rates and spreads – January 1972 to December 1990.

Table 7.3b. *International correlations of series (1972–9)[a]*

	France	Germany	Italy	US	UK
Excess stock-market returns					
France	1.000				
Germany	1.270	1.000			
Italy	0.130	0.195	1.000		
US	0.199	0.357	0.281	1.000	
UK	0.118	0.437	0.329	0.618	1.000
Change in long-term interest rates					
France	1.000				
Germany	0.153	1.000			
Italy	0.135	0.040	1.000		
US	0.174	0.203	−0.022	1.000	
UK	0.044	0.200	0.245	−0.092	1.000
Change in short-term interest rates					
France	1.000				
Germany	0.276	1.000			
Italy	0.294	0.089	1.000		
US	0.272	0.268	0.312	1.000	
UK	0.149	0.137	0.154	0.192	1.000
Long–short interest rate spread					
France	1.000				
Germany	0.654	1.000			
Italy	0.597	0.072	1.000		
US	0.777	0.736	0.404	1.000	
UK	0.379	0.497	0.054	0.367	1.000

Note: [a]The sample period is from January 1972 to February 1979.

repeated for both sub-samples. The only intra-European correlation which is strong throughout the period is that of France–Germany; however, the correlation of both these countries' returns with the US is, in all cases, greater as is the German–UK correlation for all samples (the latter perhaps reflecting the pivotal role of the city of London as a financial center). Interestingly, this pattern tends to be repeated for the changes in shorts and longs and the yield gap. The implication of these results would seem to be that the European countries have closer capital-market integration with the US than with each other and this result seems to persist despite the existence of the EMS.

Table 7.3c. *International correlation of series (1979–90)^a*

	France	Germany	Italy	US	UK
Excess stock-market returns					
France	1.000				
Germany	0.365	1.000			
Italy	0.142	0.340	1.000		
US	0.456	0.437	0.310	1.000	
UK	0.333	0.421	0.355	0.542	1.000
Change in long-term interest rates					
France	1.000				
Germany	0.516	1.000			
Italy	0.205	0.110	1.000		
US	0.343	0.493	0.095	1.000	
UK	0.173	0.184	0.811	0.216	1.000
Change in short-term interest rates					
France	1.000				
Germany	0.097	1.000			
Italy	0.018	0.025	1.000		
US	0.148	0.049	0.038	1.000	
UK	0.041	0.045	0.051	0.061	1.000
Long–short interest rate spread					
France	1.000				
Germany	0.364	1.000			
Italy	−0.075	−0.318	1.000		
US	0.392	0.683	−0.379	1.000	
UK	0.412	0.154	0.391	0.152	1.000

Note: ^{a}Sample periods are as follows: excess stock returns – March 1979 to May 1990.
Interest rates and spread – March 1979 to December 1990.

V Multivariate cointegration tests

As discussed in section III, we also conducted some multivariate cointegration tests. Our purpose here is to test whether there is greater evidence of cointegration for our European countries during the EMS period relative to the non-EMS period and whether adding the non-European countries to this set makes a difference. To this end, we set up six different groupings of

Table 7.4. Multivariate cointegration tests[a]

	Shorts						Longs				
	1A			1B			2A			2B	
	λMax	Trace		λMax	Trace		λMax	Trace		λMax	Trace
Full sample											
$r \leq 4$	55.37	105.41	$r \leq 2$	28.54	40.35	$r \leq 4$	39.72	78.35	$r \leq 2$	10.21	18.20
$r \leq 3$	28.06	50.04	$r \leq 1$	10.79	11.81	$r \leq 3$	17.48	38.63	$r \leq 1$	4.20	7.98
$r \leq 2$	12.88	21.68	$r \leq 0$	1.01	1.01	$r \leq 2$	12.68	21.16	$r \leq 0$	3.78	3.78
$r \leq 1$	8.70	8.80				$r \leq 1$	16.32	8.46			
$r = 0$	8.09	8.09				$r = 0$	2.14	2.14			
Sub-sample 1											
$r \leq 4$	34.42	81.42	$r \leq 2$	22.66	35.47	$r \leq 4$	35.63	103.56	$r \leq 2$	19.75	26.14
$r \leq 3$	22.34	46.99	$r \leq 1$	8.81	12.81	$r \leq 3$	32.70	67.93	$r \leq 1$	4.88	6.40
$r \leq 2$	15.21	24.65	$r \leq 0$	3.99	3.99	$r \leq 2$	22.96	35.22	$r \leq 0$	1.51	1.51
$r \leq 1$	5.48	9.44				$r \leq 1$	9.73	12.25			
$r = 0$	3.95	3.95				$r = 0$	2.52	2.52			
Sub-sample 2											
$r \leq 4$	29.29	71.22	$r \leq 2$	12.75	21.17	$r \leq 4$	35.94	71.38	$r \leq 2$	20.59	28.59
$r \leq 3$	22.46	41.93	$r \leq 1$	6.12	8.42	$r \leq 3$	19.14	35.44	$r \leq 1$	6.27	8.01
$r \leq 2$	14.09	19.48	$r \leq 0$	2.29	2.29	$r \leq 2$	12.54	16.29	$r \leq 0$	1.73	1.73
$r \leq 1$	4.99	5.57				$r \leq 1$	3.02	3.74			
$r = 0$	0.38	0.38				$r = 0$	0.71	0.71			

Stocks

	3A			3B			5% Significance levels				
	λMax	Trace		λMax	Trace		λMax	Trace		λMax	Trace
Full sample											
r≤4	34.03	63.64	r≤4	16.44	21.72	r≤4	34.39	75.33	r≤2	21.89	35.07
r≤3	18.05	28.70	r≤3	5.13	5.27	r≤3	28.16	53.35	r≤1	15.75	20.17
r≤2	6.40	10.64	r=0	0.14	0.14	r≤2	21.89	35.07	r=0	9.09	9.09
r≤1	4.05	4.24				r≤1	15.75	20.17			
r=0	0.18	0.18				r=0	9.09	9.09			
Sub-sample 1											
r≤4	37.00	79.08	r≤2	15.12	21.15						
r≤3	20.54	42.08	r≤1	4.54	6.02						
r≤2	16.01	21.53	r=0	1.48	1.48						
r≤1	4.51	5.52									
r=0	1.01	1.01									
Sub-sample 2											
r≤4	31.66	63.28	r≤2	13.88	21.11						
r≤3	14.99	31.61	r≤1	6.33	7.22						
r≤2	9.66	16.62	r=0	0.89	0.89						
r≤1	4.96	6.97									
r=0	2.01	2.01									

Note: r denotes the number of cointegrating vectors. The 5% critical values of the maximum eigenvalue (λMax) and the Trace statistics are taken from Johansen and Juselsius (1990). The vector autoregressions included a constant term.

our variables: group 1a consists of all five short-term interest rates, whilst group 1b consists only of the European short-term rates; group 2a contains all five long-term interest rates, whilst group 2b consists of only the European long-term rates; group 3a consists of all five share indices, whilst group 3b consists only of the European share indices. Additionally, we consider these six different groupings for our three sample periods.

The results of our multivariate cointegration exercise are reported in table 7.4. In particular, we report there maximum eigenvalue statistics (λMax), which is a test for at most r cointegrating vectors against the alternative of $r + 1$ cointegrating vectors, and the trace statistic which is the stochastic matrix trace test (T) for at most r cointegrating vectors. The estimated values of these statistics suggest that there is one unique cointegrating vector for short-term interest rates over the full and first sample. This result is unchanged when the UK and US short rates are included in the set (group 1a) so the result would seem to be driven by the interaction of the European rates. What is especially interesting about this effect is that it does not appear in the EMS sample period for either the group 1a or 1b data sets. The results for longs differ from the shorts in that cointegrating vectors are unearthed for the group 2a set for the full and first samples, but there is no evidence of cointegration for group 1b, the European set. In contrast to the short results, there is some evidence of cointegration for the long rates during the "EMS sample" on the basis of the λMax statistic for group 2a, but not for the European set. The results for stocks seem even less encouraging since there is only evidence of one cointegrating vector for all five stock indices over sub-period 1.[8] These results seem somewhat counter-intuitive since they reveal no clear pattern of capital market integration, especially for the EMS period.

VI   The power of domestic and international variables to forecast excess returns

In this section we examine the extent to which a variety of domestic and international variables help to predict our excess stock returns series. In table 7.5 we present some statistics from regressions of our five countries' excess returns on a variety of "domestic" variables. In particular, we present the coefficient(s) of the explanatory variable(s), and the associated standard error(s), and the adjusted coefficient of determination. The first set of regressions [1] simply involve regressing a country's excess returns on a January dummy.[9] This return is significant at the 5 percent level for both the US and UK, and, although it is statistically insignificant at this level for the other countries, both France and Italy have t-ratios above unity.[10] The second set of regressions contain the January dummy and the change in the

Table 7.5. *Forecasting excess stock market returns with domestic variables (with January dummy)*[a]

		France	Germany	Italy	US	UK
[1]	Jan.	0.038	0.016	0.026	0.018	0.031
		(0.025)	(0.010)	(0.014)	(0.009)	(0.013)
	$\bar{R}^2$	0.016	0.008	0.006	0.012	0.017
[2] Δi^{SR}	Jan.	0.035	0.012	0.024	0.019	0.029
		(0.023)	(0.011)	(0.014)	(0.009)	(0.012)
	Δi^{SR}	−35.313	−11.248	−16.474	−7.512	−32.330
		(13.113)	(7.873)	(7.016)	(4.331)	(6.208)
	$\bar{R}^2$	0.071	0.017	0.026	0.026	0.134
[3] Δi^{LR}	Jan.	0.035	0.016	0.015	0.019	0.021
		(0.025)	(0.010)	(0.014)	(0.008)	(0.009)
	Δi^{LR}	−55.782	−24.026	−48.847	−29.590	−78.903
		(21.438)	(15.436)	(17.494)	(9.026)	(13.116)
	$\bar{R}^2$	0.057	0.020	0.045	0.071	0.292
[4] Spread	Jan.	0.038	0.016	0.026	0.019	0.031
		(0.025)	(0.010)	(0.014)	(0.010)	(0.013)
	Spread	9.881	4.262	−0.123	5.391	1.471
		(3.860)	(1.599)	(2.800)	(1.585)	(1.960)
	$\bar{R}^2$	0.034	0.029	0.002	0.067	0.015
[5]	Jan.	0.036	0.013	0.023	0.019	0.029
		(0.023)	(0.011)	(0.014)	(0.009)	(0.012)
	Δi^{SR}	5.740	3.873	−0.967	4.980	0.502
		(4.473)	(1.539)	(2.799)	(1.587)	(1.819)
	Spread	−31.813	−8.975	−16.887	−5.128	−32.154
		(14.293)	(7.657)	(7.125)	(4.016)	(6.148)
	$\bar{R}^2$	0.073	0.033	0.022	0.071	0.131
[6]	Jan.	0.036	0.015	0.014	0.019	0.022
		(0.026)	(0.010)	(0.014)	(0.009)	(0.009)
	Δi^{LR}	7.039	3.928	−6.484	5.106	1.563
		(3.811)	(1.540)	(2.635)	(1.547)	(1.570)
	Spread	−49.703	−20.929	−48.995	−27.204	−78.958
		(22.229)	(14.996)	(17.616)	(8.807)	(12.997)
	$\bar{R}^2$	0.064	0.038	0.041	0.117	0.292

Note: [a]Heteroscedasticity – consistent standard errors are reported in parentheses. $\bar{R}^2$ is the coefficient of determination adjusted for degrees of freedom. Figures in parentheses below the Ljung-Box statistic are marginal significance levels. For sample periods see table 7.1a.

short rate. The coefficient on the interest rate is negative across all countries and has explanatory power in three, namely France, Italy, and the UK. The change in the long rate (regression block three) also has a negative effect on returns and is significant at the 5 percent level in all but Germany. In regression four, the long–short spread is used to forecast returns and this also has explanatory power for three countries. Interestingly, when the changes in short rates are added to the spread (regression block five) the adjusted coefficient of determination in three cases is above that for either of the regressions consisting of the change in shorts or the change in the spread, suggesting that the combination of both variables helps to forecast returns. This is consistent with Campbell and Shiller's model of the term structure of interest rates (Campbell and Shiller, 1987); a similar pattern emerges when long rates are combined with the spread, instead of shorts. For the two sub-samples (not reported) the picture is very similar for the first three sets of regressions, although there is quite a marked difference between the predictive power of the spread over the two samples: the spread is statistically significant at the 5 percent level across all five countries for the period 1972–9 but is only significant in the case of Italy for the second sub-sample. This is perhaps indicative of domestic variables having less predictive power in the EMS period, a period in which we would expect greater integration and therefore a greater role for non-domestic variables. We turn now to an examination of the effects of international variables on excess returns.

In tables 7.6a–7.6c we present some regressions of excess returns on the change in home and foreign interest rates and home and foreign spreads. The "S" statistics are linear Wald statistics which in the case of S (All) tests for the joint significance of all the coefficients, S (Country) tests the significance of only the home country, whilst S (Foreign) tests only for the significance of the foreign country; none of the S statistics test for the significance of the constant and seasonal dummy. Consider each of the countries in turn. Although the S (All) statistic is significant at the 5 percent level for France, its significance is attributable to domestic variables; the S (Foreign) statistic is insignificant for all countries. For Germany, US and UK variables have explanatory power, but other European countries' variables do not. French and UK variables have explanatory power for Italy, but Germany and the US do not. Somewhat surprisingly, only French variables have any explanatory power in explaining US excess returns (at the 6 percent level). Foreign variables have their greatest impact for the UK, with all four countries having a significant impact on UK returns. The contrast between the UK and the other countries presumably reflects the importance of the UK as a financial center and cojointly the fact that the UK had fewer restrictions on capital-account transactions relative to the other countries.

Table 7.6a. *Forecasting excess stock returns with international variables*
(short-term interest rates and long–short spreads)[a]

	France	Germany	Italy	US	UK
France					
Δi^{SR} (France)		−37.610	−34.736	−28.365	−32.729
		(15.372)	(13.745)	(13.562)	(14.297)
Δi^{SR} (Foreign)		22.895	0.081	−7.602	4.604
		(15.131)	(9.592)	(5.349)	(7.349)
Spread (France)		2.859	2.728	5.701	6.274
		(5.656)	(4.965)	(5.322)	(4.694)
Spread (Foreign)		2.003	3.497	0.750	−1.338
		(0.655)	(3.080)	(3.097)	(2.342)
$\bar{R}^2$		0.080	0.071	0.071	0.068
S (All)		11.020	15.224	12.201	12.481
		(0.026)	(0.004)	(0.016)	(0.014)
S (France)		9.286	9.268	7.771	11.835
		(0.010)	(0.010)	(0.021)	(0.003)
S (Foreign)		2.292	1.941	2.590	0.720
		(0.318)	(0.379)	(0.274)	(0.698)
Germany					
Δi^{SR} (Germany)	−8.182		−9.064	−8.371	−8.911
	(9.095)		(7.657)	(7.509)	(7.606)
Δi^{SR} (Foreign)	−6.229		−0.933	−0.512	−5.673
	(6.498)		(3.611)	(2.479)	(4.251)
Spread (Germany)	2.515		3.830	0.792	5.350
	(1.605)		(1.532)	(1.950)	(1.671)
Spread (Foreign)	2.838		0.331	3.904	−3.146
	(2.843)		(1.206)	(1.510)	(1.182)
$\bar{R}^2$	0.036		0.025	0.042	0.053
S (All)	10.809		7.701	13.659	11.943
	(0.029)		(0.103)	(0.008)	(0.018)
S (Germany)	3.487		7.451	1.377	10.618
	(0.175)		(0.024)	(0.502)	(0.005)
S (Foreign)	3.406		0.179	7.293	7.518
	(0.192)		(0.915)	(0.026)	(0.023)
Italy					
Δi^{SR} (Italy)	−15.840	−18.605		−16.324	−13.682
	(7.293)	(7.199)		(7.341)	(6.778)
Δi^{SR} (Foreign)	14.918	15.473		3.433	−21.618
	(11.653)	(10.435)		(5.637)	(8.183)
Spread (Italy)	−4.118	−1.511		−1.098	1.619
	(3.091)	(2.818)		(2.748)	(2.701)
Spread (Foreign)	14.021	−2.467		1.864	−6.683
	(5.227)	(3.125)		(3.000)	(2.017)
$\bar{R}^2$	0.050	0.026		0.016	0.078
S (All)	12.244	9.218		6.250	22.044
	(0.016)	(0.056)		(0.181)	(0.000)
S (Italy)	5.705	6.683		4.950	5.212
	(0.058)	(0.035)		(0.084)	(0.074)
S (Foreign)	7.229	3.437		0.567	15.233
	(0.027)	(0.179)		(0.753)	(0.000)

Table 7.6a. (*cont.*)

	France	Germany	Italy	US	UK
US					
Δi^{SR} (US)	-5.947	-4.630	-5.425		-4.762
	(4.239)	(4.012)	(4.001)		(3.969)
Δi^{SR} (Foreign)	-3.259	-2.453	0.780		0.108
	(5.367)	(7.290)	(3.835)		(3.710)
Spread (US)	2.722	5.659	4.987		5.476
	(1.679)	(2.378)	(1.591)		(1.628)
Spread (Foreign)	5.988	-1.257	0.982		-2.320
	(3.255)	(2.528)	(1.510)		(1.186)
$\bar{R}^2$	0.081	0.063	0.064		0.074
S (All)	19.663	13.562	13.977		16.904
	(0.001)	(0.009)	(0.077)		(0.002)
S (US)	5.224	9.342	13.241		15.097
	(0.073)	(0.009)	(0.001)		(0.001)
S (Foreign)	5.682	0.320	0.424		3.973
	(0.058)	(0.852)	(0.809)		(0.137)
UK					
Δi^{SR} (UK)	-30.260	-32.526	-31.431	-30.597	
	(6.041)	(5.856)	(5.890)	(5.934)	
Δi^{SR} (Foreign)	-8.471	-2.081	-13.552	0.584	
	(6.804)	(12.500)	(8.169)	(4.269)	
Spread (UK)	-1.034	-1.765	-0.948	-0.644	
	(1.779)	(1.862)	(2.168)	(1.869)	
Spread (Foreign)	13.710	5.993	3.082	7.791	
	(3.788)	(2.304)	(2.618)	(1.959)	
$\bar{R}^2$	0.201	0.149	0.163	0.178	
S (All)	59.335	36.417	35.881	41.633	
	(0.000)	(0.000)	(0.000)	(0.000)	
S (UK)	25.368	30.849	28.610	26.673	
	(0.000)	(0.000)	(0.000)	(0.000)	
S (Foreign)	27.041	7.172	8.265	17.599	
	(0.000)	(0.028)	(0.016)	(0.000)	

Note: [a]All regressions include a constant and a January Dummy Heteroscedastic – consistent standard errors are reported in parentheses. S(*) denotes the joint significance levels of first, all the coefficients in the regression with the exception of the constant and January Dummy, second, the significance of the domestic variable and third, the significance of the international variable. See note to table 7.1a for sample periods.

Table 7.6b. *Forecasting excess stock returns with international variables,* (*short-term interest rates and long–short spreads*) *1972–9[a]*

	France	Germany	Italy	US	UK
France					
Δi^{SR} (France)		−29.926	−30.789	−23.607	−21.191
		(22.349)	(18.170)	(17.701)	(18.364)
Δi^{SR} (Foreign)		3.122	−0.990	−10.169	1.590
		(24.490)	(11.859)	(31.290)	(12.098)
Spread (France)		15.300	5.745	16.496	9.154
		(7.687)	(8.349)	(9.009)	(5.379)
Spread (Foreign)		−5.384	4.152	−4.752	7.507
		(4.481)	(6.616)	(6.906)	(6.458)
$\bar{R}^2$		0.115	0.113	0.108	0.116
S (All)		9.565	13.246	9.800	9.845
		(0.048)	(0.010)	(0.044)	(0.032)
S (France)		6.969	3.599	5.471	6.793
		(0.031)	(0.165)	(0.065)	(0.033)
S (Foreign)		2.276	1.259	0.493	1.537
		(0.321)	(0.533)	(0.782)	(0.464)
Germany					
Δi^{SR} (Germany)	−28.819		−24.767	−23.938	−19.652
	(8.825)		(8.066)	(8.048)	(7.372)
Δi^{SR} (Foreign)	1.685		−2.106	−8.615	−15.039
	(5.625)		(3.282)	(7.606)	(4.814)
Spread (Germany)	1.163		4.609	0.392	4.523
	(2.412)		(1.947)	(2.368)	(1.796)
Spread (Foreign)	8.490		2.943	6.219	0.412
	(2.733)		(1.210)	(2.046)	(1.991)
$\bar{R}^2$	0.288		0.279	0.293	0.306
S (All)	26.177		24.544	31.677	31.499
	(0.000)		(0.000)	(0.000)	(0.000)
S (Germany)	12.576		18.082	9.956	12.930
	(0.002)		(0.000)	(0.007)	(0.016)
S (Foreign)	9.951		7.584	12.563	11.116
	(0.007)		(0.023)	(0.002)	(0.004)
Italy					
Δi^{SR} (Italy)	−18.076	−16.846		−17.076	−13.167
	(8.318)	(8.251)		(8.799)	(7.167)
Δi^{SR} (Foreign)	17.092	22.833		−8.152	−33.307
	(14.898)	(16.661)		(18.096)	(12.860)
Spread (Italy)	5.308	4.182		5.155	6.232
	(4.598)	(3.412)		(3.727)	(3.161)
Spread (Foreign)	−1.638	−3.695		−2.319	−9.037
	(7.232)	(4.057)		(4.559)	(4.906)
$\bar{R}^2$	0.044	0.067		0.033	0.112
S (All)	9.181	12.276		8.072	15.228
	(0.057)	(0.015)		(0.089)	(0.004)
S (Italy)	7.741	7.987		7.300	9.744
	(0.021)	(0.018)		(0.026)	(0.008)
S (Foreign)	2.023	3.665		0.539	7.895
	(0.364)	(0.160)		(0.764)	(0.019)

Table 7.6b. (*cont.*)

	France	Germany	Italy	US	UK
US					
Δi^{SR} (US)	−18.889	−12.844	−17.119		−12.174
	(13.129)	(11.722)	(11.321)		(12.149)
Δi^{SR} (Foreign)	7.962	1.619	1.481		1.782
	(7.796)	(9.858)	(4.245)		(6.506)
Spread (US)	4.148	10.778	7.241		8.875
	(3.049)	(3.966)	(2.384)		(2.868)
Spread (Foreign)	8.308	−2.948	2.692		−0.649
	(3.899)	(3.517)	(1.651)		(3.434)
$\bar{R}^2$	0.202	0.180	0.189		0.170
S (All)	19.581	21.026	18.138		16.633
	(0.001)	(0.000)	(0.001)		(0.002)
S (US)	7.682	12.001	14.623		14.530
	(0.021)	(0.002)	(0.001)		(0.001)
S (Foreign)	4.562	1.172	2.876		0.161
	(0.102)	(0.557)	(0.237)		(0.923)
UK					
Δi^{SR} (UK)	−45.847	−39.328	−38.095	−36.091	
	(11.853)	(11.626)	(9.830)	(12.026)	
Δi^{SR} (Foreign)	−11.441	−8.086	−22.746	−14.796	
	(10.987)	(22.274)	(12.751)	(22.796)	
Spread (UK)	−3.402	−1.259	−3.655	−2.952	
	(4.957)	(5.951)	(5.545)	(5.258)	
Spread (Foreign)	21.442	6.800	5.574	15.544	
	(4.253)	(3.595)	(3.616)	(3.599)	
$\bar{R}^2$	0.288	0.152	0.264	0.267	
S (All)	44.924	18.963	35.175	35.674	
	(0.000)	(0.001)	(0.000)	(0.000)	
S (UK)	15.047	13.054	17.859	9.019	
	(0.001)	(0.001)	(0.000)	(0.001)	
S (Foreign)	33.529	4.531	15.244	23.346	
	(0.000)	(0.104)	(0.016)	(0.000)	

Note: [a]See note to table 7.6a. Sample period is from January 1972 to February 1979.

Table 7.6c. *Forecasting excess stock returns with international variables, 1979–90 (short-term interest rates and long–short spreads)*[a]

	France	Germany	Italy	US	UK
France					
Δi^{SR} (France)		−42.674	−37.766	−31.482	−36.179
		(17.599)	(16.976)	(16.507)	(16.511)
Δi^{SR} (Foreign)		32.642	10.158	−6.137	10.693
		(19.139)	(13.495)	(4.938)	(10.393)
Spread (France)		−10.786	−5.486	−5.019	−1.493
		(7.549)	(7.331)	(7.664)	(8.294)
Spread (Foreign)		10.583	−0.162	2.057	−1.528
		(4.271)	(3.783)	(2.890)	(3.871)
$\bar{R}^2$		0.092	0.038	0.041	0.042
S (All)		9.582	4.977	7.480	5.043
		(0.048	0.289)	(0.113)	(0.283)
S (France)		6.118	4.976	3.688	4.983
		(0.047)	(0.083)	(0.158)	(0.083)
S (Foreign)		7.058	0.058	2.456	1.355
		(0.029)	(0.753)	(0.293)	(0.508)
Germany					
Δi^{SR} (Germany)	6.999		2.344	7.071	0.981
	(13.242)		(11.219)	(11.633)	(10.865)
Δi^{SR} (Foreign)	−12.271		10.144	2.222	1.233
	(9.933)		(8.930)	(3.141)	(6.548)
Spread (Germany)	3.428		2.814	−2.214	3.988
	(2.856)		(3.077)	(4.087)	(3.003)
Spread (Foreign)	−4.026		−3.692	5.068	−4.528
	(4.716)		(2.303)	(2.117)	(1.880)
$\bar{R}^2$	−0.012		−0.008	−0.012	−0.004
S (All)	4.373		5.914	8.401	7.894
	(0.358)		(0.207)	(0.078)	(0.096)
S (Germany)	2.243		1.151	0.438	2.202
	(0.326)		(0.563)	(0.803)	(0.364)
S (Foreign)	1.694		4.102	5.956	5.954
	(0.429)		(0.129)	(0.051)	(0.051)
Italy					
Δi^{SR} (Italy)	−4.589	−10.218		−8.948	7.495
	(15.274)	(16.105)		(16.060)	(15.089)
Δi^{SR} (Foreign)	10.770	−0.159		0.056	−18.842
	(15.123)	(14.188)		(5.719)	(10.482)
Spread (Italy)	−10.374	−10.592		−10.046	−7.433
	(5.184)	(5.075)		(5.278)	(4.764)
Spread (Foreign)	20.386	−1.472		0.341	−6.138
	(7.733)	(5.546)		(4.159)	(3.293)
$\bar{R}^2$	0.085	0.034		0.034	0.071
S (All)	11.106	4.825		4.554	8.665
	(0.025)	(0.306)		(0.336)	(0.070)
S (Italy)	4.113	4.740		3.842	2.789
	(0.128)	(0.093)		(0.146)	(0.248)
S (Foreign)	8.138	0.071		0.007	5.730
	(0.017)	(0.965)		(0.996)	(0.057)

Table 7.6c. (*cont.*)

	France	Germany	Italy	US	UK
US					
Δi^{SR} (US)	−3.304	−4.870	−5.309		−4.437
	(4.504)	(4.393)	(4.290)		(4.172)
Δi^{SR} (Foreign)	−12.422	−11.489	8.524		0.663
	(8.126)	(12.491)	(5.743)		(4.625)
Spread (US)	1.395	1.194	2.037		2.942
	(2.268)	(2.878)	(2.265)		(1.895)
Spread (Foreign)	0.283	1.239	−3.181		−4.027
	(5.307)	(4.390)	(2.726)		(1.979)
$\bar{R}^2$	0.019	0.010	0.018		0.022
S (All)	7.956	3.238	6.319		8.326
	(0.093)	(0.519)	(0.177)		(0.080)
S (US)	0.853	1.613	2.181		3.619
	(0.653)	(0.446)	(0.336)		(0.164)
S (Foreign)	2.971	0.847	3.089		4.240
	(0.226)	(0.655)	(0.213)		(0.120)
UK					
Δi^{SR} (UK)	−24.743	−26.493	−26.818	−25.077	
	(7.238)	(6.847)	(7.088)	(6.978)	
Δi^{SR} (Foreign)	−9.846	3.543	19.469	0.925	
	(7.779)	(12.013)	(6.478)	(2.949)	
Spread (UK)	−0.113	−0.889	1.912	0.286	
	(2.263)	(1.968)	(1.980)	(2.119)	
Spread (Foreign)	1.017	2.210	−5.376	2.499	
	(5.611)	(3.233)	(2.551)	(2.001)	
$\bar{R}^2$	0.116	0.112	0.157	0.109	
S (All)	28.981	18.572	31.942	13.436	
	(0.000)	(0.001)	(0.000)	(0.009)	
S (UK)	12.250	15.010	15.892	12.978	
	(0.002)	(0.001)	(0.000)	(0.002)	
S (Foreign)	3.242	0.904	12.298	1.592	
	(0.198)	(0.636)	(0.002)	(0.451)	

Note: [a]See note to table 7.6a. Sample period is from March 1979 to December 1990.

The sub-sample results for the regressions of excess returns on home and foreign variables are reported in tables 7.6b and 7.6c. These results are of interest since they indicate that the influence of German financial variables on French excess returns has increased dramatically for the period of the EMS, whilst, although all foreign variables have significant explanatory power for Germany in sub-sample 1, such explanatory power disappears in the EMS period. The only other country which exhibits a dramatic change over the two periods is the UK. Thus, the high explanatory power of foreign variables, noted above, would seem to have its source in the early sub-sample; only German variables have an influence in the EMS sub-sample. This perhaps indicates the dominance of the German economy within Europe.

VII Some estimates of observable and unobservable factor models

In tables 7.7a–7.7c we present estimates of equation (13), the observable factor model. As we have seen, this model offers a simple extension of our previous model: if the predictability of domestic returns is simply due to the changing risk of an international risk factor, rather than the domestic and foreign forecast variables, then the addition of such a variable to our previous regression should render the other variables insignificant. As is clear from our tables, the international factor is highly significant across countries and time periods and, in a few cases (UK – full sample, and UK, France, and Italy – sub-sample) the coefficient on the international factor is insignificantly different from unity (the S1's). What is less clear, however, is the difference the international variable makes to the significance of the other variables: in some cases the significance drops (see France for the full sample) whilst for others the significance remains largely unchanged (see, for example, the UK for the full sample). A broadly similar pattern emerges for the two sub-samples.

Finally, we examine some results for the unobservable factor model, (14), over our full- and sub-sample periods. As we have seen, this model imposes the testable restriction that expected excess stock returns are perfectly correlated across countries. The results are reported in table 7.8 for two different center countries (namely, the US and Germany) using the same forecasting variables as in table 7.7. All the equations have been normalized on the center country; that is, the β for the center country is set equal to one. The remaining free coefficients are the β on the "home country" and the θ's on the forecasting variables. On the basis of a 5 percent significance level, there are a number of rejections of the restrictions when short rates are used as instruments. The model rejects less often for the UK when Germany is the center country, but there is no clear cut pattern for the EMS countries:

Table 7.7a. *Observable factor model for excess stock returns on stock returns, interest rates and long–short spreads*[a]

	France	Germany	Italy	US	UK
France					
Constant		−0.004	−0.001	−0.001	−0.003
		(0.005)	(0.005)	(0.005)	(0.005)
XR st/mkt (Foreign)		0.530	0.157	0.557	0.245
		(0.106)	(0.086)	(0.174)	(0.247)
Δi^{SR} (France)		−34.327	−37.511	−26.893	−30.621
		(14.784)	(14.019)	(12.538)	(13.457)
Δi^{SR} (Foreign)		27.146	2.437	−4.392	11.998
		(14.607)	(9.944)	(5.332)	(9.272)
Spread (France)		1.296	0.664	2.457	2.884
		(5.391)	(5.166)	(5.418)	(6.167)
Spread (Foreign)		0.676	3.926	−0.832	−1.075
		(2.993)	(3.100)	(3.239)	(2.484)
$\bar{R}^2$		0.161	0.086	0.156	0.095
S (0) All		9.245	15.032	6.731	9.282
		(0.055)	(0.004)	(0.151)	(0.054)
S (0) Δi^{SR}		6.100	7.205	5.042	5.676
		(0.047)	(0.027)	(5.042)	(5.676)
S (0) spread		0.322	2.137	0.206	0.251
		(0.851)	(0.344)	(0.902)	(0.882)
S (1)		19.809	96.053	6.454	9.290
		(0.000)	(0.000)	(0.011)	(0.002)
Germany					
Constant	−0.003		−0.003	−0.002	−0.001
	(0.003)		(0.003)	(0.003)	(0.003)
XR st/mkt (Foreign)	0.173		0.181	0.381	0.270
	(0.067)		(0.059)	(0.123)	(0.110)
Δi^{SR} (Germany)	−11.983		−11.864	−7.437	−8.350
	(8.095)		(6.943)	(6.500)	(6.631)
Δi^{SR} (Foreign)	0.304		2.435	1.249	3.098
	(5.392)		(3.710)	(2.665)	(6.288)
Spread (Germany)	2.159		4.277	1.270	3.734
	(1.567)		(1.483)	(1.863)	(1.728)
Spread (Foreign)	2.457		0.605	1.751	−2.670
	(2.807)		(0.163)	(1.791)	(1.251)
$\bar{R}^2$	0.122		0.115	0.170	0.177
S (0) All	5.489		11.907	6.102	9.798
	(0.241)		(0.018)	(0.192)	(0.044)
S (0) Δi^{SR}	2.729		3.832	1.881	2.612
	(0.255)		(0.147)	(0.390)	(0.271)

Table 7.7a. (*cont.*)

	France	Germany	Italy	US	UK
S (0) spread	3.908		8.933	3.553	5.898
	(0.142)		(0.011)	(0.169)	(0.052)
S (1)	154.694		192.650	25.299	43.964
	(0.000)		(0.000)	(0.000)	(0.000)
Italy					
Constant	−0.001	−0.002		−0.004	−0.003
	(0.006)	(0.006)		(0.005)	(0.005)
XR st/mkt (Foreign)	0.135	0.534		0.530	0.339
	(0.089)	(0.103)		(0.124)	(0.094)
Δi^{SR} (Italy)	−14.966	−18.106		−16.738	−9.084
	(6.921))	(6.933)		(6.958)	(7.047)
Δi^{SR} (Foreign)	22.302	20.312		6.307	−10.957
	(11.992)	(10.094)		(5.737)	(8.175)
Spread (Italy)	−3.196	−1.689		−1.618	0.574
	(2.759)	(2.696)		(2.544)	(2.608)
Spread (Foreign)	12.739	−4.512		−0.778	−6.361
	(5.082)	(3.007)		(2.763)	(1.949)
$\bar{R}^2$	0.068	0.116		0.098	0.141
S (0) All	10.841	12.451		6.853	13.597
	(0.028)	(0.014)		(0.114)	(0.009)
S (0) Δi^{SR}	6.454	9.457		6.674	3.268
	(0.040)	(0.009)		(0.036)	(0.195)
S (0) spread	6.308	3.085		0.560	10.903
	(0.043)	(0.214)		(0.756)	(0.004)
S (1)	93.789	20.369		14.264	49.213
	(0.000)	(0.000)		(0.000)	(0.000)
US					
Constant	−0.006	−0.003	−0.003		−0.001
	(0.003)	(0.003)	(0.003)		(0.002)
XR st/mkt (Foreign)	0.172	0.362	0.166		0.428
	(0.060)	(0.081)	(0.043)		(0.046)
Δi^{SR} (US)	−4.455	−4.444	−5.994		−5.012
	(4.319)	(3.823)	(3.892)		(3.367)
Δi^{SR} (Foreign)	2.228	0.574	3.486		13.212
	(4.971)	(6.194)	(3.775)		(3.222)
Spread (US)	2.710	4.247	4.668		2.139
	(1.724)	(2.327)	(1.462)		(1.439)
Spread (Foreign)	4.842	−1.543	1.164		−2.044
	(3.244)	(2.378)	(1.391)		(0.920)
$\bar{R}^2$	0.164	0.188	0.142		0.385

Table 7.7a. (*cont.*)

	France	Germany	Italy	US	UK
S (0) All	9.800	7.581	14.815		28.724
	(0.044)	(0.108)	(0.005)		(0.000)
S (0) Δi^{SR}	1.111	1.363	3.134		17.976
	(0.574)	(0.506)	(0.209)		(0.000)
S (0) spread	8.417	4.637	10.246		5.498
	(0.015)	(0.098)	(0.006)		(0.064)
S (1)	187.823	61.616	374.667		153.747
	(0.000)	(0.000)	(0.000)		(0.000)
UK					
Constant	−0.006	−0.004	0.000	−0.002	
	(0.003)	(0.003)	(0.004)	(0.003)	
XR st/mkt (Foreign)	0.139	0.499	0.214	0.791	
	(0.125)	(0.164)	(0.082)	(0.134)	
Δi^{SR} (UK)	−30.783	−29.692	−26.801	−30.683	
	(5.701)	(5.403)	(5.884)	(4.768)	
Δi^{SR} (Foreign)	−4.117	2.370	−10.621	4.350	
	(7.296)	(11.024)	(7.910)	(3.636)	
Spread (UK)	−0.874	−0.194	0.483	1.191	
	(1.713)	(2.053)	(2.290)	(1.620)	
Spread (Foreign)	12.962	3.321	2.735	3.461	
	(3.664)	(2.385)	(2.530)	(2.019)	
$\bar{R}^2$	0.223	0.260	0.220	0.454	
S (0) All	36.213	36.353	32.446	51.257	
	(0.000)	(0.000)	(0.000)	(0.000)	
S (0) Δi^{SR}	29.162	32.074	21.751	46.203	
	(0.000)	(0.000)	(0.000)	(0.000)	
S (0) spread	12.889	2.496	2.769	6.424	
	(0.000)	(0.287)	(0.250)	(0.040)	
S (1)	47.580	9.299	92.901	2.447	
	(0.000)	(0.002)	(0.000)	(0.118)	

Note: [a]All regressions include a constant and January dummy, Heteroskedastic-consistent errors are reported in parentheses. S (0) All denotes the joint significance of the short-run interest rates and interest rate spreads under the null hypothesis of zero significance while S (0) Δi^{SR} denotes the joint significance of the short run interest rates, and S (0) spread denotes the joint significance of interest rate spreads. S (1) denotes the significance of the observable international factor under the null hypothesis that the coefficient is equal to 1. See table 7.1a for sample periods.

Table 7.7b. *Observable factor model for excess stock returns on stock returns, interest rates, and long–short spreads (1972–9)[a]*

	France	Germany	Italy	US	UK
France					
Constant		−0.003	−0.010	−0.010	−0.035
		(0.010)	(0.088)	(0.011)	(0.020)
XR st/mkt (Foreign)		0.467	0.117	0.177	−0.068
		(0.256)	(0.110)	(0.362)	(0.324)
Δi^{SR} (France)		−30.712	−32.793	−25.016	−21.972
		(22.030)	(18.202)	(17.808)	(17.858)
Δi^{SR} (Foreign)		16.571	1.129	−6.826	−1.537
		(22.259)	(11.439)	(27.761)	(16.249)
Spread (France)		11.339	5.937	15.026	10.617
		(7.411)	(8.484)	(8.604)	(9.193)
Spread (Foreign)		−5.926	3.529	−5.486	7.275
		(4.445)	(6.771)	(7.018)	(6.839)
$\bar{R}^2$		0.132	0.112	0.103	0.107
S (0) All		7.543	12.689	8.116	6.693
		(0.110)	(0.013)	(0.087)	(0.153)
S (0) Δi^{SR}		2.149	3.248	1.975	1.865
		(0.342)	(0.197)	(0.373)	(0.394)
S (0) spread		2.453	3.947	3.733	5.494
		(0.293)	(0.139)	(0.155)	(0.064)
S (1)		4.354	64.482	5.519	10.837
		(0.037)	(0.000)	(0.023)	(0.001)
Germany					
Constant	−0.009		−0.010	−0.007	−0.009
	(0.005)		(0.004)	(0.004)	(0.007)
XR st/mkt (Foreign)	0.067		0.119	0.170	0.114
	(0.048)		(0.039)	(0.079)	(0.040)
Δi^{SR} (Germany)	−29.029		−27.481	−24.213	−18.728
	(9.169)		(7.654)	(7.650)	(6.956)
Δi^{SR} (Foreign)	3.698		−0.103	−6.430	−10.541
	(5.656)		(2.980)	(8.336)	(4.860)
Spread (Germany)	1.525		5.049	0.893	3.745
	(2.388)		(1.874)	(2.237)	(1.698)
Spread (Foreign)	7.460		2.446	4.386	0.268
	(3.005)		(1.186)	(2.093)	(2.143)
$\bar{R}^2$	0.302		0.326	0.318	0.349
S (0) All	19.261		25.670	23.793	20.571
	(0.001)		(0.000)	(0.000)	(0.000)
S (0) Δi^{SR}	10.117		12.902	13.291	14.226
	(0.001)		(0.002)	(0.001)	(0.001)

Table 7.7b. (*cont.*)

	France	Germany	Italy	US	UK
S (0) spread	13.048		13.193	10.737	5.741
	(0.001)		(0.001)	(0.005)	(0.057)
S (1)	384.096		519.452	111.196	493.501
	(0.000)		(0.000)	(0.000)	(0.000)
Italy					
Constant	−0.011	−0.000		−0.006	0.021
	(0.008)	(0.010)		(0.008)	(0.017)
XR st/mkt (Foreign)	0.098	0.664		0.541	0.198
	(0.110)	(0.240)		(0.168)	(0.068)
Δi^{SR} (Italy)	−17.980	−15.447		−17.876	−8.669
	(8.708)	(7.512)		(8.351)	(7.385)
Δi^{SR} (Foreign)	20.101	39.283		17.409	−25.774
	(15.224)	(15.656)		(19.593)	(13.236)
Spread (Italy)	4.902	2.227		3.699	5.130
	(4.523)	(3.323)		(3.545)	(3.023)
Spread (Foreign)	−2.199	−6.757		−6.235	−9.760
	(7.401)	(4.024)		(4.222) .	(4.807)
$\bar{R}^2$	0.043	0.129		0.099	0.132
S (0) All	8.680	18.626		7.162	9.436
	(0.069)	(0.001)		(0.128)	(0.051)
S (0) Δi^{SR}	4.650	8.450		4.606	4.624
	(0.098)	(0.015)		(0.100)	(0.099)
S (0) spread	1.897	2.958		2.322	6.486
	(0.387)	(0.228)		(0.313)	(0.039)
S (1)	66.722	1.963		7.496	82.348
	(0.000)	(0.161)		(0.006)	(0.000)
US					
Constant	−0.010	−0.006	−0.008		−0.009
	(0.005)	(0.005)	(0.005)		(0.009)
XR st/mkt (Foreign)	0.040	0.277	0.148		0.322
	(0.083)	(0.137)	(0.054)		(0.434)
Δi^{SR} (US)	−18.482	−10.454	−18.325		−7.405
	(13.467)	(11.915)	(11.577)		(8.518)
Δi^{SR} (Foreign)	8.905	8.260	4.005		13.414
	(7.870)	(9.722)	(4.063)		(5.263)
Spread (US)	4.338	9.052	7.584		3.864
	(3.024)	(4.060)	(2.227)		(2.264)
Spread (Foreign)	7.649	−3.056	1.930		0.302
	(4.167)	(3.318)	(1.491)		(2.811)

Table 7.7b. (*cont.*)

	France	Germany	Italy	US	UK
$\bar{R}^2$	0.197	0.209	0.244		0.415
Q (27)	48.997	45.737	48.055		29.308
	(0.006)	(0.014)	(0.008)		(0.346)
S (0) All	17.182	17.468	16.887		11.834
	(0.002)	(0.002)	(0.002)		(0.019)
S (0) Δi^{SR}	2.955	1.308	3.318		8.075
	(0.228)	(0.520)	(0.190)		(0.018)
S (0) spread	14.159	6.740	13.126		3.580
	(0.001)	(0.343)	(0.001)		(0.167)
S (1)	133.146	27.983	249.919		243.326
	(0.000)	(0.000)	(0.000)		(0.000)
UK					
Constant	0.000	−0.009	0.016	0.008	
	(0.017)	(0.017)	(0.017)	(0.014)	
XR st/mkt (Foreign)	−0.046	0.659	0.177	0.942	
	(0.229)	(0.269)	(0.116)	(0.257)	
Δi^{SR} (UK)	−45.775	−29.566	−32.213	−37.769	
	(11.653)	(10.915)	(9.323)	(9.598)	
Δi^{SR} (Foreign)	−12.411	4.671	−20.420	−3.332	
	(12.309)	(18.591)	(11.897)	(14.328)	
Spread (UK)	−3.058	0.992	5.251	−2.341	
	(5.525)	(6.119)	(5.731)	(4.385)	
Spread (Foreign)	21.862	3.863	4.473	7.188	
	(4.812)	(3.969)	(3.770)	(4.233)	
$\bar{R}^2$	0.281	0.205	0.281	0.483	
S (0) All	27.903	11.823	36.462	26.329	
	(0.000)	(0.019)	(0.000)	(0.000)	
S (0) Δi^{SR}	15.525	8.105	14.445	15.491	
	(0.000)	(0.017)	(0.001)	(0.000)	
S (0) spread	20.753	1.715	3.511	3.004	
	(0.000)	(0.424)	(0.173)	(0.223)	
S (1)	20.896	1.694	50.699	0.052	
	(0.000)	(0.193)	(0.000)	(0.820)	

Note: [a]See note to table 7.7a. See table 7.1b for sample periods.

Table 7.7c. *Observable factor model for excess stock returns on stock returns, interest rates, and long–short spreads, 1979–90*[a]

	France	Germany	Italy	US	UK
France					
Constant		0.000	0.010	0.005	0.003
		(0.007)	(0.008)	(0.006)	(0.007)
XR st/mkt (Foreign)		0.490	0.207	0.731	0.582
		(0.120)	(0.121)	(0.160)	(0.103)
Δi^{SR} (France)		−36.609	−40.938	−23.096	−30.522
		(16.989)	(17.403)	(15.698)	(15.928)
Δi^{SR} (Foreign)		28.988	10.449	−3.804	24.694
		(17.260)	(12.781)	(5.361)	(10.097)
Spread (France)		−8.930	−9.804	−5.116	−2.168
		(7.148)	(7.669)	(7.185)	(7.291)
Spread (Foreign)		8.839	1.381	0.945	−1.561
		(4.321)	(3.807)	(3.407)	(3.628)
$\bar{R}^2$		0.190	0.065	0.225	0.182
S (0) All		6.301	5.616	3.642	8.612
		(0.178)	(0.230)	(0.457)	(0.716)
S (0) Δi^{SR}		4.685	5.534	3.091	8.257
		(0.096)	(0.063)	(0.213)	(0.161)
S (0) spread		4.412	1.637	0.511	0.549
		(0.110)	(0.441)	(0.775)	(0.760)
S (1)		18.191	42.848	2.813	16.584
		(0.000)	(0.000)	(0.093)	(0.000)
Germany					
Constant	0.002		−0.001	0.001	−0.001
	(0.004)		(0.004)	(0.003)	(0.003)
XR st/mkt (Foreign)	0.236		0.217	0.492	0.458
	(0.109)		(0.097)	(0.170)	(0.178)
Δi^{SR} (Germany)	−0.240		2.379	12.728	−6.434
	(10.091)		(9.906)	(11.411)	(7.926)
Δi^{SR} (Foreign)	−2.315		12.359	4.620	13.376
	(8.301)		(9.489)	(3.194)	(8.215)
Spread (Germany)	1.064		3.133	−2.824	2.700
	(3.333)		(3.048)	(3.929)	(2.633)
Spread (Foreign)	−1.246		−1.396	4.480	−4.121
	(4.157)		(2.467)	(2.078)	(1.908)
$\bar{R}^2$	0.098		0.095	0.176	0.198
S (0) All	0.255		2.950	8.005	11.204
	(0.993)		(0.566)	(0.091)	(0.024)
S (0) Δi^{SR}	0.128		1.718	2.390	2.812
	(0.938)		(0.424)	(0.303)	(0.245)

Table 7.7c. (*cont.*)

	France	Germany	Italy	US	UK
S (0) spread	0.179		1.595	5.935	5.488
	(0.914)		(0.450)	(0.051)	(0.064)
S (1)	49.475		65.673	8.885	9.272
	(0.000)		(0.000)	(0.003)	(0.002)
Italy					
Constant	−0.020	−0.006		−0.006	−0.005
	(0.008)	(0.008)		(0.007)	(0.006)
XR st/mkt (Foreign)	0.175	0.502		0.496	0.488
	(0.120)	(0.127)		(0.364)	(0.148)
Δi^{SR} (Italy)	−3.179	−15.312		−13.172	−16.990
	(11.367)	(16.353)		(15.672)	(14.355)
Δi^{SR} (Foreign)	21.895	−1.336		2.687	−5.762
	(15.563)	(12.077)		(6.614)	(10.065)
Spread (Italy)	−7.411	−8.738		−8.470	−4.811
	(4.300)	(5.117)		(4.916)	(4.569)
Spread (Foreign)	21.775	−2.885		−0.669	−7.070
	(7.369)	(5.476)		(3.970)	(8.156)
$\bar{R}^2$	0.111	0.133		0.108	0.156
S (0) All	9.781	3.955		4.156	8.334
	(0.044)	(0.412)		(0.385)	(0.080)
S (0) Δi^{SR}	2.000	0.909		0.935	2.084
	(0.369)	(0.635)		(0.627)	(0.353)
S (0) spread	9.052	3.050		3.312	6.842
	(0.011)	(0.218)		(0.209)	(0.033)
S (1)	(0.000)	(0.000)		(0.002)	(0.001)
US					
Constant	−0.002	0.000	−0.002		−0.002
	(0.003)	(0.004)	(0.004)		(0.003)
XR st/mkt (Foreign)	0.272	0.389	0.168		0.550
	(0.061)	(0.098)	(0.006)		(0.066)
Δi^{SR} (US)	−1.522	−5.734	−5.319		−4.946
	(4.452)	(3.936)	(4.298)		(3.484)
Δi^{SR} (Foreign)	−2.910	−14.241	10.029		14.457
	(7.321)	(11.066)	(5.862)		(3.823)
Spread (US)	0.961	−0.778	1.979		1.567
	(2.423)	(2.732)	(2.158)		(1.901)
Spread (Foreign)	1.496	2.100	−1.491		−4.184
	(4.839)	(4.062)	(2.652)		(1.605)
$\bar{R}^2$	0.204	0.194	0.093		0.383
S (0) All	1.578	3.853	5.384		27.239
	(0.813)	(0.426)	(0.250)		(0.000)

Table 7.7c. (*cont.*)

	France	Germany	Italy	US	UK
S (0) Δi^{SR}	0.400	3.587	3.823		15.189
	(0.819)	(0.166)	(0.148)		(0.001)
S (0) spread	0.390	0.289	0.989		6.804
	(0.823)	(0.865)	(0.370)		(0.033)
S (1)	140.703	38.737	191.595		46.095
	(0.000)	(0.000)	(0.000)		(0.000)
UK					
Constant	−0.001	−0.001	−0.002	0.000	
	(0.004)	(0.003)	(0.004)	(0.003)	
XR st/mkt (Foreign)	0.263	0.451	0.202	0.679	
	(0.099)	(0.196)	(0.108)	(0.144)	
Δi^{SR} (UK)	−26.870	−27.049	−23.014	−25.527	
	(6.324)	(5.789)	(7.337)	(5.438)	
Δi^{SR} (Foreign)	−0.223	3.101	20.982	3.937	
	(6.575)	(9.267)	(6.345)	(2.848)	
Spread (UK)	0.459	1.154	3.151	3.020	
	(2.171)	(2.143)	(1.875)	(1.750)	
Spread (Foreign)	1.551	1.011	−3.875	0.502	
	(4.904)	(3.066)	(2.695)	(2.227)	
$\bar{R}^2$	0.239	0.290	0.234	0.437	
S (0) All	20.208	26.977	38.197	37.896	
	(0.000)	(0.000)	(0.000)	(0.000)	
S (0) Δi^{SR}	18.379	21.954	27.549	26.575	
	(0.000)	(0.000)	(0.000)	(0.000)	
S (0) spread	0.261	0.661	4.033	4.139	
	(0.878)	(0.740)	(0.133)	(0.126)	
S (1)	55.250	7.832	54.468	4.940	
	(0.000)	(0.005)	(0.000)	(0.026)	

Note: [a]See note to table 7.7a. See note to table 7.1c for sample periods.

there are two rejections for Italy, regardless of the center country, a sub-sample 1 rejection for Germany when the US is the center country and a full sample rejection for France when Germany is the center country. Interestingly, there are no rejections of the model when the spread specification is used and, additionally, there are a greater number of significant β's with this specification. This is perhaps a reflection of the richer information set provided by the spread. However, given our methods of control, these results do not aid in our understanding of capital-market integration in Europe, since on this basis capital-market integration would seem to be as strong for the non-ERM participants.

Summary and conclusions

In this chapter we have been concerned to examine two themes relating to excess stock returns: first, the extent to which excess stock returns in certain key European countries are predictable and, second, the interrelatedness of such stock returns between our chosen countries. Different methods were used to assess each of these factors and different sample periods were used to address the effect that the EMS has had on the integration process in Europe. Given the large amount of results generated in the chapter, we now highlight our salient findings and present an overall conclusion which we believe to be representative of our results.

Some simple descriptive statistics, presented in section IV, indicated a substantial amount of international capital-market integration and this seemed strongest for European countries relative to the US, compared to the intra-European relationships.

Using the multivariate cointegration methodology of Johansen (1988), we examined the issue of capital-market integration from a slightly different perspective to our main testing methodology (this was viewed as an extension of our simple sample correlations). Using this methodology we found evidence of capital-market integration in terms of cointegration of short and long interest rates and stock prices. For short rates such integration seemed to be driven by the interaction of the European countries; however, for the stock price set, US prices appeared to be important in providing a unique cointegrating relationship. Furthermore, little evidence could be adduced from these results that capital-market integration had increased during the EMS period.

Some simple regression based tests, presented in section VI, indicated that domestic variables, such as the yield spread, do have significant explanatory power for excess returns (and, in particular, the yield spread had forecasting power over and above that provided independently by short and long interest rates). Thus in common with the vast US literature (see note 3) excess returns in Europe would seem to have a predictable element. Further, some evidence of the effect of the EMS could be adduced from these regressions since they indicated that domestic variables had less predictive power during the EMS period relative to the pre-EMS period. On introducing foreign variables into these regressions we found that, in terms of the full sample, there was clear evidence of such variables affecting domestic excess returns for the UK, perhaps reflecting the importance of

Table 7.8. *Unobservable factor model*[a]

1A Short rate specification (US center)

	France			Germany			Italy			UK		
	Full	1	2	Full	1	2	Full	1	2	Full	1	2
β	2.45	0.62	2.15	0.73	0.76	0.00	0.53	0.58	−0.28	1.36	1.91	−0.09
	(2.48)	(0.38)	(2.26)	(1.68)	(1.51)	(0.02)	(0.88)	(0.92)	(0.24)	(1.89)	(2.11)	(0.12)
R1	0.98	3.94	0.01	2.53	9.04	0.00	4.35	4.22	0.54	25.48	6.97	8.17
	(0.32)	(0.47)	(0.92)	(0.11)	(0.00)	(1.00)	(0.04)	(0.04)	(0.46)	(0.00)	(0.01)	(0.00)

1B Short rate specification (Germany center)

	France			Italy			UK			US		
	Full	1	2	Full	1	2	Full	1	2	Full	1	2
β	1.52	0.18	3.16	0.06	−0.21	−1.52	3.08	1.85	−6.28	0.78	0.21	16.85
	(1.46)	(0.21)	(1.37)	(0.08)	(0.38)	(0.48)	(2.49)	(3.64)	(0.49)	(1.73)	(0.68)	(0.08)
R1	3.71	3.16	0.09	5.71	7.78	1.07	7.54	2.54	0.24	2.13	2.92	3.39
	(0.05)	(0.08)	(0.76)	(0.02)	(0.01)	(0.30)	(0.01)	(0.11)	(0.62)	(0.14)	(0.09)	(0.07)

2A Spread specification (US center)

	France			Germany			Italy			UK		
	Full	1	2	Full	1	2	Full	1	2	Full	1	2
β	0.67	1.33	1.57	0.75	0.64	1.07	0.50	0.96	0.58	1.15	1.85	1.86
	(0.67)	(0.44)	(1.14)	(3.03)	(2.87)	(1.49)	(0.94)	(1.67)	(0.34)	(3.72)	(4.13)	(0.64)
R1	0.25	3.48	0.08	0.03	0.14	0.12	0.42	1.85	0.13	0.34	0.12	1.40
	(0.62)	(0.06)	(0.78)	(0.86)	(0.71)	(0.73)	(0.52)	(0.17)	(0.72)	(0.56)	(0.73)	(0.24)

2B Spread specification (Germany center)

	France			Italy			UK			US		
	Full	1	2	Full	1	2	Full	1	2	Full	1	2
β	4.05	2.18	2.76	0.79	1.99	3.42	0.69	1.34	−0.69	1.33	1.52	0.89
	(0.78)	(2.15)	(1.13)	(0.59)	(1.68)	(0.58)	(1.48)	(2.49)	(0.71)	(3.02)	(2.93)	(1.46)
R1	0.18	0.52	0.03	3.11	0.18	0.44	0.33	0.01	1.17	0.04	0.23	0.09
	(0.67)	(0.47)	(0.86)	(0.08)	(0.67)	(0.51)	(0.57)	(0.92)	(0.78)	(0.84)	(0.63)	(0.76)

Note: $^a\beta$ denotes the estimated country loading of the excess stock return on a single unobserved factor (standard error in parentheses) and R1 denotes a test of the overidentifying restrictions discussed in the text (marginal significance level in parentheses).

the UK as a financial centre (although this effect was most prominent for sub-sample 1): there was little evidence of international variables influencing our other countries' excess returns. The results from these regressions do, however, change quite dramatically for the sub-sample periods. Thus, for the EMS period we find that the influence of German financial variables on French excess returns increases dramatically for the EMS period and the significance of foreign variables in German excess returns for the pre-EMS period disappears completely for the EMS period.

Our estimates of the observable factor models suggest that the explanatory power of domestic variables had as its source the changing risk of an international factor and this result seemed to hold regardless of the foreign country taken to represent the international factor. This finding seemed to be reinforced by our unobservable factor model where an international factor seemed to be important for the European countries regardless of the source of this factor, i.e., US or Germany (although the model seemed to reject less often for the UK when the German factor is taken to be the international factor).

In conclusion, we have found fairly strong evidence that excess returns for a number of European countries contain a substantial predictable element. Our tests also showed that one interpretation of our predictability could be seen in terms of a common international risk factor. European capital markets do indeed, therefore, seem to exhibit a substantial degree of capital-market integration. However, such integration seems, by and large, to be as strong for European countries relative to the US as it is relative to the commonly accepted anchor of the EMS, namely Germany. Additionally, this integration does not seem to have been greatly affected by the EMS. Perhaps, then, closer integration within Europe has to await the political decision by the member countries of the EC to subsume their national currencies into a common currency.

Notes

We are very grateful to Colin Fraser for his efficient research assistance.

1 In efficient capital markets, integration can arise either through the perfect mobility of financial assets which firms then use to finance real investment projects, or, more directly, via foreign direct investment of savings and real investment projects. Mergers with foreign firms and foreign listings would also serve to reduce the segmentation of national capital markets. This is discussed in more detail in section II.

2 A large amount of research has been conducted on the predictability of US excess returns, but, to our knowledge, none has been conducted for the European countries considered in this chapter.

3 See Fama and French, 1989, for a discussion of the interrelatedness of stock returns and the business cycle.

4 We do not review the literature on the predictability of excess returns in this chapter; see Balvers, Cosimano, and McDonald, 1990, for a useful survey.

5 See Jeon and Furstenberg (1990) for a discussion of the issues and limitations of recent research on the "segmented market" issue in the finance literature.

6 We have not incorporated dividends in our measure of returns because, given the way they are reported (i.e., annually or semi-annually), we do not believe they would add much to the variability of the overall returns series (see Lo and MacKinley, 1990, for supporting evidence). Further, obtaining dividend series for all the countries in our sample is somewhat problematic.

7 We also conducted unit root tests on the spread series (not reported). In every case the statistics suggested the series were stationary.

8 This result would seem to confirm the result of Artis and Taylor (1990) discussed above.

9 A number of researchers (see, for example, Fraser and Power, 1991) have suggested that the stock returns exhibit a January seasonal effect.

10 In all future regressions we include the January effect, even when this is not explicitly noted.

References

Aliber, R. (1973), "The Interest Rate Parity Theorem: A Re-interpretation," *Journal of Political Economy*, 81, pp. 1451–9.

Artis, M. and M.P. Taylor (1989), "Some Issues Concerning the Long-Run Credibility of the European Monetary System," in R. MacDonald and M.P. Taylor (eds.), *Exchange Rates and Open Economy Macroeconomics*, Oxford: Basil Blackwell.

(1990), "International Financial Stability and the Regulation of Capital Flows," in G. Bird (ed.), *The International Financial Regime*, Surrey University.

Balvers, R.J., T.F. Cosimano, and B. McDonald (1990), "Predicting Stock Returns in an Efficient Market," *Journal of Finance*, 45(4), pp. 1109–28.

Bayoumi, T. (1989), "Savings-Investment Correlations: Immobile Capital, Government Policy or Endogenous Behaviour?" International Monetary Fund, August.

Campbell, J.Y. and Y. Hamao (1989), "Predictable Stock Returns in the United States and Japan: A Study of Long-Term Capital Market Integration," L.S.E. Financial Markets Group, Discussion Paper No. 69.

Campbell, J.Y. and R.J. Shiller (1987), "Cointegration and Tests of Present Value Models," *Journal of Political Economy*, 95, pp. 1062–88.

Canzoneri, M. (1982), "Exchange Intervention in a Multiple Country World," *Journal of International Economics*, 13, pp. 267–89.

Cooper, S. (1991), "Cross-Border Savings Flows and Capital Mobility in the G7 Economies," Bank of England, Discussion Paper No. 54.

Cumby, R.E. and M. Obstfeld (1984), "International Interest Rates and Price Level Linkages Under Flexible Exchange Rates: A Review of Recent Evidence," in J. Bilson and R. Marston (eds.), *Exchange Rate Theory and Practice*, Chicago: University of Chicago Press.

Dean, A., M. Durand, J. Fallon, and P. Hoeller (1989), "Savings Trends and Behaviour in OECD Countries." OECD Department of Statistics, Working Paper No. 67.

Engle, R.F. and C.W.J. Granger (1987), "Cointegration and Error Correction Representation, Estimation and Testing," *Econometrica*, 34(5), pp. 1243–50.

Fama, E. and K.R. French (1989), "Dividend Yields and Expected Stock Returns," *Journal of Financial Economics*, 22, pp. 3–25.

Feldstein, M. (1983), "Domestic Saving and International Capital Movements in the Long Run and the Short Run," *European Economic Review*, 21(1/2).

Feldstein, M. and C. Horioka (1980), "Domestic Saving and International Capital Flows," *Economic Journal*, 90, pp. 314–29.

Frankel, J. (1989), "Quantifying International Capital Mobility in the 1980s," NBER, Working Paper No. 2856.

Frankel, J. and A. MacArthur (1988), "Political vs Currency Premia," *European Economic Review*, 23(5).

Frankel, J., M. Dooley, and D. Mathieson (1989), "International Capital Mobility in Developing Countries vs Industrial Countries: What do Savings Investment Correlations Tell Us?" NBER, Working Paper No. 2043.

Fraser, P. and M.P. Taylor (1990a), "Modelling Risk in the Interwar Foreign Exchange Market," *Scottish Journal of Political Economy*, 37(3), pp. 241–58.

  (1990b), "Some Efficient Tests of International Real Interest Parity," *Applied Economics*, 22(8), pp. 1083–92.

  (1991), "Some 'News' on Covered Interest Parity," forthcoming in M.P. Taylor (ed.), *Financial Markets*, Money Study Group.

Fraser, P. and D. Power (1991), "Predictability, Trends and Seasonalities: An Empirical Analysis of UK Investment Trust Portfolios 1970–1990," University of Dundee Discussion Papers in Accountancy and Business Finance, No. Fin/9101.

Frenkel, J.A. and R.M. Levich (1975), "Covered Interest Arbitrage: Unexploited Profits?", *Journal of Political Economy*, 83, pp. 325–38.

  (1977), "Transaction Costs and Interest Arbitrage: Tranquil versus Turbulent Periods," *Journal of Political Economy*, 85(6), pp. 1209–25.

Goodhart, C. (1988), "The International Transmission of Asset Price Volatility," in *Financial Market Volatility*, A Symposium Sponsored by the Federal Reserve Bank of Kansas City, Jackson Hole, Wyoming, pp. 79–119.

Hansen, L.P. (1982), "Large Sample Properties of Generalized Method of Moments Estimators," *Econometrica*, 50(4), pp. 1029–54.

Howe, J.S. and J. Madura (1989), "The Impact of International Listings on Risk Implications for Capital Market Integration," *Journal of Banking and Finance*, No. 14, pp. 1133–42.

Isard, P. (1983), "An Accounting Framework and Some Issues for Modelling How Exchange Rates Respond to News," in J.A. Frenkel (ed.), *Exchange Rates and International Macroeconomics*, NBER.

Jeon, B. and G. Furstenberg (1990), "Growing International Co-movement In Stock Price Indexes," *Quarterly Review of Economics and Business*, 30(3), pp. 15–30.

Johansen, S. (1988), "Statistical Analysis of cointegrating Vectors," *Journal of Economic Dynamics and Control*, No. 12, pp. 231–54.

Johansen, S. and K. Juselsius (1990), "Maximum Likelihood Estimation and Inference on Cointegration – With Applications to the Demand for Money," *Oxford Bulletin of Economics and Statistics*, No. 52, pp. 169–210.

King, M. and S. Wadhwani (1989), "Transmission of Volatility Between Stock Markets," Paper presented at NBER Conference on Stock Market Volatility and the Crash, Dorado, Puerto Rico.

MacDonald, R. and M.P. Taylor (1988), "The Term Structure of Forward Exchange Premia: The Interwar Experience," *The Manchester School*, 56(1), pp. 69–76.

(1989), "Economic Analysis of Foreign Exchange Markets: An Expository Survey," in R. MacDonald and M.P. Taylor (eds.), *Exchange Rates and Open Economy Macroeconomics*, Oxford: Basil Blackwell.

(1991), "The Monetary Approach to the Exchange Rate: Long-Run Relationships and Coefficient Restrictions," *Economics Letters*, 37, pp. 179–85.

MacDonald, R. and T.S. Torrance (1989), "Some Survey Based Tests of Uncovered Interest Parity," in R. MacDonald and M.P. Taylor (eds.), *Exchange Rates and Open Economy Macroeconomics*, Oxford: Basil Blackwell.

(1990), "Expectations Formation and Risk in Four Foreign Exchange Markets," *Oxford Economic Papers*, 42, pp. 544–61.

Mishkin, F.S. (1981), "The Real Interest Rate: A Multi-Country Empirical Study," *Canadian Journal of Economics*, 17, pp. 283–311.

(1984), "Are Real Interest Rates Equal Across Countries? An Empirical Investigation of International Parity Conditions," *Journal of Finance*, 39, pp. 1345–57.

Obstfeld, M. (1986), "Capital Mobility in the World Economy: Theory and Measurement," *Carnegie-Rochester Conference Series on Public Policy*, Vol. 24.

Perron, P. (1988), "Trends and Random Walks in Macroeconomic Time Series: Further Evidence from a New Approach," *Journal of Economics Dynamics and Control*, 12, pp. 297–332.

Summers, L. (1989), "Tax Policy and International Competitiveness," in J. Frenkel (ed.), *International Aspects of Fiscal Policies*, University of Chicago Press.

Taylor, M.P. (1987), "Covered Interest Parity: A High Frequency, High Quality Data Study," *Economica*, 4, pp. 429–38.

(1989a), "Covered Interest Arbitrage and Market Turbulence: An Empirical Analysis," *Economic Journal*, 99, pp. 376–91.

(1989b), "Expectations Risk and Uncertainty in the Foreign Exchange Market: Some Results Based on Survey Data," *The Manchester School*, 57, pp. 142–53.

Wolfe, C.P. (1987), "Forward Exchange Rates, Expected Spot Rates, and Premia: A Signal Extraction Approach," *Journal of Finance*, 52, pp. 395–406.

IV EMU: The road from Maastricht

8 The European System of Central Banks after Maastricht

CHARLES A.E. GOODHART

Introduction

I shall start by asking in section I what *new* decisions about the structure and operations of the European System of Central Banks (ESCB) have emerged from Maastricht, besides the fact that previous outline drafts and proposals have now been transmuted into a signed Treaty. I identify four such innovations, of which the most important is the fixed timetable for starting stage 3 by January 1, 1999 at the latest (Article 109J, Para. 4 of the Treaty).

With the signing of the Treaty, and the protocol on the Statute of the European System of Central Banks, the objectives, structure, and governance of the ESCB have now been clearly spelt out and agreed. What still remains to be done is to work out exactly how the ESCB shall operate. This planning exercise is to be the job of the European Monetary Institute (EMI) over the next four years. Some of the issues that it will need to address on market operations, clearing and settlement, and prudential regulation are discussed in section II.

Arrangements for the EMI during stage 2, and for member states who have a derogation, i.e., they are unable to meet the convergence criteria, or unwilling in the case of the UK and Denmark to join stage 3, are set out in the Treaty and the relevant protocols. One important transitional issue has not yet been fully discussed. This concerns the move from the establishment of irrevocably fixed exchange rates (stage 3A) to a single European currency (stage 3B). I argue in section III that this move will take longer and be more difficult and costly than seems heretofore to have been realized. Note issue engenders seigniorage receipts, and I also criticize the agreed method of allocating these.

The Treaty establishes the independence of the ESCB, but leaves important questions open about the inter-relationships between domestic monetary policy and exchange-rate policy. I have, however, dealt with this subject at some considerable length, in a companion paper on "The External Dimension of the EMU" (1992). There is also the equally important question of the relationship with, and coordination of, (national) fiscal policies in conjunction with the ESCB's single European monetary policy. Once again, however, this is the subject of a companion paper on "Relationships between Monetary and Fiscal Policies in EMU" (1992). So I shall deal exceedingly briefly with these issues in section IV.

Finally, the central elements in the strategy of the ESCB are that it shall give over-riding priority to the achievement of price stability, and shall be independent of any political, or other public sector, body, or authority. While I am in broad agreement with the strategy, it does raise questions both about flexibility of operation and democratic accountability that are not necessarily answered in the best possible way in this Treaty. This is discussed in the concluding section V.

I   What was decided at Maastricht?

Considering the length and intensity of the discussions, relatively little that was new, with respect to the structure and role of the European System of Central Banks (ESCB), emerged from the process of negotiations culminating in the Maastricht Treaty of December 1991. The basic strategy had been outlined in the Delors Committee Report of May 1989, and agreed at the Rome Summit of October 1990. This was that the European Community (EC) should move through stages to the adoption of a single currency (ECU).

Given the elimination of exchange controls on capital movements as part of the 1992 process, a single currency implies a single EC interest rate. In order, therefore, to maintain proper monetary order in the EC, and to control both monetary growth and interest rates, a single currency requires a single locus, one center, for the determination of monetary policy. This locus must be the European central bank. Since this would be established from the voluntary union of national central banks, and with the example of the Federal Reserve System in the USA, this led naturally on to the concept of the European System of Central Banks, involving a European central bank (ECB) together with member national central banks forming the system, with a central board to run the ECB on a day-by-day basis, under the instructions and oversight of the council, consisting of the (six) board members and the individual national central bank governors. So much was largely an inevitable consequence, within the present policial context, of the prior decision to adopt a single currency.

That decision, to adopt a single currency, in turn could be presented as a logical concomitant and extension of the 1992 process to establish a single market. A single currency not only reduces barriers to trade (transactions costs and risks of currency fluctuations), but also makes (national) price differentials much more transparent, thereby potentially extending and improving the working of markets. What is less clear to me is how far the adoption of a single currency will in turn facilitate and induce pressures for further unification and centralization at the federal center, for example, in fiscal policy (briefly addressed subsequently in section IV), and also how far such subsequent, and partly consequential, steps were consciously foreseen and intended by the authors of the Delors Committee Report.

Had the ESCB been founded at an earlier date, if, say, the Werner Committee Report proposal had been successfully implemented, then its structural form, of ECB plus member NCBs, would in my view have been much the same.

Such a system is a natural consequence of a voluntary union of previously independent entities. What is different now, from what might have occurred twenty years ago, are two main features. The first is the absolute primacy placed upon the achievement of price stability. Twenty years ago there would more likely have been a list of objectives, including probably maintaining the internal and external value of the currency, the establishment of full employment, and ensuring the health and smooth working of the financial system. There would have been little guidance to central bankers in these earlier decades on the weight to place on these various objectives. Now the ordering of objectives is to be clearly lexicographic. As set out in Article 2, of the Protocol on the Statute of the ESCB agreed at Maastricht, "the primary objective of the ESCB shall be to maintain price stability." Only then, when this is achieved, i.e., "without prejudice to the objective of price stability," is the ESCB to "support the general economic policies . . . [and] the objectives of the Community as laid down in Article 2 of this Treaty" [i.e., the Maastricht Treaty]. Furthermore, the ESCB is specifically required "to act in accordance with the principle of an open market economy with free competition," an instruction which would not have figured before 1980 at least, but there is no mention now among the "Objectives" of the ESCB having any special responsibility for looking after the health of the financial (or banking) system, which would probably have been included in a similar pre-1980 document.

The second respect in which the present Treaty differs from that which could have been written two decades ago relates to the insistence of the present text on the absolute political independence of the ESCB, e.g., Article 7 of the Protocol and Article 107 of the Treaty. In view of the rather complicated political structure of the EC, e.g., involving Council, Commission and Parliament, it is quite difficult to imagine quite what form the relationships between the ESCB and the various Community and national political authorities might have taken twenty years ago, but it is unlikely that there would have been quite such emphasis on total independence from political control, then as now.

There are two reasons for both these new developments. The first is the key position of Germany in these negotiations. The independence of the Deutsche Bundesbank, and its concentration on the achievement of price stability,[1] are held to be responsible for its comparative success, and that of the German economy, in achieving a successful combination of comparatively low inflation and high economic growth. Partly because of its success (but also partly because of the relative size and position of the German economy), the EMS had become a system in which the Bundesbank and the deutsche mark were increasingly the hegemonic leader, as is again illustrated by the timing and pattern of interest-rate increases in December 1991. An alternative to the establishment of an ECU system would be one in which a deutsche mark bloc evolved, perhaps an increasingly likely outcome following the events in recent years in Eastern Europe. In any case it was patently clear that in economic terms the Germans have most to lose in abandoning their monetary independence to join the ECU/ESCB systems. Since Germany not only had most to lose, but also was the foremost (in both population and GDP per head) member of the EC, it was to be expected that they would insist that the ECB be constructed largely along the lines of the Bundesbank as a condition for their acceptance of the agreement.

The second reason, which is, perhaps, more ephemeral (as will be discussed further in section V), is that current academic theories about the optimal constitution and role of central banks provide complete support for the Bundesbank's, somewhat more intuitive, position. With there being no trade-off in the medium and longer-term between growth and employment on the one hand and inflation on the other (a vertical Phillips curve), the best that any authority with responsibility for controlling nominal variables can do is to achieve price stability. But the politicians, with increasingly short horizons and high discount rates, as elections loom ever closer, are likely to want them to kick-start the economy, to engineer a temporary boom, even at the expense of endangering not only current inflation, but, even worse, of imperilling expectations of future inflation (time inconsistency). This argument leads directly on to advocacy of a politically independent central bank, with long and non-renewable periods in office for the Board and Council members, in order to reinforce such independence (Articles 11 and 14 of the Protocol).

The outlines of the above were clearly visible in the Delors Committee Report, fleshed out in the Draft Treaty of the Committee of Central Bank

Governors completed toward the end of 1990, and effectively agreed at the Rome Summit. What then has Maastricht added? In one sense the question is invalid. Even though the basic structure of the ESCB may have been set out in the Committee's Draft, and agreed at Rome, it had yet to be confirmed in a solemn Treaty. The very fact that the Treaty has now been signed is, of itself, a new and important development.

Beyond that, I would claim that there are five additional elements in the Treaty that were not already in the 1990 Draft. First, there had remained certain areas of disagreement between the governors on the structure and constitution of the ESCB, which were flagged in the Draft by the use of square brackets. These have now mostly been resolved. One such disagreement was the relative weight to be given to the Board, as compared to the Council in the formulation of monetary policy, with the Bundesbank preferring to give more weight to the board and most other central banks preferring to assign the prime role to the council.[2] On this the Germans appear to have conceded to the others. Another area of some disagreement relates to the role of the ECB and ESCB in regulation, prudential arrangements, and lender of last resort functions (the latter term was *never* mentioned in the preparation of the Treaty). As discussed further in section II, such prudential questions have been left open for further evolutionary decision by the Treaty.

The second major additional decision incorporated into the Treaty is the precise definition of the convergence criteria, as set out in the two Protocols, the first on excessive deficits (with the 3 percent PSBR/GDP and 60 percent Debt/GDP ratios) and the second on the other criteria, as mentioned in Article 109F (average rate of inflation not more than 1.5 percent over the three best countries in the preceding year; exchange rate in the narrow margins without a downwards realignment against any other member, or any severe tension, for at least the previous two years; average long-term interest rates not more than 2 percent above the best three members for the previous year). Another criterion is that each member state must have ensured, at the latest by the date of the establishment of the ESCB, that its national legislation, including the statutes of its national central bank, is compatible with the Treaty and the Protocol of the ESCB (Article 14.1 of the Protocol of the ESCB).

The Protocol specifically relating to the UK (i.e., the opt-out clause), however, states that Article 14, *inter alia*, of the Protocol on the ESCB shall not apply to the UK until Parliament has taken its separate decision to move to the third stage. Consequently, the government here can continue to maintain the existing relationship between the Bank and Whitehall, until Parliament decides to enter the third stage. Once this decision has been taken, however, the UK would not be allowed to enter stage 3, even if all the other criteria were met until the independence of the Bank had been established by Act of Parliament. In the meantime all other EC countries, including Denmark, which has a Protocol providing for a referendum before entry, are committed to (any necessary) legislation to give their national central banks full independence from political control by the date of the formation of the ESCB, January 1, 1999 at the latest.

Of these convergence criteria, the debt ratio of 60 percent looks the highest hurdle, with many EC countries who might otherwise seem prime candidates for early entry, e.g., Belgium, Denmark, and Ireland, stranded well above that level. But both the reference values for the PSBR/GDP and debt/GDP ratios are subject to further assessment, in the case of the deficit:

Whether the ratio has not declined substantially and continuously, and has not reached a level that comes close to the reference value;
or alternatively whether the excess over the reference value is only exceptional and temporary and the deficit remains close to the reference value.

And in the case of the debt ratios, "whether the ratio is not sufficiently diminishing and not approaching the reference value at a satisfactory pace" [Article 104C, Para. 2].

These qualifying clauses are full of adverbs, such as "substantially," "continuously," "exceptional," "sufficiently," etc., so that the decision on whether the criteria have been met, or not, will be in some large part a discretionary judgment.

The third major advance, achieved at Maastricht, has been to establish not only a procedure for making such judgments, but also a timetable with a fixed terminus ad quem for moving from stage 2 to stage 3. Thus stage 2 is to start on January 1, 1994 (Article 109E). At the start of stage 2 the European Monetary Institute (EMI) will be established. Among its other functions (to be considered shortly below), the EMI will be responsible, alongside the Commission, for preparing a report to the Council on progress made in achieving the convergence criteria. Such a report must be put before the Council not later than December 31, 1996. Then, the Council, of Heads of State, must decide, by a qualified majority, "whether a majority of the Member States fulfils the necessary conditions for the adoption of a single currency" (i.e., seven out of thirteen), and, if so, "whether it is appropriate for the Community to enter the third stage of economic and monetary union." The second decision does not necessarily follow automatically if the first condition is met. A single currency group which excluded the deutsche mark would be somewhat problematical, and it is conceivable, just, in theory that Germany might not meet all the criteria, e.g., because of an excessive deficit, while seven other member states did meet them.

More likely is that a combination of debt ratio and inflation differential criteria might have prevented a majority of seven countries becoming eligible for some, potentially open-ended, long period of time. Indeed it had, perhaps, been the expectation (hope) of the UK authorities that stage 2 would, perforce, continue so long that the momentum to EMU would wither on the vine. Certainly *the* innovation, in the context of EMU/ESCB, achieved at the Maastricht Treaty negotiations is contained in Article 109J, Para. 4, whereby, if by end 1997 a date for stage 3 has not been set, it will start, come what may, on January 1, 1999 with whatever states are then eligible for membership. Whilst this extra clause, in effect, blows up the majority requirement and ensures a "two-speed Europe," its success does in practice depend on both Germany and one other large member state being part of the core. As earlier asserted, without the deutsche mark, such a group would be broken-backed: while if Germany was the only large eligible member state, the new group would just be seen as a deutsche mark bloc.

One of the main gaps in the 1990 Draft Treaty of the central bank governors had related to the transitional steps for moving from stage 2 to stage 3. As noted above, the procedures, and timetable, for moving to stage 3 have now been agreed. Indeed my fourth choice for one of the key decisions and developments agreed at Maastricht related to the transitional arrangements, both with respect to stage 2 itself, and to the treatment of member states with a derogation, i.e., unable (or in the case of UK and Denmark unwilling) to join stage 3 after its inception.

With respect to the latter, a third body will be formed called the *General* Council, on which governors of all the national central banks, with and without a derogation, will be represented. It will not participate in determining the monetary policy of the single currency group in stage 3, which will be the prerogative of the *Governing* Council.[3] It will, however, deal with more administrative matters, such as the collection and use of statistics, pay, and rations, etc., and will contribute to the preparations for entry into stage 3 of those countries still with a derogation (Articles 41-8 of the Protocol of the ESCB).

Reverting to stage 2, the main body to be established to prepare the passage to stage 3 will be the EMI, whose main duties will be discussed in section II below. There is, however, a surprise here in that a further advisory body, the Monetary Committee, has also been established by the Treaty (Article 109C). During stage 2 it (also) is to "review the monetary and financial situation of the Member States . . . and the general system . . . and to examine the situation regarding the movement of capital and the freedom of payments." Once stage 3 has begun, the Monetary Committee is to be transmogrified into an Economic and Financial Committee which will, however, continue to review the "economic and financial situations" of countries without a derogation, and "the monetary and financial situations" of countries with a derogation. In all cases it will continue to examine, at least once a year "the movement of capital and the freedom of payments." It is not at all clear to me how the dividing lines for its remit and responsibilities are to be drawn relative to the EMI/ESCB on the monetary side, or to the Commission on the economic side, nor what the specific purpose of its establishment is perceived to be (and who were its sponsors among the member states, and why).

Thus the strategy, timetable, and structure of governance, both in stage 3 and in the transitional period, have all now been largely established. But what still is left a blank is how the ESCB shall actually operate in order to achieve its strategic objectives. Indeed even the site of its headquarters, let alone the site of its market operations, or other functions (e.g., payments and settlement arrangements), remains undecided. Thus Article 37 of the ESCB's protocol requires that "Before the end of 1992, the decision where the seat of the ECB will be established shall be taken by common accord . . . of Heads of State." On this subject common discord is far more likely than accord, and the trading process should be fascinating to behold.

The fifth decision is a revised basis for the transfer of foreign exchange reserves to the ECB. At an earlier stage there had been proposals that all foreign exchange reserves held by national central banks should be transferred to the ECB, partly to cement the new system by making any unilateral withdrawal more costly. Now, however, although the ESCB shall "hold and manage the official foreign reserves of the Member States" (Article 105.2, Indent 2, of the Treaty and Article 3.1 of the ESCB's Protocol), the very next clause (105.3 and 3.2 respectively) states that this "shall be without prejudice to the holding and management by the Governments of Member States of foreign exchange working balances." This will place much weight on the precise definition of what balances are needed for "working" purposes, and when balances may be distinguished as excessive to "working" needs.

Moreover, the transfer of foreign reserve assets from the national central banks to the ECB is not to be complete, but in proportion with their share in the subscribed capital of the ECB (Article 30.2 of the Protocol), "up to an amount equivalent to ECU 50.000 million," set out in Article 30.1. Consequently national central banks with reserve assets in excess of those required to be transferred can presumably keep them. (Quite what happens to those central banks with insufficient reserves to meet the call for proportionate transfer is not made clear; presumably they would have to borrow.)

II EMI and the future operations of the ESCB

Quite what the role and functions of the EC's federal monetary body (now named the European Monetary Institute) was to be in stage 2 had never been clear in the original Delors Committee Report, since responsibility for monetary policy was then to remain with the national central banks. That role is now made much clearer; it is to plan how the ESCB shall operate when it starts work.

As noted earlier, the strategic objectives, constitution, structure, and governance of the ESCB have now been agreed by Treaty. But quite how the ESCB should operate, and what its prudential duties, if any, should be have all been left for future decision, recommendations on which have largely been made the responsibility of the EMI. It all reminds me somewhat of the poem (among the "100 Poems on the Underground" in London, an example of a true public good) which went:

> I wanna be the leader
> I wanna be the leader
> Can I be the leader?
> Can I? I can?
> Promise? Promise?
> Yippee, I'm the leader
> I'm the leader
>
> OK what shall we do?

The key clause is Article 109F, Para. 3 of the Treaty. This states that:

For the preparation of the third stage the EMI shall:
  prepare the instruments and the procedures necessary for carrying out a single monetary policy in the third stage;
  promote the harmonisation . . . of the conditions governing the collection, compilation and distribution of statistics in the areas within its field of competence;
  prepare the rules for operation to be undertaken by the national Central Banks in the framework of the ESCB;
  promote the efficiency of EC cross-border payments;
  supervise the technical preparation of ECU banknotes.
At the latest by 31st December 1996 the EMI shall specify the regulatory, organisational and logistical framework necessary for the ESCB to perform its task in the third stage. This framework shall be submitted to the ESCB at the date of its establishment.

Thus, after Maastricht we know what the objectives of the ESCB shall be, roughly the date of its establishment, and how it will be governed, but quite how it will actually operate, in virtually every field of central bank action, has been passed on to the EMI for further consideration (and what role, if any, is the Monetary Committee to have in all this?). In this sense the decisions at Maastricht cover only a limited area.

What remains to be decided? Virtually *all* operational details, and also the range of ECB responsibilities, notably in the prudential field. I am going to touch here on five operational issues that remain for decision in the remainder of this section. These will be:

1 Central banks as government banks;
2 Open market operations for monetary policy;
3 Reserve ratios;
4 Clearing and settlement;
5 Prudential and regulatory issues.

Then in section III I shall consider some problems connected with the move to the use of the ECU as a single currency, and relating to the division and utilization of seigniorage receipts, which have not yet been given, in my view, a satisfactory assessment yet.

Central Banks as bankers to their governments

Central banks were originally established in many countries, including the UK, France, and Prussia, to provide finance on favorable terms to their own government. They have subsequently remained in most cases the banker to the government, providing where necessary short-term finance by way of purchase of bills, or other paper directly from government, or direct loans and overdrafts (ways and means advances in UK). Now such assistance with (short-term) direct finance must stop; under Article 21.1 of the Protocol of the ESCB, "overdrafts or any other type of credit facility by the ECB or by the national central banks to [any public sector body of the EC or Member States] and the purchase directly from them of debt instruments shall be prohibited" (also see Article 104 of the Treaty).

Like other economic agents, public sector expenditures, revenues, debt sales, and redemptions are lumpy and subject to uncertainty, e.g., owing to strikes, communication failures, etc. So no government, or other public body, can be certain of retaining a positive balance in its bank account at all times. Consequently all public bodies, including the central government of all member states (and the Commission?), will need to arrange for stand-by loan finance from *private sector banks*.

It is theoretically perfectly possible for a public sector body to leave a deposit account – on which no overdraft can ever be allowed – with one (central) bank, and to arrange for overdrafts with other bank(s). But, given the economies of centralization, etc. (not to speak of compensating balances), the logic of Article 21.1 is clear, which is that public sector banking services should be privatized by whichever private commercial bank offers the best deal. It is remarkable that this logical conclusion has virtually nowhere been spelt out, perhaps because the authors of most of the technical sections are central bankers who would prefer to keep the business themselves.

Open market operations for monetary policy

Indeed the above transfer of public sector business to private bank(s) would somewhat simplify the conduct of monetary policy, since unpredictable fluctuations in the monetary base usually arise from unforeseen transfers between public sector accounts held at the central bank and private sector accounts held at commercial banks. If both sets of accounts were with commercial banks, such fluctuations would not affect the monetary base.

Even then many other factors would influence the banking system's reserve base, and differentially between national centers, e.g., shifts in note demand, net balances at the clearing (discussed below) and foreign exchange transactions. How then is the ESCB to operate to establish a single interest rate (or rate of monetary growth) throughout the EC? In part, because of the difficulties in estimating the net shortage/surplus of bank reserves in the various member states, a policy of trying to choose a given quantitative market intervention in several different markets would be inefficient, and would leave differentials between national reserve base net shortages/interest rates which would induce (and be resolved by) inter-bank flows.

An alternative would be to try to operate in several (many) national centers simultaneously to try to fix interest rates at a common level. But that will be difficult if the instruments dealt in are not identical, since they will have differing characteristics, e.g., liquidity, risk premia, etc. (i.e., a French TB is not identical to a UK TB, nor an ICI three month bill to a Siemens three month bill), and the markets are not currently identical, in that there are varying "emergency" lending arrangements by the national central banks. On the other hand if the ECB was to deal in an *identical* instrument in each center, e.g., ECU TB's issued by the German government, why not make the operation more efficient by centralizing in one center?

But that raises the question (if market operations were to be centralized in one center), whether inter-bank transfers and markets would be good enough to enable the interest rate established in the one center to be closely matched and efficiently established in all the other national markets. The answer is, perhaps, "yes" if London was to be the one center, but more dubious otherwise.

One of the factors influencing liquidity is intervention, or other operations, by the central bank in the foreign exchange market. Again the question arises whether such operations should be spread around centers, with some possible inefficiency and confusion, or centralized, once the ESCB is established. One obvious point is that it would not make much sense to centralize market operations in domestic assets in one EC center and have forex operations in another.

Perhaps even more important, the structure and nature of money markets in the various financial centers of the EC differ, and this affects the nature and form of national central bank support (lender of last resort) arrangements to deal with (unforeseen) liquidity crises as they occur, especially late in the working day when wholesale markets are closely down. Such support arrangements (e.g., working through the discount market in London, via Lombard arrangements in some other countries) are somewhat arcane, but nevertheless play an important role in present national money markets. What is to become of them? Are they to be abandoned, made uniform, taken over by the ECB, or what? In particular, if in stage 3 the large clearing banks in London suddenly find, late in the afternoon in London (n.b. after the rest of continental Europe has closed because of the hour's difference, or will London have to go onto a common European time schedule?), that they have a cash deficit, what will they do? At present they can obtain funds via the discount houses who turn to the Bank of England for help. But what will happen in stage 3?

Reserve ratios

In some part the question of how to deal with late-in-the-day swings in bank cash positions is bound up with the decisions to be taken on (required) reserve ratios. If such reserve ratios are relatively high, but only have to be met *on average* over some period, then a larger proportion of such unforeseen fluctuations on any day in bank cash positions can be absorbed by fluctuations between zero and some upper bound in such reserves. So less specific support for money markets needs to be arranged.

On the other hand such required reserves involve a pecuniary penalty on banks, to the extent that interest paid by the central bank on them is below market rates. To some extent the loss to banks from such a penalty can be offset by receiving other central bank services in return at below market cost, as I believe happens in Germany. Be that as it may, there are national differences not only in required reserve ratios, but how they are calculated (e.g., the averaging procedure, if any), remunerated (if at all), and, per contra, how other central bank services to their banks are priced. These may appear to be technical minutiae, but they will influence comparative banking profits and money markets in member states.

There is, therefore, likely to be a call for harmonization (of required reserve ratios, the costing of central bank transactions with their national banking system, market support mechanisms, etc.). Beyond this, there are those who will call for variations in reserve ratios to be used as a further instrument (besides open market operations) of monetary policy, e.g., to allow two objectives (perhaps an external objective, in addition to domestic price stability) to be achieved. In effect this would be akin to applying a variable tax rate on banking intermediation. While such measures to vary required reserves could be introduced, under Article 19.1 of the Protocol of the ESCB, and would have some macroeconomic effects, those effects would be diluted and distorted by disintermediation. In that respect variations in reserve ratios suffer from the same basic disadvantages as virtually all other direct controls. In this latter respect, "The Governing Council may, by a majority of two-thirds of the votes cast, decide upon the use of such other operational methods of monetary control as it sees fit . . .," presumably including controls on required collateral, terms of lending, controls on interest rates, and quantitative limits on lending, etc., though the Council should respect Articles 2 and 34 (from Article 20 of the Protocol of the ESCB). Article 34 simply defines what a legal act of the ESCB shall be, but Article 2 (on objectives) requires the ESCB to "act in accordance with the principle of an open market economy with free competition, favouring an efficient allocation of resources." Whether, and which, direct controls on banking (other than required reserve ratios) would be consistent with Article 2 has yet to be determined, perhaps in the European Court of Justice?

Clearing and settlement

Under Article 22 of the ESCB's Protocol, "The ECB and national central banks may provide facilities, and the ECB may issue ECB regulations to ensure efficient and sound clearing and payment systems within the Community and with other countries." The permissive use of the word "may," implying also "may not" if the ECB so desires, will be noted. This article might seem to imply that decisions on this function may be taken at leisure, but I wonder whether this Article will not in practice be overtaken by the subsequent Article 52 included in chapter IX on "Transitional and Other Provisions for the ESCB."

This article states that, "Following the irrevocable fixing of exchange rates, the Governing Council shall take the necessary measures to ensure that bank-notes denominated in currencies with irrevocably fixed exchange rates are exchanged by the national central banks at their par value." As noted in section IV, there will have to be a stage 3A, during which currencies are irrevocably fixed, but before they are all replaced by the single ECU currency, stage 3B. As discussed below, stage 3A could last for some time, perhaps several years. Article 52 stipulates that the ECB achieve par clearance of bank notes among the participating countries in stage 3A. Since a requirement for the acceptability of deposits is that they should be convertible at par into notes, a necessary (but not sufficient) condition for the par clearance of such notes would seem (to me) to be par clearance of cheque payments drawn on deposit balances[4] (or overdrafts).

Since par clearing of deposits will not necessarily happen naturally, and will, I suggest, be a requisite condition for par clearing of notes (plus some extra arrangements to deal with the higher cost of the latter, see note 4), it seems to me to be necessary for the ESCB to establish, in stage 3A, a wholesale clearing and payments mechanism in the EC.

Moreover, the EMI is given the task, in Article 109F, Para. 2, of the Treaty to "facilitate the use of the ECU and oversee the development, including the smooth functioning of the ECU clearing system." Admittedly this is a relatively small part of the overall system *at present*, and operates largely through close-of-business inter-bank credits without any overt official support. Yet, this responsibility is bound to be passed on to the ESCB. As and when the ECU clearing system explodes in size, and becomes the single EC payments mechanism (stage 3B), it would hardly seem practical, or possible, to have the safety and smooth functioning of the ECU clearing system in its present, somewhat *ad hoc*, and immature condition.

For all these reasons, I believe that the permissive, and apparently quite distant, wording of Article 22 of the Protocol on the ESCB will soon be overtaken by a realization that the ESCB will have to plan on inaugurating clearing systems for (wholesale) deposits both in ECU and in participating member states' national currencies at the outset of stage 3A. This will involve considerable prior planning on the structure, e.g., the netting arrangements and the mechanics of the system.

Among the problems to be resolved, two stand out. The first is that in each clearing there is bound to be a net deficit/surplus position relating to claims on each irrevocably fixed currency. Presumably the ESCB will have to be the counterparty to ensure overall balance each day for each currency at the clearing, in order to ensure par clearing at all times (and places).[5] Thus the ESCB will, as I see it, have to participate directly in the clearing(s).

Second, even if, somehow, the ESCB were to manage to abstain from participation, it would have to ensure that the payments system was not brought to a standstill by the failure, or the fear of a failure, of a member commercial bank. This would suggest that at some stage the ESCB would have to guarantee that a payment was "good," in the sense that should the paying bank fail to honor its debt, the payee would still get good funds. This entails the ESCB having to assume such debts, and clearly would involve it in risk.

As Garber and Folkerts–Landau (1992) have argued, the need to support the clearing and payments system in this way is bound to lead the ECB into establishing rules and regulations for, and entering into a prudential relationship with, those commercial banks participating in the European, and ECU, clearings.

Prudential and regulatory issues

The question of what prudential functions, if any, the ESCB, and within it the constituent ECB and national central banks should severally perform, appeared to be a bone of some contention in the 1990 Central Bank Governors' Draft Treaty. The question has not been resolved at Maastricht. Indeed it has been comprehensively smothered.

Thus, Article 105, Para. 5, of the Treaty states that "The ESCB shall contribute to the smooth conduct of policies pursued by the competent authorities relating to the prudential supervision of credit institutions and the stability of the financial system," a phrase repeated word for word in Article 3.3 of the Protocol of the ESCB. This is then fleshed out slightly in Article 25, which in Paragraph 25.1 enables the ECB to "offer advice to and be consulted by the Council, the Commission and the competent authorities of the Member States on [all relevant legislation]." The ECB can, however, only go beyond a consultative role, to assume a prudential function of its own, after the lengthy, and quite problematical, procedure outlined in Article 105, Para. 6 of the Treaty, whereby "The Council may, acting unanimously on a proposal from the Commission and after consulting the ECB and after receiving the assent of the European Parliament, confer upon the ECB specific tasks concerning policies relating to the prudential supervision of credit institutions," and Article 25.2 of the Protocol enables the ECB to fulfil such tasks. Notice the requirement for unanimity in the Council here, which suggests to me adamant opposition from the Germans to giving the ECB *any* prudential functions.

If so, how is the European deposit (or note) clearing to be organized? Can the national central banks (and other competent authorities?) provide the necessary support to ensure the smooth functioning of a federal European clearing mechanism? At present, the national central banks, in concert with their own commercial banks, and ultimately their governments, have the ability to undertake costly lender of last resort activities. Will that ability persist into stage 3 (A or B)?[6]

If the member national central banks should feel increasingly constrained in support operations, and the ECB is prevented from assuming such responsibilities by the unanimity requirement of Article 105.6, must we expect the whole banking and financial system of the EC to become more fragile in stage 3? Will it require a financial collapse in Europe to sort out the disagreements evident among central banks on who should do what in the prudential field?

The combination of the phraseology about "the competent authorities" – but who exactly are the competent authorities? – and Article 105.6, suggests that there will be, for the time being, neither harmonization nor centralization of prudential systems and responsibilities. Each member state authority will go on doing its own thing in this field. But as every other aspect of monetary policy becomes both more harmonized and centralized in stage 3, does this standfast position on prudential supervision make sense?

I foresee that this will be a subject of continuing contention and dispute in the operations of the ESCB.

III   Note issue and seigniorage

The first step in stage 3 (stage 3A) will be the irrevocable fixing of exchange rates among participating member states. Only subsequently (stage 3B) will it be practically possible to move on to a single currency, the ECU. As already noted in section II, the maintenance of par clearing for notes and deposits for the participating members will be quite complicated to handle, and both for operational and administrative convenience, and also to cement the single currency system into place, the most rapid transfer possible from stage 3A to 3B would seem desirable.

There are, however, some practical problems (and there are also possible problems of political acceptability, which will not be discussed further here). There have been many examples of currency exchanges (reforms) in history, but most have involved either the removal of zeros, perhaps as an element in a plan to check (hyper) inflation, and/or a shift in political governance (as is presently occurring in certain East European states), whereby the public/government is voluntarily rejecting its previous currency (e.g., the rouble or dinar).

One of the few occasions when a unit of currency was changed for another reason neither by a factor of 10 nor by political rejection, occurred in the case of decimalization in the UK. Although the £ was retained as the large unit, the subsidiary units, shillings and pence, were exchanged for new p, at a rate of 24/10 and 12/5 respectively, i.e., in fractions. This took some five years, or so, to plan and involved considerable redesign of school-books, vending machines, etc.

Such fractions will be childs' play compared with the seven, or so, figure decimals in which each currency's parity with the ECU is presently stated.

This will cause a problem. Conversion into ECU of national currencies will be made much easier if the relevant fraction (decimal) is user friendly, as it is *not* at present. This would argue for a final realignment to achieve that; for some ideas and illustrative numbers, see Giovannini (1991). However, Article 109J requires, for the convergence criteria to be met, that countries shall not have devalued against any other Member States' currency for the previous two years (Article 109J.1, indent 3), and Article 109L, Para. 4, notes that "At the starting date of the third stage, the Council shall . . . adopt the conversion rates at which their currencies will be irrevocably fixed . . . This measure shall by itself not modify the external value of the ECU." *But* any user friendly realignments of the ECU value of participating countries is bound to modify the external value of the ECU a little bit. Is there any room at all between Article 109J and L for a final realignment?

If not, the conversion fractions (decimals) will be barbarous indeed. How are people to react when their goods worth 10 deutsche marks suddenly become worth 4.91ECU? The confusion among the old and the educationally sub-normal will be horrendous. It is not good enough to suggest that we can all cope by carrying around pocket calculators with us for a few weeks. The problems will be intense even if the conversion fractions are user friendly, more so if they are not.

There are, perhaps, two alternatives. One is cold turkey, whereby *all* payments, calculations, etc., are in local currency one day, all in ECU the next. That would presumably require an immediate exchange not only of notes, but also of subsidiary coin. Since there can be, presumably, only one set of ECU coins, all the vending and slot machines, telephone kiosks, etc., of at least eleven out of the twelve member countries would immediately become unusable, and have to be replaced. The chaos would be intense, and many mistakes would be made.

The alternative would be a phased, side-by-side introduction. First each local note, say French franc, would be issued with its ECU value (a nasty fraction), on the reverse. All notes, issued in whichever local currency, would be legal tender, all prices expressed in dual form. Then, after some period, the notes would have a round number of ECU on one side, and the fraction of local currency on the other (for notes issued initially in each member state). Then, one would move on to replacing the subsidiary local coins by subsidiary ECU coins. Finally one could remove the local fraction, leaving a completely ECU based system, with no reference whatsoever to the prior national currency.

How long would all this last? At a guess three years to plan and three to complete. If so, and if this is seen as a better alternative to cold turkey, stage 3A could easily last some five or six years. Even cold turkey would probably involve a three to four year planning introduction. If so, hopes and suggestions that the EC can move rapidly to the use of a single currency seem to me to be very wide of the mark. We will need to expect a lengthy stage 3A.

Moreover, the transition will, as argued above, lead to considerable costs, both psychological and in terms of real resources. Yet no mention was made, or assessment attempted, of such potentially heavy costs in the study "One Market, One Money." It seems a peculiar oversight.

Be that as it may, there is no doubt at all about the final objective, of having a single ECU currency. The issue of such currency, which will presumably remain non-interest-bearing, will entail and provide seigniorage for the issuing authority, the ESCB. The central bank governors reached a decision on how such seigniorage was to be allocated during the course of 1991, and this decision was ratified in the Protocol of the ESCB, and is set out in Articles 32 and 33. Effectively, after a transfer to reserves for the ECB, the net profits of the monetary income of the ESCB, derived from seigniorage, shall be split up among the participating central banks according to a formula set out earlier in Article 29.1, whereby

Each national central bank shall be assigned a weighting in this key which shall be equal to the sum of:
   50% of the share of its respective Member State in the population of the
      Community in the penultimate year preceding the establishment of the ESCB;
   50% of the share of its respective Member State in the [GDP of the EC over the
      previous 5 years] preceding the penultimate year before the establishment of
      the ESCB.

The formula is somewhat arbitrary. Thus it disregards entirely the fact that the initial usage, or outstanding value, of currency per head differs substantially between countries, e.g., being much higher in Germany than in the UK. Consequently the formula will benefit the UK relative to Germany.

My concern is rather whether the allocation of seigniorage to national central banks, by this or any other formula, is appropriate. The ECU will be a single European currency, and its comparative usage in one, or another, member state will be unknown and unknowable. The central budget of the EC is comparatively tiny relative to that of all other federal states. The seigniorage receipts of the ESCB (after due transfer to reserves) should in my view have gone, as is the case in all other federal countries, to the central EC government. It is difficult to find a more obvious case for the transfer of fiscal receipts to the EC.

What is *not* spelt out in Article 32 is exactly what the national central banks shall then do with their seigniorage receipts. If they are to be fully independent of governments, Article 14.1, does this mean that national governments cannot require their own central bank to pass on the seigniorage receipts to the national Treasury? What then would the national central banks do with the funds? In practice, I cannot believe that the national central banks can really do other than pass on the greater proportion of such seigniorage to their own national government, but who will decide what reserves the central bank need to retain? If they are to be independent, presumably the central bank itself. A licence to print money, indeed. The question of accountability, for their usage of seigniorage funds, arises here also, though less important than the accountability of the ESCB for its policy actions, discussed further in section V.

IV   Policy coordination: the external dimension

Although the ESCB is to be independent, and to focus on the achievement of price stability as its over-riding priority, there remain some questions about the coordination of monetary policy with such other main policy instruments as remain within the control of the political authorities.

The greatest potential for conflict has been seen as arising in the field of external monetary relationships, since decisions on the choice of external exchange-rate regime, e.g., fixed, or float, or managed float, were left in the hands of the political authorities. If the Ministers of Finance, for example, were to instruct the ECB to peg the ECU to the (assumed inflationary) \$, how could the ESCB simultaneously give primacy to achieving price stability?

The potential for conflict was, however, so patent that some form of compromise was always likely to ensue. The Treaty requires that the Council shall consult the ECB, in those cases where the recommendation does not derive directly from the ECB, and that any "general orientations" shall be "without prejudice" to the maintenance of "price stability." The key sections (in Article 109, Paras. 1 and 2) read:

The Council may, acting by unanimity on a recommendation from the ECB or from the Commission, and after consulting the ECB . . . conclude formal agreements on an exchange rate system for the ECU *vis-à-vis* non-Community currencies.
In the absence of an exchange rate system . . . the Council may, acting by a qualified majority on a recommendation from the Commission and after consulting the ECB, [or] on a recommendation from the ECB, formulate general orientations for exchange rate policy . . . without prejudice to the primary objective [of] price stability.

One of my concerns, however, with the formulation of the constitution of the ESCB is that the definition of price stability is nowhere strictly defined, as discussed below in section V. As a sceptic I believe that this is a purposeful omission by the central bankers involved in the drafting process to avoid the exercise of a close public accountability (the kinder interpretation would be to allow for residual flexibility). Nevertheless it opens room for differing interpretations of whether some exchange rate "orientation" would, or would not, be inconsistent with "price stability." Moreover, the Council only needs to "consult" the ECB and, having consulted, can decide as the politicians prefer.

Be that as it may, I should be quite surprised if there was, in practice, either much conflict between the ESCB and the Council or an attempted reassertion of political supremacy through this route, at least in the foreseeable future. The independent ESCB is bound to challenge any threat to the achievement of the primary objective which it has been allocated, i.e., price stability. It is difficult to see the Council being prepared to ignore or over-ride such objections unless broader political support for the whole concept of an independent central bank targeted on the achievement of price stability had already been eroded to such an extent that the politicians would also envisage a wholesale revision to the Treaty. This would then just represent a quick back-door route to such a revision under certain circumstances.

Instead, I would expect greater problems to arise from the interplay of fiscal policies, largely still under the command of the national authorities, and monetary policy. As is well known, the interaction of monetary and fiscal policy helps to determine the exchange rate. Thus a combination of a lax fiscal policy and a tight monetary policy, as in the US in the first half of the 1980s and in Germany since reunification, tends to lead to exchange-rate appreciation. Thus, if the EC should wish to achieve some particular outcome for the exchange rate, and with monetary policy predicated to the achievement of internal price stability, then EC fiscal policy *in aggregate* has to be adjusted to that end.

Can that be done, given the decentralized fiscal process in the EC? (Again sceptics can question whether it could be done even in a centralized system; note the many economic and political problems of achieving a desired macroeconomic stance for fiscal policy.)

Even though the process of achieving an "ever closer union" is likely to lead to more fiscal competencies being transferred to the federal center, e.g., an eco tax and greater expenditures to assist cohesion, for the foreseeable future the greater bulk of fiscal powers, and the roles and functions of stabilization and redistribution are likely to remain primarily in the hands of the national authorities. How, then, can the EC hope to achieve any desired *aggregate* fiscal outcome for the Community as a whole?

There are two main Articles relating to the conduct of national fiscal policy in the Treaty. These are Article 104C which sets out measures to prevent and to rein back excessive government deficits, as defined in the accompanying Protocol, and Article 103, which relates to the general coordination of policies. Whereas measures to limit "excessive deficits" in certain member countries may, on occasions, also lead to an improved aggregate Community fiscal stance, there are no good grounds for expecting that generally and normally to be the case. Hence, the main reliance has to be placed on Article 103.

Under this Article, the Council, acting by qualified majority on a recommendation from the Commission, may adopt, and make public, broad guidelines for the economic policies of member states (Para. 2), and monitor the consistency of national policies with such guidelines (Para. 3). No doubt one of the elements of such broad guidelines would relate to national fiscal policies. Given that the monetary policy of the ECB was predicated primarily to the achievement of price stability, that would leave a multitude of objectives for national (and Community) fiscal policies, among them stabilization of output, a sustainable balance of payments, optimal allocation of resources, redistribution, etc. So, it is not clear exactly what weight the Commission (and Council) either could, or should, give to the external dimension (e.g., to the achievement of some preferred exchange rate and/or current account) in setting broad guidelines. In any case, as partly implied above, given the uncertainty about the impact of fiscal deficit(s) on the external dimension, it would be difficult to be clear exactly how changes in such deficits would affect it, and hence how to take account of such external considerations, except in a very broad way.

Let us, however, assume that this difficult task has been done and that, say, in order to strengthen the current account and/or to depreciate the ECU, the Council set out in its broad guidelines that fiscal policies should become more restrictive. Then in so far as any national member states were transgressing the Protocol relating to Article 104C, there would be a series of steps, and associated enforcement measures that could, though probably only after some considerable delay, be followed (Article 104C, Paras. 6–11). But, let us for our present purposes, assume that none of the countries have "excessive deficits" as thus defined. How then, if at all, can the Council try to ensure that its broad guidelines are met?

At present this is not clear. Under Article 103, Para. 3, the Council, with the support of the Commission, should be in a position to monitor whether each member state is complying with the broad guidelines, and, if not (Para. 4), to recommend changes in its policies, and to do so publicly, not least in a report to the European Parliament. There will, therefore, be a power of public censure. Given, however, the tendency for the journalistic media in each country to support their own nationalistic viewpoint, it is quite hard to see whether public censure by a qualified majority of other Community countries would represent that much of an inducement to comply. There is, however, a possibility, as set out in Para. 5, that the rules for mutual surveillance could *in future* perhaps be given greater definition and bite.

That said, there is, of course, the question of the reference point for any comparison. Whereas the ability of the EC either to establish, or to achieve, an aggregate fiscal outcome for the Community as a whole, notably with respect to some desired common external outcome, will be *extremely* limited, even such limited progress as it may be able to take in that direction would represent greater coordination than exists at present.

V   The overall strategy

The ESCB has been given the remit of achieving domestic price stability as an over-riding priority, and the independence from political pressures to achieve that end without fear or favor.

That strategy is predicated on an analytical economic theorem, which is that, in a world without money illusion and/or systematic errors in expectations, there will be no medium-, or longer-, term trade-off between higher inflation and higher growth/output, i.e., a longer-term vertical Phillips curve. Consequently the best outcome that the authorities can hope to achieve, over the longer term, is price stability. The exploitation of the possibility of shorter-term gains, from unanticipated inflation, leading to higher output in the short run only leads over a period of years to a worse situation with the same output and higher inflation.

I cannot fault the logic of the underlying analysis, though I have some reservations. First, the concept of the medium-/longer-term vertical Phillips curve does not seem to have any stable empirical embodiment. It shifts around in an apparently insubstantial fashion, but usually seeming, in the UK at least, to follow quite closely where the current level of actual unemployment has moved. Second, older economists will have seen so many changes in the basic models and analyses of macroeconomics (much less so in microeconomics), to be doubtful about the proposition that the current state of the art has at last discovered the eternal verities.

Be that as it may, the present objectives and strategy of the ESCB are in accord with current best practice economic analysis. Even so, there may be some crisis circumstances, when some re-ordering of priorities, or adjustment in policies, may be needed, for example a major financial collapse, a banking panic, or perhaps a political disaster, war, or insurrection.

Alternatively, future politicians might want to shift from a (managed) float between blocs, to a fixed rate or some form of cooperative management, which would place limits on the ESCB's ability to give over-riding priority to domestic price stability.

At present, there is *no* flexibility built into the Articles of the Treaty and Protocol. The objective of price stability gets absolute priority among objectives in Article 3A of the Treaty and Article 2 of the Protocol. These are *not* among the Articles subject to a simplified amending procedure

(Article 41 of the Protocol). Instead, it would require the completion of a new Treaty in its entirety to change the objectives of the ESCB. This is not only an enormously time consuming exercise, but would require unanimity among member states. Such a revision of the priorities among objectives cannot be done in a hurry, and can hardly be done at all.

On the other hand an important feature of the Treaty and Protocols, which has surprisingly escaped much notice, is that there is no definition whatsoever of "price stability." "Excessive deficits" are defined in a special protocol. But the convergence criterion on price stability is only in *relative* terms, i.e., within 1.5 percent of the annual average of CPI of the three best performing states.

Consequently, there is some room for flexibility. The ESCB can choose how it prefers to define its (path toward) price stability. If there is, say, an immediate (banking) crisis, the ESCB may claim that an immediate easing of monetary policy in response to the crisis would be more consistent with longer-term sustainable price stability than continuing monetary restraint, which might lead to future price falls (as in the 1930s).

Thus the (I assume) purposive refusal to quantify what should be regarded as price stability, or a date by which it should be reached, does provide the ECB and the ESCB with a modicum of flexibility in response to crises. But by the same token it reduces their exposure to external accountability. If there is no quantification of price stability, how can success or failure be measured?

The ECB has certain reporting responsibilities. Thus under Article 109 B.3, "The ECB shall address an annual report on the activities of the ESCB and on monetary policy of both the previous and current year to the European Parliament, the Council and the Commission, and also to the European Council"; and under Article 15 of the Protocol, "The ECB shall draw up and publish reports on the activities of the ESCB at least quarterly."

But such Reports are occasions for the expressions of *ex-post* justification of whatever, for good or ill, those in authority have chosen to do. Without a clear definition of price stability, and preferably some incentive in the form of bonus payment for achieving that outcome, there is no firm basis for accountability. The ECB's report is *bound* to state that their actions were consistent, as they saw best, with the achievement of price stability over the appropriate horizon. Most central bank reports have made that claim year after year for decades! In the uncertain world of macroeconomics, how are outsiders to demonstrate that the ESCB is wrong in its judgments? Even then, the ESCB is protected against any criticism by its independence. Everyone hates criticism, and even an independent Governing Council and Board will listen to outside comment. Nevertheless, as Montagu Norman once said, "The dogs may bark, but the caravan moves on."

The failure to define price stability provides flexibility at the cost of relaxing accountability. This is a structure and system constructed by, with, and for central bankers, to give them an easier life. It is neither necessary nor desirable.

A much better alternative procedure is available, and is embodied in the Reserve Bank of New Zealand Act. Under this Act the government and the Reserve Bank sign a treaty specifying a quantitative definition of price stability, e.g., 0–2 percent rise in the CPI and a date for its achievement. The reappointment of the governor depends on success in obtaining that goal (the additional possibility of linking the governor's salary to the outcome was considered, but rejected on the political grounds that a pecuniary award to the governor for imposing restrictive policies could have been too inflammatory). Some limited flexibility for disregarding CPI increases resulting from indirect tax increases, interest-rate increases, and oil shocks is written into the Treaty.

For the rest, the RBNZ has a clear numerical objective and an incentive to achieve it. The ESCB will not have such a clear objective or associated incentive unless it decides to impose one on itself. Given its numerical objective the RBNZ does *not* have much flexibility in its operations, but the government *does*. It has the ability to over-ride the Treaty, and to set the RBNZ new objectives (e.g., perhaps to peg to the Australian $), but it can only do so in a totally transparent manner, by laying an Order before Parliament.

Thus under the RBNZ Act, there is a clearly specified numerical target, providing clear incentives to the Reserve Bank to achieve it. Flexibility remains in the hands of the democratically elected politicians, but can only be exercised in a transparent manner. Both accountability and flexibility are achieved. Under the Maastricht Treaty some room for flexibility is achieved by being careful to fudge the question of how exactly price stability shall be measured, but that same fudge blurs and reduces the accountability of the ESCB. If I was to run the ESCB myself I would, indeed, propose a structure whereby both my objective and accountability were left blurred and fuzzy. But for the rest of us, I suggest that this part of the Treaty and Protocol is deficient.

Notes

1 Both the extent of the tactical flexibility, and reaffirmation of strategic focus, in achieving this aim were illustrated by the postponement of the interest-rate increase by the Bundesbank till after the Maastricht summit meeting, but its subsequent hike by more than had been generally expected.

2 The voting pattern, of one council member, one vote, i.e., unweighted by relative
   size of country, has remained unchanged from the 1990 Draft. This, however,
   raises the question of how to deal with the likely accession of future members to
   the EC, which would swell the size of the council, perhaps to an unmanageably
   large size, and dilute the weight of each present member's single vote. This
   problem is very similar to that faced (or perhaps not faced) with the accession of
   the five Eastern Lander to the German Federal Republic. While (the speed of)
   this latter was not foreseen, the accession of further members to the EC is clearly
   foreseeable. Nevertheless the Treaty contains no guidance about how the
   structure of governance might (need to) be adjusted in such an event.
3 The distinction between the General and the Governing Councils will be hard to
   remember. I would have wished the drafting officials to have turned to their
   Thesaurus to find a synonym for Council in one of the two cases – perhaps, a
   General Eisteddfod of Central Bankers?
4 The additional problem with notes is the extra expenditures involved for banks in
   collecting, sorting, and shipping them home with appropriate insurance and
   protection, plus the added interest lost meanwhile (since one cannot expect the
   population of country A willingly to accept the notes of country B during stage
   3A). If par clearing of notes is to be achieved, someone, the commercial banks, the
   national central banks, or the ECB will have to meet this cost.
5 What will happen outside European business hours? If there is a net surplus of
   French francs and deficit of deutsche mark in Tokyo, will there be a minute shift
   in the exchange rate in Tokyo, or will the ESCB arrange for correspondents to
   offset imbalances occurring in other centres also?
6 There is a provision in Article 32.4 of the Protocol whereby "The Governing
   Council may . . . in exceptional circumstances [indemnify national central
   banks] for specific losses arising from monetary policy operations undertaken for
   the ESCB." I wonder whether, and what, lender of last resort actions that might
   cover.

References

D. Folkerts-Landau and P. Garber (1992), "The ECB: a bank or a monetary policy
    rule," in *Establishing a Central Bank: Issues in Europe and Lessons from the US*,
    Eds. M.B. Canzoneri, V. Grilli and P.R. Masson Cambridge University Press,
    pp. 86–110.
A. Giovannini (1991), "The Currency Reform as the Last Stage of Economic and
    Monetary Union: Some Policy Questions", National Bureau of Economic
    Research, Warning Paper No 3917.
C.A.E. Goodhart (1992), "The External Dimension of EMU" and "National Fiscal
    Policy within EMU: The Fiscal Implications of EMU" in *EMU and ESCB
    after Maastricht*, Ed. C.A.E. Goodhart, Financial Markets Group, London
    School of Economics, pp. 267–300 and 315–335.

9 A European money demand function

MICHAEL J. ARTIS,
ROBIN C. BLADEN-HOVELL
and WENDA ZHANG

Introduction

As a result of the increasing degree of European integration and exchange-rate stability within the European Monetary System, spillover effects and currency substitution can be expected to affect single-country estimates of the money demand function. If not properly taken into account, such misspecification will lead to bias in the estimated parameters of the model and potential instability in the estimated function. It has recently been suggested that estimation of an area-wide (EMS) demand for money function may provide an appropriate solution to such misspecification, although the benefits thereby achieved may only be obtained at the cost of introducing aggregation bias into the relationship.

This chapter examines the issues underlying the estimation of such an area-wide money demand function in the context of two alternative monetary aggregates, M1 and M2. A two-stage cointegration methodology is applied to provide estimates of money demand over both the period preceding and following the introduction of the EMS framework. In addition, the chapter also reports upon the effect of disaggregating the relationship to the individual country level and reveals that, not only might the conditions for complete aggregation not be met within the system, but that the desirable characteristics attributed to the aggregate relationship appear to depend upon behavior within individual countries. The implications of this result for monetary policy within a complete monetary union are discussed in the final section of the chapter.

Background

The structure and performance of European financial markets has changed considerably since the introduction of the European Monetary System. The

240

increased stability of intra-ERM exchange rates, together with the almost complete removal of capital controls over the period, has resulted in a quickening pace of financial liberalization throughout Europe, with capital markets becoming increasingly integrated across the region. It is generally argued that, as a consequence of these developments, national European currencies have become increasingly substitutable for one another in the private sector's portfolio, thereby giving rise to an attendant loss of opportunity for national monetary authorities to insulate domestic monetary conditions from developments that originate elsewhere in the rest of Europe.

The potential impact of currency substitution for the operation of domestic monetary policy has, of course, long been recognized in the literature. Early work by McKinnon (1982), for example, identified currency substitution as having first-order implications both for the efficacy of domestic monetary targets and for movements of the exchange rate between the major trading blocs. The basis for McKinnon's claim and the policy conclusions that flow from it, was relatively straightforward. Where currency substitution occurs, inflation rates across countries will be determined by movements in world, rather than domestic, monetary aggregates and, as a consequence, greater efficiency in demand management may be obtained by abandoning domestic monetary targets in favor of targets expressed at the world (G-3) level. Although the general validity of McKinnon's argument for developments in the global economy was subsequently placed in doubt by Spinelli (1983), recent work by Bekx and Tullio (1987) concerning the determination of the deutsche mark–dollar exchange rate suggests that the hypothesis may hold for the EMS.

The essence of the Bekx and Tullio analysis was to demonstrate that, over the period of the Exchange Rate Mechanism, the deutsche mark–dollar exchange rate appeared to be better determined by aggregate EMS monetary conditions than by developments in domestic monetary conditions within Germany itself. The analysis was based upon the proposition that, as capital controls between member states fall, expectations of realignment will lead to a transfer of funds from countries which are likely to depreciate to strong-currency countries within the system. Under these conditions, currency substitution on the demand-side and central bank intervention on the supply-side, may combine to render domestic monetary stocks more volatile and less important as determinants of domestic inflation than would otherwise be the case. Indeed, independent evidence concerning the potential significance of the supply-side channel for transmitting the effects of disturbances between EMS members has been produced by Mastropasqua, Micossi, and Rinaldi (1988) and by Bayoumi and Kenen (1992). The former authors found that movements in the German monetary base are correlated with lagged values of the monetary bases for other EMS member states, with German monetary movements providing a partial compensation for expansionary or contractionary monetary disturbances that originate elsewhere within the EMS. Bayoumi and Kenen find that, in the late-EMS period, when there have been no realignments, the aggregate ERM money supply performs at least as well as and arguably better than the individual national aggregates in predicting inflation and the price level.

The most common interpretation applied to the Bekx and Tullio result is that their findings are consistent with the view that the aggregate money demand function for the EMS region as a whole is both well behaved and stable. Such an interpretation, if true, would be significant in two respects. First, it confounds the great body of literature relating to the apparent lack of stability of the money demand function estimated at the single-country level, where the instability is interpreted to mean either a lack of constancy for parameter estimates or failure for the estimated function to provide accurate out-of-sample forecasts. Second, stability of an aggregate EMS money demand function satisfies the well-known necessary, but not sufficient, condition for policy-makers to seriously consider directing monetary policy at the aggregate EMS level, the importance of this possibility obviously increasing in the run-up to any agreement concerning complete monetary union within Europe.

Direct evidence concerning the stability of a European money demand functions has, to our knowledge, only been provided by two studies to date. Kremers and Lane (1991) have examined the stability of the function on the basis of a narrow (M1) definition of money whilst Monticelli and Strauss-Kahn (1991) have investigated the problem in the context of a broader (M3) definition. Not only did each study find substantial evidence apparently confirming the intrinsic stability of the aggregate relationship, but also the preferred specification in each case was remarkably simple from the point of view of the limited number of explanatory variables required. In the current paper we concentrate upon the demand for narrow money balances within Europe, as defined in terms of M1 and M2. We believe, however, that many of the points that are made in the following sections are likely to be applicable with equal force to the demand for money under broader definitions.

Cointegration and the Kremers and Lane study

Kremers and Lane essentially adopt a two-stage cointegration methodology for estimating the aggregate demand for money within Europe. Consistently applied this procedure requires that, at stage one, individual series be screened for their univariate stationarity properties and, in this context, a series is said to be integrated of order one, $I(1)$, if it requires first differencing for it to become covariance stationary. Two or more non-stationary variables are subsequently considered to be cointegrated if there exists some linear combination of them that is itself stationary. The properties of this first stage process are, by now, well understood. Stock's (1987) theorem demonstrates that OLS estimates of the cointegrating vector are super-consistent whilst Stock and Watson (1988) and Campbell and Perron (1991) review the problems that nuisance parameters, such as serial correlation in the residuals or endogeneity of the regressors, may pose for statistical inference within the model.[1]

The conventional interpretation of the first stage cointegrating vector is that it represents the long-run relationship between the regressors;[2] the short-run dynamics of the process subsequently being determined in the second stage through an application of the Granger Representation Theorem (see Engle and Granger, 1987). This theorem demonstrates that, for any cointegrating relationship, there exists an error correction formulation for the dynamic structure. The regressors in this second stage comprise transformed series from stage one, differenced to an appropriate degree in order to induce stationarity, together with an error correction term involving the residuals from the first-stage equation itself, thereby effectively imposing the long-run properties of the model upon the dynamic structure.

Kremers and Lane originally estimated their model over the period 1978:4–1987:4, using aggregate quarterly information for seven countries. The data related to M1, real income, the consumer price index together with two measures of the opportunity cost of holding money, the short-term and long-term interest-rate respectively. The countries involved in the study were Germany, France, Italy, Netherlands, Denmark, Belgium, and Ireland, with Luxembourg being omitted on the grounds of inadequate data.[3] EMS aggregates for M1 and real income were subsequently constructed as the sum of the deutsche mark equivalent of the national currency series, where the conversion factor involves OECD estimates of the purchasing power parity (PPP) exchange rates for each country.[4] Aggregate values for the ERM interest rate and consumer price index were similarly obtained; the former being calculated as the weighted average of the national rates with weights derived from the shares of national currency in the ECU, defined to exclude Luxembourg and the United Kingdom; the latter using the share of national GDP in the ERM aggregate as weights. A final variable, the ECU–Dollar exchange rate, was also included in the study.

Broadly similar procedures for constructing aggregate values of the regressors are adopted in the current paper, the principal exception being the choice of exchange rate used to convert national currency values into a common currency – in our case US dollars. Specifically, we report results derived from aggregate data constructed using a fixed-base exchange rate, initially calculated as the average dollar exchange rate for each country in 1980.

This method was originally utilized by McKinnon (1982), Spinelli (1983), and Bekx and Tullio (1987) but was rejected by Kremers and Lane on the basis that it induced misspecification in the Bekx–Tullio model.[5] This claim is somewhat surprising given that casual inspection of the graphs showing the effects of the alternative conversion procedures in the Kremers and Lane study suggests that series converted using either the PPP and fixed-base method are almost identical.[6] Moreover, PPP exchange rates are notoriously difficult to construct and frequently rely upon assumptions concerning the nature of the underlying economies that are often violated. In contrast, the main advantage of the fixed-base exchange rates is the ease with which they may be constructed; the disadvantage is that the choice of base period itself is arbitrary. In order to examine the potential significance of this arbitrary choice we conduct a limited sensitivity analysis in the study and present results derived from the use of an alternative base period, namely 1988. Complete details of the variable definitions, together with the various weights and conversion factors used throughout the study are presented in appendix A.

The evidence

Prior to examining the relationships between variables, univariate time series properties need to be established. These are described in table 9.1. This table presents evidence relating to both the Dickey–Fuller (DF) and Augmented Dickey–Fuller (ADF) test applied to the logarithms of M1 and M2 (denoted $m1$ and $m2$), consumer prices (p), real income (y), the ECU–dollar exchange rate (ecu), real money balances $(m1 - p$ and $m2 - p)$ and the level of short-term interest rates (R) respectively. The tests for integration of order zero, I(0), are tests conducted on the levels of variables; tests for integration of order one, I(1), are conducted on the first difference of the variables. The DF and ADF tests are constructed as t-tests with a non-standard distribution which is tabulated in Fuller (1976).

The results of the exercise clearly indicate that, with the exception of consumer prices, all the variables considered by the study qualify as I(1), the majority passing both the DF and ADF tests at the 1 percent level. The tests indicate, however, that consumer prices are I(2) over the period, a finding which is consistent with a large body of evidence contained in the literature.[7] A major consequence of this result is that the consumer price

Table 9.1. *Unit root tests*

Series	DF[Z]	ADF[Z]	DF[DZ]	ADF[DZ]
$m1$	-1.89	-0.70	-10.74**	-5.81**
$m2$	-0.79	-0.75	-7.38**	-3.79*
p	-2.58	-2.29	-3.07	-2.45
y	-0.85	-0.66	-6.95**	-4.85**
R	-2.49	-3.50†	-3.76*	-4.18**
ecu	-1.15	-1.51	-4.63**	-3.72**
$m1-p$	-2.34	-2.28	-9.56**	-5.29**
$m2-p$	-2.63	-2.60	-6.90**	-4.38**

Notes: Significant at the 1% level (**), 5% level (*) and 10% level (†). DF and ADF refer to the Dickey–Fuller and Augmented Dickey–Fuller test statistics computed for the level [Z] and first difference [DZ] in a regression including a constant, time trends and the first lag of the dependent variable. Critical values are given in Fuller (1976).

index should not appear as independent regressor in a cointegrating relationship involving nominal money balances, but rather, may only appear in the context of a transformed variable, such as real money balances. This would have the effect of imposing long-run price homogeneity on the relationship, but would allow homogeneity with respect to real income to be determined by the data since the I(1) nature of the latter permits an independent, cointegrating role for this variable in the real balance relationship. Finally, of course, a role may exist for the rate of consumer price inflation in the cointegrating vector, since, by definition, this variable will also be I(1).

In the results that follow, we have chosen to model the cointegrating relationship from the point of view of a real money balance equation. The general specification of the relationship is given in equation (1) and OLS estimates for alternative sample periods and definitions of both narrow money and the ERM countries involved in the study are presented in table 9.2, where figures in parentheses relate to coefficient standard errors. The critical values for the Dickey–Fuller and Augmented Dickey–Fuller tests reported in the table were taken from Engle and Granger (1987).

$$(m-p)_t = \alpha_0 + \alpha_1 y_t + \alpha_2 R_t + \alpha_3 ecu_t + \mu_t \tag{1}$$

Our preferred estimate for the model, obtained for approximately the same sample period as that covered by the Kremers and Lane study, is

Table 9.2. *Full aggregation money demand equations*

Equation	Dependent variable	Period	Independent variables				R^2	D–W	$\hat{\sigma}$
			const.	y_t	R_t	ECU_t			
2	$(m1-p)_t$	79:2–87:4	−3.739 (0.66)	0.842 (0.10)	−1.455 (0.22)	0.085 (0.02)	0.96	1.97	1.44
3	$(m1-p)_t$	79:2–90:2	−4.691 (0.30)	0.987 (0.05)	−1.207 (0.15)	0.093 (0.01)	0.98	1.90	1.42
4(d.w.)	$(m1-p)_t$	79:2–90:2	−3.952 (0.34)	0.810 (0.05)	−1.083 (0.17)	0.136 (0.01)	0.97	1.38	1.58
5	$(m2-p)_t$	79:2–90:2	−5.342 (0.18)	1.199 (0.03)	−0.698 (0.09)	0.034 (0.01)	0.99	1.59	0.90
6	$(m1-p)_t$	73:1–79:1	−4.989 (0.66)	1.043 (0.10)	−1.963 (0.62)	0.191 (0.08)	0.93	1.20	1.92
7(+UK)	$(m1-p)_t$	79:2–87:4	−6.372 (0.72)	1.236 (0.11)	−1.564 (0.25)	0.093 (0.02)	0.97	1.71	1.52

Tests:

Equation	Cointegration		Serial correlation			Normality
	D–F	AD–F	AR[1]	AR[4]	AR[8]	NORM[2]
2	−5.50**	−3.34†	0.00	3.92	8.11	0.28
3	−6.27**	−4.16**	0.05	5.73	6.66	0.79
4	−5.05**	−3.61*	3.31†	8.33†	9.20	1.33
5	−5.70**	−5.75**	1.11	5.37	8.74	0.82
6	−3.08	−3.10	3.75†	7.69	17.94*	1.27
7	−4.98**	−3.00	0.54	5.65	11.25	0.20

Equation	Heteroscedasticity		Stability	
	HET[1]	ARCH[4]	CHOW[n1,n2]	CHOW[n1,n2]
2	0.00	1.50	1.11 [10,20]	1.85 [6,25]
3	0.66	0.97	0.90 [10,31]	1.14 [6,35]
4	0.00	1.06	2.05 [10,31]	1.97 [6,35]
5	0.93	2.72	0.81 [10,31]	1.19 [6,35]
6	1.12	2.53	3.01* [10,11]	3.93* [6,15]
7	0.00	4.16	1.49 [10,21]	2.28 [6,25]

Note: Significant at the 1% level (**), 5% level (*), and 10% level (†).

shown as equation (2) in the table. In many respects this compares favorably with the original. Despite the absence of any role for consumer price inflation in the model and our choice of long-term, rather than short-term, interest rates, the model continues to cointegrate, albeit only at the 10 percent level. Moreover, the relationship appears particularly robust in terms of the pattern for serial correlation. Lagrange multiplier tests, denoted $AR(i)$, where i represents the order of serial correlation, indicate a complete absence of first-, fourth-, and eighth-order serial correlation at conventional levels.

According to Campbell and Perron (1991), the absence of serial correlation from the first-stage equation removes one of the major nuisance parameters which essentially prevent standard statistical inference being conducted on the static relationship. Therefore, subject to the caveat that the asymptotic distribution, and hence the usual critical values, may not apply due to the potential endogeneity of regressors, we have followed Kremers and Lane in reporting the results of test statistics for heteroscedasticity, denoted $HET(j)$, and normality, denoted $NORM(k)$ together with a series of Chow tests, denoted $CHOW(n,m)$, for parameter stability over the last n observations of the current sample.

Inspection of the accompanying equations in the table indicates that the results illustrate a remarkably consistent pattern which is most apparent when the sample is extended beyond 1987:4, or where it is either modified to cover the period prior to 1979:2 or redefined to include the United Kingdom. The results for the former are shown in equations (3)–(5), initially on the basis of an $m1$ definition of money and using the 1980 fixed-base exchange-rate conversion; subsequently, in equation (4), for $m1$ using the alternative 1988 base, and in equation (5) for $m2$ balances. In each case the relationship cointegrates and, with the exception of equation (4), remains free of serial correlation. Moreover, although conventional tests of significance are inappropriate at this stage, casual inspection of coefficients suggests a behavior response in the model that runs in accordance with theoretical priors, notably in terms of the reduced value of the coefficient on interest rates in the $m2$ equation.

The two remaining equations in table 9.2 relate to results obtained when the model is either re-estimated over a third, sample period, 1973:1–1979:1, or where the range of countries incorporated into the aggregate ERM definition is amended to include the United Kingdom.[8] In neither case does the relationship cointegrate, at least on the basis of the calculated ADF statistic, suggesting that the presumed stability of the aggregate, long-run, money demand function relates to both a particular group of countries and a very specific time period. This naturally raises the question of what the characteristics of behavior were in each of these countries over the period from 1979:2 onwards, an issue we shall address later in the chapter.

The preferred specifications of the error correction formulation of the model for real $m1$ and $m2$ balances over the period are given as equations (8) and (9) below.

$$\Delta(m1-p)_t = -0.001 + 0.251\Delta(m1-p)_{t-2} + 0.897\Delta y_{t-3} - 0.817\Delta R_t - 0.727\hat{u}_{t-1}$$
$$\qquad\quad (.003)\quad (0.095)\qquad\qquad\quad (0.338)\qquad\quad (0.394)\qquad (0.151)\quad (8)$$

T: $80{:}3-90{:}2 R^2 = 0.60$ D$-$W$=2.17$ $\hat{\sigma}=1.17\%$
AR(1)$=0.93$ [3.84] AR(4)$=3.40$ [9.49] AR(8)$=4.11$ [15.51]
NORM(2)$=0.90$ [5.99] HET(1)$=0.94$ [3.84] ARCH(4)$=1.68$ [9.49]
CHOW(10, 25)$=0.68$ [2.21] CHOW(6, 29)$=0.97$ [2.43]

$$\Delta(m2-p)_t = 0.001 + 0.359\Delta(m2-p)_{t-2} + 0.383\Delta y_{t-2} + 0.253\Delta y_{t-3} - 0.375\hat{u}_{t-1}\quad (9)$$
$$\qquad\quad (0.001)\ (0.110)\qquad\qquad\quad (0.146)\qquad\quad (0.143)\qquad (0.109)$$

T: $80{:}3-90{:}2$ R$^2 = 0.48$ D$-$W$=2.09$ $\hat{\sigma}=0.52\%$
AR(1)$=0.32$ [3.84] AR(4)$=5.63$ [9.49] AR(8)$=12.32$ [15.51]
NORM(2)$=0.48$ [5.99] HET(1)$=1.33$ [3.84] ARCH(4)$=2.16$ [9.49]
CHOW (10, 25)$=1.24$ [2.21] CHOW(6, 29)$=1.83$ [2.43]

With few modifications, equation (8) corresponds very closely to the dynamic structure originally estimated by Kremers and Lane. In particular, the coefficient on the error correction term remains high – a finding consistent with the general absence of serial correlation in the first stage. Moreover, the diagnostics for the equation, notably those relating to tests of parameter stability, all indicate that the equation is well determined over the sample period. A somewhat counter-intuitive finding, however, is that the implied rate of adjustment embodied in the M2 equation is significantly lower, being only half the value estimated for real M1 balances, but more in line with the values obtained from single-country estimates.

Taken together these results suggest that the behavior of ERM participants, over the period since the inception of the framework, has been extraordinary. This particularly so in view of the well-known difficulty that has been experienced in fitting a stable money demand function for the individual countries concerned. Boughton (1991), for example, provides some evidence of a structural break affecting the demand for M1 in Germany in 1988:1 whilst Atkinson et al. (1984) failed to find any stable M1 equation for France over the period 1973:2–1983:1.[9]

The question arises as to what interpretation should be placed on these results. We can think of two main contenders, not necessarily wholly mutually exclusive. One possibility is that the aggregation works because currency substitution is a prominent characteristic of financial behavior in ERM countries; as discussed below, it may be difficult to capture such behavior at the individual country level. If so, aggregation is beneficial. By working at the aggregate level, we can legitimately circumvent the specification problem. Moreover, since currency substitution invalidates

Table 9.3. *Disaggregated money demand equations (1979:2–1990:2)*

Dependent var. $(m1-p)_t$

Equation	Country	Independent variables					R^2	D–W	$\hat\sigma$
		const.	y_t	R_t	exc_t	D79Q4			
10	France	-3.658 (0.52)	0.744 (0.10)	-0.724 (0.23)	-0.064 (0.03)	0.129 (0.03)	0.83	2.18	2.96
11	Germany	-8.965 (0.35)	1.763 (0.06)	-1.504 (0.31)	0.172 (0.02)		0.97	1.07	2.44
12	Italy	2.272 (0.46)	-0.064 (0.08)	-0.710 (0.16)	0.249 (0.02)		0.84	0.72	2.74

Tests:

Equation	Cointegration		Serial correlation			Stability			
	D–F	AD–F	AR[1]	AR[4]	AR[8]	CHOW[n1,n2]	CHOW[n1,n2]	CHOW[n1,n2]	CHOW[n1,n2]
10	-7.06**	-4.02*	0.43	3.63	14.46	0.25 [14,26]	0.49 [10,30]	0.23 [6,34]	
11	-3.91	-3.42+	9.61**	10.39**	12.87	3.97** [14,27]	3.21** [10,31]	1.92 [6,35]	
12	-3.18+	-3.72*	17.26**	19.34**	22.29**	3.03** [14,27]	3.11** [10,31]	3.40** [6,35]	

Addition of variable (LM test)

Equation	$\chi^2(1)$	variable	Cointegration[b]	
			D–F	AD–F
10	5.49*	short-term ERM rate[a]	-7.71**	-4.27**
11	5.03*	short-term ERM rate[a]	-3.89*	-3.38+
12	11.31**	short-term ERM rate[a]	-4.16**	-5.05**

Note: [a]Weighted average short-term ERM rate. [b]D–F and AD–F are recomputed after adding the short-term ERM rate.

the pursuit of monetary targets at the national level and transfers the legitimacy of such targeting to the aggregate level, it is the aggregate demand for money function which is of policy interest.

Although currency substitution may be an attractive explanation, that does not make it correct. Another candidate must be aggregation bias: that is, that the stability and properties of the aggregate function arise simply from the process of aggregation, are unrepresentative of behavior at the individual country level and could be misleading at the level of policy formation. Of course, aggregation can be beneficial if what is going on is adding up over individually thin data streams, or over data streams containing idiosyncratic disturbances which for some reason cannot be partialled out: then we could rely on aggregation to reveal the true demand for money function. Clearly the currency substitution hypothesis can be thought of as a special case of this, where the disturbances are by definition negatively correlated, and aggregation is especially beneficial.

Testing for aggregation bias

It would be nice to test for aggregation bias by a procedure which nested the individual country functions in the aggregate, but strict conformity with this route is not open to us because of the fact that the aggregate is expressed in logarithms and the data are logs-of-sums, not sums-of-logs. Moreover, even when the pre-weighted functions are estimated, inference about parameter constancy between samples is hindered by reason of the serial correlation and other problems revealed by the diagnostics for the individual equations. We have therefore fallen back upon two alternatives. The first is the relatively straightforward procedure of estimating the long-run money–demand relationship separately for the three largest participants in the ERM, namely Germany, France, and Italy, the results being presented in table 9.3.[10]

Clearly, in this context, a necessary condition for aggregation is that the structure of the individual country equations be sufficiently close for meaningful averages to be defined. The evidence suggests, however, that although all three equations cointegrate, albeit only at the 10 percent level in the case of Germany, substantial differences exist across countries in coefficient values and error structure of the relationship. Of the three, only the estimate for France is completely free from serial correlation, whilst the coefficient estimates for the income elasticity range from -0.06 in the case of Italy to 1.76 in Germany. Even if allowance is made for the effect of nuisance parameters in the long-run model, it is difficult to believe that these values represent similar behavioral responses across the three countries. Moreover, the statistics given at the bottom of table 9.3

Table 9.4. *Partial aggregation money demand equations (79:2–90:2)*

Dependent Var. $(m1 - p)_t$

Equation	Aggregation	const.	y_t	R_t	ECU_t	D79Q4	R^2	D-W	$\hat{\sigma}$	Normality NORM[2]
3	Full ERM	−4.691 (0.30)	0.987 (0.05)	−1.207 (0.15)	0.093 (0.01)		0.98	1.90	1.42	0.79
13	France excluded	−5.497 (0.29)	1.129 (0.05)	−1.147 (0.16)	0.150 (0.01)		0.98	1.31	1.44	1.52
14	Germany excluded	−2.701 (0.30)	0.670 (0.05)	−0.958 (0.13)	0.086 (0.01)	0.063 (0.02)	0.97	1.84	1.41	0.19
15	Italy excluded	−6.473 (0.37)	1.257 (0.05)	−1.316 (0.20)	0.058 (0.02)	0.048 (0.02)	0.97	1.70	1.75	0.67

Tests:

Equation	Cointegration		Serial correlation		
	D–F	AD–F	AR[1]	AR[4]	AR[8]
3	−6.27**	−4.16**	0.05	5.73	6.66
13	−4.93**	−5.49**	4.20*	8.84†	10.79
14	−6.43**	−4.40**	0.03	1.98	4.20
15	−5.72**	−3.44†	0.83	5.10	10.88

Equation	Heteroscedasticity		Stability		
	HET[1]	ARCH[4]	CHOW[n1,n2]	CHOW[n1,n2]	CHOW[n1,n2]
3	0.66	0.97	1.48 [14,27]	0.90 [10,31]	1.14 [6,35]
13	0.26	10.95*	2.55* [14,27]	1.73 [10,31]	1.33 [6,35]
14	0.28	3.89	1.88 [14,26]	1.31 [10,30]	1.99 [6,34]
15	4.44*	5.12	0.84 [14,26]	0.43 [10,30]	0.47 [6,34]

Note: Significant at the 1% level (**), 5% level (*) and 10% level (†).

demonstrate the impact of augmenting each country's equation with the ERM short-term interest rate, where the ERM is redefined to exclude the home country itself. The effect of this is to significantly increase the DF and ADF statistics estimated for the model in two of the three countries, the exception being Germany.

The second procedure adopted for investigating the properties of the aggregate function involve redefining the aggregate ERM in several different ways, suppressing one country from the aggregate each time. Thus, we redefine the ERM aggregate sequentially, as excluding France, excluding Germany, excluding Italy, etc. In the present context, it might have been expected that this procedure would show that the stability revealed in the aggregate ERM results depends upon stability in Germany and Germany's dominant size. But, as the results reported in table 9.3 show, Germany is not the most stable of the three countries considered.

The results of the partial aggregation exercise are given in table 9.4 and overall present a rather mixed picture as to the effects of aggregation. First the diagnostics printed at the foot of the table indicate that the relationship continues to cointegrate irrespective of the excluded country – albeit only at the 10 percent level when Italy is omitted. Problems concerning serial correlation and parameter constancy arise when France and Germany are omitted from the aggregation, a result particularly apparent for the parameter estimated on the ECU exchange rate and real income in the model. The implication that the demand for money is particularly stable in France appears to bear out the results obtained in the cointegrating equation estimates shown – for the three largest countries – in table 9.3 above.

Currency substitution

Testing for currency substitution with aggregate monetary data is less straightforward. What term adequately captures the gains from moving into another currency (or, more generally, assets denominated in another currency)? If uncovered interest parity prevails, then the gains from moving into a foreign bond – the interest rate minus expected depreciation – are reflected in the domestic interest rate, already part of the money demand function. In the estimates presented so far we have included the ECU exchange rate vis-à-vis the dollar, on the basis that Kremers and Lane found this variable to be important, as have we. Its presence can be rationalized as a reflection of currency substitution, on certain (though not necessarily very attractive) assumptions. A more direct approach appears to be as follows. The monetary magnitude under study here is M1, a relatively narrow money, for which the own rate of return may not be particularly important

– certainly, we have not found it necessary to incorporate such a measure. It might be that for such a definition, speculation about the exchange rate itself is the key to currency substitution. The results shown in appendix B reflect this approach. Expected exchange-rate gains were defined from the three-month forward premia logged for sterling against other currencies, assuming triangular arbitrage. Demand functions for the individual countries were then re-estimated incorporating this variable; a partial adjustment form was assumed to take care of the dynamics. Exchange-rate gains against all other ERM currencies individually, and against an appropriately weighted index were incorporated, along with exchange-rate gains against the US dollar.

There are two powerful uniformities in the results. Currency substitution is significant with the right (negative) sign in every case except for France. The dynamic term is important – large and significant – in every case, except for France. The significance of the currency substitution term, interestingly, is confined to the European currencies and – except for Italy – does not embrace the US dollar.

Conclusions

The results presented in this chapter provide confirmation of the robustness of the result obtained earlier by Kremers and Lane: an aggregate ERM money demand function for the M1 definition of money can be estimated which appears structurally stable and to have nice properties. By contrast, comparable money demand equations estimated for the individual countries tend to be less well behaved. Contrasting interpretations are available. On the one hand, the results may reflect the presence of currency substitution at the individual country level, with aggregation being an appropriate response. If this is the correct interpretation, the policy response implied in the move to EMU is well founded. But it may be that the results reflect aggregation bias. The explanations are not mutually exclusive and indeed we do find some presumptive evidence of currency substitution. However, it also seems quite clear that the behavior of the aggregate reflects behavior of the underlying country-specific money demand functions. The stability of French monetary relationships, remarked upon in other studies, is clearly a powerful influence on the form and stability of the aggregate money demand function; whilst, unlike the case for the other countries, we could find no evidence for currency substitution in France.

The implications for policy within a complete monetary union reflect these results. The apparent dependence of the aggregate function upon inclusion of the French data for its stability properties is especially worrying. To what extent, if at all, is the stability of the French relationship dependent upon French monetary policy? How far would that form of monetary policy carry across to aggregate policy specified within a monetary union? There must be a nagging doubt that underlying this apparently stable relationship are aspects of the Lucas critique and Goodhart's law which are simply waiting to have a further laugh at the expense of monetary economists.

Appendix A: The Data

1 Data sources

Data are mainly taken from the International Monetary Fund, International Financial Statistics (IMF–IFS).

2 Interpolation procedure

Quarterly GDP are interpolated using the information of annual GDP and quarterly index of industrial production (Chow and Liu, 1971), if they are not available.

3 Definition of the series

M1 & M2   Money stock, seasonally adjusted. IMF definition for M1 and national definition for M2.

P   Consumer price index.

Y   GNP/GDP, seasonally adjusted.

R   Long term interest rate, period average, fraction.

ECU   US\$·P_{ERM}/ECU·P_{us}, period average.

EXC   US\$·P/National currency·P_{us}, period average.

4 Weights for aggregation

See Table 9A.

Table 9A. *Weights for aggregation*

Variable	Method 1		Method 2
M1, M2 & Y	change to US$		change to US$
	at 1980 exchange rate		at 1988 exchange rate
	DM/US$	1.8177	1.7562
	francs/US$	4.2260	5.9569
	lire/US$	856.5	1,301.6
	guilders/US$	1.9881	1.9766
	kroner/US$	5.6359	6.7320
	B-francs/US$	29.243	36.768
	Irish p.	0.4859	0.6553
P	National GDP (1980) weights		National GDP (1988) weights
	Germany	35.267%	35.756%
	France	28.807%	27.122%
	Italy	19.760%	21.714%
	Netherlands	7.342%	7.014%
	Denmark	2.875%	2.970%
	Belgium	5.116%	4.503%
	Ireland	0.833%	0.921%
R & ECU	ECU weights		ECU weights
	at Dec. 1988 exchange rate		at Dec. 1988 exchange rate
	DM	40.198%	40.198%
	francs	21.292%	21.292%
	lire	11.073%	11.073%
	guilders	12.695%	12.695%
	kroner	3.174%	3.174%
	B-francs	10.277%	10.266%
	Irish p.	1.290%	1.290%

Appendix B: Currency substitution

Table 9B-1. *Currency substitution in the German money demand equation*

Const.	$(m1-p)_{t-1}$	y_t	R_t	E_{US}	E_{FF}	E_{LI}	E_{ERM}	$\bar{R}^2$	$\hat{\sigma}$	D–W	h
-0.97	0.89	0.20	-1.09	-0.04	-0.11			0.99	1.37	2.05	-0.19
(1.8)	(17.2)	(1.9)	(6.2)	(0.3)	(1.5)						
-1.18	0.88	0.24	-1.13	-0.05		-0.14		0.99	1.36	2.17	-0.62
(2.2)	(17.9)	(2.4)	(6.4)	(0.4)		(1.8)					
-1.05	0.89	0.22	-1.09	-0.03			-0.19	0.99	1.38	2.07	-0.24
(1.9)	(17.1)	(2.1)	(6.2)	(0.3)							
							-0.19	0.99	1.38	2.07	-0.24
(1.9)	(17.1)	(2.1)	(6.2)	(0.3)			(1.4)				
-1.01	0.89	0.21	-1.09				-0.19	0.99	1.36	2.08	-0.27
(2.0)	(17.7)	(2.2)	(6.2)				(1.5)				

Note: Figures in parentheses are *t*-statistic in absolute value.

Table 9B-2. *Currency substitution in the French money demand equation*

const.	$(m1-p)_{t-1}$	y_t	R_t	D79Q4	E_{US}	E_{DM}	E_{LI}	E_{ERM}	$\bar{R}^2$	$\hat{\sigma}$	D-W	h
-3.96	-0.02	0.82	-0.72	0.11	-0.19	0.30			0.78	3.23	1.90	1.61
(5.4)	(0.1)	(5.7)	(2.2)	(3.2)	(0.6)	(0.9)						
-3.75	-0.09	0.79	-0.57	0.10	-0.08		0.37		0.79	3.18	1.79	—
(5.4)	(0.6)	(5.8)	(1.9)	(2.9)	(0.5)		(1.4)					
-3.87	-0.03	0.81	-0.71	0.11	-0.19			0.34	0.78	3.23	1.90	2.37
(5.4)	(0.2)	(5.7)	(2.2)	(3.2)	(0.6)			(0.9)				
-3.75	-0.01	0.78	-0.68	0.11				0.13	0.78	3.21	1.94	0.69
(5.5)	(0.1)	(5.8)	(2.1)	(3.3)				(0.7)				

Table 9B-3. *Currency substitution in the Italian money demand equation*

const.	$(m1-p)_{t-1}$	y_t	R_t	E_{US}	E_{DM}	E_{FF}	E_{ERM}	$\bar{R}^2$	$\hat{\sigma}$	D-W	ρ
0.34	0.85	-0.06	-0.22	0.23	-0.38			0.95	1.42	2.10	-0.17
(1.5)	(22.5)	(1.2)	(2.3)	(1.8)	(2.5)						
0.18	0.87	-0.02	-0.31	0.01		-0.14		0.95	1.49	2.12	-0.13
(0.8)	(19.2)	(0.5)	(3.3)	(0.2)		(1.4)					
0.31	0.87	-0.05	-0.23	0.22			-0.44	0.95	1.41	2.13	-0.17
(1.5)	(22.7)	(1.2)	(2.5)	(1.8)			(2.7)				
0.15	0.85	-0.02	-0.23				-0.19	0.95	1.45	2.13	-0.16
(0.8)	(22.1)	(0.4)	(2.4)				(1.9)				

Table 9B-4. *Currency substitution in the Dutch money demand equation*

Const.	$(m1-p)_{t-1}$	y_t	R_t	E_{US}	E_{DM}	E_{FF}	E_{ERM}	$\bar{R}^2$	$\hat{\sigma}$	D–W	ρ
-0.51	0.90	0.14	-0.90	-0.08	-0.60			0.98	2.02	1.84	-0.23
(0.8)	(14.6)	(0.9)	(3.8)	(0.4)	(1.9)						
-0.59	0.92	0.16	-0.78	-0.18		-0.11		0.98	2.07	1.86	-0.22
(0.9)	(13.8)	(1.0)	(3.3)	(1.0)		(1.2)					
-0.48	0.94	0.14	-0.86	-0.11			-0.37	0.98	2.02	1.86	-0.27
(0.8)	(15.0)	(0.9)	(3.8)	(0.6)			(1.9)				
-0.35	0.95	0.10	-0.85				-0.40	0.98	2.00	1.91	-0.30
(0.6)	(15.7)	(0.7)	(3.9)				(2.2)				

Table 9B-5. *Currency substitution in the Belgian money demand equation*

const.	$(m1-p)_{t-1}$	y_t	R_t	E_{US}	E_{DM}	E_{FF}	E_{ERM}	$\bar{R}^2$	$\hat{\sigma}$	D–W	ρ
0.12	0.89	-0.07	-0.25	0.13	-0.41			0.91	1.79	2.13	-0.28
(0.5)	(24.1)	(1.1)	(1.5)	(0.8)	(2.1)						
-0.13	0.90	0.01	-0.34	-0.13		-0.12		0.90	1.87	2.14	-0.31
(0.6)	(23.0)	(0.1)	(2.1)	(0.9)		(1.0)					
-0.01	0.90	-0.03	-0.26	0.06			-0.55	0.91	1.77	2.16	-0.31
(0.1)	(25.2)	(0.6)	(1.6)	(0.4)			(2.3)				
-0.04	0.89	-0.03	-0.24				-0.51	0.91	1.75	2.15	-0.30
(0.2)	(26.9)	(0.5)	(1.6)				(2.5)				

Table 9B-6. *Currency substitution in the Danish money demand equation*

	const.	$(m1-p)_{t-1}$	y_t	R_t	D83Q4	E_{US}	E_{DM}	E_{FF}	E_{LI}	E_{ERM}	
	-2.90	0.71	0.85	-0.81	-0.17	-0.34	0.03				B-1
	(3.2)	(11.6)	(3.1)	(2.7)	(5.3)	(1.2)	(0.1)				
	-2.11	0.75	0.61	-0.98	-0.18	-0.18		-0.25			B-2
	(2.2)	(11.9)	(2.1)	(3.3)	(5.8)	(0.9)		(1.8)			
	-2.15	0.75	0.62	-1.05	-0.18	-0.20			-0.28		B-3
	(2.3)	(12.0)	(2.2)	(3.4)	(5.9)	(1.0)			(1.8)		
	-2.31	0.73	0.67	-0.93	-0.18					-0.42	B-4
	(2.4)	(11.8)	(2.3)	(3.1)	(5.6)					(1.9)	

Equation	$\bar{R}^2$	$\hat{\sigma}$	D-W	h
B-1	0.99	2.99	1.93	0.25
B-2	0.99	2.87	2.03	-0.12
B-3	0.99	2.87	2.09	-0.35
B-4	0.99	2.91	1.99	0.03

Notes to appendix B

1 Money demand equation is specified as follows (Bordo and Choudhri, 1982):

$$(m1 - p)_t = \beta_0 + \beta_1 (m1 - p)_{t-1} + \beta_2 y_1 + \beta_3 RL_t + \beta_4 RL_{f,t} + \ldots + u_t$$

where RL is the domestic interest rate (short- or long-term rate) and RL_f is the foreign interest rate. Under conditions of interest rate arbitrage, $RL = RL_f + E$, where E is expected depreciation. Substituting in the above equation, we have

$$(m1 - p)_t = \beta_0 + \beta_1 (m1 - p)_{t-1} + \beta_2 y_t + (\beta_3 + \beta_4) RL_t + \beta_4 E + \ldots + u_t$$

β_4 provides a measure of the degree of currency substitution.

2 E_{DM} is defined as follows:

$$E_{DM} = 4(F - S)/S$$

F is the 3-month forward rate, S is the spot rate. (Both are the national currency per DM.)

E_{US} E_{FF} E_{LI} are defined in the same way (FF: French franc, LI: lire).

E_{ERM} is defined in the same way and ECU weights are used to construct that series (e.g., in the German money demand equation, E_{ERM} stands for DM appreciation against other countries within the ERM).

3 In the French money demand equation, the term $(m - p)_{t-1}$, which was found to be negative and insignificant, is omitted.

4 Cochrane–Orcutt and Hildreth–Liu (grid search) procedures are used where serial correlation is detected.

Notes

We should like to thank Stefano Micossi and Brian Henry for assistance in providing data. Work on the paper was facilitated by financial support from the Leverhulme Foundation under the terms of a project administered by the Centre for Economic Policy Research, London. We are grateful to both institutions.

1 Engle and Sam Yoo (1987) illustrate a three-stage estimation procedure that allows the standard errors in the model to be corrected for this bias.

2 See Johansen (1988), however, for difficulties with this interpretation.

3 Consistent quarterly estimates for real income were only available for Germany, France, and Italy, information for the remaining countries being interpolated from annual figures. An identical problem exists for the current study and quarterly values have been interpolated on the basis of the annual relationship between GDP or GNP and industrial production for the countries concerned.

4 Kremers and Lane also experiment with alternative methods of conversion including current exchange rates and fixed-base exchange-rate values. The results they report, however, all relate to data constructed using purchasing power parity rates.

5 Kremers and Lane also note that the intrinsic properties of PPP exchange rates are quite appealing, most notably that the weight of each country in the ERM aggregate reflects the size of its real economy.
6 Indeed, upon detailed inspection it would appear that the claim concerning misspecification is not well founded at all, but rather is based upon an inappropriate interpretation of a (presumably) non-cointegrating first-stage equation, where inference about homogeneity and stability of the relationship is drawn from T- and F-statistics that, at best, have non-standard distributions.
7 Both Stock (1987) and Stock and Watson (1989), for example, comment upon this result. The latter, in particular, suggest that the finding derives from the sharp upward movement in prices administered by the oil price shocks of 1973 and 1979.
8 The choice of sample period in this case was dictated by the availability of a consistent series for M1 in the United Kingdom.
9 For a contrary view, however, see Artis *et al.* (1992) where an evolutionary spectrum analysis of monthly velocity series for five European countries and the US only finds evidence of instability in the case of the US and UK.
10 It was found necessary to include an additional dummy variable for 1979:4 in the French equation in order to reflect what appears to be a data error affecting the French M1 series on the IMF tape currently available in Manchester.

References

Artis, M.J., R.C. Bladen-Hovell, and D. Nachane (1992), "Instability of the Velocity of Money: A New Approach Based on the Evolutionary Spectrum," Mimeo, University of Manchester.

Atkinson, P., A. Blundell-Wignall, M. Rondoni and H. Ziegelschmidt (1984), "The Efficacy of Monetary Targeting: The Stability of Demand for Money in Major OECD Countries," OECD *Economic Studies*, pp. 145–76.

Bekx, P. and G. Tullio (1987), "The European Monetary System and the Determination of the DM–Dollar Exchange Rates," Unpublished; Brussels: Commission of the European Communities.

Bayoumi, T. and P. Kenen (1992), "Using an EC-wide Monetary Aggregate in Stage Two of EMU," mimeo, Bank of England.

Bordo, M.D. and E.U. Choudhri (1982), "Currency Substitution and the Demand for Money," *Journal of Money, Credit and Banking*, 14, pp. 48–57.

Boughton, J. (1991), "Long-Run Money Demand in Large Industrial Countries," IMF Staff Papers, Vol. 38, pp. 1–32.

Campbell, J. and P. Perron (1991), "Pitfalls and Opportunities: What Macroeconomists Should Know about Unit Roots," NBER Technical Paper No. 100.

Chow, G. and A. Lin (1971), "Best Linear Unbiased Interpolation, Distribution and Extrapolation of Time Series by Related Series," *Review of Economics and Statistics*, 53, pp. 372–5.

Engle, R. and C. Granger (1987), "Cointegration and Error Correction: Representation, Estimation and Testing," *Econometrica*, 55, pp. 251–76.
Engle, R. and B.S. Yoo (1987), "Forecasting and Testing in Cointegrated Systems," *Journal of Econometrics*, 135, pp. 143–59.
Fuller, W. (1976), *Introduction to Statistical Time Series*, New York: John Wiley.
Granger, C. (1986), "Developments in the Theory of Cointegrated Variables," *Oxford Bulletin of Economics and Statistics*, 48, pp. 213–28.
Johansen, S. (1988), "Statistical Analysis of Cointegrating Vectors," *Journal of Economic Dynamics and Control*, 12, pp. 231–54.
Kremers, J. and T.D. Lane (1991), "Economic and Monetary Integration and the Aggregate Demand for Money in the EMS," International Monetary Fund, Washington, *Staff Papers*, Vol. 37, pp. 777–805.
McKinnon, R. (1982), "Currency Substitution and Instability in the World Dollar Standard," *American Economic Review*, 72, pp. 320–33.
Mastropasqua, C., S. Micossi, and R. Rinaldi (1988), "Intervention, Sterilization and Monetary Policy in European Monetary System Countries, 1979–87," in F. Giavazzi, S. Micossi, and M. Miller (eds.), *The European Monetary System*, Cambridge.
Monticelli, C. and M. Strauss-Kahn (1991), "European Integration and the Demand for Broad Money," *Mimeo*, Economic Unit of the Committee of Governors of EEC Central Banks.
Spinelli, F. (1983), "Currency Substitution, Flexible Exchange Rates and the Case for International Monetary Cooperation," International Monetary Fund, Washington, *Staff Papers*, Vol. 38, pp. 1–32.
Stock, J. (1987), "Asymptotic Properties of Least-squares Estimates of Cointegrating Vectors," *Econometrica*, 55, pp. 1035–56.
Stock, J. and M. Watson (1988), "Variable Trends in Economic Time Series," *Journal of Economic Perspectives*, 2, pp. 147–74.
(1989), "Interpreting the Evidence on Money-Income Causality," *Journal of Econometrics*, 40, pp. 161–81.

10 Monetary union and fiscal union: a perspective from fiscal federalism

JÜRGEN VON HAGEN

I Introduction

The theory of optimal currency areas seeks to determine the optimal geographical domain of a currency. The theory of fiscal federalism seeks to determine the optimal regional organization of government within the boundaries of a geographical area. The former starts from the presumption that one money, administered by a single monetary authority, should circulate in a region. The latter holds that the authority over fiscal policy should be divided between governments of various regional levels, each with its own functions and responsibilities. Thus, the theory of optimal currency areas embodies a paradigm of centralizing policy functions, fiscal federalism embodies a paradigm of decentralized government.

The modern version of the theory of optimal currency areas lists a variety of criteria for choosing the size of a currency area or monetary union.[1] In a nutshell, the benefits from monetary union result from the lower costs of transactions in international trade with one money or completely fixed exchange rates, from the implementation of a common monetary policy in response to exogenous shocks, and, provided that the institutional design of the monetary union's central bank is right, from a more credible central bank commitment to price stability. The main costs associated with monetary union result from the loss of the exchange rate as an instrument of macroeconomic adjustment. These costs will be small, if the size of transitory, country-specific shocks within the union is small compared to common shocks and permanent shocks, if capital and labor mobility are high within the union, and if the majority of the members' trade occurs with other members of the monetary union.

The main criteria for the optimal regional distribution of government as established by the traditional literature on fiscal federalism (e.g., Buchanan, 1950; Oates, 1972; Musgrave, 1986) are summarized in Oates (1972, p. 35):

Decentralization theorem:

For a public good – the consumption of which is defined over geographical subsets of the total population, and for which the costs of providing each level of output of the good in each jurisdiction are the same for the central or the respective local government – it will always be more efficient (or at least as efficient) for local governments to provide the Pareto-efficient levels of output for their respective jurisdictions than for the central government to provide *any* specified and uniform level of output across all jurisdictions.

The theorem applies not only to public good in the narrow sense, but, more generally, to the provision of macroeconomic stability and distributional justice.[2] Regional diversity of preferences over public goods and proximity of the responsible administration to the concerned citizens call for entrusting a local rather than a central authority with their production. In contrast, cost-savings from enlarging the group of joint consumers, spillovers and externalities between local jurisdictions, and inefficient competition among local governments justify delegating their provision to the central government.

What is the relationship between optimal currency areas and the optimal regional organization of government? A common answer is that monetary union must be matched by fiscal union. We will call this the

Parallel unification proposition:

Currency unification requires fiscal policy unification.

There are various ways to justify this contention. In the case of Canada, for example, many of the fiscal functions of the central government have been put in place to assure an equitable distribution of the welfare gains from monetary (and economic) union among the provinces (Cumming, 1986). In the context of European Monetary Union, it is often argued today that a monetary union without fiscal union would entail important allocative inefficiencies and insufficient macroeconomic stabilization. These concerns have made the proposition an important tenet in the current debate. For example, Lamfalussy (1989, p. 93) concludes that "fiscal policy coordination appears to be a vital component of a European economic and monetary union." De Larosière (1990) argues that "monetary union implies strongly convergent economic policies in the broadest sense, notably with regard to fiscal policy . . ." Similarly, Pöhl (1991) claims that "monetary union is only viable . . . [with] . . . consistent fiscal policies." These are claims with wide-ranging political consequences. Since the authority over public finances is at the heart of government, fiscal union would mark a much greater step toward creating a unified polity than monetary union. Countries may, therefore, be ready and willing to join in a monetary union, but unwilling to unify their fiscal policies at the same time.

In this chapter, we discuss the parallel-unification proposition from a perspective of fiscal federalism. Section II reviews the relevant principles of fiscal federalism. Section III evaluates the main aspects of monetary union currently debated in their light. The final section spells out our main conclusions. We will argue that there are three main fallacies behind the proposition. One is the focus solely on increasing regional spillovers and externalities which neglects the countervailing tendency of a monetary union to raise the heterogeneity of preferences, incomes, political views, and information of consumers and governments using the same money, which justifies decentralization of fiscal policy. The second is to argue solely on the basis of two-country models, where all fiscal policy spillovers can be corrected by centralizing fiscal functions. If the monetary union contains more than two members, spillovers may affect subsets of, but not all, members, making fiscal union an inefficient response to the problem. Finally, the focus solely on static efficiency arguments neglects that decentralization entails dynamic gains from competition among governments and that policy games played repeatedly have larger sets of equilibria than the single-shot games that are typically considered.

For the sake of clarity, we will follow conventional terminology and define a federation as a country or nation consisting of several federal states each of which contains a number of municipalities. Subsequently, a federation will be understood to have a central government and to use one money in all federal states. We will be interested primarily in monetary unions formed by groups of nationals. In view of the current debate in Europe, we will speak of fiscal union either in the sense of creating a unified fiscal authority at the center of the monetary union or in the sense of the close coordination of the members' fiscal policies.

II   Principles of fiscal federalism

Fiscal equivalence

The traditional theory of fiscal federalism deals with the distribution of fiscal responsibilities across regional jurisdictions to achieve an optimal allocation of resources in the provision of public goods. Its basic allocative tenet is the principle of reciprocity (Musgrave, 1986) or fiscal equivalence (Olson, 1969). It says that the geographical incidence of the benefits of a public program should coincide with the jurisdiction of the government operating and financing the program.[3] Otherwise, the benefits or the costs of the program would spill over to other jurisdictions and create external effects. The government operating the program, which, by assumption, cares only about its own jurisdiction, would disregard these externalities and would fail to achieve a welfare optimum for the society as a whole. Nor are there *internalities* (Olson) which would lead to similar welfare reductions.[4] The exact correspondence of the region benefiting from a public program and the region financing it assures Pareto-efficient outcomes in the provision of public goods.

Fiscal equivalence establishes a preference neither for centralized nor for decentralized government *per se*. On the contrary, it implies that too much centralization is just as inefficient as too much decentralization. The principle justifies the coexistence of various governments and levels of government, including governments with overlapping jurisdictions, in a country according to the regional incidence of the programs they administer. Furthermore, the equivalence principle requires that regional levels of activity in a public program vary in response to regional differences in preferences. Coexistence of regional governments providing different packages of taxes and public goods allows consumers to select the combinations they like best by locating in their most preferred jurisdiction.[5]

While the equivalence principle is an important yardstick for the design of a federation, its practical implementation suffers from several difficulties. One is the mobility of the tax base. If residents of other jurisdictions cannot be excluded from the consumption of a public good provided by a local government, taxpayer mobility creates free-riding problems. Taxpayers will tend to move to jurisdictions with low taxes and low levels of public services and enjoy the benefits of public goods provided by governments in jurisdictions charging higher taxes. Local governments confronted with mobile taxpayers must compete for tax resources. The result is a *prisoners' dilemma*: each local government finds it optimal to keep taxes and service levels low, although all governments together would find it preferable to raise taxes and provide a higher level of services. This leads to inefficient equilibria in which the level of taxes and the production of public goods are both too low.

Another impediment of fiscal equivalence arises from economies of scale in the production of public goods. As long as tastes over a public good are uniform in the population, economies of scale in its production would justify making the jurisdiction producing it large enough to exhaust all cost advantages. But, if tastes differ and enlarging the jurisdiction diminishes the responsiveness of the public administration to private preferences, a trade-off exists between the welfare gain due to a larger scale of production

Table 10.1. *Vertical fiscal structure in six federations (1981)*

Government units	Austria	Germany	Switzerland	Canada	US	Australia
State	9	11	26	10	50	7
Local	2301	9000	3000	8000	79913	900
own revenue as percentage of total expenditure						
State	55.0	71.6	72.6	81.2	77.8	38.9
local	77.6	61.7	84.5	48.5	61.7	66.3
net transfers received as percentage of current revenue plus grants						
State	39.2	1.9	15.8	1.5	−8.0	56.1
local	8.8	27.6	9.4	47.7	41.8	22.6

Source: Bird (1986), table 1.2.

and the welfare loss from a larger jurisdiction. Finally, all existing federations are shaped by historical and political processes instead of efficiency considerations, making violations of fiscal equivalence the rule rather than the exception.[6]

The traditional view of fiscal federalism responds to these problems with an efficiency-based theory of tax harmonization among local governments and a theory of vertical grants or transfers from higher to lower-level governments. Both provide remedies if fiscal equivalence cannot be implemented in practice (Olson, 1969; Break, 1980). Limiting regional differences in tax rates reduces the importance of tax considerations in locational choices and, thus, inefficient competition for tax sources.[7] Higher-level governments can use grants to lower-level governments to encourage them to produce at cost-minimizing levels and to compensate them for the difference between the internal and the external benefit of a public good. Once this allocative role of vertical transfers has been acknowledged, it is straightforward to argue that fiscal equivalence does not imply the assignment of individual taxes to specific jurisdictions. Instead, the collection of taxes can be governed by efficiency criteria, too (Spahn, 1988). Economies of scale in the collection and administration of taxes suggest to entrust the highest-level government with the collection of important taxes such as income or sales taxes. Centralized tax collection can be combined with revenue sharing and vertical transfers assuring the matching of revenues and expenditures for all levels of government. Since the provision of most public goods would remain the responsibility of the lower-level governments, such a system entails that the latter are left with only weak tax sources and rely heavily on transfers from higher-level government. Table 10.1 illustrates this so-called tax gap empirically. Vertical fiscal imbalance can thus be justified as the outcome of designing federal public finances along efficiency standards.

Inter-jurisdictional externalities and mobility are particularly important for macroeconomic stabilization and income and wealth redistribution. Individual states in a federation are generally considered unable to execute stabilization efficiently. Inter-state trade and financial flows would cause the additional demand created by a fiscal expansion in one state to dissipate quickly to the neighboring states. The individual government would bear the full cost of a stabilization program, but reap only a small part of the benefits. The result is another *prisoners' dilemma*: each individual state would refrain from policies to counteract macroeconomic shocks, although all states together would find such policies desirable. Thus, the literature generally agrees that macroeconomic stabilization would be insufficient, if left to regional governments. For similar reasons, it generally concludes that redistribution should be a central government function, too. If not, rich taxpayers would try to evade taxation by moving to regions with low tax rates and low benefits for the poor, leaving those regions with more generous benefits with low-income taxpayers and the need for high tax rates. Again, the resulting equilibrium would yield insufficient redistribution.

Entrusting the central government with stabilization policies implies that stabilization programs are geared at national aggregates rather than regional variables. This does not deny that, in practice, stabilization policies do have regional effects, unless the regional distribution of productive activities is perfectly uniform.[8] However, the assignment of stabilization policies to the central government must assume that the desire for stability of the national aggregates is approximately the same in all parts of a federation and that the regional effects are small compared to the national effects. Similarly, the assignment of redistribution to the central government presumes that the desire for income and wealth equality is approximately the same in all regions of the federation. On a national level, these assumptions are commonly accepted as realistic.

Equalization

Equalization is an implication of the ethical principle that equal citizens deserve equal fiscal treatment regardless of where they live in a federation (Buchanan, 1950). It is generally interpreted as meaning that citizens have a right to the same basic level of *public services* with a similar tax burden in all parts of a federation. For example, the report of the Rowell-Sirois Commission, the first explicit statement of this principle for Canada in the 1940s, argued that equalization was an important aspect of national solidarity and emphasized its strong nation-building character (Cumming, 1986). The constitutional mandate to maintain uniformity of living conditions for all citizens throughout the Federal Republic is the basis for the German system of equalization, the *Länderfinanz-ausgleich* (Bird, 1986). In practice, equalization is oriented at the provision of public goods rather than individual incomes. For the discussion below this is important to note, for it implies that equalization is compatible with regional differences in real income or real growth.

Equalization requires transfers from richer to poorer jurisdictions. Vertical transfers are payments from the central to the local governments financed by central government taxes collected in all parts of the federation. This is the case in Canada, where "Parliament and the Government of Canada are committed to the principle of making equalization payments to ensure that provincial governments have sufficient revenues to provide reasonably comparable levels of public services at reasonably comparable levels of taxation."[9] Alternatively, transfers can be horizontal among local governments without involving the central government, as in Germany.

Competition among Leviathans

The efficiency considerations behind fiscal equivalence are derived from the traditional view of government as a neutral body maximizing public welfare. The modern theory of public choice takes a radically different view. It regards politicians as rent-seeking individuals using their public office to pursue private, selfish goals. This view of government as a "Leviathan" emphasizes the importance of institutions such as constitutional rules forcing politicians to serve the public interest in the pursuit of their own goals and limiting their discretionary power (Brennan and Buchanan, 1977).

The "Leviathan" view of government leads to a different perspective of the optimal regional structure of government. Brennan and Buchanan (1977) argue that, competition among local governments constrains government spending and taxation in a similar way as constitutional restraints. By creating such competition, federalism puts a check on the growth of Leviathan and on rent-seeking politicians. In Hirshman's (1970) terms, federal structures give citizens the opportunity for "exit" – for moving themselves or their assets to jurisdictions whose economic and fiscal policies they prefer – in addition to the "voice" of their democratic votes. Faced with the threat of losing parts of their constituency to other jurisdictions, politicians have to conduct fiscal policies in close accordance with the public's preferences and refrain from excessive rent-extraction. This implies that decentralized government is beneficial even if preferences are homogeneous and economies of scale in the production of public goods are large. Tax harmonization and vertical transfers are, from this perspective, forms of inter-governmental collusion which limit beneficial competition and generate more discretionary power for the politician.[10]

Rogoff (1985) and Kehoe (1989) point to another benefit from competition among governments. In a world of nominal and real rigidities, such as wage contracts or costs of reallocating real capital, public expectations about future government actions are important determinants of macroeconomic outcomes. Collusion among governments, even if it is well-intended to internalize some international spillover, often lowers the cost of deviating from *ex-ante* optimal policies. This would lead the public to expect larger deviations than with independent, competitive policy-making. The result is that, if governments cannot commit formally to *ex-ante* optimal policies, the equilibrium outcomes are worse with cooperating governments.

Finally, in a world of imperfect information and uncertainty, competition has the character of a search process for optimal solutions. The value of this search mechanism extends not only to private markets, but also to governments. Competition among governments means that different policy approaches to a particular problem are tried out. In the end, democracy allows successful approaches to dominate, because only successful governments survive the challenge of elections (Vaubel, 1992). In this sense, decentralized government achieves a higher degree of dynamic efficiency than centralized government.

III   Economic union, monetary union, and fiscal federalism

An economic union is a group of countries with no artificial internal trade barriers, neither tariff nor non-tariff, and no artificial internal barriers to factor mobility, such as capital controls or restrictive work permits. A monetary union is a group of countries using the same currency or linked by irrevocably fixed exchange rates. Since much of the current debate over the European monetary union involves important aspects of economic union as well, we will discuss, in the following, economic and monetary union (EMU) together.

EMU changes the economic ties between countries in important ways.[11] The European program to complete the Single European Market by 1992 exemplifies the effects of economic integration. Economic union, by eliminating trade barriers, enhances trade, and raises the share of intra-union imports in each member's consumption. Increased intra-union competition makes producers and consumers more responsive to regional relative price differentials. The revoking of national-purchase clauses for public procurement in the union implies that government spending in one member country creates direct demand for products of other member countries. Capital market integration gives individual members easier access to the savings and to the investment opportunities in other member countries and makes investors react more swiftly to changes in financial market conditions across the union. All these changes intensify the links between national markets. Monetary union amplifies these effects by lowering the cost of transactions in international trade in goods, services, and assets, by eliminating nominal exchange-rate risk, and by increasing the transparency of the international price system.

The elimination of capital and exchange controls raises capital mobility in an economic union. Labor mobility increases due to the mutual recognition of education and training standards and the right to seek and find employment in any part of the union. Greater factor mobility intensifies competition among governments by creating new "exit" opportunities. Greater mobility also increases the spillovers of public goods across national borders, as consumers find it easier to enjoy the benefits of public goods provided by governments in the adjacent regions of the neighboring countries. As a result, political borders lose much of their economic relevance in an EMU.

How, then, does the creation of an EMU affect the optimal regional allocation of fiscal responsibilities among a group of countries? In particular, is there an unambiguous case for creating a central fiscal institution for the union? Advocates of the parallel-unification proposition answer with a clear "yes." In their view, EMU brings new international externalities and spillovers particularly in the areas of stabilization policy, taxation, and government borrowing in the capital markets. Applying fiscal equivalence, they conclude that EMU demands fiscal unification as a complement. In the remainder of this section, we will look at the main arguments put forth to make this case.

Macroeconomic stabilization

One important argument is that efficient macroeconomic stabilization in an EMU requires a fiscal authority at the center of the union endowed with a sizeable spending power, or, if this is deemed politically unattractive, the close coordination of the members' stabilization policies by a central authority. It rests on two grounds, namely that monetary union eliminates the individual government's option to use monetary policy for stabilization and that EMU increases the spillovers of fiscal stabilization policies among countries.

Before indulging in the argument, we may pause to ask, does fiscal policy still merit attention, today, as a tool for macroeconomic stabilization? Surely, economists and economic policy-makers have lost much of their earlier confidence in its usefulness to fine-tune the economy (e.g.s Chouraqui and Price, 1984), as its instruments are generally too unwieldy to counteract short-term fluctuations. Yet, it is likely that governments will try to resuscitate fiscal policy instruments, once they lose the monetary ones for stabilization in an EMU. Furthermore, even in the absence of "active" counter-cyclical policies, public spending, taxation and borrowing have important macroeconomic effects including international spillovers. Such spillovers may include "growth externalities," i.e., long-run effects on investment and income, in addition to the short-run stabilization externalities usually considered in the literature. Therefore, arguments for fiscal unification based on macroeconomic externalities deserve attention, even if fine-tuning is not the primary fiscal policy goal, today.

The loss of the monetary stabilization instrument for the individual governments raises the importance of a dichotomy of economic shocks hitting the union, namely the distinction between symmetric shocks, i.e., shocks that affect all members in the same way, and asymmetric shocks, which affect some member(s) in a different way than others. It is well known from the literature on monetary policy coordination that union monetary policy can address symmetric shocks, but not asymmetric ones.[12] One might argue, then, that the individual member countries of an EMU have no need for fiscal responses to symmetric shocks. However, this is not necessarily true. The union central bank may be committed strongly to a monetary rule or a "conservative" policy and, from the governments' point of view, pay too little attention to short-run fluctuations. The European example shows that such a design of the common central bank may be attractive to contain long-run inflation trends. Furthermore, as monetary policy is assigned to stabilize the union's price level and output, national balance-of-payments or current-account constraints become the responsibility of fiscal policy. The implication is that the national governments may wish to use fiscal policy instruments to add to the monetary policy response to symmetric shocks and achieve an appropriate policy mix (Lamfalussy, 1989).

Proponents of fiscal unification argue that this cannot be achieved efficiently with independent national fiscal policies, because of the gap between the individual and the group's benefit from stabilization policies conducted by national governments in an EMU. Fiscal unification is necessary to overcome this externality problem.[13] However, by focusing entirely on the size of the spillovers, this position overlooks other, important attributes of an EMU. One is that, as an arrangement among a group of nations, EMU entails significant heterogeneity among policy-makers and their constituencies within the same currency area. An important aspect of this are differences in the interpretations of fiscal policy and its economic effects. Driven largely by different political views, such disagreements are likely to be large in an EMU of countries governed by different political systems and parties. Frankel and Rockett (1988) show that, with disagreements of this kind among the policy-makers, it is possible that policy coordination yields worse outcomes than independent decision-making. Policy-makers may agree on coordinated policies, but the results will make at least one partner worse off. In contrast, refraining from coordination may be viewed as a strategy to reduce the risk of entering a cooperation in which (at least) one partner has a "wrong" view of the world.[14]

Preferences over the objectives of stabilization policies may also differ significantly across member countries. For example, a region whose unemployment rate for structural reasons is much more volatile than the union's average rate – such as Michigan in the US (Eichengreen, 1990b) –

Table 10.2. *Spillover effect of a German fiscal expansion*

Country affected	Germany	France	Italy	UK
Multimod simulation				
real GDP effect	1.04	0.34	−0.36	−0.32
price level effect	1.20	−0.62	−0.76	−0.36
Quest simulation				
real GDP effect	2.10	0.14	0.18	0.38
price level effect	4.50	−1.50	−0.90	−1.70

Notes: German fiscal expansion is two percent of German GDP. All effects are in percent of baseline simulation. Real GDP effects are first-year effects, price level effects, measured on the basis of absorption deflators, are fifth-year effects.
Source: EC (1990), tables 5.5 and 5.6.

may place greater emphasis on policies stabilizing employment than others. The relative performance of the European economies in the past two decades suggests that there is ample disagreement over such issues as the choice between output, employment, or price stability as the primary stabilization objective, or the optimal speed of adjustment to aggregate shocks (De Grauwe, 1990a). Furthermore, prior to the emergence of a unified political body, EMU economic aggregates will seem meaningless at the national level and will not be accepted as objectives for stabilization by the citizens of the EMU. But fiscal unification requires uniform macro-economic policies throughout the union and leaves no room for diversification in accordance with the national preferences. This implies a welfare loss which works against the efficiency gains from resolving potential externality problems.

    Proponents of fiscal unification commonly derive their argument based on models in which only two countries form a union. Unification then internalizes all possible fiscal externalities. But the application of this paradigm to an EMU of more than two countries is quite misleading. Many externalities will be strong among adjacent countries, but weak or non-existent among countries that are further apart. For example, it is plausible to assume that a fiscal expansion in the Netherlands creates extra demand for output in Belgium, but, given the greater (economic) distance, that the spillover to Greece, Portugal, or Spain is zero. Macroeconomic simulations by the European Commission indicate a large variation in the size of bilateral spillovers of unilateral fiscal expansions among the EC countries. This is illustrated in table 10.2, which shows that spillovers of a

Table 10.3. *Standard deviations of real exchange-rate changes in Germany and Europe*

	German Länder						European countries							
	BA	BE	BW	HE	NRW	SA	A	B	DK	F	I	L	NL	UK
Monthly growth rates														
1973–8	17	22	17	18	18	20	55	103	126	186	271	105	111	256
1979–82	12	17	13	14	13	14	39	112	97	111	108	115	53	261
1983–6	12	22	12	13	12	14	30	48	64	72	81	49	34	239
1987–9	9	9	9	12	8	9	23	20	49	38	64	25	25	163
Quarterly growth rates														
1973–8	28	35	26	29	28	31	110	219	222	397	564	207	206	512
1979–82	18	26	18	19	18	19	84	211	183	234	219	257	108	522
1983–6	14	30	15	17	16	19	46	82	113	143	140	82	69	555
1987–9	12	21	12	14	11	12	33	38	87	65	123	41	45	289
Annual growth rates														
1973–8	49	60	45	54	46	49	262	544	409	823	902	502	362	1035
1979–82	30	48	32	35	31	30	217	470	362	563	463	456	195	1133
1983–6	25	49	24	29	25	29	110	288	256	444	279	244	101	929
1987–9	14	27	21	19	17	18	64	62	117	213	286	115	87	808

Note: Entries are averages of real exchange rates based on consumer price indices with 6 German *Länder*, times 1000. BA Bavaria, BE Berlin, BW Baden-Württemberg, HE Hesse, NRW Northrhine-Westphalia, SA Saarland, A Austria, B Belgium, DK Denmark, F France, I Italy, L Luxembourg, NL Netherlands, UK United Kingdom.
Source: von Hagen and Neumann (1991).

German fiscal expansion vary substantially in size and even in sign among the largest partners of Germany in the EC. In view of such differentiated spillovers, uniform responses to macroeconomic shocks would be inadequate to capture the externalities correctly. Instead, a network of bi- and multilateral forms of coordination is required to achieve unambiguous welfare gains from internalizing the spillovers.

Cohen and Wyplosz (1989) and van der Ploeg (1991) claim that the current account of the union becomes "a public good."[15] In their view, a fiscal expansion in one member country causes a real appreciation of the common currency and, consequently, a real income gain over the rest of the world for the entire union, as well as a deficit in the union's current account. As independent national governments do not fully account for the real income benefit of other countries' residents, they do not use spending and tax policies sufficiently to smooth aggregate spending over time in response to exogenous shocks. Again centralized stabilization policies would achieve more efficient outcomes. Their argument, however, hinges critically on the empirically unwarranted assumption that real exchange rates are fixed in an EMU. Table 10.3 shows that, in contrast, the variance of real exchange rates among Germany, the Netherlands, Belgium, and Luxembourg in the late 1980s was of the same order of magnitude as the variance of real exchange rates between the West German *Länder* in the 1970s. The same observation holds for the persistence of real exchange-rate changes over time.[16] Consequently, the empirical strength of the "public goods" character of the EMU current account remains in doubt.

Bilateral, intra-union real exchange rates and current accounts do not mysteriously disappear by the act of economic and monetary unification. One might think that they lose importance, since individual members can finance persistent current-account deficits more easily in an EMU and do not face foreign exchange shortages. But current-account deficits imply wealth transfers and, possibly, differential rates of real capital accumulation. Thus, they remain linked to the location of economic activity and the distribution of wealth in the EMU (Masson and Melitz, 1991) and, therefore, valid constraints of national fiscal policies.

Stabilization of regional shocks

The traditional literature on the optimal currency area (e.g., Kenen, 1969), pointed out that the countries entering a monetary union lose their bilateral exchange rates as instruments to adjust to asymmetric shocks. In the absence of government intervention, adjustment to country-specific shocks requires changes in regional relative prices. With a flexible exchange rate, such changes can be obtained rapidly through exchange-rate adjustment.

But with a common currency, real exchange-rate adjustment must operate through output price changes and changes in factor prices, which are sluggish in reality. Unless EMU fosters price and wage flexibility significantly, fiscal policy, therefore, sees its importance increase in dealing with asymmetric shocks in a monetary union (Wyplosz, 1991).

Suppose a recessionary shock hits a single country of an EMU but no other member directly. With flexible exchange rates, the country's currency would soon depreciate, and the resulting real depreciation would raise export demand and help the economy recover from the shock. In a monetary union, in contrast, relative price changes, and, therefore, the recovery would be very slow. More rapid adjustment can occur either by regional movements of labor and capital, by a domestic fiscal expansion, or by using EMU fiscal policies to direct a greater portion of EMU aggregate demand toward the country originally affected, e.g., by reducing this country's burden of EMU taxes or by increasing EMU public spending in that country. But, for the transactions costs involved, factor movements are an inefficient way to respond to *transitory* regional shocks. In the context of Europe, migration is rendered particularly difficult by language and cultural differences, and may even be considered politically unacceptable as a means of adjustment (Doyle, 1989).

The lack of adequate fiscal mechanisms would expose the EMU to prolonged spells of regional economic disparities unrelated to the underlying trends of regional development, causing strain and dissatisfaction with the EMU and undermining its proper functioning. A centralized fiscal policy could serve as the main mechanism to absorb such shocks. Thus, Jacques Delors, the chairman of the committee for the Study of Economic and Monetary Union (1989, p. 89), argues:

in all federations the different combinations of federal budgetary mechanisms have powerful "shock-absorber" effects, dampening the amplitude either of economic difficulties or of surges in prosperity of individual states. This is both the product of, and the source of the sense of national solidarity which all relevant economic and monetary unions share.

The traditional theory disregards the possibility of domestic fiscal policies to absorb transitory asymmetric shocks for much the same reasons that it ascribes global stabilization policy to the central government. Consequently, the same criticism applies here: a centralized fiscal policy is not obviously more efficient than independent stabilization policies. While it would help overcome the externality problems affecting all union members, it would also widen the gap between regional preferences and regional outcomes produced by a centralized system.

In the European context, the call for a sizeable centralized fiscal budget to stabilize transitory regional shocks in a EMU goes back to the MacDougall Report (European Commission, 1977). It estimated that a budget of about 5 percent of the Community's GNP would be required for a viable EMU, a large expansion compared to the current budget of about 1 percent. The Delors Report (para. 30) foresaw that a central budget of that size was not politically feasible in the near future and, therefore, called for greater coordination of fiscal policies among the members to achieve the same purpose. Von Hagen and Fratianni (1990a) point out that the fiscal mechanism dealing with asymmetric shocks can be based on transfers among the participating countries, channeling income from countries enjoying a positive relative shock to countries suffering from a negative relative shock. Since all relative shocks are zero on average, such a scheme would demand no increase in the overall spending power of the central bureaucracy. From the perspective of fiscal federalism, this would have the advantage that the actual spending authority remains with the national governments, which can use the funds received in accordance with national preferences and priorities.

It is interesting to ask, how relevant the stabilization of asymmetric shocks is in existing monetary unions. Several recent empirical studies come to the conclusion that fiscal redistribution mechanisms from the central government to the state level play only a small role in existing EMUs. Von Hagen (1991b) finds that a transitory 1-dollar loss in real income of a state in the US relative to the average of the union is offset by a reduction of about 8 cents in federal income taxes and 2 cents in federal transfers to individuals. This result is confirmed by Atkeson and Bayoumi (1991), who, studying a much longer time period and more disaggregated data, find an offset of 13.6 cents to a dollar's loss in income relative to the US average.[17] Masson and Taylor (1991) report an offset of 13 percent for Canada. Most of the offsetting transfers operate through the federal income tax system rather than central government spending. Note, finally, that the automatic cross-state "financial equalization" in Germany is designed to respond only to permanent differences in state incomes; its elasticity with regard to transitory asymmetric shocks is small.[18] Most vertical and horizontal transfers in existing federations seem to be of a more permanent nature and not a response to transitory regional shocks.

Von Hagen and Fratianni (1991, 1992, chapter 6) analyze the importance of transfer payments among the members of an EMU in the presence of asymmetric shocks and propagation mechanisms. Transfer payments compensate members of a monetary union hit by adverse idiosyncratic shocks for the loss of their monetary policy instrument. One important result of their study is that trade and capital-market integration alleviates the tensions from asymmetric shocks and reduces the importance of transfer payments to keep the members in the union. This suggests that the absence of large-scale transfer mechanisms to buffer transitory regional shocks in existing federations is due to the high degree of economic integration. A closely related question is, what are the sources of asymmetric shocks in a group of countries? Autonomous, discretionary interventions of the national governments at the macro and micro levels are certainly among the main causes. But, to the extent that greater international competition and mobility reduce their domestic benefits, the incentives for government interventions should be much diminished in an EMU. This suggests that, in addition to providing better propagation mechanisms for dealing with them, EMU also dampens the frequency and strength of asymmetric shocks among the member countries.

Krugman (1990) and De Grauwe (1992) offer the opposite hypothesis, namely that EMU augments the importance of regional shocks. They argue that, in a large region of free labor and capital mobility, individual industries will tend to locate in geographical clusters to exploit intra-industry economies of scale. If this were the case, then preference shifts among individual goods would translate quickly into regional shocks. However, there is no reason to believe that national borders would still play a role in the boundaries of such clusters. The northern European coal and steel region, which extends from northern France over Belgium and the southern Netherlands to the Ruhr, exemplifies this point. This implies that fiscal transfers among the member countries of an EMU, which are still defined by national borders, are not efficient to deal with such shocks.

Insurance against regional shocks

Begg and Wyplosz (CEPR, 1989, p. 23) and Williamson (1991) propose a common EMU unemployment insurance system as a minimal fiscal set-up to tackle regional shocks in a European EMU. This also seems to be the institutional framework behind van der Ploeg's (1991) proposal of a "European Federal Transfer System." Similar to the tax-transfer scheme discussed above, an insurance system would have the political advantage of being budget-neutral in the aggregate.

Wyplosz (1991) argues that an insurance system is preferable to a system of transfers among governments because "we need to recognize that it is individuals who are hit, not States or regions" (p. 181), which is undeniably true. By insuring individuals rather than states against asymmetric shocks, one would also circumvent the problem posed by shocks affecting regions which comprise parts of more than one state. However, it is also clear that unemployment insurance is not the adequate solution. One important reason is that unemployment insurance would benefit only one type of economic activity and only workers; yet, asymmetric shocks affect owners of capital and land and, indirectly, non-employed people in a region just as well. Thus, an unemployment insurance buffering asymmetric shocks would pose severe inequity problems. Even a tax and transfer system based on a federal individual income tax would leave inequities between residents of different states, since there is variation in (and there are incentives to increase) the non-taxable share of total income (Boadway, 1986). If the proper individual insurance scheme cannot be implemented, transfers among the members of an EMU need not be less equitable than unemployment insurance.[19]

Second, there are well-known incentive problems with unemployment insurance. Apart from working against labor mobility within the EMU, because people have fewer incentives to move in response to asymmetric shocks, the availability of an insurance system financed by other countries would make governments less eager to implement efficient labor market policies (van der Ploeg, 1991) and tempt unions into more aggressive wage demands. Van der Ploeg (1991) dismisses these concerns with the remark that they can also be raised against national unemployment insurance, which exists after all. But this rebuttal misses the point. National unemployment insurance with its moral hazard problems is carried by the solidarity of the citizens of a country. As Masson and Melitz (1991) rightly point out, it is very questionable that the same degree of solidarity exists among citizens of countries as different in their culture and ethics as those of the European Community. Ultimately, an EMU unemployment insurance system that lacks the support of solidarity might become a source of political destabilization of the union itself.

Once again, it is interesting to look at the experience of existing monetary unions. The German unemployment insurance system is an example of what Wyplosz, Williamson, and van der Ploeg may have in mind: one system for the entire federal country is administered by a central institution. Unemployment contributions and benefits obey uniform standards in all states. Significant regional differences only kick in when unemployed persons go off the federal unemployment insurance and become eligible for welfare, which is administered locally. The US provides the counter-example (von Hagen, 1991b). Here, unemployment insurance is strictly under the authority and financial responsibility of the states, which operate under federal guidelines demanding minimum standards. Table 10.4 shows that there are significant differences in the benefits of unemployment insurance across states. The main role of the federal government is to be the lender-of-last resort for the individual state insurance system. The US approach has the clear advantage of leaving each state with the possibility to design its system according to the preferences of its population.

Table 10.4. *Variation across states of unemployment insurance in the US*

1989		1988		1989		1988		1989 required minimum	
potential benefits (dollars)		average benefits (dollars)		potential duration (weeks)		average duration (weeks)		base-year earnings (dollars)	
min.	max.	min.	max.	min.	max.	min.	max.	min.	max.
5	382	100	186	1	30	5	21	150	3640

Source: von Hagen (1991b).

To summarize, the importance of fiscal mechanisms to deal with asymmetric shocks has probably been exaggerated in much of the current discussion about a European EMU. If monetary integration proceeds much faster than economic integration, asymmetric shocks may be significant particularly early on. If so, the implementation of a tax-based redistribution mechanism among the member states would be more appropriate than both the creation of a large spending power at the center of the union and a system based on unemployment insurance.

Harmonization of tax policies

Numerous authors have recently discussed tax harmonization in an EMU.[20] In the simplest – popular – interpretation, tax harmonization stands for the close convergence of tax rates in the different regions of the EMU.[21] The traditional argument about inefficient tax competition among governments suggests that EMU demands a high degree of tax harmonization, since EMU raises the mobility of the tax base.[22] With regard to the European EMU, it has been argued that differences in taxes on labor and capital incomes would trigger migration and capital flows and lead to inefficient regional production patterns. Different sales tax rates would distort relative prices that may cause lasting trade imbalances, with the consequence that the monetary union may become unsustainable at some point. The EC (1990, p. 130) concludes that, in a European monetary union, harmonization is most important for value-added and corporate income taxes, which, eventually, should become the EC's own, central tax source.

Several implicit assumptions behind these arguments deserve attention. Regional tax differentials are clearly a source of misallocation in an EMU in which regions are equal in all respects except tax rates on incomes or output. But such extreme homogeneity is unrealistic. First, taxes must be considered as one side only of a larger package of taxes and public goods. For example, if taxes on income finance social security, health insurance, and unemployment insurance, regional income tax differences are justified by differences in those benefits and the public's demand for them. To the extent that the demand for a social safety network is a positive function of real income, regional differences in real income levels entail regional differences in the demand for such services. Fiscal equivalence then implies not only that regional tax differences are justified, but also that regional differences in services are justified and that services should not be administered centrally. Similar considerations apply to other public goods and the taxes raised to finance them.

Second, optimal tax theory teaches that the tax structure should be a function of the structure of price elasticities of demand and supply. There is no reason to assume that EMU equalizes such elasticities.[23] To the extent that demand functions are non-homothetic, price elasticities vary with income levels, so that differences in member states' incomes justify different tax structures (Vaubel, 1992). In an EMU, inefficient trade flows can be avoided by the agreement to levy sales taxes at the point of sale, making the consumer indifferent about the sales tax rate at the point of origin of the good. Finally, countries have different degrees of tax evasion and shadow economies of different sizes as a result.[24] With equal nominal tax rates, effective tax rates would still vary across countries. Since migration, capital flows, and trade flows respond to effective tax rates, nominal tax harmonization would not prevent distortions.

Empirical evidence for the US shows that sizeable variation in tax rates across states can exist in an EMU. Table 10.5 provides some illustrative data. Although these data are not exactly comparable, it is interesting to point out that the standard deviations and ranges of effective direct government tax rates as percentages of national GDP within the EC reported in Eichengreen (1990a) are of similar order of magnitude as those reported in table 10.5.

Even if the case for tax harmonization in an EMU is weak, a strong case can be made for coordination of the *collection* of taxes in an EMU. Economies of scale in the administration of taxes increase, as the volume of trade and income flows across national borders increase. Individual tax payers would spend less time filing their tax liabilities to different member countries, if tax forms are uniform and tax formulae comparable. Similarly, a common tax administration would find it easier and less costly than

Table 10.5. *Characteristics of state taxes in the US*

	average (percent)	standard dev. (percent)	range (percent)
State personal income tax			
marginal rate in lowest bracket	2.5	2.2	10.0
marginal rate in highest bracket	6.6	4.4	14.0
average effective rate on incomes above one million dollars	6.7	3.7	12.9
State corporate income tax:			
marginal rate in lowest bracket	5.1	3.0	11.5
marginal rate in highest bracket	6.4	3.2	12.0
State sales tax rate	4.4	1.8	8.8

Source: ACIR (1990) and Wildasin (1991).

individual, national administrations to monitor and enforce taxes across national borders. Obviously, this would be simplified greatly, if the norms of tax collection are somewhat uniform. For example, the Canadian Central Government – under the Tax Collection Agreements – collects taxes on behalf of the provinces, provided the latter adhere to the same definitions of the tax base (Boadway, 1986). Coordinated tax administration would raise overall tax revenues by reducing tax evasion (Wyplosz, 1991). However, efficient, coordinated tax collection does not require that tax rates be harmonized at all (Break, 1980).

Isard (1990) points to the risk of large real exchange-rate swings due to changes in corporate taxes, which explain some of the movements of the US dollar in the 1980s. In an EMU, such real exchange-rate changes require fluctuations in output prices which could become disruptive for the union as a whole. That is, there is a potential benefit from coordinating the timing of tax reforms among the members of an EMU, without implying that taxes be harmonized.

Coordination of government borrowing

In an EMU, governments of all participating countries are able to borrow in an integrated, union-wide capital market. Governments obtain easier access than before to the savings of other member economies, and all governments borrow in the same currency. These implications have caused the fear that EMU might entail an "undue appropriation" of union savings by individual members. "There is a danger that without coordinated fiscal policies individual member countries might run excessive national deficits and absorb a disproportionate proportion of Community savings" (Lamfalussy, 1989, p. 95).

In an EMU, an increasing deficit of one member government would raise interest rates union-wide and attract savings from all parts of the union to finance the deficit. As interest rates increase, borrowing costs for all governments increase, raising their cost of refinancing outstanding debt and discouraging deficit-financing expenditures. That is, the rising deficit in one country crowds out private investment and consumption and public expenditures in other member countries. However, as long as one member's public does not represent a future tax liability for consumers in other member countries, the nature of this crowding out is different from the traditional, domestic crowding out of private investment by government deficits. For citizens of an EMU member country, the purchase of another member's newly issued government debt increases net private wealth. In their view, the fact that public deficits in the borrowing country crowd out domestic investment is irrelevant since, at the margin, the expected future revenue stream from the investment projects that would have been undertaken otherwise must be equal to the expected future revenue stream from the borrowing country's bonds.

The increase in the domestic government's debt financing cost due to a foreign government's borrowing complicates the situation.[25] Define the domestic government's budget constraint as

$$G - T + iB_{-1} = \Delta B + \Delta M, \tag{1}$$

where G is government expenditure, T tax revenue, B government debt outstanding, ΔM seigniorage revenue, and i the rate of interest paid on public debt, both domestic and foreign. Assuming that monetary policy is run by the EMU's central bank, let seigniorage revenue $\Delta M = 0$ for simplicity, and assume that governments finance fixed ratios of their expenditures G by issuing bonds, i.e., $\Delta B = \alpha G$. This implies that an increase in the government's cost of refinancing the current debt leads to an immediate increase in taxes. The domestic households' wealth constraint, abstracting from real capital and assuming that there are only two countries in the union, is

$$W = W_{-1} + (Y - C) + i(\theta B_{-1} + \theta^* B^*_{-1}) - T, \tag{2}$$

where Y is labor income, C consumption, and θ and θ^* are the shares of domestic and foreign debt outstanding held by domestic households. Consider now the effect of an increase in the foreign government's borrowing, $\Delta B^* = \alpha^* G^*$ on the domestic household's wealth. It consists of two parts, the impact on the interest rate, i, and the increase in the household's tax payments, T. Denoting the elasticity of the interest rate with respect to foreign borrowing as β, and the growth rate of foreign debt as $\lambda^*, \lambda^* = \Delta B^*/B^*_{-1}$, households can choose a portfolio such that the total wealth effect is positive:

$$\theta^* \geq (1 - \theta)[\beta/(\lambda^* + \beta)]B_{-1}/B^*_{-1}. \tag{3}$$

That is, domestic households can hedge against the risk of a negative wealth effect of foreign borrowing by diversifying their portfolios. Expression (3) shows that, to do so, their share of foreign debt should increase with the strength of the interest-rate elasticity and the ratio of domestic to foreign debt outstanding, and decrease with the growth rate of foreign debt.

The domestic government can do its part to protect domestic households from the interest-rate effect of foreign borrowing further by consolidating its debt in long-term bonds, so that the current cost of financing the debt remains largely unaffected by changes in interest rates. Governments in an EMU thus have a greater incentive to choose a high proportion of long-term debt (Bishop, 1991). In sum, crowding-out considerations do not justify caps on or coordination of government borrowing.

Fiscal discipline in an economic and monetary union

If market participants fail to identify the individual government's riskiness and make all governments in an EMU pay the same premium for default risk, another externality from public borrowing arises: a government's raising additional debt affects the common risk premium and, consequently, other governments' cost of borrowing. This has led to the call for borrowing constraints on the individual governments in an EMU to prevent excessive debts (e.g., EC, 1990, Delors Report, para. 33).

However, the common currency denomination alone does not imply that all governments of equal maturity are perfect substitutes. Goldstein and Woglom (1991), for example, show that there are significant interest differentials for municipal debt in the US, and that such differentials can be explained to a large extent by differences in borrowing patterns and policies. Partial and complete default of individual governments in the future can still change the relative values of government obligations, even if they are all denominated in the same currency. The crucial factor behind the potential externality is not the common currency *per se*, but the implicit assumption that the member governments in an EMU will come to each other's help in the case of a financial crisis. If this is true, EMU provides an implicit insurance against illiquidity, which gives rise to a moral hazard problem. Counting on the solidarity among the members of the union, a government may be tempted to run up debt to levels deemed unsustainable in the absence of a union, expecting that the monetary union will monetize its debt in the case of a liquidity crisis rather than letting it face bankruptcy or burden its citizens with large tax increases. Thus, the assumed solidarity of an EMU has two effects: it creates a risk-premium externality and weakens the fiscal discipline of the member governments. Neither one depends on the assumption that markets price risk inappropriately, as alleged, e.g., in the Delors Report (para. 30) or by the EC (1990).

Theoretically, both effects could be avoided by firm no-bail-out rules in the EMU statutes. But such a clause may not be credible. Market participants may not believe that governments would not help each other out in a debt crisis. Systems of regional and structural programs justified on the basis of solidarity and "cohesion" such as in the EC do their part to undermine the credibility of a no-bail-out clause (EC, 1990). In the US, the fact that neither the Federal Government nor the Federal Reserve bailed out the City of New York in its crisis demonstrates that, in contrast, an EMU with a no-bail-out clause is possible. The proof can only be in the practice of EMU.

There are other incentives at work in an EMU that strengthen the fiscal discipline of the member governments. One is that interest-rate differentials are no longer affected by nominal exchange-rate risk and, therefore, are more informative market indicators of the relative quality of the governments as borrowers. Another one is that, without access to the domestic money printing press, national governments in an EMU operate under a "harder" budget constraint (De Grauwe, 1990b; Fratianni and von Hagen, 1990). Moesen and van Rumpuy's (1990) finding that decentralized governments tend to produce smaller aggregate deficits and debts than centralized governments can be interpreted as supporting this point. Thus, even if solidarity prevails, the net effect of EMU on fiscal discipline is ambiguous.

The other important question is, are deficit or debt constraints effective to mitigate the externality and discipline effect? In the US, most states have deficit and debt restraints of varying degrees of stringency. Yet, states with stringent deficit or debt constraints are equally likely to be found in the group of states with the largest deficits or debts (measured as a percentage of gross state products or per capita) as those without or with weak constraints. That is, formal fiscal constraints have not prevented extreme debts and deficits. On the contrary, debt and deficit restraints induce off-budget activities, which reduce the quality of published budget data and, therefore, make it harder for market participants to assess individual government risk appropriately (von Hagen, 1991a). Thus, even if a risk-premium externality exists, it is unlikely that it can be resolved on the basis of borrowing or debt constraints.

IV   The parallel-unification proposition: an assessment

The parallel-unification proposition contends that fiscal unification is a necessary complement to economic and monetary union. Our discussion of the main arguments put forth in the current debate over European monetary union has shown that this proposition focuses entirely on the potential increase of international spillovers in a monetary union. Other consequences of monetary unification which touch on the regional organization of government are neglected. One is that a large degree of heterogeneity of preferences, incomes, political views, and information in a monetary union justifies a large degree of decentralization of fiscal policies. The other is that, in a union of more than two countries, fiscal unification may replace inefficient externalities with equally inefficient internalities. Therefore, to hold up the parallel-unification proposition, increased spillovers must be the only or the dominant characteristic of an EMU. For a union combining a group of nations, this is unrealistic. As a result, the efficiency argument for fiscal unification is not convincing.

At the same time, there are alternative ways to tackle international externalities in a monetary union. Certainly, the union should foster cooperation between governments if they believe that this is in their interest. Institutions to disseminate information throughout the union and to facilitate communication between governments would improve the basis for efficient outcomes. Similarly, the union should support the sharing of administrative functions where this allows exploiting economies of scale, as well as the joint provision of local public goods across borders. None of these possibilities, however, requires unification or coordination imposed from above.

The case for fiscal unification becomes even weaker, once the underlying interpretation of the policy problem is revisited. Arguments about inefficient outcomes produced by externalities and tax competition are based on the view that the interaction of governments is best characterized by a prisoners' dilemma. In this paradigm, independent government policies are undesirable, because it is always in the best interest of the individual government to adopt strategies leading to inefficient equilibria. But it is important to remember that this paradigm rests on the absence of communication among the participating governments and a very short time horizon of the relevant interaction. Both assumptions are highly contrived for an EMU. The very existence of a common central bank facilitates regular communication and mutual consultation. The EMU members certainly expect the union to be a lasting arrangement. The prisoners' dilemma paradigm is, therefore, not a good description of the situation. Instead, game theory leads us to expect that repeated interaction among governments yields efficient outcomes without formal policy coordination nor unification.

One might object to this that fiscal unification is still necessary, even with repeated interaction, to prevent individual governments from defecting from such efficient policy solutions. Unification would reduce avoidable uncertainty about the future of the fiscal regime, allowing governments to commit to long-run policies predicated on the expected fiscal performance of other governments. But this requires that the fiscal union be enforceable, i.e., that the union have the power to penalize members wanting to withdraw sufficiently to assure that the cost of leaving the union is larger than the perceived cost of staying in it. In the international context and in the absence of a firm political union, it seems unlikely that such penalties exist. Domestic voters may "punish" an incumbent government for withdrawing from the union, yet, if the government believes that the cost of membership exceeds the benefits and convinces the voters of its view, the opposite will be true. Foreign governments, in contrast, will have little power to exert credible threats. With no powerful enforcement mechanisms, the fiscal union would have to rely largely on voluntary cooperation, anyway.

Thus, the traditional theory of fiscal federalism does not lend unambiguous support to the parallel-unification proposition. Whether or not unification is desirable can only be determined empirically and by criteria which pose difficult measurement problems. If the case for unification is weak, is there a strong case against it? The modern, public choice-oriented theory of fiscal federalism forcefully asserts that there is. The argument is that fiscal unification, including the international coordination of fiscal policies, tax harmonization, and coordinated borrowing policies must be regarded as forms of collusion among governments that limit competition among governments. Fiscal unification reduces the citizens' opportunities for "exit" and impedes the functioning of competition among public policies as a mechanism for searching optimal policies in a world of uncertain events. In doing so, fiscal unification lowers the quality of government in an economic and monetary union.

Competitive policy-making, on the other hand, does not necessarily

290   Jürgen von Hagen

imply disorderly policy-making. The public-choice interpretation of fiscal federalism entails that the rules of the monetary union should stipulate the regulations under which competitive policy-making may evolve best. This requirement for the fiscal arrangements in a monetary union has been neglected so far. The creation of a framework for fiscal policy competition is entirely consistent with the principle of *subsidiarity* – the principle that decentralized arrangements should be adopted where possible – now embedded in the European economic and monetary union. The rules governing policy competition would include requirements of mutual exchange of information, rules of interaction, such as procedures to initiate and to end bilateral and multilateral forms of cooperation, and other provisions to reduce uncertainty and to direct the competitive process toward efficient outcomes. They may even include explicit rewards for policies deemed beneficial for the union as a whole, such as incentives for budgetary discipline. Rather than trying to press all members into the strait-jacket of unified fiscal policies, the monetary union would thus provide the institutional framework in which competing governments, through repeated interaction, can find the fiscal policies best suited for their countries.

Notes

1 See Masson and Taylor (1991) and De Grauwe (1992) for excellent summaries. I do not consider here the criteria for entering a currency union, such as the convergence of economic performance and policies. See Fratianni and von Hagen (1991) for a discussion.
2 See, e.g., Oates (1972) and Head (1962) for a discussion of the public goods character of stabilization and distributional justice. Oates assumed that stabilization and distribution would naturally be allocated with the central government.
3 Oates (1972), chapter 2, Break (1980), pp. 13 sq.
4 Olson (1969) speaks about internalities when the geographical area of a jurisdiction is larger than the area of incidence of the program it administers.
5 Tiebout (1956) conjectured that such coexistence would lead to an optimal allocation of resources as local governments compete for constituents. For a critique of this argument see Bewley (1981).
6 Even in the Federal Republic of Germany, where the post-war federal structure was decreed by the American, British, and French administrations and redesign of the federal states was mandated by the constitution of 1949, this redesign proved impossible against the opposition of vested interests. The Federal Republic eventually changed its constitutional mandate into a mere possibility in the 1970s. Following German unification in 1990, East Germany's federal structure revived historical boundaries rather than following the rationale of fiscal federalism.

7 Note, however, that there are alternatives to tax harmonization. Boadway (1982), for example, shows how tax systems can be designed to achieve efficient allocations.

8 For a discussion of the regional effects of US stabilization policies see Engerman (1965). Hammond (1991) shows empirical evidence of regional effects of monetary policy in the US.

9 Boadway, Robin F., and Flatters, F.R., *The Economics of Equalization Payments*, a Study for the Economic Council of Canada, in after Graham (1982), p. 247.

10 Bell (1989) shows how a trade-off can be constructed and an optimal balance be struck between the traditional efficiency gains from centralizing government in the presence of externalities and the efficiency losses from lost competition among governments.

11 For a detailed discussion of the effects of economic and monetary union, see European Commission (1990).

12 See, e.g., Fratianni and von Hagen (1991) for a review of the literature.

13 See, e.g., van der Ploeg (1991), Bredenkamp and Deppler (1990), Corden (1986).

14 Ghosh and Masson (1991) present a simulation exercise in which policy-makers are uncertain about the "true" model and, in contrast to the scenario in Frankel and Rockett (1988), take their uncertainty into account when policies are planned. They do not find evidence that international policy coordination leads to worse outcomes than uncoordinated policies. While this does not diminish the importance of Frankel and Rockett's results, it clarifies the importance of a distinction between disagreement and uncertainty. Frankel and Rockett's policy-makers each have dogmatic priors about their own view of the world. This can be interpreted in terms of ideological differences. Ghosh and Masson's policy-makers, in contrast, are merely unsure about the true structure of the world.

15 Bredenkamp and Deppler (1990) argue, however, that governments in a "hard currency regime" should lessen their attention to current-account constraints.

16 Eichengreen (1990a) presents evidence for real exchange-rate variation for the US.

17 An earlier study by Sachs and Sala-i-Martin (1989) concluded that a loss in relative income by 1 dollar was offset by approximately 40 cents, pointing to a much larger role of federal–state redistribution. This study, however, failed to account for the difference in transitory and permanent differences in relative state incomes.

18 See, e.g., Italianer and Vanheukelen (1992). For an exposition of the mechanics of financial equalization in Germany see the appendix to chapter three in Bird (1986).

19 Musgrave (1986, p. 40) argues in a similar way that regional redistribution is an important substitute for inter-personal redistribution given the lack of a perfectly just inter-personal redistribution scheme.

20 Tanzi and Ter-Minassian (1987), Giovannini (1989), Isard (1989, 1990), Eichengreen (1990a), Vegh and Guidotti (1990).

21 Isard (1989) proposes a more refined definition of tax harmonization, which recognizes that tax rates need not converge in an EMU. Instead, Isard (p. 11)

defines harmonization as "setting tax rates in a manner that does not provide strong incentives for tax bases to shift from one jurisdiction to another." The absence of '∙x harmonization in this sense is clearly a source of distortion in an EMU, theoretically and practically. Unfortunately, Isard's concept of harmonization is extremely difficult to operationalize and, hence, offers no guidance for practical policies.

22 See, e.g., van der Ploeg (1991), Wyplosz (1991), and van Rompuy et al. (1991) for a restatement of the traditional argument in the context of the European EMU.

23 For a formal discussion of the optimal tax argument see Rose (1987).

24 Note that different propensities for tax evasion may explain why some European governments have relied more on the inflation tax than others in the past. From this perspective, the convergence of inflation rates in a European EMU would tend to raise the incentive for governments in countries with high degrees of tax evasion to improve the efficiency of their tax-collection systems.

25 See also Wyplosz (1991) for a discussion of this point.

References

ACIR (Advisory Commission on Intergovernmental Relations) (1990), *Significant Features of Fiscal Federalism*, Washington DC: US Government Press.

Atkeson, Andrew and Tamim Bayoumi (1991), "Do Private Capital Markets Insure Regional Risk? Evidence From the United States and Europe," Working Paper, University of Chicago and International Monetary Fund.

Bell, Christopher R. (1989), "Between Anarchy and Leviathan," *Journal of Public Economics*, 49, pp. 207–21.

Bewley, T.F. (1981), "A Critique of Tiebout's Theory of Local Public Expenditures," *Econometrica*, 49, pp. 713–40.

Bird, Richard M. (1986), *Federal Fiscal Finance in Comparative Perspective*, Toronto: Canadian Tax Foundation.

Bishop, Graham (1991), "Public Debt: Credit Spreads or Currency Spreads? A European Perspective," London: Salomon Brothers International, mimeo.

Boadway, Robin (1982), "A Note on the Method of Taxation and the Provision of Local Public Goods," *American Economic Review*, 72, pp. 846–52.

(1986), "Federal Provincial Transfers in Canada: A Critical Review of the Existing Arrangements," in Mark Krasnick (ed.), *Fiscal Federalism*, Toronto: University of Toronto Press.

Branson, William H. (1989), "Financial Market Integration and Monetary Policy in 1992," Working Paper, Marstrand, September.

Break, George F. (1980), *Financing Government in a Federal System*. Studies of Government Finance, Washington DC: Brookings Institution.

Bredenkamp, Hugh and Michael Deppler (1990), "Fiscal Constraints of a Fixed Exchange Rate Regime," in Victor Argy and Paul De Grauwe (eds.), *Choosing an Exchange Rate Regime – The Challenge for the Smaller Industrial Countries*. Washington DC: International Monetary Fund.

Brennan, Geoffrey and James M. Buchanan (1977), "Towards a Tax Constitution for Leviathan," *Journal of Public Economics*, 8, pp. 255–73.

Buchanan, James M. (1950), "Federalism and Fiscal Equity," *American Economic Review*, 40, pp. 583–99.

BMWi (Bundesministerium für Wirtschaft) (1989), *Europäische Währungsordnung*. Gutachten des Wissenschaftlichen Beirats beim BMWi, Bonn.

Center for European Policy Research (CEPR) (1989), *The EMS in Transition*, London.

Chouraqui, Jean C. and Robert W.R. Price (1984), "Medium Term Financial Strategy: The Coordination of Fiscal and Monetary Policies," *OECD Economic Studies*, 2, pp. 7–49.

Cohen, Daniel and Charles Wyplosz (1989), "The European Monetary Union – An Agnostic Evaluation," in Ralph C. Bryant, David A. Currie, Jacob A. Frenkel, Paul Masson, and Richard Portes (eds.), *Macroeconomic Policies in an Interdependent World*, Washington DC: International Monetary Fund.

Corden, W. Max (1986), "Fiscal Policies, Current Accounts, and Real Exchange Rates: In Search of a Logic for International Policy Coordination," *Weltwirtschaftliches Archiv*, 122.

Cumming, Peter (1986), "Equitable Fiscal Federalism: The Problems in Respect of Resources Revenue Sharing," in Mark Krasnick (ed.), *Fiscal Federalism*, Toronto: University of Toronto Press.

De Grauwe, Paul (1990a), "The Cost of Disinflation and the European Monetary System," *Open Economies Review*, 1, pp. 147–74.

(1990b), "Fiscal Disciplines in Monetary Unions," International Economics Research Paper 71, Centrum voor Economische Studiën, Leuven.

(1992), *The Economics of Monetary Integration*, Oxford: Oxford University Press.

Delors, Jacques (1989), "Regional Implications of Economic and Monetary Integration," in Committee for the Study of Economic and Monetary Union, *Report on Economic and Monetary Union in the European Community*, Collection of Papers, Luxembourg: Office for Official Publications of the EC, pp. 81–90.

De Larosiere, Jacques (1990), Speech delivered to the Belgium Royal Society for Political Economy, Brussels, December 12 in BIS *Review*, 251.

Delors Report (Committee for the Study of Economic and Monetary Union) (1989), *Report on Economic and Monetary Union in the European Community*, Luxembourg: Office for Official Publications of the EC.

Doyle, Maurice F. (1989), "Regional Policy and European Economic Integration," in Committee for the Study of Economic and Monetary Union, *Report on Economic and Monetary Union in the European Community*, Collection of Papers, Luxembourg: Office for Official Publications of the EC, pp. 69–80.

Eichengreen, Barry (1990a), "One Money for Europe? Lessons from the US Currency Union," *Economic Policy*, 10, April, pp. 119–86.

(1990b), "Is Europe an Optimum Currency Area?" CEPR Discussion Paper 478.

Engerman, Stanley (1965), "Regional Aspects of Stabilization Policy," in Richard A. Musgrave (ed.), *Essays in Fiscal Federalism*, Studies in Government Finance, Washington DC: Brookings Institution.

European Commission (1977), "Report of the Study Group on the Role of Public Finance in European Integration" (MacDougall Report), Brussels.

European Commission (Commission of the European Communities, Directorate-General for Economic and Financial Affairs) (1990), "One Market, One Money – An Evaluation of the Potential Benefits and Costs of Forming an Economic and Monetary Union," *European Economy*, 44.

Frankel, Jeffrey and Katharine Rockett (1988), "International Macroeconomic Policy Coordination When Policymakers Do Not Agree on the True Model," *American Economic Review*, 78, pp. 318–40.

Fratianni, Michele and Jürgen von Hagen (1990), "Adjustment to Central Bank Dominance," Working Paper, Indiana University Graduate School of Business.

    (1991), *The European Monetary System and European Monetary Union*, Boulder: Westview Press.

Frenkel, Jacob and Morris Goldstein (1990), "Monetary Policy in an Emerging European Economic and Monetary Union: Key Issues," Working Paper WP/90/73, Washington DC: International Monetary Fund.

Ghosh, Atish R. and Paul R. Masson (1991), "Model Uncertainty, Learning, and the Gains from Coordination," *American Economic Review*, 81, pp. 466–79.

Giovannini, A. (1989), "National Tax Systems versus the European Capital Market," *Economic Policy*, 9, pp. 345–86.

Glick, Reuven and Michael Hutchison (1990), "Fiscal Constraints and Incentives with Monetary Coordination: Implications for Europe 1992," Working Paper presented at the Conference "Financial Regulation and Monetary Arrangements After 1992," Marstrand.

Goldstein, Morris and Geoffrey Woglom (1991), "Market-Based Fiscal Discipline in Monetary Unions: Evidence from the U.S. Municipal Bond Market," Working Paper, International Monetary Fund.

Graham, John F. (1982), "Equalization and Canadian Federalism," *Public Finance Publique*, 37, pp. 246–62.

Gros, Daniel (1991), "Fiscal Issues in EMU," *Moneda Y Credito*, No. 193, pp. 11–45.

Hammond, George (1991), "Money and Regional Price Dispersion in the US," Working Paper, Indiana University School of Business.

Head, John (1962), "Public Goods and Public Policy," *Public Finance*, 17, pp. 197–219.

Hirshman, Albert O. (1970), *Exit, Voice, and Loyalty*, Cambridge, Mass.: Harvard University Press.

Isard, Peter (1989), "The Relevance of Fiscal Conditions for the Success of European Monetary Integration," IMF Working Paper WP/89/6.

    (1990), "Corporate Tax Harmonization and European Monetary Integration," *Kyklos*, 43, pp. 25–51.

Italianer, Alexander and Marc Vanheukelen (1992), "Proposals for Community Stabilisation Mechanisms: Some Historical Applications," in European Commission (ed.), *The Economics of Community Public Finance. European Economy* Special Issue 3, Brussels.

Kehoe, Patrick (1989), "Policy Cooperation among Benevolent Governments may be Undesirable," *Review of Economic Studies*, 56, 289–96.

Kenen, Peter B. (1969), "The Theory of Optimum Currency Areas: An Eclectic View," in Robert A. Mundell and Alexander K. Swoboda (eds.), *Monetary Problems of the International Economy*, Chicago: University of Chicago Press.

Krugman, Paul (1990), *Geography and Trade*, mimeo.

Lamfalussy, Alexandre (1989), "Macro-coordination of Fiscal Policies in an Economic and Monetary Union in Europe," in Committee for the Study of Economic and Monetary Union (ed.), *Report of Economic and Monetary Union in the European Community* (Delors Report), Luxembourg: Office for Official Publications of the EC.

Masson, Paul R. and Jacques Melitz (1991), "Fiscal Policy Independence in a European Monetary Union," *Open Economies Review*, 2, 113–36.

Masson, Paul R. and Mark P. Taylor (1991), "Common Currency Areas and Currency Unions: An Analysis of the Issues," Chapter 1 this volume.

Moesen, Wim and Paul van Rompuy (1990), "Government Size, Budget Deficits and Fiscal Decentralization," Public Economics Research Paper 10, Centrum voor Economische Studien, Leuven.

Musgrave, Richard (1959), *The Theory of Public Finance*, New York: McGraw-Hill.

  (1986), "The Economics of Fiscal Federalism," in *Public Finance in a Democratic Society*, Collected Papers of Richard A. Musgrave, Vol. 2, New York: New York University Press.

Oates, Wallace E. (1972), *Fiscal Federalism*, New York: Harcourt Brace Jovanovich.

Olson, Mancur Jr. (1969), "The Principle of 'Fiscal Equivalence': The Division of Responsibilities among Different Levels of Government," *American Economic Review*, Papers and Proceedings, 59, 479–87.

Pauly, Mark V. (1973), "Income Redistribution as a Local Public Good," *Journal of Public Economics*, 2, 35–58.

Pöhl, Karl O. (1991), Statement to the Committee on Economic and Monetary Matters and Industrial Policy of the European Parliament, Brussels, March 18, in BIS *Review*, 65.

Rogoff, Kenneth C. (1985), "Can International Monetary Policy Coordination be Counterproductive?" *Journal of International Economics*, 8, 199–217.

Rose, Manfred (1987), "Optimal Tax Perspective on Tax Harmonization," in Sijbren Cnossen (ed.), *Tax Coordination in the European Community*, Deventer: Kluwer Law and Taxation Publishers.

Sachs, Jeffrey D. and Xavier D. Sala-i-Martin (1989), "Federal Fiscal Policy and Optimum Currency Areas," Working Paper, Harvard University.

Spahn, P. Bernd (1988), "On the Assignment of Taxes in Federal Polities," in Geoffrey Brennan, Bhagan S. Grewal, and Peter Groenewegen (eds.), *Taxation and Fiscal Federalism*, Sydney: Australian National University Press.

Tanzi, Vito and Teresa Ter-Minassian (1987), "The European Monetary System and Fiscal Policies," in S. Cnossen (ed.), *Tax Coordination in the European Community*, Deventer: Kluwer.

Tiebout, Charles (1956), "A Pure Theory of Local Expenditures," *Journal of Policial Economy*, 64, 416–24.

van der Ploeg, Frederick (1991), "Macroeconomic Policy Coordination Issues During the Various Phases of Economic and Monetary Integration in Europe," in *The Economics of EMU*, *European Economy*, Special Edition 1, Brussels: European Communities.

van Rompuy, Paul, Filip Abraham, and Dirk Heremans (1991), "Economic Federalism and the EMU," in *The Economics of EMU*, *European Economy*, Special Edition 1, Brussels: European Communities.

Vaubel, Roland (1992), "Die politische Oekonomie der wirtschaftspolitischen Integration in der Europäischen Gemeinschaft," forthcoming in *Jahrbuch für Neue Politische Oekonomie*, 11.

von Hagen, Jürgen (1991a), "A Note on the Empirical Effectiveness of Formal Fiscal Restraints," *Journal of Public Economics*, 14.

(1991b), "Fiscal Arrangements in a Monetary Union – Evidence from the U.S.," in Don Fair and Christian de Boissieux (eds.), *Fiscal Policy, Taxes, and the Financial System in an Increasingly Integrated Europe*, Deventer: Kluwer.

von Hagen, Jürgen and Michele Fratianni (1990), "Monetary and Fiscal Policy in a European Monetary Union – Some Public Choice Considerations," in: Paul J. Welfens (ed.): *The European Monetary System – From German Dominance to European Monetary Union*, Berlin: Springer.

(1991), "Policy Coordination in the EMS with Stochastic and Structural Asymmetries," in Clas Wihlborg, Michele Fratianni, and Thomas D. Willett (eds.), *Financial Regulation and Monetary Arrangements after 1992*, Amsterdam: North-Holland.

(1992), *The European Monetary System and European Monetary Union*, Boulder, CO: Westview Press.

von Hagen, Jürgen and Manfred J.M. Neumann (1991), "Real Exchange Rate Variability Within and Between Monetary Unions: How far Away is EMU?" Working Paper, Indiana University School of Business.

Wildasin, David E. (1991), "State Income Taxation with Mobile Labor," Working Paper, Indiana University Department of Economics.

Williamson, John (1991), "Britain's Role in EMU," mimeo.

Wyplosz, Charles (1991), "Monetary Union and Fiscal Policy Discipline," in *The Economics of EMU*, *European Economy*, Special Edition 1, Brussels: European Communities.

Index

ADF *see* Dickey-Fuller
Agenor, P.-R. 101
aggregation *see under* money demand
    function
A'Hearn, B. 146, 148
aid 102, 106
Aitken, D. 72
Aizenman, J. 41, 106
Alesina, A. 43
Alexander, W.E. 41
Algeria 98
Aliber, R. 166
Allen, P.R. 40
appreciation of currency 42
arbitrage
    onshore–offshore 167
    former Soviet Union 56–7
ARCH (Autoregressive Conditional
    Heteroscedasticity) 174–7
    in money demand function analysis 247,
        249, 252
Argentina: trade 62–3, 72
Argy, V. 41
Armstrong, H. 139
Artis, M.J. ix, 209
    on exchange controls 169
    on monetary targets 5
    on money demand function, European
        xiv, 240–63
    on price stability 34
    on RIP 167
    on speculative attacks 36
    on substitutability 44
Asian republics of former Soviet Union
    63, 67, 69, 71
asymmetric shocks 17–18
    in Europe 125
        employment 120–2
        and labor mobility 116–18
        output 119–20

and real exchange-rate flexibility
    122–4
and fiscal federalism 274, 277–82
Atkeson, A. ix, 279
    on United States xii, 75–85
Atkinson, P.A. 249
Attanasio, O.P. 147, 148, 157
Australia 14
    fiscal policy 43, 268–9
Austria 12, 105
    exchange rates 128
    fiscal federalism 268–9, 276–7
Autoregressive Conditional
    Heteroscedasticity *see* ARCH

Backus, D. 91
Balassa, B. 72
Baltic Republics of former Soviet Union
    63, 66–7, 69
Balvers, R.J. 209
banks
    Bank for Central African States 96
        see also CFA franc zone
    Bank of England 226
    Banque de donnés régionales see Eurostat
    and CFA franc zone 96, 101, 102
    European Investment Bank 23
    private sector 224–5
    see also central banks; ESCB
Barro, R. 31, 40, 43, 147
Basle–Nyborg Agreement (1987) 36
Bauwens, L. 72
Bayoumi, T. ix, 158
    on capital mobility 10, 166
    on house prices 43
    on money demand function 241–2
    and S-I correlations 43, 165–6
    on shocks 18, 131, 279
    on United States xii, 75–85
BEA *see* Bureau of Economic Analysis

Begg 280
Bekx, P. 241–2, 244
Belgium
  and ESCB 220
  exchange rate 113, 128
  fiscal federalism 275–7, 280
  issues, currency union 15
  labor market migration 116–17
  money demand function 243, 256, 259
  optimum currency theory 113, 116–17,
    124, 128
  output 15
  see also EC
Bell, C.R. 291
Belorussia 63, 67, 69
Benin *see* CFA franc zone
Bertola, G. 42
Bewley, T.F. 290
Bhandari, J. 10
Bianchi, P. 158
Bird, R.M. 268, 270, 291
Bishop, G. 25, 43–4, 286
bivariate vector autoregressive
    methodology 168
Bladen-Hovell, R.C. ix
  on money demand function, European
    xiv, 240–63
Blanchard, O. 92
Blanchard, O.J. 33
Blank, S. 43
Blundell-Wignall, A. 14
Boadway, R. 43, 281, 284, 291
Bofinger, P. 67
Bordo, M.D. 261
borrowing *see* deficits and debts;
    government borrowing
Boughton, J.M. ix, 249
  on CFA franc zone xii, 96–107
Bovenberg, A.L. 42, 43
Boyer, R. 41
Branson, W. 36, 138
Brazil: trade 62–3, 72
Break, G.F. 269, 284, 290
Bredenkamp, H. 44, 291
Brennan, G. 271
Britain
  and ESCB 215, 232, 236
    EMI and 224, 226, 230
    and Maastricht decisions 219, 221
  excess stock returns and capital market
    see capital market intergration
  exchange rate 113–14, 123
  fiscal policy 43, 275–7
  issues, currency union 43
    monetary union, transition to 35, 38
    traditional criteria 10, 11, 14–15, 42

labor markets 132
  data 155–6
  employment and unemployment and
    shocks 121–2, 123, 133–4, 138–9,
    141, 144, 145, 155, 158–9
  mobility/migration 116, 146, 148,
    149–50, 155, 159
  restoring equilibrium 151–4, 160
  money demand function 248, 262
  optimum currency theory 113–14, 116,
    119, 121–2, 123, 127
  output 15, 119, 123
  regions listed 127
  trade 14
  see also EC
Bruno, M. 17
Buchanan, J.M. 264, 270, 271
budgetary policy *see* fiscal policy
Buiter, W.H. 44
Bundesbank 5–6, 34, 44
  and ESCB 218, 219, 239
Bureau of Economic Analysis (US) 83–4,
    89, 92
Burkina Faso 104
  see also CFA franc zone
BVAR methodology 168

Calvo, G. 44
CAMA *see* Central African Monetary
    Area
Cameroon 97, 98, 103–4, 105, 106
  see also CFA franc zone
Campbell, J. 243, 248
Campbell, J.Y. 169–70, 171–2, 188
Canada
  exchange rates 128
  fiscal federalism 265
    and economic and monetary union
      279, 284, 291
    fiscal policy 25, 26–8, 29
    principles of 268–9, 270–1
  issues, currency union 4
    fiscal policy 25, 26–8, 29
    traditional criteria 8–9, 11–16, 17, 41
  output 15–16
  trade 14
  unemployment 8–9
Canzoneri, M. 40, 168
capital market
  in CFA franc zone 102
  intergration and European excess stock
    returns xiii, 163–211
    data and descriptive statistics 173–83
    factor models, observable and
      unobservable 195–205
    forecasting and domestic and

international variables 186–95
methodology 170–3
multivariate cointegration tests 183–6
recent evidence reviewed 164–70
mobility 8, 10, 21
and fiscal federalism 278, 280
portfolio diversification 16
private *see under* United States
speculative attack 35–7
speculative efficiency 167
Caribbean *see* Eastern Caribbean
Currency Area
Caroleo, F.E. 159
Caroll, C. 91
Central African Monetary Area 6
see also CFA franc zone
Central African Republic *see* CFA franc
zone
Central Bank for West African States 96
see also CFA franc zone
central banks
and CFA franc zone 96, 102
and convergence 33
and fiscal policy 22–3, 264, 274
and monetary policy 6, 38
former Soviet Union 66
see also banks; ESCB
centralization in former Soviet Union
56–8, 72
CFA franc zone (Communauté Financière
Africaine) xii, 96–107
currency arrangements 100–5
economic performance 97–100
issues, currency union 6, 12–13, 25, 40
Chad 103
see also CFA franc zone
Chapman, P.G. 160
Chile: trade 62
Choudhri, E.U. 261
Chouraqui, J.C. 273
Chow, G. and CHOW in money demand
function analysis 247, 248–50, 252,
255
CIP *see* covered interest parity
clearing by ESCB 227–9
Cochrane, J. 16, 91
Cohen, D. 18, 112, 158, 277
cointegration
and labor market analysis 150–4
money demand function 242–4, 250, 252
multivariate tests of capital market
integration 183–6
collection of taxes 283–4
COMECON, former 63–5, 66
Commerce Department (US) 89, 91, 92
see also Bureau of Economic Analysis

Commission, EC
and ESCB 217, 220, 235, 237
and fiscal federalism 275, 279, 291
and issues, currency union 3, 7, 16, 20,
42
and optimum currency theory 112, 118,
124, 128
and former Soviet Union 55, 63, 72–3
Communauté Financière Africaine *see*
CFA franc zone
competition
among governments and fiscal
federalism 271–2
in former Soviet Union, 56–8, 72
Condé, J. 104
Congo 103–4, 105
consumption fluctuations in United States
76–7, 88–90, 92–3
convergence
defined 30
and ESCB 219–20
issues in currency unions 29–33, 39, 44
Cooper, R.N. 5
Cooper, S. 165, 167
coordination
fiscal policy 28–9
government borrowing 285–6
of policy and ESCB 233–6
Corden, W.M. 40, 42, 43, 101, 291
Cosimano, T.F. 209
Côte d'Ivoire 97, 98, 101, 103, 104, 105
see also CFA franc zone
Council, EC 23, 40
and ESCB 217, 220, 234, 235, 237
covered interest parity and capital market
integration 166–7
credibility of monetary policy 5
Creedy, J. 159
Cumby, R.E. 168
Cumming, P. 265, 270
currency
substitution and money demand
function 241, 251, 253–4, 257–60
unions
defined 3
see also CFA franc zone; European
monetary union; existing currency
unions; fiscal federalism; fiscal
policy; issues; monetary union;
optimum currency area
Currie, D.A. 5
customs union in former Soviet Union
59–65, 72

Damrau, D. 25, 43–4
De Grauwe, P. ix, 290

300   **Index**

De Grauwe (*cont.*)
  on budget constraint 287
  on optimum currency area xiii, 111–29
  on shocks 16, 158, 275, 280
  on single-criterion approach 41
De Larosière, J. 266
de Melo, J. 106
Dean, A.M. 165
decentralization and fiscal federalism 265,
    267, 278–9, 290
defecits and debts
  in CFA franc zone 100
  and ESCB 219, 237
  and fiscal policy 23–5, 285–8
  incentives for excessive 24
  and monetary union, transition to 35–6,
    44
  ratio and ESCB 220–1, 229
  see also government borrowing
Delors, J.: Delors Committee Report 10,
    23, 38
  and ESCB 216, 217, 218–19, 223
  and fiscal federalism 278–9, 286–7
Denmark
  and ESCB 215, 220, 221
  exchange rate 113
  fiscal federalism 276–7
  issues, currency union 15, 25
  labor market 116
  money demand function 243, 256, 260
  optimum currency theory 113, 116
  output 15
  see also EC
Deppler, M. 44, 291
depreciation of currency 42, 278
Devarajan, S. 100, 103, 105, 106
Dickey–Fuller and Augmented
    Dickey–Fuller tests (DF and ADF)
    151, 178–9
  and money demand function 244–5, 247,
    248, 250, 252–3
diversification 4
  output 13–16
  portfolio 16, 81–8
Dominguez, K. 37
Dooley, M. 10, 165
Dornbusch, R. 7, 42, 43, 44
Doyle, M.F. 278
Driffill, J. 44

East Germany 3, 39, 42, 290
Eastern Caribbean Currency Area 13, 41
Eastern Europe 3, 12, 39, 41, 218, 290
EC (European Community)
  central bank *see* ESCB
  excess stock returns and capital market

  see capital market integration
fiscal federalism 272, 275–82, 286, 291
issues, currency union 4
  convergence 29–33
  fiscal policy 23, 25, 26, 28, 43
  monetary policy 6, 7, 40
  monetary union, transition to 33–8,
    44
  traditional criteria 8–12, 14–16, 19–20,
    41–2
labor *see* labor markets
output 15–16
and former Soviet Union 55–6, 59, 62–4,
    69, 70–1, 72–3
trade 14
unemployment 8–9
see also Commission; Council; money
    demand function; optimum
    currency area *and also* individual
    countries
ECB (European Central Bank) 33, 237,
    239
  and EMI 226, 228, 229
  and Maastricht decisions 216, 218–19,
    222
  and note issue 232
  and policy coordination 233–4
econometric analysis *see* capital market
    integration
economic performance 97–100
economic union
  defined 270
  see also currency unions; fiscal
    federalism
economies of scale in production of public
    good 267, 269
ECU 12, 38
  and ESCB 216, 218, 225, 235
  clearing 228
  transition to 230–3
  Hard Ecu proposal 38, 40
  and money demand function, European
    243, 244–5, 246, 252–3
efficiency
  gains and monetary union, transition to
    37
  Pareto-efficiency 267
  speculative 167
EFTA 12
Eichengreen, B. ix, 3, 40, 43, 44
  on exchange rate 291
  on labor markets and European
    monetary unification xiii, 130–62
  on labor mobility 8
  on optimum currency area 128
  on price flexibility 41

on shocks 112
on tax 283
on unemployment 274
Emerson, M. 59
EMI *see* European Monetary Institute
emigration *see* mobility/migration *under*
labor markets
employment *see* unemployment and
employment
EMS *see* European Monetary System
EMU *see* European Monetary Union
energy price and labor market shocks
138–46, 156, 157, 160
Engerman, S. 291
Engle, R. 160, 169, 171, 243, 245, 261
equalization and fiscal federalism 270–1
Equatorial Guinea 106
see also CFA franc zone
equivalence, fiscal 266–70
ERM *see* Exchange Rate Mechanism
ESCB (European System of Central
Banks) after Maastricht xiii–xiv,
215–39
Maastricht decisions 216–22, 239
note issue and seigniorage 230–3, 239
overall strategy 236–8
policy coordination 233–6
see also European Monetary Institute
Europe
and CFA franc zone 99, 101–2, 103, 105
excess stock returns *see* capital market
integration
see also EC; issues, currency unions;
labor markets; optimum currency
area *and* entries beginning
European
European Central Bank *see* ECB
European Commission *see* Commission,
EC
European Council *see* Council, EC
European Currency Unit *see* ECU
European Federal Transfer System
suggested 280
European Investment Bank 23
European Monetary Fund 33
European Monetary Institute suggested 33,
34
and ESCB 215, 220, 223–30
central banks as banks to
governments 224–5
clearing and settlement 227–9
open market operations for monetary
policy 225–6
prudential and regulatory issues 219,
229–30
European Monetary System

excess stock returns and capital market
see capital market integration
and issues, currency union 4, 30, 39
fiscal policy 21–2, 29, 42
monetary policy 5–6, 40
monetary union, transition to 34–6,
44
traditional criteria 10, 11, 18–20
and former Soviet Union 71
see also ESCB; Exchange Rate
Mechanism; money demand
function; optimum currency area
European Monetary Union 33–4, 125
after Maastricht *see* ESCB; fiscal
federalism; money demand
function, European
issues, currency union 3, 4, 6, 16, 20, 26,
34, 37
and optimum currency area, Europe as
124–6
see also currency unions; ESCB; fiscal
federalism; labor markets and
European monetary unification;
money demand function
European Parliament 217, 235
European System of Central Banks *see*
ESCB
Eurostat 113–16, 119, 123
excess stock returns *see* capital market
integration
exchange rate
and capital market integration 163, 166,
167, 169, 174
and ESCB 219, 226, 227–8, 230, 234
fixed to French franc *see* CFA franc
zone
and issues, currency union convergence
31, 39
fiscal policy 21, 24, 29, 41–2
monetary union, transition to 35–7
traditional criteria 7–8, 15, 18–19
real
and fiscal federalism 264, 272, 276,
277–8, 284, 291
flexibility and asymmetric shocks
122–4
and labor market shocks 138–46, 156,
157, 160
variability 112–16, 128
and former Soviet Union 65, 68, 72–3
union *see* monetary union
see also Exchange Rate Mechanism;
money demand function
Exchange Rate Mechanism
and capital market integration 164,
173–4

Exchange Rate Mechanism (*cont.*)
  and issues, currency union 30
    monetary policy 5, 40
    monetary union, transition to 34–6,
      44
    traditional criteria 10, 11, 18
  and money demand function 241–3, 245,
    248–54, 262
  see also exchange rate
existing currency unions *see* CFA franc
    zone; Soviet Union, former *and*
    private capital markets *under*
    United States
exports *see* trade

facilitating transactions 5
factor
  mobility 7–11, 104, 272
  models, observable and unobservable
    and capital market integration
    195–205
Fama, E. 209
federal systems
  fiscal *see* fiscal federalism
  see also Australia; Canada; Germany;
    regionalism; Soviet Union; United
    States
Feinstein 156
Feldstein, M. 10, 165
financial markets *see* capital market
    integration
finance based tests and capital market
    integration 168–70
Finland 12
  trade 62–3, 69
fiscal discipline 286–8
fiscal equivalence 266–70
fiscal federalism xiv, 26–8, 39, 264–96
  decentralization 265, 267, 278–9, 290
  and economic and monetary union
    272–88, 291–2
    fiscal discipline 286–8
    government borrowing coordination
      285–6
    harmonization of policies 282–4
    shocks 277–8, 280–2
    stabilization 269–70, 273–8
  and government borrowing 24
  principles 266–72, 290–1
    competition among Leviathans 271–2
    equalization 270–1
    fiscal equivalence 266–70
  former Soviet Union 58–9
  see also fiscal policy; parallel unification
fiscal policy
  and ESCB 217, 234–5

and issues, currency union 4, 48–9
and labor market 150
unification *see* fiscal federalism
within currency areas 21–9, 42–4
  budget discipline prospects 23–6
  coordination 28–9
  flexibility and interregional transfers
    26–8
  government borrowing in fiscal
    federalism 24
  spillovers from national policies 21–3
  see also fiscal federalism
fiscal reciprocity 266–70
fiscal union *see* fiscal federalism
Flatters, F.R. 291
flexibility
  fiscal and interregional transfers 26–8
  lacking in ESCB plans 237
  price 4, 16–17, 41
  of real exchange rate 122–4
  and successful currency union 16–17
  wages 4, 7–8, 41
Flood, R.P. 41, 106
Folkerts-Landau, 229
forecasting excess returns 186–95
France
  central bank 224
  and CFA franc zone 99, 101–2, 104–5
  excess stock returns and capital market
    see capital market integration
  exchange rate 113
  fiscal federalism 275–7, 280
  inflation 99
  issues, currency union 13–15, 18, 42
  labor market
    employment and unemployment 121,123
    migration 116–17, 131
  money demand function 243, 249–53,
    254, 256, 258, 261, 262
  optimum currency theory 113, 116–17,
    119, 121, 123, 126
  output 15, 119
  regions listed 126
  trade 14
  see also CFA franc zone
  see also EC
Frankel, J.
  on capital mobility 10
  on CIP 167
  on policy coordination 274, 291
  on PPP 168
  and S-I correlation 10, 165, 166
  on time series tests 160
Fraser, P. ix
  on capital market integration xiii,
    163–211

Fratianni, M. 279–80, 287, 290, 291
French, K.R. 209
Frenkel, J.A. 18, 41, 42, 106, 166
Friedman, M. 32
Fuller, W. 245
see also Dickey-Fuller
Furstenberg, G. 169, 209

Gabon 97–8, 104, 105, 106
see also CFA franc zone
Gambia 98, 106
Garber, P. 229
GARCH 167
GDP and GNP *see* output; product
Gellner 144
Generalized Model of Moments 173
Germany
and ESCB 226, 232, 234, 239
and Maastricht decisions 218, 219,
221
excess stock returns and capital market
see capital market integration
exchange rate 113–14, 123, 128
fiscal policy and fiscal federalism 21, 43
and economic and monetary union
275–7, 279–80, 291
principles of 268–9, 270–1, 290
issues, currency union 3, 39
fiscal policy 21, 43
monetary policy 5–6, 7, 14–15, 40
traditional criteria 10, 14–15, 18, 41–2
labor market
employment and unemployment
120–2, 123
migration 116–17, 131
monetary policy 5–6, 7, 14–15, 40
money demand function 241, 243,
249–53, 256–7, 261
optimum currency theory 113–14,
116–17, 119, 120–2, 123, 126, 128
output 15, 119, 120, 123
regions listed 126
trade 14, 62
see also EC
Ghana 98
Ghosh, A.R. 291
Giavazzi, F. 7, 18, 35, 40, 43, 44, 101
Giersch, H. 128
Giovannini, A. 35, 40, 43, 44, 231, 291
Goldstein, M. 18, 43, 158, 286
Goodhart, C.A.E. ix, 4, 40, 169
on central banks, European xiii–xiv,
215–39
Goodman, J. B. 43
Gordon, D. 40, 43
Gordon, J. 43

Gordon, R.J. 33
government
banks to *see* central banks; ESCB
borrowing 24, 36
coordination 285–6
see also deficits and debts
Leviathan view of 271–2
see also fiscal federalism; fiscal policy
Graham, J.F. 43, 291
Granger, C.W.J. 169, 171, 243, 245
Greece
exchange rate 113
fiscal policy 43, 275
issues, currency union
convergence 31–2
fiscal policy 43
monetary policy 4, 7, 40
monetary union, transition to 34
traditional criteria 15–16
optimum currency theory 113
output 15–16
trade 62–3
see also EC
Greenwood, M.J. 147
Gregory, R.G. 14
Grilli, V. 7, 43
Gros, D. ix, 40
on former Soviet Union xii, 55–74
gross capital position, measurement of
inter-regional 76, 81–8, 92
Gualtieri, G. 158
Guidotti, P.E. 44, 291
Guillaumont, P. 106
Guinea 106
Guinea-Bissau 98, 106

Hall, R. 151
Hamada-Iwata ratio 99
Hamao, Y. 169–70, 171–2
Hammond, G. 291
Hansen, L.P. 173
Hard Ecu proposal 38, 40
harmonization of fiscal policy 282–4, 292
Hart, R.A. 159
Head, J. 290
Helpman, E. 72
Henderson, D.W. 36, 41
Hertzberg, M. 89
heteroscedasticity (HET) in money
demand function analysis 248–9,
252
see also ARCH
Hirshman, A.O. 271
Horioka, C. 10, 165
Horry, I.D. 44
Howe, J.S. 169

Hughes, G. 146
hyperinflation 66

IMF *see* International Monetary Fund
Imlah, A. 92, 93
immigration *see* mobility/migration *under*
    labor markets
imports *see* trade
income
    and product
        in CFA franc zone 97, 104
        in United States
            inter-regional gross capital position
                76, 81–8, 92
            net capital flows 75–6, 77–81, 91–2
            regional consumption fluctuations
                76–7, 88–90, 92–3
            see also output
    real *see* money demand function
    see also wages
industrial diversification and successful
    currency union 13–16
inflation
    in CFA franc zone 99, 100
    and ESCB 219, 221
    and issues, currency union 4, 5, 42
        and convergence 29–30, 32
        and fiscal policy 22
        and shocks 19–20
    in former Soviet Union 66
    tax 292
        see also seigniorage
    see also money demand function; price
        instability sources and monetary
        union 34–7
    see also shocks
insurance against shocks and fiscal
    federalism 280–2
integration *see* capital market integration
inter-regional gross capital position,
    measurement of 76, 81–8, 92
interest rates
    and capital market integration
        data and statistics 173, 174–7, 181–3
        factor models 196–207
        forecasting 188–95
        recent evidence 165–8
    and ESCB 216, 219, 225, 233
    and fiscal federalism 285, 287
    and issues, currency union 30, 37
    real interest-rate parity 167–8
    see also money demand function
International Monetary Fund
    and Africa 97, 100
    and ERM and inflation 30
    and exchange rates 97, 102

and money demand function 255–60
and MULTIMOD model 18–20, 21, 42
and trade 62, 64, 65
investment *see* capital market
Ireland
    and ESCB 220
    fiscal policy 25, 43
    money demand function 243, 256
    see also EC
Isard, P. 168, 284, 291–2
Ishiyama, Y. 41
issues, currency union xi–xiii, 1–51
    convergence 29–33, 44
    fiscal policy within currency areas 21–9,
        42–4
    monetary policy 5–7, 40
    monetary union: .transitional issues
        33–8, 44
    traditional criteria for successful 7–20,
        40–2
Italianer, A. 291
Italy
    excess stock returns and capital market
        see capital market integration
    exchange rate 113
    fiscal federalism 275–7
    issues, currency union 7, 43
        traditional criteria 11, 14–15, 41, 42
    labor markets 116–17, 118, 132
        data 156–7
        employment and unemployment and
            shocks 120–2, 133, 134–6, 140–3,
            144, 145, 156, 158–9
        migration 146–7, 148–50, 156–7, 159
        restoring equilibrium 151–4, 160
    monetary policy 7
    money demand function 243, 249–53,
        256, 258, 261
    optimum currency theory 113, 116–17,
        118, 120–2, 126–7
    output 15
    regions listed 126–7
    trade 14
    see also EC

Japan
    and European capital market integration
        169–70
    exchange rate 113
    fiscal policy 22
    issues, currency union 11, 14, 15, 22
    optimum currency theory 113
    output 15
    trade 14
Jeon, B. 169, 209
Johansen, S. 171, 185, 261

Jurgensen, P.: Report 37
Juselius, K. 171, 185

Kaser, M.C. 72
Katz, L. 92
Kehoe, P. 91, 271
Kenen, P. 41, 128, 241–2, 277
King, M. 169
King, R. 158
Krasker, W.S. 44
Kremers, J.
   on aggregate demand for money 242–4,
      245, 248–9, 253–4, 261–2
   on currency substitution 35
   on fiscal policy 42
Krugman, P. 31, 64, 125, 128, 280
Kydland, F. 91

labor markets
   and European monetary unification xiii,
      130–62
   data 155–8
   income see income; wages
   mobility/migration 4, 8, 43, 116–18,
      130–2, 146–50, 159
   and regions 131–2, 138–46, 158–9
      restoring equilibrium 150–4, 160
   see also unemployment
mobility/migration
   in CFA franc zone 104
   and fiscal federalism 278, 280
   limited in former Soviet Union 70, 73
   in United States 93
   see also under European above
Lagrange multiplier (AR) in money
      demand function analysis 247,
      248–50, 252
Lamfalussy, A. 265, 274, 285
Lane, T.D. 35
   on aggregate demand for money 242–4,
      245, 248–9, 253–4, 261–2
Langley, P.C. 159
Latin America: trade and regional
      integration 61–3, 72
lender of last resort function 219
Leviathan view of government 271–2
Levich, R.M. 166
Levy, V. 103
Liberia 100, 106
Libya 98, 106
Lipton, D. 72
Lithuania 63, 67, 69
Lo 209
local government and fiscal federalism
      267–9, 271
long-run considerations of Soviet common

currency 69–70
Love, J. 138
Luxembourg
   exchange rates 128
   fiscal federalism 276–7
   see also EC

Maastricht
   and issues, currency union 3, 23, 30, 33,
      34, 38
   see also ESCB
MacArthur, A. 168
McCormick, B. 146
McDonald, B. 209
MacDonald, R. ix, 44
   on capital market integration xiii,
      163–211
MacDougall Report 279
Mace, B. 91
MacKinley 209
McKinnon, R. 11, 128, 241, 244
McMaster, I. 146–8, 155, 159
Madura, J. 169
Mali 103, 104
   see also CFA franc zone
Marion, N. 41, 106
Masciandaro, D. 43
Massarotto, G. 156
Masson, P.: on currency union issues ix,
      xi–xiii, 1–51, 290, 291
   current account deficits 277
   offset 279
   private capital markets 88
   unemployment insurance 281
Mastropasqua, C. 241
Mathieson, D. 10, 165
Mauritiania 98
Mayer, T. 10
measurement
   of exchange rate 113–15
   of inter-regional gross capital position
      76, 81–8, 92
medium-run considerations of Soviet
      common currency 67–8
Mélitz, J. 22, 40, 43, 44, 277, 281
Meltzer, A. 111
Meredith, G. 42
Mexico 12, 13
Micossi, S. 241
Middle East: trade with former Soviet
      Union 63
migration see mobility/migration under
      labor markets
Miller, E. 147
Miller, M. 25, 43–4
Mishkin, F.S. 168

Mitchell, B.R. 156
mobility
    capital market 8, 10, 21, 278, 280
    see also factor mobility and also
        mobility/migration under labor
        markets
Möbius, U. 72
Moesen, W. 287
Monaco 102
monetary policy
    and convergence 29–30
    and ESCB 225–6, 234–5, 239
    and issues, currency union 5–7, 40
    and monetary union, transition to 37
    see also monetary union
monetary union
    defined 272
    distinct from currency union 3
    and fiscal policy see under fiscal
        federalism
    transition to 39
    transitional issues 33–8, 44
    see also European Monetary Union;
        monetary policy; Soviet Union,
        former
money demand function, European xiv,
        24, 240–63
    aggregation 246–51, 256
        bias, testing for 251–3
    cointegration 242–4, 250, 252
    currency substitution 241, 251, 253–4,
        257–60
    data 255–60
    evidence 244–5
money markets 226
    see also capital market
Monte Carlo method 171
Monticelli, C. 242
Morocco 98
MULTIMOD model 18–20, 21, 42
multinationals 101
multivariate cointegration tests of capital
        market integration 183–6
Mundell, R. 7–8, 72, 111, 130, 131
    Mundell–Fleming model 21, 165
Musgrave, R. 264, 266, 291
Mussa, M. 36
Myrdal, G. 30, 128

net capital flows in United States 75–6,
        77–81, 91–2
Netherlands
    exchange rate 113–14, 123, 128
    fiscal federalism 275–7, 280
    issues, currency union 15–16
    labor market

employment and unemployment 123
    migration 116–17
money demand function 243, 256, 259
optimum currency theory 113–14,
        116–17, 119, 123, 124, 127, 128
output 119, 123
regions listed 127
see also EC
Neumann, M.J.M. 112, 128, 276
neutrality, risk 167
New Zealand 14
    Reserve Bank 238
Newman, J.L. 103
Niger 104
    see also CFA franc zone
Nigeria 98
no-bail-out rules 287
nominal shocks 17
NORM (normality) in money demand
        function analysis 247, 248–9, 252
Norman, M. 238
Norway 12
note issue and ESCB 230–3, 239

Oates, W.E. 264, 290
observable factor models 172–3
    and capital market integration 196–204
Obstfeld, M. 37, 44, 166, 168
OCS regression 165
ODA (official development assistance) 102,
        106
OECD
    and capital market integration 166, 168
    and CFA franc zone 106
    and exchange rate 113–16
    and money demand function 243
    and output 119
    and production 15
    and trade 62–3
official development assistance 102, 106
Olson, M. Jr. 266–7, 269, 290
onshore-offshore arbitrage 167
open market operations and ESCB 225–6
openness and successful currency union
        11–13
Operations Accounts (France) 102
optimal tax theory 283
optimality of customs union in former
        Soviet Union 60–5
optimum currency area, Europe as xiii,
        111–29, 130, 264
    and EMU, implications for 124–6
    labor mobility 116–18
    real exchange rate
        flexibility 122–4
        variability 112–16, 128

and shocks *see* Europe *under*
asymmetric shocks
see also capital market integration; labor
markets and European monetary
unification
Organization for Economic Cooperation
and Development *see* OECD
Oudiz, G. 42
output 275
in CFA franc zone 97, 99, 102, 103, 104,
106
diversification 13–16
and Europe as optimal currency area
119–20, 123, 128
and issues, currency union
and convergence 21–3
and diversification 13–16
and fiscal policy 42
and shocks 19–20
and labor market 158
former Soviet Union 61, 69
see also product

Padoa Schioppa, F. 147, 148, 157
Pagano, M. 35, 101
parallel unification proposition 265–6, 291
assessment of 288–90
and economic and monetary union
272–88
principles of 266–72
Pareto-efficiency 267
Paris Club 100
parity conditions and capital market
integration 166–8
permanent shocks 17
Perron, P. 170, 178, 243, 248
Perroux, F. 30
Pissarides, C. 146–8, 155, 159
Pöhl, K.O. 43, 265
Poland: trade 64–5
policy
coordination and ESCB 233–6
see also currency unions; fiscal policy;
monetary policy
political independence of ESCB 217, 218
political risk 166
Poloz, S. 41, 122, 128
portfolio diversification 16, 81–8
Portugal
exchange rate 113
fiscal federalism 275
issues, currency union
convergence 31–2
fiscal policy 43
monetary policy 4, 7
monetary union, transition to 34

traditional criteria 15–16
optimum currency theory 113
output 15–16
see also EC
Powder, D. 209
PPP *see* Purchasing Power Parity
Price, R.W.R. 273
price
and fiscal federalism 264, 275, 283
flexibility 4, 16–17, 41
and issues, currency union 4, 7–8, 34, 41
and labor market shocks 43, 138–46,
156, 157, 160
reform in former Soviet Union 56–7
stability 264
in CFA franc zone 97–8, 99–100, 103,
104, 106
ensuring 5
and ESCB 217, 218, 233–4, 235,
237–8
see also exchange rate; inflation; money
demand function
prisoners' dilemma 267, 269
private capital markets *see under* United
States
private sector banks 224–5
product *see* income and product; output
protectionism in former Soviet
Union 59–60, 61, 72
prudential issues and ESCB 219, 229–30
public good concept 265, 277, 283
economies of scale in production of 267,
269
public service equalization 270–1
Purchasing Power Parity 167, 168, 243–4,
262

rationality 167
Razin, A. 42
real exchange rate *see under* exchange rate
real interest-rate parity 167–8
real shocks 17
reciprocity, fiscal 266–70
regionalism
integration in Latin America 61–2
interdependence and successful currency
union 11–13
interregional transfers and fiscal
flexibility 26–8
and issues, currency union 4, 16
fiscal policy 26–9, 39
traditional criteria 8–9, 10–11, 40–1
and labor market shocks 131–2, 138–46,
158–9
restoring equilibrium 150–4, 160
and optimum currency areas, Europe as

regionalism (*cont.*)
    asymmetric shocks 118–22, 125
    exchange-rate variability 112–16
    and labor mobility 116–18
    protectionism in former Soviet Union
        59–60
    in United States xii, 75–95
        consumption fluctuations 76–7, 88–90,
           92–3
        inter-regional gross capital position
           76, 81–8, 92
        net capital flows 75–6, 77–81, 91–2
    see also federal systems; fiscal federalism
regression analysis
    and capital market integration 165–6,
        168, 170
    of income and product in United States
        81–8, 89–90, 93
    of labor markets 150–4
    see also money demand function
regulatory issues and ESCB 219, 229–30
required reserves of ESCB 226–7
Reserve Bank of New Zealand Act 238
reserve ratios and ESCB 226–7
Ricardian equivalence 165
Rinaldi, R. 241
RIP *see* real interest-rate parity
risks and capital market integration 166,
    167, 169
Rockett, K. 291
Rodrik, D. 100, 103, 105, 106
Rogers, C.A. 40
Rogoff, K. 43, 271
Rose, A. 10, 91
Rose, M. 292
Roubini, N. 42
Rowell-Sirois Commission 270
Russian Federation and Republic 13, 67
Russo, M. 158

Sachs, J.D. 17, 26–7, 33, 42, 72, 88, 291
Sala-i-Martin, X. 26–7, 31, 88, 147, 291
sales fluctuations in United States 76–7,
    88–90, 92–3
Salvatore, D. 146
savings-interest correlations 10, 77
    and capital market integration 164,
        165–6, 167
Schumacher, D. 72
Scytovsky, T. 128
seigniorage 6–7, 24
    and ESCB 230–3, 239
Sénégal 103, 104
    see also CFA franc zone
settlement by ESCB 227–9
shadow economies 283–4, 292

Shiller, R. 72, 188
shocks
    and fiscal federalism 264, 274, 277–82
        insurance against 280–2
    and issues, currency union 4, 7
        fiscal policy 24, 27, 44
        traditional criteria 7–9, 13–14, 16,
           17–19, 41–2
    and optimum currency area, Europe as
        see Europe *under* asymmetric shocks
    and former Soviet Union 65, 68
    and successful currency union 17–20
    terms-of-trade in CFA franc zone 96,
        97–9, 104, 105
    see also unemployment *and also* labor
        markets and European monetary
        unification
short-run considerations of Soviet
    common currency 66–7
S-I models *see* savings-interest correlations
Sierra Leone 98, 100
Smaller Industrial Country Region 42
'Snake in Tunnel' system of exchange-rate
    fixity 174
Soviet Union, former
    costs and benefits of economic and
        monetary union xii, 55–74
    centralization of competition 56–8
    common currency 65–70, 72–3
    contrast with Europe 70–1
    customs union 59–65, 72
    fiscal federalism 58–9
    trade 59–65, 66–9, 72
    issues, currency union 4, 13
Spahn, P.B. 269
Spain
    exchange rate 113–14, 123
    fiscal policy 43, 275
    issues, currency union 7, 15, 31–2, 43
    labor market
        employment and unemployment
           120–2
        migration 116, 118
    monetary policy 7
    optimum currency theory 113–14, 116,
        118, 119, 120–2, 123, 127–8
    output 15, 119, 123
    regions listed 127–8
    see also EC
Spaventa, L. 18
speculation *see* capital market
spillover effects
    and fiscal federalism 266, 271, 273–5,
        277
    of fiscal policy 21–3, 28–9, 42
    of goods arbitrage 57

Spinelli, F. 241, 244
stabilization and fiscal federalism
  macroeconomic 269–70, 273–7
  of regional shocks 277–8
Stanley, G. 43
state *see* government
Steinherr, A. 72
sterilized foreign exchange market
  intervention 36–7
stickiness of wages and prices 7–8, 16–17
Stock, J. 243, 262
stock markets 169–70
  see also capital market integration
Stockman, A. 91
Straubhaar, T. 117
Strauss-Kahn, M. 242
Structural Funds, EC 25
subsidiarity *see* decentralization
substitutioncurrency 35
Sudan 100, 106
Summers, L. 33, 91, 165
Sweden 12
Switzerland 43
  fiscal federalism 268–9
Symansky, S. 42
symmetric shocks 17–18, 274

Tabellini, G. 43
Tanzi, V. 43, 291
tax
  evasion 283–4, 292
  inflation *see* seigniorage
  see also fiscal policy
Taylor, J. 139
Taylor, M.P. ix, 166–70, 279, 290
  on issues, currency union xi–xii, 1–51
temporary shocks 17
Ter-Minassian, T. 291
Tesar, L. 91
Tiebout, C. 290
time series regression 165–6
Togo 98
  see also CFA franc zone
Torrance, T.S. 167
Tower, E. 41
Townsend, A.R. 159
Townsend, R. 91
trade 14, 62–5, 72, 283
  in CFA franc zone 96–9, 101–5
  IMF on 62, 64, 65
  and issues, currency union 11–13, 14
  in former Soviet Union 59–65, 66–9, 72
  in United States 14
    inter-regional gross capital position
      76, 81–8, 92
    regional consumption 76–7, 88–90,

92–3
  see also exchange rates
trans-Caucasian republics of former Soviet
  Union 63, 67, 69
transfers *see* fiscal policy
Treaty of Rome amendments 6
  see also Maastricht
Trivellato, U. 156
Tullio, G. 241–2, 244
two-country models of fiscal federalism
  275
'two-track' approach to monetary union
  34

Uibopuu, H.-J. 71
UIP *see* uncovered interest parity
Ukraine 67, 69, 72
uncovered interest parity and capital
  market integration 167, 168
unemployment and employment 132,
  133–8, 158, 160
  and fiscal federalism 274–5, 280–2
  insurance 280–2
  and issues, currency union 7, 8–9, 33, 41
  and migration 146–50
    see also mobility/migration *under*
    labor markets
  and optimum currency area, Europe as
    120–2, 123, 125
  regional 138–46, 158–9
Ungerer, H. 40
unification *see* parallel unification
unit root tests 178–80, 245
United States 125
  aid from 102
  excess stock returns *see* capital market
    integration
  Federal Reserve 216, 287
  fiscal federalism
    and economic and monetary union
      274, 279, 281–4, 286–7, 291
    principles of 268–9
    see also fiscal policy *under* issues
    below
  issues, currency union 4, 39
    convergence 31–2
    fiscal policy 21–2, 24–5, 26–8, 43–4
    traditional criteria 8–9, 11–15, 17, 18,
      40–1
  labor markets 131
    data 157–8
    employment and unemployment and
      shocks 133, 136–8, 144–6, 157,
      158–9
    migration 147–8, 149–50, 157, 159
    restoring equilibrium 151–2, 153, 160

United States (*cont.*)
    unemployment 8–9, 281
    output 15
    private capital markets and adjustments
       in currency unions xii, 75–95
       measurement of inter-regional gross
          capital position 76, 81–8, 92
       net capital flows 75–6, 77–81, 91–2
       regional consumption fluctuations
          76–7, 88–90, 92–3
       trade 14, 62, 76–7, 81–90, 92–3
       wages and prices 17
unobservable factor models and capital
    market integration 195, 206–7

van der Ploeg, F. 277, 280–1, 291, 292
van Rumpuy, P. 287, 292
Vanhaverbeke, W. ix, 16, 158
    on optimum currency area xiii, 111–29
Vanheukelen, M. 291
VAR methodology 168
variability of real exchange rate 112–16,
    128
Vaubel, R. 41, 111, 272, 283
Vegh 291
Venables, A. 31
Von Hagen, J. ix, 27, 88, 112, 128
    on fiscal federalism xiv, 264–96

Wadhwani, S. 169
wages
    in CFA franc zone 103
    flexibility 4, 7–8
       and successful currency union 16–17
       and labor mobility 146–50, 157, 158,
          159–60
    see also income
Wald statistics 188
Walker, M.A. 44

WAMO *see* West African Monetary Union
Watson, M. 243, 262
Weber, A. 44, 112, 158
Werner Committee Report 217
West African Monetary Union 6
    see also CFA franc zone
West Germany 290
    and optimum currency theory 114,
       116–17, 119, 120–1, 125, 128
    see also Germany
Wildasin, D.E. 284
Willett, T.D. 41
Williamson, J. 280, 281
Wenda Zhang *see* Zhang
Winston, C. 89
Woglom, G. 43, 158, 286
Wolf, M. 34
Wolfe, C.P. 167
World Bank
    and Africa 98, 100
    and exports 14
Wyplosz, C. 158
    on monetary integration 18
    on public good 277
    on shocks 112, 278, 280, 281
    on tax evasion 284
    on tax harmonization 292

Xafa, M. 40, 43

Yoo, B.S. 160, 261
Yugoslavia 28
    trade 62–3, 64

Zacharia, K.C. 104
Zaïre 97, 98, 100
Zhang, Wenda ix
    on money demand function, European
       240–63